Global Pandemics and International Law

This book reviews the efficacy of Global Health Law, assessing whether its legal framework based on the International Health Regulations represents a valid tool in the containment of modern global pandemics such as COVID-19. The volume provides an introduction to the international legal framework surrounding epidemics and pandemics and the main global governance issues that have been generated by the COVID-19 outbreak. It highlights the main shortcomings of global health law while also including practical proposals to improve the World Health Organization (WHO)'s mechanism to prevent and respond to disease such as the WHO Pandemic Agreement. Emphasis is placed on what has not worked in the international, regional, and national responses to COVID-19. It is argued that the pandemic has shed light on the weaknesses of global and domestic health law. Against this backdrop, the book also considers the relevance and potential application of concepts from other legal regimes, such as wildlife law, human rights, and animal law in line with the One Health concept. By identifying legal gaps and providing legal arguments, this work contributes to the historical and conceptual foundation and the practical development of international law in the new age of COVID-19, with the goal of stimulating legal reform in this vital new era. The work is essential reading for academics, researchers and policy-makers working in International Law, Health Law, Environmental Law, Animal Law, Biolaw, Human Rights Law, and the Law of International Organizations.

Ilja Richard Pavone is Senior Researcher of International Law at the National Research Council of Italy, Rome, where he coordinates the research unit in International, European, and National Biolaw. He is Professor of European Law and Biotechnologies at the Catholic University of the Sacred Heart, Rome.

Global Pandemics and International Law

An Analysis in the Age of Covid-19

Ilja Richard Pavone

Routledge
Taylor & Francis Group

LONDON AND NEW YORK

First published 2024
by Routledge
4 Park Square, Milton Park, Abingdon, Oxon OX14 4RN

and by Routledge
605 Third Avenue, New York, NY 10158

Routledge is an imprint of the Taylor & Francis Group, an informa business

© 2024 Ilja Richard Pavone

British Library Cataloguing-in-Publication Data
A catalogue record for this book is available from the British Library

Library of Congress Cataloging-in-Publication Data
Names: Pavone, Ilja Richard, author.
Title: Global pandemics and international law : an analysis in the age of
   Covid-19 / Ilja Richard Pavone.
Description: Abingdon, Oxon [UK] ; New York, NY : Routledge,
   2023. | Includes bibliographical references and index.
Identifiers: LCCN 2023034118 (print) | LCCN 2023034119 (ebook) |
   ISBN 9780367608224 (hardback) | ISBN 9781003100645 (ebook)
Subjects: LCSH: COVID-19 (Disease)—Law and legislation. |
   COVID-19 Pandemic, 2020– | Pandemics.
Classification: LCC K3575.C68 P38 2023 (print) | LCC K3575.C68
   (ebook) | DDC 344.04/3624144—dc23/eng/20230929
LC record available at https://lccn.loc.gov/2023034118
LC ebook record available at https://lccn.loc.gov/2023034119

ISBN: 978-0-367-60822-4 (hbk)
ISBN: 978-0-367-60829-3 (pbk)
ISBN: 978-1-003-10064-5 (ebk)

DOI: 10.4324/9781003100645

Typeset in Galliard
by Apex CoVantage, LLC

to my beloved children Edoardo and Sveva

Contents

Acknowledgments

This volume entitled "Global Pandemics and International Law in the Age of COVID-19" is a collaborative effort in many respects and is the result of the active contributions of friends and colleagues. First, it is the product of an institutional collaboration between the Biolaw Unit at the Interdepartmental Center for Research Ethics and Integrity (CID Ethics) of the National Research Council of Italy (CNR) and the Department of Political Sciences of Sapienza University, both located in Rome, Italy. "Global Health Law" was identified as a joint thematic area of interest within both institutions. In order to define a concrete field of research, the COVID-19 pandemic, and its impact on the global architecture for health emergency preparedness, response, and resilience (HEPR) represented a global event that deserved great attention and with it, a post-pandemic consensus (namely, the new pandemic treaty, WHO CA+).

First, I would like to thank Cinzia Caporale who is the Head of the CID Ethics (CNR), to which I belong. Cinzia played a crucial role in Italy during the pandemic: she chaired the national ethics committee for clinical trials on COVID-19 and was one of the 10 members of Prime Minister Mario Draghi's technical-scientific committee for the management of the pandemic crisis. I therefore had the opportunity to extensively discuss with her some aspects present in the volume from a privileged perspective.

I also particularly thank Raffaele Cadin who along with Cinzia Caporale gave a decisive contribution to the birth of the cooperation between CNR and Sapienza University in the field of health law.

Most of the chapters of this book are the object of the lessons in my course on Law and Biotechnologies at the Catholic University of the Sacred Heart in Rome.

This volume has come to life after engaged discussions with Pia Acconci, Gianluca Burci, Cinzia Caporale, Donato Greco Jr., Stefania Negri (who I met during my research stay at the Max Planck Institute for Comparative Public Law & International Law in Heidelberg in early 2020 just before the pandemic began), Rumiana Yotova, Pedro Villarreal, and my colleagues at CNR (in particular, Giorgia Adamo, Andrea Grignolio Corsini, Emanuela Midolo, Giulia Sciolli). I wish to thank all of them for having instilled the passion for health law and for their aid in the writing and revision of the single chapters of this book.

Foreword

The COVID-19 pandemic has deeply shaken countries, societies and health systems worldwide and put into question global health governance, calling for a more robust international health architecture. With the forthcoming approval by the World Health Organization (WHO) of the revised International Health Regulations (IHR) and the much-heralded Global Pandemic Treaty, it is to be expected that 2024 will mark a turning point in global health law and the international binding framework for prevention, preparedness and response to public health emergencies of global concern.

In light of the significance and groundbreaking nature of such reforms and innovations, Ilja Pavone's book represents an important and timely contribution to the field and to the ongoing debate on the development of international health law as triggered by the COVID-19 pandemic.

The book has three key objectives. First, to highlight the major challenges posed by the COVID-19 outbreak, which unveiled serious flaws and shortcomings in preparedness and response capacities at both national and international levels. Second, to provide a critical assessment of the appropriateness and effectiveness of relevant legal instruments and tools, as well as WHO practice, face to this unprecedented and unparalleled global health emergency. Third, to explore and discuss the ongoing reform and normative processes while suggesting arguments and solutions for incremental improvements and the necessary strengthening of prevention, preparedness and response to possible future pandemics.

After setting the scene with a useful preliminary presentation of the basic legal and institutional issues related to the WHO and the protection of the right to health in international law, Dr. Pavone's book offers an interesting critical analysis of the global health architecture seen through the lens of the impact that the COVID-19 outbreak has had on institutions, governance mechanisms and the law. The critical perspective adopted flows consistently throughout the work and also opportunely extends to other interrelated fields such as human rights, bioethics, intellectual property, environmental law and security. In this respect, the book fleshes out key concepts and brings accurate insights on the issues which are at the core of the contemporary debate.

In sum, Dr. Pavone's thought-provoking book represents an important contribution to the current debate on the evolution of the international legal framework governing the prevention and response to public health emergencies of global concern and I'm confident that it will become a reference work for anyone interested in global health security and the role of international law.

Stefania Negri

Preface

COVID-19 was declared a pandemic by the World Health Organization (WHO) in March 2020. It is the main health challenge faced by humankind since the Great Influenza Pandemic of 1918. The global 2009 H1N1 Influenza Pandemic, the growing spread of zoonotic diseases such as Middle East Respiratory Syndrome (MERS), monkeypox, and Severe Acute Respiratory Syndrome (SARS), and the over-exploitation of the environment had unequivocally revealed to the entire world that it was not an issue of whether but when a new global pandemic would occur.

COVID-19 is neither the first nor will it be the last pandemic with major consequences for health, the economy, and human rights.

Although infectious diseases cause more victims than wars, they have never received adequate attention by the international community, and legal scholars have not elevated them to the same level as other threats to humankind such as wars, international terrorism, climate change, drought, and nuclear disasters.

The purpose of this volume is therefore to examine the topics "epidemics", "pandemics", and international law in the age of COVID-19 and in the current post-pandemic scenario (in May 2023, the WHO declared the end of the emergency), with a view of generating new insights and reflections on the state of global health governance.

The lack of interest in the prevention and management of disease outbreaks by the international community – although State cooperation in the field of health is ancient and dates to the XIX century – led to a weakness in the Global Architecture for Health Emergency Preparedness, Response, and Resilience (HEPR architecture). This resulted in the WHO ineffectively implementing the International Health Regulations IHR – the Organization's legal framework for dealing with disease outbreaks – that severely hampered their response to the pandemic. COVID-19 has clearly demonstrated that pandemics pose potential existential threats to humanity and must be elevated to the highest level of attention. Reform of the global health architecture through a new treaty on pandemic preparedness and response or an amendment to the IHR is necessary in order to adjust the shortcomings of the previous reform of the IHR in 2005.

Since its founding, the WHO has been on the frontlines in the struggle against infectious diseases, and it has achieved several successes, such as the complete eradication of smallpox in 1979 and the almost complete elimination of the polio virus. However, the WHO has also been criticized for an overdependence on Member States, excessive bureaucratization, and structural weaknesses ("design gaps").

Since the onset of the COVID-19 pandemic in early 2020, these charges have been repeated with greater vehemence.

Undoubtedly, in this instance, the Organization failed to meet its overarching objective, notably "the attainment by all peoples of the highest possible level of health". It not only declared a public health emergency of international concern (PHEIC) one month after being notified of a disease cluster in Wuhan but also provided imprudent advice, such as not recommending that States ban travel from China even after a lockdown had been imposed in Wuhan.

However, the WHO's efforts have undoubtedly been hindered by competing economic, political, and social interests: in short, a lack of political cooperation. As clearly shown by other issues of common concern – such as climate change – domestic and economic considerations prevail over the necessity to find shared solutions.

However, the WHO's mistakes betray a more fundamental issue: the very design of the WHO is not fit for its purpose in relation to the serious challenges that it faces.

This book describes the main design imperfections of the WHO – such as lack of an enforcement mechanism, limited authority, and limited funding – by focusing on what went wrong in the early phases of COVID-19. To substantiate this claim, I argue that the vision behind the creation of the WHO was flawed in its key assumptions. The WHO was set up on premises that revealed themselves fallacious. The founding fathers of the WHO were convinced that the attainment of the highest standard of health was a shared goal of all nations, that the prevention and containment of the spread of infectious diseases were an effort to which all States were committed, and that industrialized countries would help those with limited resources in this complex task. They therefore presumed that States would have a concrete interest in cooperating in the prevention and containment of disease outbreaks.

The system that was established to provide a global response to epidemics and pandemics – based on the IHR – has failed miserably, and the call for reform certified its collapse.

It is easy to highlight responsibilities and multiple failures on three levels. With reference to China, growing evidence shows a violation of the duties of timely notification and information sharing under Articles 6 and 7 of the IHR and at least of the obligation under customary international law of due diligence in the prevention and containment of disease outbreaks and in informing the international community. Furthermore, China has not prohibited but has instead tolerated the trade in wild animals protected under the Convention on the Trade on Endangered Species (CITES), which may have contributed to the origin of the disease outbreak in the wet market of Wuhan.

This is not the first case of a coronavirus appearing in South-East Asia; in the precedent of the SARS virus, which caused a disease outbreak in China and overseas in 2002–2003, Chinese authorities tried to cover up evidence of the virus for months, resulting in avoidable deaths and disruption at home and abroad. In the aftermath, the WHO updated its IHR precisely with the purpose of preventing future cover-ups.

As to the WHO, it is clear how it failed in its responsibilities: it relied excessively on the information provided by China regarding the extent of the first clusters of COVID-19 and declared a PHEIC with extreme delay (about one month after China notified the WHO Regional Office that a pneumonia of unknown origin had been recorded in the region of Hubei in Wuhan). Then, the first technical guidelines to its Member States were blatantly erroneous (such as the initial denial of human-to-human transmission or the recommendation not to consider asymptomatic patients as possible carriers of the disease, since asymptomatic transmission was underappreciated).

Eventually, instead of openly criticizing China for succumbing to the temptation to cover up the extent of the outbreak (as the former Director-General (DG) did in the precedent of SARS), the WHO's DG praised China for its transparency and proper reaction to the contagion.

Several reasons have been put forward to explain the WHO's failure in managing in an appropriate and timely manner the early stages of the spread of COVID-19, when it had not yet reached the threshold of pandemic, such as political ties with China and the lack of political independence. The main cause is more likely a design flaw of the WHO, which has not been equipped with the necessary authority to adequately fulfill its mission.

Indeed, the WHO does not have the power to carry out investigations *in loco* without the territorial State's consent, unlike arms control treaties, and must therefore strongly rely on the information that should be provided *bona fide* by a Member State. In addition, it does not have the faculty to impose sanctions against a Member State that does not comply with its obligations under the IHR, such as early warnings or the establishment of appropriate core capacities. The WHO also cannot impose lockdowns or distribute beds, ventilators in ICU units, drugs, or vaccines (and none of these issues were solved by the Accord on Pandemic Prevention, Preparedness and Response – WHO Pandemic Agreement)

The WHO has mainly normative functions, setting norms and standards and providing technical support and scientific advice. Its Constitution does not envisage an operational role that provides an on-the-ground response during a serious disease outbreak.

The WHO operates within a Westphalian system, according to which health is a matter that rests within the jurisdiction of each State, which mainly responds to the health needs of its citizens. The WHO solely provides technical advice and recommends measures; that is, the WHO supports the States – in particular developing countries – but they should be able to react autonomously to a disease outbreak through stronger health systems, adequate funding, and equitable distribution of medicines and vaccines.

The third level of responsibility is that of the WHO Member States. With few exceptions – such as New Zealand, Singapore, Vietnam, and Taiwan – most States were unprepared to tackle the new coronavirus. It is important to clarify that domestic governments are not obliged to wait for a "green light" by the WHO (meaning a declaration of PHEIC and the DG's temporary recommendations) in order to adopt stringent measures with the goal of preventing the diffusion of a given infectious disease. States waited until the pandemic was unfolding before reacting with the enforcement of lockdowns and severe limitations of personal freedoms and civil liberties.

Even though we are in the age of globalization, States' reactions to COVID-19 presented more similarities than differences with the great plagues of the XIX Century (such as the case of the Hamburg plague). First, they were characterized by a lack of coordination, also at a regional or sub-regional level. The dominant approach among affected countries was to lock down or restrict "non-essential" activities and impose sharp curbs on international (and in some cases, national) travel.

The securitization of COVID-19 in terms of two distinct "referent objects" (humankind vs. citizens) reflects the political tension between the progressive erosion of *Domaine Réservé* in light of the globalization process and the political will in the age of populism to regain some essential functions, among which is health. COVID-19 was indeed perceived as an occasion for seeking political or economic advancement.

Further lessons are related to the need to codify the One Health approach that would recognize the linkage among human health, environmental degradation, and animal welfare. That is, COVID-19 is a health crisis with serious ecological implications, since it has its roots in the failures of environmental law and, specifically, wildlife law.

Moreover, vaccine nationalism has widened the inequalities between North and South and amplified discrimination on access to essential health services. The issues of vaccine nationalism and distributive justice that emerged during the pandemic have shown that solidarity and commitment to multilateralism is less forthcoming during a health emergency.

I The World Health Organization (WHO) and the global governance of diseases

Part I The birth of the WHO and the International Health Regulations (IHR)

1. Introduction

This chapter begins in Part I with a historical reconstruction of the development of global health law in its early phases. Its path has roots in the second half of the XIX century, when early sanitary conventions – although with few successes and several false starts – marked the inception of State cooperation in the field of public health. This was an intense phase of institutionalization – where the establishment of the WHO represents the most significant achievement. The WHO has passed through the XX century up to the revision of the IHR in 2005, which has opened a new season oscillating between new aspirations and the recurrence of ancient flaws.

The main argument of the chapter is that the global health security architecture since its origins, which dates back to the first international sanitary conference (Paris, 1851) up to the IHR (2005), is grounded on a "systemic flaw".

As widely discussed in the present chapter, the IHR (2005) – which are a modern version of the early conventions on infectious diseases – are based on a containment rather than on a preventive logic. Although during the XIX and XX centuries, science did not yet understand the dynamics behind the spillover of a pathogen from an animal to a human being, but now, the mechanisms of transmission of a zoonotic disease are clear. Despite the advancement of science, there are no binding rules in either health law or environmental law that impose a specific obligation of prevention of zoonotic diseases. Therefore, the IHR are built on the assumption that disease outbreaks are a matter of fact and the product of natural events; therefore, they apply only once a disease outbreak is already spreading around the world (and the WHO Director-General declares a public health emergency of international concern – PHEIC)

Against this backdrop, I underline in Chapter II that the parallel negotiations for a new pandemic treaty (WHO Pandemic Agreement) and for

DOI: 10.4324/9781003100645-1

amending the IHR will have a concrete impact on future disease outbreaks only if grounded on the concept of "deep prevention".[1]

This examination is preparatory to evaluate in Chapter II (the WHO's practice concerning the management and containment of disease outbreaks) and in Chapter III (the WHO's response to the COVID-19 pandemic) whether the WHO has exerted or not its international public authority in the management of infectious diseases; whether strong limitations have instead emerged in its capacity to respond; and if, in particular, the restraints faced during the COVID-19 pandemic were somehow predictable. Indeed, the choice to devote a part of this early chapter to the history of health cooperation seemed functional not only to fully comprehend the context in which the analysis is situated but also to investigate in a prospective way the main legal issues raised by the COVID-19 pandemic.

Part II of this chapter then focuses on the content and scope of the right to health. This is central to the WHO that has the specific goal of the attainment by all peoples of the highest possible level of health (Art. 1, WHO Constitution). Part II discusses the emergence of health in international human rights law. It covers the right to health in both the WHO and the UN (in particular, Article 12 of the International Covenant on Economic, Social and Cultural Rights), in sectorial and in regional treaties. Against this backdrop, I highlight that the WHO has failed to adopt a treaty on the right to health, which constitutes a significant normative gap of the WHO that has undermined its actions.

2. The international health regime prior to the creation of the WHO

2.1. The phase of health unilateralism

Human history is characterized by infectious diseases, which have flourished at the same pace as the development of human civilization. Early disease outbreaks were facilitated by early human settlements, where large number of people used to live in close proximity to one another and to animals, often in conditions of poor sanitation and nutrition.[2] Many significant diseases of human civilization, such as measles, tuberculosis, smallpox, and cholera, probably arose concurrently with the advent of agriculture and domestication of animals in human society,[3] although a key role has also been played by environmental factors.[4]

---

1 Jorge Vinuales, Suerie Moon, Ginevra Le Moli, Gian-Luca Burci, "A Global Pandemic Treaty Should Aim for Deep Prevention", *The Lancet* (2021): 1791–1792.
2 Mirko D. Grmek, "Géographie médicale et histoire des civilisations", *Annales E.S.C.* 18 (1963): 1071–1097; William H. Mcneill, *Plagues and Peoples* (Blackwell: 1977); William H. Mcneill, *The Human Condition. An Ecological and Historical View* (Princeton University Press: 1980).
3 Andrew A. Dobson, E. Robin Carper, "Infectious Diseases and Human Population History: Throughout History the Establishment of Disease has been a Side Effect of the Growth of Civilization", *Bioscience* (1996): 115–126; Jessica M.C. Pearce-Duvet, "The Origin of Human Pathogens: Evaluating the Role of Agriculture and Domestic Animals in the Evolution of Human Disease", *Biological Review* (2006): 369–382.
4 Jared Diamonds, *Guns, Germs and Steel: The Fates of Human Society* (W.W. Norton: 1997), 195–214.

The plague of Athens (429–426 BC) was the first ever recorded epidemic of human history, causing about 100,000 victims. The affliction was described in detail by Thucydides – who contracted the disease but eventually survived – in "the Plague of Athens". The "Thucydides trap" forced the Spartan troops that were ready to invade Athens to refrain from entering in the city.

The word "epidemic" derives from ancient Greek, with *epi* that means "upon" or "above" and *demos* that designates "people". Epidemic refers to an infectious disease that will probably infect a large amount of people in one or more countries.[5]

The death of Pharaoh Ramses V in 1157 BC was caused by smallpox, which is evidenced by the still visible marks on the mummy's face.[6] However, smallpox was not the only infectious disease of that time: polio was also widespread among the ancient Egyptians, as shown by a stila of the 18th Dynasty (1403–1365 BC) that depicts a victim with a right leg hit by the infectious disease. For millennia, only natural (unwanted) infections immunized the human being from the most serious contagious diseases.

During the Roman Empire and the Middle Ages, the spread of infectious diseases was very slow.

The first global epidemics and pandemics, such as plague (1347–1357), black death (1349), and cholera (from 1817), were then related to the new overseas trading routes (such as the Silk Road).

Conquest and colonization – which are at the roots of modern international law – also contributed to the diffusion of contagious diseases.[7] Measles, smallpox, and influenza were brought and transmitted by the European conquerors to the native populations of the "New World" in South America, killing thousands of them. The settlers then exporting farming to these populations and destroying their original lifestyle and their natural habitats contributed to the current degradation of the environment.[8]

5 According to the United States Centers for Disease Control (CDC), the term is defined as "a rate of disease incidence clearly above the normal expectancy for a specified area", which refers to "the baseline disease incidence in an area among the same population at the same time of the year". U.S. Department of Health and Human Services, Centers for Disease Control and Prevention, "Principles of Epidemiology in Public Health Practice", in *An Introduction to Epidemiology and Biostatistics* 3rd ed. (2012), cdc_6914_DS1%20(3).pdf.
6 Smallpox (variola major) is a viral disease that emerged 3,000/4,000 years ago in East Africa, presumably due to close contact (domestication) with camels and cattle (or mice). It belongs to the genus of the Ortho-pox-virus, family pox-viridae (double DNA). Disease-like forms of smallpox are caused in humans by the virus of monkeys (monkeypox) and cattle (cow-pox). The infection occurs through the secretions of the nose, breathing, sneezing and coughing, skin contact, clothes, and blankets. Yu Li, Darin S. Carroll, Shea N. Gardner, Matthew C. Walsh, Elizabeth A. Vitalis, and Inger K. Damon, "On the Origin of Smallpox: Correlating Variola Phylogenics with Historical Smallpox Records", *Proceedings of the National Academy of Sciences* 104 (40) (2007): 15787–15792.
7 Antony Anghie, "The Evolution of International Law: Colonial and Postcolonial Realities", *Third World Quarterly* (2006): 739–753.
8 Anne Peters, "International Law between Covid-19 and the Next Pandemic", *MPIL Research Paper Series, No. 2022–18* (Max Planck Institute for Comparative Public Law and International Law: 2002), 1–18, at 2.

An acceleration happened, however, in the XIX century due to growth in trade through the sea (harbors were the main entry point of new viruses) and the Industrial Revolution. In fact, the steamship and railways played a crucial role in facilitating the spread of disease outbreaks.

The building of the Suez Channel (1869) then determined an increase of movement of goods and persons, such as travelers, Muslim pilgrims, and migrants. Migration from Europe to America severely contributed to the outbreak of contagious diseases. Industrialization comported a rapid urbanization and concentration of people overcrowding cities.

Many diseases, however, originated from Asia (such as the SARS-CoV-2 pandemic). When the British Empire colonized the North of India, it opened new trade routes. Cholera, for instance, originated in North-East India (the first outbreak dates to 1817). Railways facilitated a rapid diffusion of cholera when it first arrived in Europe following the inception of the trade routes between Afghanistan and Persia. Around 1819–1820, cholera was eventually stemmed a first time, realistically due to a *cordon sanitaire* imposed by the Russian authorities, but spread once again towards the West in the years immediately following, hitting Germany in 1830 and Great Britain in 1832.

The scientific community was divided on how to react in an appropriate manner to the cholera outbreak. The inefficiency of quarantine practices and *cordon sanitaires* to block the spread of the disease – which were the most common measures put in place by States to protect themselves from foreign diseases – convinced most scientists that cholera did not have an infectious source but rather was transmitted under the form of miasma. The miasma was an imperceptible steam – according to scientists led in 1870 in Munich by Max von Pettenkofer – that emanated from water tables and stagnant waters under determined climate conditions. The supporters of the miasma theory were opposed to any State intervention, with the dogmatic belief of *laissez-faire*.

It was not yet clear at the time that such measures, in order to be efficient, should have been accompanied by an improvement of sanitary conditions, widespread immunization of the population, and health literacy.

This belief mainly broke through liberal States, while authoritarian countries of the Old Continent adopted similar policies to those used to cope with plague, such as restrictions to movement, isolation and forced hospitalization, and quarantines in the harbor cities and in inhabited areas with outbreaks of the contagious diseases.

The city of Hamburg, Germany experienced a large-scale cholera epidemic in 1892, at a time when the disease had largely vanished from most of Europe.[9] Disease outbreaks comported devastating impacts on human societies including wars and conflicts.

---

9 Attila Tàrnok, "The Cholera Epidemics in Hamburg and What to Learn for COVID-19 (SARS-CoV-2)", *Citometry A* (2020): 337–339.

Considering the transboundary dimension of these infectious diseases, States realized that unilateral measures were insufficient and that a stricter cooperation was necessary.

Against this backdrop, Goodman highlighted three steps in the process that lead to an increased inter-governmental cooperation in the health field.[10] In the first stage, diseases were simply interpreted as divine punishment, and societies reacted through sacrifices and prayers.[11] The second stage is represented by the adoption of concrete measures aimed at containing the spread of disease outbreaks, which was then indicated by the strategy of *cordon sanitaire* in medieval times; this implied the complete isolation of a given community to prevent both the importation and exportation of a specific infectious disease.[12] Then, the most common courses of action were quarantines of incoming travelers and ships.[13]

It is no surprise that this same type of initiative, namely, the well-known lockdowns and social distancing in the age of COVID-19 ("non-pharmaceutical interventions" – NPIs), is still the only viable solution to mitigate the spread of a given infectious disease.

The concept of modern public health was developed as result of quarantines. This means a growing interconnection between societies insofar as a health event in a given part of the world has consequences for other States.

In more general terms, the XIX century marks the birth of the phenomenon of intergovernmental organizations (IGOs) with the establishment of the early proto-IGOs,[14] such as the river commissions, the first typology of an international entity. The Central Commission for the Navigation of the Rhine (Vienna Congress, 1815) and the European Commission of the Danube (Paris Agreement, 1856)[15] are two examples of early IGOs.

10 Neville M. Goodman, *International Health Organizations and Their Work* (Churchill Livingstone: 1971), 38;

11 Véronique Eicher, Adrian Bangerter, "Social Representations of Infectious Diseases", in Gordon Sammut, Eleni Andreouli, Milton Keynes, George Gaskell, Jaan Valsiner (eds.), *The Cambridge Handbook of Social Representation* (Cambridge University Press: 2015), 385–396.

12 The *cordon sanitaire* is a French term that means "sanitary cordon". It denotes a disease outbreak-control method where a quarantine zone is established and those inside are not allowed to leave. Traditionally, the line around a *cordon sanitaire* was quite physical and represented by a fence or a wall that was built and armed troops to patrol it; inside, the inhabitants were left to tackle the disease outbreak without outside help.

13 Eugenia Tognotti, "Lessons from the History of Quarantine, from Plague to Influenza", *Emerging Infectious Diseases* 19 (2013): 254–260. Quarantine policies were set up for the first time as a protective measure on the European continent in 1377 in the city of Ragusa (now Dubrovnik) on Croatia's Dalmatian Coast. A specific order stipulated that travelers coming from areas affected by plague were prohibited from entering the city, unless they spent a period of isolation on the island of Mrkan or in the city of Cavtat. This measure put the city of Ragusa at the forefront in the prevention of epidemic outbreaks.

14 Anne Peters, "Le cheminement historique des organisations internationals: entre technocratie et démocratie", in Pierre-marie Dupuy, Vincent Chetail (eds.), *The Roots of International Law: Liber Amicorum Peter Haggenmacher* (Brill: 2013), 486–529.

15 This Commission was then put beside by the International Commission for the Danube established by the Versailles Treaty of 28 June 1919.

The main goal of these commissions was to ensure the freedom of navigation of commercial ships, to supervise the works necessary to guarantee this navigation, and to collect taxes on the basis of the ship tonnage. To these aims, the commissions were empowered with legal, executive, and judicial powers.

The year 1865 has been defined as the *annus mirabilis* of IGOs,[16] with the institutions of the International Telegraphic Union (1865) and the International Commission of the Cape Spartel Light in Tanger (1865), which is the first intergovernmental institution in which the United States participated.[17]

The Washington Conference of 1889–1890 marked the creation of the first IGO with a regional character, the International Union of American Republics, which is at the root of Pan-Americanism.[18]

However, the spread of infectious diseases, notably, zoonotic diseases, can be placed at the very foundations of international law, since early IGOs were created in the specific sector of health. The *Conseil Supérieur de Santé* – set up in Constantinople in 1838 in response to repeated cholera outbreaks in the Mediterranean region – is the ancestor of modern IGOs.[19] It was not an IGO with a secretariat and specific organs but in general a *conseil* made of representatives of both Islamic and European countries concerned by the rapid spread of infectious diseases.[20]

The international community of this period was characterized as an equal society devoid of the lack of a central government apparatus and based on the model, dating back to the Westphalian Peace of 1648, of the relationship between independent States *superiorem non recognoscentes.* This phenomenon, as a whole, was analyzed as "the legal organisation of the international society".[21]

The aim of these first attempts of inter-State collaboration marked a historical step from "cohabitation" to "cooperation", although they did not have the genuine goal of coordinating the efforts in dealing with issues of common concern, such as the freedom of navigation or prevention of disease outbreaks, that is, they did not overcome the limits of the Westphalian order. States mainly

---

16 Madeleine Herren, *Internationale Organisationen seit 1865: eine Globalgeschichte der internationalen Ordnung, Wissenshcaftliche Buchgesellschaft* (Wissen verbindet: 2009), 18.

17 David J. Bederman, "The Souls of International Organizations: Legal Personality and Lighthouse at Cape Spartel", *Vanderbilt Journal of International Law* 36 (1996): 275–377.

18 Joseph B. Lockey, "The Meaning of Pan-Americanism", *The American Journal of International Law* (1925): 104–117.

19 Jean-David Mizrahi, "Politique Sanitaire et impérialisme à l'heure de la revolution pastorienne: Le Conseil sanitaire de Costantinople 1839–1923", in Walid Arbid et al. (eds.), *Méditerranée. Moyen Orient: Deux siècles de relations internationales. Recherche en homage à Jacques Thobie* (L'Harmattan: 2003), 221–242.

20 Joep Schenk, *The Rhine and European Security in the Long Nineteenth Century: Making Lifelines from Frontlines* (Routledge: 2021).

21 Pasquale Fiore, "L'organisation juridique de la société international", *Revue de droit international et de législation comparée* 2 (1889): 105–126 and 209–242, Angelo Golia Jr., Anne Peters, "The Concept of International Organization", in Jan Klabbers (ed.), *Cambridge Companion to International Organizations Law* (Cambridge University Press: 2022), 25–49.

aimed at harmonizing the measures adopted unilaterally by other countries that were considered an undue restriction on international trade and travel. Different policies regarding the prevention of disease outbreaks arising from the Far East had a negative effect on trade.[22]

However, some scholars have argued that the necessity of State cooperation in the field of prevention and containment of disease outbreaks was not just driven by the egoistic goal of avoiding excessive damage to free trade. Harrison contends, for instance, that the new diplomatic context and the climate of *appeasement* after the Congress of Vienna (1815) were the key drivers in fostering health diplomacy.[23]

In the XIX century, the rapid spread of the Asiatic Cholera outbreaks (in 1830–1832, 1848–1851, 1865–1874, 1884–1886, and 1892–1895),[24] and a steady growth of international trade, stimulated the necessity to cooperate.

States, through international collaboration, tried to prevent, on the one hand, importing exotic epidemics from the Asian continent due to the circulation of people from Asia to Europe, who were mainly pilgrims; on the other hand, States wanted to avoid excessive limitations to the free circulation of goods and restrictive measures such as quarantines.[25]

States were concerned not only about Asian diseases but also about the illegal trade of opium and alcohol. The trade of opium from the British colonies in India to China was highly lucrative. Its deleterious effects on health, however, were the object of a growing concern and led to the adoption of the International Opium Convention (The Hague, 23 January 1912).

Alcohol and alcoholism in territories under colonial occupation and its effects on the health of indigenous populations were also a matter of interest. This led to the enactment of the Convention Relating to the Liquor Traffic in Africa (Saint-Germain-en-Laye, 10 September 1919).

As the main global mode of transportation was by sea, the first health conferences were focused on measures restricting maritime transportation, particularly at the moment of arriving at foreign ports.

Notably, after more than a century, States have been animated by the same goals, whereas the Preamble of the revised text of the IHR of 1969 clearly

---

22 Neville M. Goodman, *International Health Organizations and Their Work* (Churchill Livingstone: 1971), Valeska Huber, "The Unification of the Globe by Disease? The International Sanitary Conferences on Cholera, 1851–1894", *The Historical Journal* (2006): 453–476; Stefania Negri, "Communicable Disease Control", in Gian Luca Burci, Brigit Toebes (eds.), *Research Handbook on Global Health Law* (Edward Elgar: 2018), 265–302.

23 Mark Harrison, "Disease, Diplomacy and International Commerce: The Origins of International Sanitary Regulations in the Nineteenth Century", *Journal of Global History* 1 (2006): 197–217.

24 Gordon C. Cook, "The Asiatic Cholera: An Historical Determinant of Human Genomic and Social Structure", in B.S. Drasar, B.D. Forrest (eds.), *Cholera and the Ecology of Vibrio Cholera* (Springer: 1996), 18–53.

25 Mark W. Zacher, Tania J. Keefe, *The Politics of Global Health Governance: United by Contagion* (Palgrave Macmillan: 2008), 25–38.

stated that their objective was to ensure "the maximum security against the international spread of diseases with a minimum interference with world traffics".

On the basis of these expectations, 12 States met at the First International Sanitary Conference (1851), convened by France against cholera, plague, and yellow fever, with the intention of standardizing quarantine regulations and managing maritime communications in the Mediterranean and Black Sea (the main entry points of these diseases).[26]

Outcome of the conference was an international health agreement signed by all delegates on 16 January 1852, which never entered into force. Only France and Sardinia ratified the treaty, followed by Portugal. The project was therefore unsuccessful. At the diplomatic level, several States were simply unwilling to cave into their police powers to confront outbreaks. What remained was the understanding that agreements would become necessary. Indeed, very specific conventions on the spread of some infectious diseases were then agreed to in the following decades, but few of them entered into force.

These treaties strictly adhered to the Westphalian tradition of positivist international law,[27] since they were responsive to specific needs. First, they were based on mutual benefits: they were agreed among States with the simple purpose of avoiding the transmission of infectious diseases at the border entry points between them. Second, their design was not aimed at challenging State sovereignty but rather to reinforce it, since countries agreed to yield only a small portion of their sovereignty consistent with the achievement of the mutual benefits sought. Third, the sanitary conventions responded to the "power" paradigm, that is the perception of the external danger to national security represented by infectious diseases imported from the Far East – such as plague, cholera, and yellow fever. This threat was mainly addressed to France, Great Britain, and the United States, the most powerful countries at that time.[28]

2.2. The shift of the XX century

The XX century marked the establishment of the first IGOs or proto-organizations with a specific mandate in the field of public health.

In 1902, the Pan-American Sanitary Bureau (then the Pan-American Health Organization, PAHO), headquartered in Washington, D.C., was set

---

26　Yves Beigreder, *L'Organisation Mondiale de la Santé* (Nouvelle Edition International: 2015).
27　David P. Fidler, "Caught Between Paradise and Power: Public Health, Pathogenic Threats, and the Axis of Illness", *McGeorge Law Review* 35 (2004): 45–101, at 58–59.
28　Fidler connected the first 100 years of international health diplomacy to "the heyday of the 'Westphalian' system of international relations"; hereinafter Paradise and Power; David P. Fidler, "The Globalization of Public Health: The First 100 Years of International Health Diplomacy", *Bulletin of the World Health Organization* 79 (2001): 842–849.

up.[29] A few years later, in 1907, the first permanent office on health matters, the *Office Internationale d'Hygiène Publique* (OIHP), emerged. The mandates of both organizations included issues of disease outbreak control.[30]

After the Pandemic Influenza of 1918–1919 – caused by an H1N1 virus – which ultimately led to nearly 15 million deaths, the Health Organization of the League of the Nations (HOLN) based in Geneva was established in 1920. Its foundation can be traced to Article 23 (lect. *f*) of the Covenant of the League of the Nations, which stated that its member "will endeavour to take steps in matters of international concern for the prevention and control of disease".

The Health Organization of the League of Nations (1921–1945) played a key role in the dissemination of information and in providing technical assistance to Member States.[31]

The *Office International des Epizooties* (OIE) was founded in 1924 initially among 24 countries in response to an outbreak of rinderpest in Belgium. One of the core missions of OIE was (and is still) to provide a mechanism for the prompt reporting of disease outbreaks with a zoonotic source.

These five organizations, although overlapping in their functions and lacking appropriate cooperation, witnessed the necessity of multilateral cooperation in the health field.[32]

They are the precursors of the WHO and showed the way to the post-First World War "move towards institutions".[33]

The International Sanitary Convention (Paris, 21 June 1926), which set up specific requirements for port sanitation and quarantine with the goal of limiting the global diffusion of infectious diseases, "changed the way that the world approached international epidemic control".[34] It established requirements for notification of each Member States if even a single case of plague, cholera, or yellow fever was discovered in their territories or in case of an "epidemic of typhus or smallpox" (Art. 1, Para. 3). It provided a specific duty to establish a sanitary defense around harbours.

The 1926 International Sanitary Convention had a particular "imprinting", since it addressed only the threat represented by imported infectious diseases from Eastern countries. The internal health conditions of other States also with respect to the particular diseases identified were not dealt with at all.

29 Norman Howard-Jones, *World Health Organizations. The Pan American Health Organizations: Origins and Evolution* (WHO, History of International Public Health Series: 1981).
30 Alexa M. Stern, Howard Markel, "International Efforts to Control Infectious Diseases, 1851 to Present", *Journal of the American Medical Association* (2004): 1474–1479.
31 For details on the origin of international cooperation in the field of health, see Xavier Seuba Hernandez, "Los Orígenes de la Cooperacion Sanitaria Internacional", in Xavier Pons Rafols (ed.), *Salute Pública Mondial Y Derecho Internacional* (Marcial Pons: 2010), 67–84.
32 Makane Moïse Mbengue, "Public Health, International Cooperation", in Rüdiger Wolfrum (ed.), *Max Planck Encyclopedia of Public International Law* (Oxford University Press: 2010).
33 David Kennedy, "The Move to Institutions", *Cardozo Law Review* (1987): 841–842.
34 Anne Sealey, "Globalizing the 1926 International Sanitary Convention", *Journal of Global History* (2011): 431–455, at 431.

Although it was a universal treaty, it mainly served the interests of the Great Powers: to address the vulnerability from infectious diseases imported from the Far East and to protect them from discriminatory or politically motivated trade restrictions (*cordons sanitaires*, quarantines).

A specific treaty on Dengue Fever was also created, namely, the International Convention for Mutual Protection against Dengue Fever (Athens, 25 July 1934).

Sanitary spheres of influences were shaped by but were not entirely dependent on political spheres of influence. "International health diplomacy" in the pre-WHO era also included a reflection on issues beyond the field of infectious diseases. Treaties on occupational safety and health were adopted, such as the International Labour Organization (ILO) in 1919 (it was part of the Treaty of Versailles). Its Preamble recognizes "the protection of the worker against *sickness, disease and injury* arising out of his employment, the protection of children, young persons and women, provision for old age and injury".

The Covenant of the League of the Nations provided specific goals, such as to secure fair and humane conditions of labour for men, women, and children, (Art. 23, lect. *a*) and the prevention of traffic in women and children and the traffic in opium and other dangerous drugs (Art. 23, lect. *c*); among these goals, it stated that "Members will endeavour to take steps in matters of international concern for the prevention and control of disease" (Art. 23, lect. *f*). At the beginning of World War II, when France was under German occupation, the activity of the OIHP was interrupted. Facing the emergency situation created by the War, the Allies decided in 1941 to establish a "comité de secours interallié" to prevent the return of the situation of the previous years of 1918–1920. This body was then replaced by the United Nations Relief and Rehabilitation Administration (UNRRA) headed in Washington with a specific competence in the health field.[35]

This brief history helps to explain why the UN Charter's drafters included the promotion of solutions for "health" among the goals of the Organization in Article 55(*b*) and why, in 1945, the San Francisco negotiators of the Charter unanimously approved the creation of a specialized health agency.

Developed countries, because of the establishment of welfare States, the economic rise, the consequent availability of clean water and sanitation services, and the wide accessibility to treatments and vaccines, strongly reduced the diffusion of infectious diseases.[36] High-income countries made significant strides in reducing the threat of infectious disease to their populations and

---

35 Norman Howard-Jones, *La santé publique internationale entre les deux guerres. Les problemes d'organisation* (OMS: 1975), 78–83.

36 Simon Szreter, "Economic Growth, Disruption, Deprivation, Disease, and Death: On the Importance of the Politics of Public Health for Development", *Population and Development Review* (1997): 693–728.

economies following the availability of clean water, sanitation services, and new medical technologies.

3. The WHO's foundations

The "international health" approach to infectious diseases was shaped in the mid-nineteenth century in order to protect the European and the North American continents from pathogens coming from Asia ("Asiatic diseases"). The WHO was founded in 1948 and succeeded the OIHP and the HOLN as a UN Specialized Agency with a general competence in the health field, and it aspired to solve the health problems of the entire world population.

The WHO was based not only on a holistic conception of health as a way to improve human welfare but also on the post-World War II idea that health is one of the pillars of peace.[37] Indeed, the promotion of the solution to "health problems" was included in the goals of the organization by the UN Charter's drafters (Article 55(*b*)).[38] The importance of the topic of "health" within the UN is also shown by Article 62 of the UN Charter on the Economic and Social Council (ECOSOC; one of the main UN bodies), which includes health matters within the sectors of competence of this organ.[39]

In 1945, in San Francisco, the drafters of the UN Charter unanimously endorsed the establishment of a specialized health agency. Accordingly, ECOSOC convened an international health conference with the aim of negotiating this new organization, which was held in New York from 19 June to 22 July 1946.[40]

---

37 Preamble, Paras. 3–4. Thomas Parran, Frank G. Boudreau, "The World Health Organization: Cornerstone of Peace", *American Journal of Public Health* 36 (1946): 1267; Marcos Cueto, Theodore M. Brown, Elizabeth Fee, *The World Health Organization. A History* (Cambridge University Press: 2019).

38 Article 55, lect. *b*, affirms that "the United Nations shall promote: higher standards of living, full employment, and conditions of economic and social progress and development; solutions of international economic, social, *health*, and related problems; and international cultural and educational cooperation". In a first phase at the San Francisco Conference, the UN drafters were more inclined to discuss traditional matters of peace and security. Due to the joint initiative of Brazil and China, the General Assembly (GA) unanimously approved a declaration that it pledged to convene an international conference to discuss the establishment of a health agency. See Szeming Sze, *The Origins of the World Health Organization: A Personal Memoir, 1945–1948* (JAMA: 1982).

39 Art. 62 of UN Charter states that "The Economic and Social Council may make or initiate studies and reports with respect to international economic, social, cultural, educational, health, and related matters and may make recommendations with respect to any such matters to the General Assembly, to the Members of the United Nations, and to the specialized agencies concerned".

40 The WHO Constitution was signed on 19 June 1946 by the representatives of 61 States. It entered into force on 7 April 1948 when the threshold of 26 States – according to Art. 80 – was reached. The delay in the entry into force was due to tensions among the Great Powers as consequence of the beginning of the Cold War. See Lawrence O. Gostin, *Global Health Law* (Harvard University Press: 2014), at 91.

The Preamble's ambitious agenda and the vision of the WHO as a leader in global health governance[41] were then reiterated in the discussion on the wide functions of the WHO (Art. 2). The WHO was considered "the directing and coordinating authority on international health work" (Art. 2, lect. *a*).

Its key tasks clearly encompass the classic functions envisaged in the early sanitary conventions and first health organizations, such as the International Office of Public Health (1907) and the Health Organization of the League of the Nations (1923); these include surveillance at the borders for infectious diseases, quarantine measures, harmonization of border control measures, drug standardization, and adherence to relevant scientific and technological standards.[42]

In addition, its broad mandate envisages the promotion of the "highest possible level of health" by all peoples as a fundamental right to be enjoyed without distinction of race, religion, political belief, or economic or social condition (Preamble, Para. 2). The right to health is considered a fundamental right that all governments must attain; therefore, the main functions of the WHO are not solely confined to the prevention of the spread of infectious diseases but also include the promotion of the "highest attainable standard of health".

Furthermore, the WHO Constitution states that "[u]nequal development in different countries in the promotion of health and control of disease,

41 In general terms, global governance can be defined as "the sum of the many ways individuals and institutions, public and private, manage their common affairs. It is a continuing process through which conflicting or diverse interests may be accommodated and cooperative action may be taken. It includes formal institutions and regimes empowered to enforce compliance, as well as informal arrangements that people and institutions either have agreed to or perceive to be in their interest" (Commission on Global Governance: Our Global Neighborhood: The Report of the Commission on Global Governance. 1995, New York: United Nations). Global health can in contrast be understood as an issue that requires a collective response due to its transboundary dimension, such as specific health issues (epidemics, pandemics, NCDs, and neglected diseases), specific health demands within certain regions (e.g., developing countries), or specific populations (e.g., vulnerable groups and people living with HIV).

42 To reinforce these traditional goals, Article 2 affirms that the WHO has the purpose, *inter alia*, to establish international nomenclatures of diseases (lect., *s*), standardize diagnostic procedures (lect., *t*), develop relevant international standards (lect., *u*), and consult relevant experts (lect., *k*), and it empowered the WHO with a specific treaty-making power and standard-setting functions not only "to propose conventions and agreements" but also to include "issuing regulations and recommendations as well as performing such duties as may be assigned" to the organization. Furthermore, it anticipates that the WHO would direct and coordinate activities on "international health work" (lect. *a*), assist governments upon their request in strengthening health services (lect. *b*), stimulate and advance work on "endemic and other diseases" (therefore, not only infectious diseases) (lect. *g*), promote the improvement of "nutrition, housing, sanitation, recreation, economic or working conditions and other aspects of environmental hygiene" (lect. *i*), and promote maternal and child health and welfare (lect. *l*). See Kelley Lee, *The World Health Organization* (Routledge: 2009); Jennifer Prah Ruger, Derek Yach, "The Global Role of the World Health Organization", *Global Health Governance* (2009): 1–11.

especially communicable diseases, is a common danger" (Preamble, Para. 5). States should therefore have a common interest in protecting the health of their inhabitants. "Governments have a responsibility for the health of their peoples which can be fulfilled only by the provision of adequate health and social measures".

The strategy of the WHO was consequently that of addressing at its roots the causes of infectious diseases in developing countries by promoting better health conditions rather than by simply focusing on the protection of the trade interests of Western countries. This strategy was then exemplified by the global vaccination campaigns and the Health for All Strategy launched in 1978.

Its wide functions seemed to imply a strong erosion of health sovereignty, but as indicated by the COVID-19 pandemic, the WHO presents the typical flaws and weaknesses of IGOs.[43]

Despite the far-reaching consequences of infectious diseases on human health, as they have caused more casualties than world wars, the development of global health law was quite slow compared to other sectors of international law (such as the law on disarmament and weapons of mass destruction).[44]

The WHO Constitution was considered the "paradise" paradigm in contrast with the anterior "power" paradigm that permeated the previous 100 years of international health diplomacy.[45]

According to Fidler, the international health regime, as shaped by the WHO's Constitution in a more structured fashion, marks the shift from a simple inter-state frontier patrol system to avoid the spread of certain infectious diseases to a framework that is intended to manage health as a common public good.[46]

This global health regime based on a human rights perspective has become complementary to the UN collective security mechanism. The UN Charter was the first major treaty to affirm the prohibition of the threat or use of force in international relations, to create a specific legal framework to solve disputes among States, and to centralize the *jus in bellum* in the Security Council.[47] The

---

43 The main barrier to global health governance is represented by the latent conflict between the prerogatives of States in the domain of health, which is traditionally considered a matter that falls within domestic jurisdiction, and the necessity by the WHO to take upon itself a portion of States' competences in the health field. On the tension between globalist and statist approaches in global health governance, see Sara E. Davies, "What Contribution Can International Relations Make to the Evolving Global Health Agenda"? *International Affairs* (2010): 1167–1190.

44 On this topic, see Daniel H. Joyner, *International Law and the Proliferation of Weapons of Mass Destruction* (Oxford University Press: 2009).

45 David P. Fidler, "Caught Between Paradise and Power: Public Health, Pathogenic Threats, and the Axis of Illness", *McGeorge Law Review* (2004): 45–101.

46 David P. Fidler, "Germs, Governance, and Global Public Health in the Wake of SARS", *The Journal of Clinical Investigation* (2004): 799–804.

47 Josephat Ezenwajiaku, *State Territory and International Law* (Routledge: 2023); Christian Henderson, *The Use of Force and International Law* (Cambridge University Press: 2018), 18–24.

WHO Constitution, for its part, was the first treaty to affirm a holistic conception of health as a fundamental human right and as a catalyst for peace.[48]

4. The WHO's structure and its institutional set up

The WHO has a federal structure and is based on three layers of governance: at the bottom are the headquarters located in Geneva. Then, there are six Regional Offices that represent Africa, the Americas, South-East Asia, Europe, Eastern Mediterranean, and the Western Pacific, and finally, there are 150 local offices.[49]

The DG dictates the policy of the WHO while the regional and local offices implement the WHO's programmes.

The Regional Offices enjoy a wide independence from the headquarters. First, the regional directors are formally appointed by the Executive Board (not by the DG) upon the recommendation of the States (Art. 52 of the WHO Constitution).[50]

States are divided into regional offices on the basis of the geographical collocation but with some peculiarities. Israel – due to the ongoing diplomatic tension with some neighboring countries – is included within the European regional office. South Korea belongs to the Western Pacific region with China and Japan, while North Korea is part of the South-East Asia region.[51]

This structure was chastised for increased bureaucracy, fragmented decision making, and a decreased field level of effectiveness.[52]

In particular, the high degree of fragmentation within the WHO is indicated by an excessive independence of the regional offices. This "structural-based fragmentation" is evident since the DG does not control the appointment of the regional directors who can autonomously dictate country office budgets and programmes.[53]

The WHO's institutional set up is quite conventional and adheres to the classic tripartite structure of UN specialized agencies.[54]

---

48 The cholera epidemic in Egypt in 1947 – which spread from a British military base in the Nile Delta area – was the first testing ground for the WHO. Sylvia Chiffoleau, *Genèse de la santé publique internationale: De la peste d'Orient à l'OMS* (Presses Universitaires de Rennes: 2012), 259.

49 Yves Beigbeder, *The Internal Management of United Nations Organizations: The Long Quest for Reform* (Springer: 2016).

50 Article 52 states that "The head of the regional office shall be the Regional Director appointed by the Board in agreement with the regional committee".

51 Jeremy Youde, *Global Health Governance* (Cambridge University Press: 2012), 14.

52 Erin R. Graham, "International Organizations as Collective Agents: Fragmentation and the Limits of Principal Control at the World Health Organization", *European Journal of International Relations* (2014): 366–390.

53 Tine Hanrieder, "The Path-Dependent Design of International Organizations: Federalism in the World Health Organization", *European Journal of International Relations* (2015): 223–226.

54 Henry G. Schermers, Niels M. Blokker, *International Institutional Law*, 6th revised ed. (Brill/Nijhoff: 2018), 302–304.

According to Article 9, its main bodies are the World Health Assembly, the Executive Board, and the Secretariat.

The World Health Assembly (WHA) is the supreme decision-making body of the WHO and comprises one representative from each of the 194 Member States. The delegates must be "chosen from amongst persons most qualified by their technical competence in the field of health, preferably represent-ing the national health administration of the Member" (Art. 11). Among its numerous tasks, the WHA determines the policies of the WHO, appoints the DG (on nomination of the Executive Board), and supervises the budget. As stated by Article 59,

"Each Member shall have one vote in the Health Assembly".[55]

The functions of the WHA are not dissimilar to those of the UN General Assembly (GA); it can also establish subsidiary bodies and adopt recom-mendations, and it approves the annual budget; but it can "take any other appropriate action to further the objective of the Organization" (Arts. 18 and 23).[56]

The WHA is entrusted with a specific treaty-making power – unlike the GA – since it can adopt conventions ("binding regulations") with a two-thirds majority of votes, although such treaties do not come into force for any WHO

---

55 Due to the COVID-19 pandemic, the Seventy-fourth WHA (24 May 2021–1 June 2021) was held virtually according to the Special Procedures to regulate the conduct of virtual meetings of the World Health Assembly (Special procedures Report by the Director-General, A74/45 Provisional agenda item 1.4 21 May 2021).

56 Article 18 lists the main functions of the WHA as follows: "(a) to determine the policies of the Organization; (b) to name the Members entitled to designate a person to serve on the Board; (c) to appoint the Director-General; (d) to review and approve reports and activities of the Board and of the Director-General and to instruct the Board in regard to matters upon which action, study, investigation or report may be considered desirable; (e) to establish such committees as may be considered necessary for the work of the Organization; (f) to supervise the financial policies of the Organization and to review and approve the budget; (g) to instruct the Board and the Director-General to bring to the attention of Members and of international organizations, governmental or nongovernmental, any matter with regard to health which the Health Assembly may consider appropriate; (h) to invite any organization, international or national, governmental or non-governmental, which has responsibilities related to those of the Organization, to appoint representatives to participate, without right of vote, in its meetings or in those of the committees and conferences convened under its authority, on conditions prescribed by the Health Assembly; but in the case of national organizations, invitations shall be issued only with the consent of the Government concerned; (i) to consider recommenda-tions bearing on health made by the General Assembly, the Economic and Social Council, the Security Council or Trusteeship Council of the United Nations, and to report to them on the steps taken by the Organization to give effect to such recommendations; (j) to report to the Economic and Social Council in accordance with any agreement between the Organiza-tion and the United Nations; (k) to promote and conduct research in the field of health by the personnel of the Organization, by the establishment of its own institutions or by co-operation with official or non-official institutions of any Member with the consent of its Government; (l) to establish such other institutions as it may consider desirable; (m) to take any other appropri-ate action to further the objective of the Organization".

member unless that State has accepted it "in accordance with its constitutional processes" (Art. 19).[57]

The Executive Board is composed of 34 members technically qualified in the field of health. Members are elected for three-year terms and usually meet at least twice a year.

Its main task is to provide advice to the Assembly in its decision-making process about the WHO's programmes. It is empowered, among other things, "to take emergency measures within the functions and financial resources of the Organization to deal with events requiring immediate action. In particular, it may authorize the Director-General to take the necessary steps to combat epidemics, to participate in the organization of health relief to victims of a calamity and to undertake studies and research the urgency of which has been drawn to the attention of the Board by any Member or by the Director-General" (Art. 28, lect. *i*).

As underlined by some scholars, this faculty of taking emergency measures is something very similar to Chapter VII powers of the Security Council.[58]

The Secretariat comprises the DG and technical and administrative staff.[59] The WHO Secretariat, which carries out routine operations and helps to implement strategies, consists of experts, staff, and field workers who have appointments at the central headquarters or at one of the six regional WHO offices or other offices located in countries around the world.

The DG – described as the WHO's "chief technical and administrator officer" – is subject to the authority of the Board (Art. 31).

5. The legal powers of the WHO

The Constitution of the WHO establishes the main procedures within the Organization. Compared to other IGOs, it enjoys extensive powers. In fact, its functions go well beyond the traditional standard-setting function of IGOs.[60]

---

57 Although the GA does not have the power to adopt binding regulations (its resolutions are not *per se* binding) but rather declarations or resolutions containing recommendations, its competence has been labelled "quasi-legislative"; indeed, its acts are generally considered as the basis for the formation of customary law or *jus cogens* norms. Nicholas Onuf, "Professor Falk on the Quasi-Legislative Competence of the General Assembly", *The American Journal of International Law* (1970): 349–355.

58 In this sense, see Jose E. Alvarez, *The Impact of International Organizations on International Law* (Brill/Nijhoff: 2017), 198.

59 Article 30 states, "The Secretariat shall comprise the Director-General and such technical and administrative staff as the Organization may require".

60 David P. Fidler, "International Law and Global Public Health", *University of Kansas Law Review* (1999): 1–58; see also Donato Greco, *L'Organizzazione mondiale della sanità davanti alla pandemia di COVID-19. La governance delle emergenze sanitarie internazionali* (Le Monnier Università: 2022), 44–46.

Under Article 2, lect. *k*, of the WHO's Constitution, the Organization has the goals "to propose conventions, agreements and regulations, and make recommendations with respect to international health matters".[61] The WHO also has the competence to issue treaties (Arts. 19 and 20)[62] – which is a classic function of IGOs, such as the ILO,[63] the Food and Agricultural Organization (FAO)[64] – and binding regulations without national ratification procedures (Art. 21).[65]

Under Article 20, Member States must "take action" in order to accept a convention or an agreement within 18 months after its adoption by the WHA and shall then notify the Director-General of the action undertaken. If a State decides not to accept a convention or an agreement proposed by the WHA within the time limit, then it must provide a statement of the reasons for non-acceptance. This mechanism is quite uncommon under international law, since States are usually free to decide whether to ratify or not an agreement or a treaty without providing any justification.

61 A similar disposition is contained in the United Nations Educational, Scientific and Cultural Organization (UNESCO) Constitution that grants the General Conference the power to adopt both recommendations and conventions. "The General Conference shall, in adopting proposals for submission to the Member States, distinguish between recommendations and international conventions submitted for their approval. In the former case a majority vote shall suffice; in the latter case a two-thirds majority shall be required" (Art. IV.B.4). See, in general, Abdulqawi A. Yusuf, "UNESCO Practices and Procedures for the Elaboration of Standard-Setting Instruments", in Abdulqawi A. Yusuf (ed.), *UNESCO: Volume I: Normative Action in Education, Science and Culture* (Martinus Nijhoff Publishers: 2007), 31–50.

62 Article 19 recognizes that "the Health Assembly shall have authority to adopt conventions or agreements with respect to any matter within the competence of the Organization. A two-thirds vote of the Health Assembly shall be required for the adoption of such conventions or agreements, which shall come into force for each Member when accepted by it in accordance with its constitutional processes". For further details, see Pedro A. Villareal, Claudia Nannini, "International Law and Global Health", Mario C. B. Raviglione, Fabrizio Tediosi, Simone Villa, Núria Casamitjana, Antoni Plasència (eds), *Global Health Essentials* (Springer Nature: 2023), 451–455.

63 Article 19 of the ILO Constitution ("Conventions and Recommendations") reads as follows: "When the Conference has decided on the adoption of proposals with regard to an item on the agenda, it will rest with the Conference to determine whether these proposals should take the form: (a) of an international Convention, or (b) of a Recommendation to meet circumstances where the subject, or aspect of it, dealt with is not considered suitable or appropriate at that time for a Convention".

64 Art. XV of the FAO Constitution establishes that "the Conference may, by a two-thirds majority of the votes cast approve and submit to Member Nations conventions and agreements concerning questions relating to food and agriculture".

65 Article 21 states, "The Health Assembly shall have authority to adopt regulations concerning: (a) sanitary and quarantine requirements and other procedures designed to prevent the international spread of disease; (b) nomenclatures with respect to diseases, causes of death and public health practices; (c) standards with respect to diagnostic procedures for international use; (d) standards with respect to the safety, purity and potency of biological, pharmaceutical and similar products moving in international commerce; (e) advertising and labelling of biological, pharmaceutical and similar products moving in international commerce. These different sectors have a common element represented by the global nature of public health and the consequent necessity to harmonize domestic legislations through common standards rooted on scientific considerations.

Regulations are enacted through a two-thirds majority of Members present and voting,[66] subject to a possible opt-out by dissenting countries (Art. 22).[67] Since it is a tacit acceptance procedure, if a State does not expressly "opt out" through a rejection or reservation duly notified to the Director-General, then it is automatically bound by the regulation.[68] Significantly, such regulations enter into force for all Members once approved by the Health Assembly unless a Member State does not manifestly object ("persistent objector").

This practice does not contrast with the Vienna Convention on the Law of Treaties (VCLT); as observed by Imbert, Article 11 of the VCLT envisages the possibility of a tacit consent to be bound to a treaty "especially since under international law there is no rule imposing on States to give their consent expressly".[69]

This process, which can be considered "quasi-legislative", was an intuition by the WHO's founders that maintained that the classic approach based on "hard law" (treaties and conventions) was not sufficient to address the main health issues arising at the end of World War II. Specifically, the entry into force of treaties and conventions usually requires a long period of time, while health emergencies necessitate faster solutions. These new powers of the WHO are a novelty compared to those of the *Office International d'Hygiène Publique*, which was not entrusted with the same capacity as the WHO as it was grounded on the customary rule of treaty law (as then codified in the VCLT).[70]

This reverses the traditional rule of State consent to be bound by a treaty (generally through signature and ratification),[71] insofar as a country that fails to express its lack of consent is presumptively bound.

Therefore, the WHA has a vast array of legal options if it decides to exercise its "normative authority", which is intended as its faculty to draft global health rules, in contrast to its technical role (such as providing guidelines on

---

66 Article 60, lect. *a* indicates that "a decisions of the Health Assembly on important questions shall be made by a two-thirds majority of the Members present and voting. These questions shall include: the adoption of conventions or agreements; the approval of agreements bringing the Organization into relation with the United Nations and inter-governmental organizations and agencies in accordance with Articles 69, 70 and 72; amendments to this Constitution".

67 Article 22 affirms, "Regulations adopted pursuant to Article 21 shall come into force for all Members after due notice has been given of their adoption by the Health Assembly except for such Members as may notify the Director-General of rejection or reservations within the period stated in the notice".

68 Doris König, "Tacit Consent/Opting Out Procedure", in *Max Planck Encyclopedias of International Law* (Oxford University Press: 2013); Derek W., *The law of International Institutions* (Steven & Sons: 1975), 120.

69 Pierre-Henry Imbert, "Le consentement des Etats en droit international. Réflexions à partir d'un cas pratique concernant la participation de la CEE aux traités du Conseil de l'Europe", *Revue générale de droit international public* (1995): 353–381, at 361.

70 Article 34 of the VCLT states, "A treaty does not create either obligations or rights for a third State without its consent".

71 See Malcolm M. Shaw, *International Law* (Cambridge University Press: 2003), at 88. Article 11 of the VCLT (1969) affirms that "The consent of a State to be bound by a treaty may be expressed by signature, exchange of instruments constituting a treaty, ratification, acceptance, approval or accession, or by any other means if so agreed".

the allocation of treatments or vaccines or providing statistics on the course of a disease).[72]

The legal nature of these regulations is a debated issue, since they have the characteristics of both binding acts of IGOs and treaties under the VCLT.[73]

On the one hand, it is a fair assumption to maintain that regulations are unilateral acts of the WHO since they have been formally enacted through a resolution of the WHA (that has its legal foundation in Arts. 21 and 22 of the WHO Constitution).[74]

According to this point of view, regulations might be compared to the resolutions of the Security Council as they have been defined by the International Court of Justice (ICJ),[75] which are acts enacted by a single body that are binding upon all Member States.[76]

On the other hand, the IHR have typical elements of international treaties: their adoption is subject to the consent of its Member States, although in tacit form; they are registered at the UN Secretary-General under Article 102 of the UN Charter,[77] are open to ratification by non-Member States, and allow States Parties to make reservations.

It is possible to therefore argue that the IHR are a *sui generis* act of the WHO that share the elements of both rules of the Organization and a classic treaty.[78]

72 Lawrence O. Gostin, Devi Sridharb, Daniel Hougendobler, "The Normative Authority of the World Health Organization", *Public Health* (2015): 1–10.
73 Laurence Boisson de Chazournes, "Le pouvoir réglementaire de l'Organization mondiale de la santé à l'aune de la santé mondiale: réflexions sur la portée et la nature du Règlement sanitaire international de 2005", in *Droit du pouvoir, pouvoir du droit: mélanges offerts à Jean Salmon* (Bruylant: 2007), 1157–1181.
74 In this sense, see Andrea Spagnolo, "(Non) Compliance with the International Health Regulations of the WHO from the Perspective of the Law of International Responsibility", *Global Jurist* (2017): 1–18, at 3.
75 The ICJ has defined the UN Security Council resolutions as follows: "Security Council resolutions are issued by a single, collective body and are drafted through a very different process than that used for the conclusion of a treaty. Security Council resolutions are the product of a voting process as provided for in Article 27 of the Charter, and the final text of such resolutions represents the view of the Security Council as a body. Moreover, Security Council resolutions can be binding on all Member States". ICJ, "Advisory Opinion of 22 July 2010, Accordance with International Law of the Unilateral Declaration of Independence in Respect of Kosovo", *ICJ Reports* (2010), 442, Section 94.
76 In this sense, see Roberto Virzo, "The Proliferation of Institutional Acts of International Organizations: A Proposals for their Classification", in Roberto Virzo, Ivan Ingravallo (eds.), *Evolutions in the Law of International Organizations* (Brill/Nijhoff: 2015), 293–323, at 312.
77 Article 102 of the UN Charter states that "Every treaty and every international agreement entered into by any Member of the United Nations after the present Charter comes into force shall as soon as possible be registered with the Secretariat and published by it".
78 In this sense, see Andrea Spagnolo, "Contromisure dell'Organizzazione Mondiale della Sanità come conseguenza di violazioni dei Regolamenti sanitari internazionali in contesti epidemici", in Laura Pineschi (ed.), *La tutela della salute nel diritto internazionale ed europeo tra interessi globali e interessi particolari* (Editoriale Scientifica: 2016), 391–420, at 415.

However, in its practice, the WHA has rarely relied on its treaty-making power,[79] unlike the ILO, which has adopted a vast array of treaties in the field of labor.[80]

Hence, since its founding, it has acted primarily as a technocratic institution and over-relies on soft law instruments,[81] renouncing *de facto* the task of codification of global health law. In particular, the codification of the human right to health has not been consistent with the promises of the Preamble. The WHO was the first organization to officially proclaim a human right to health, but it failed to adopt a codification treaty on this matter despite its treaty-making power. The right to health was eventually enshrined in an expressed article of the International Covenant on Economic, Social and Cultural Rights (ICESCR) that was drafted within the UN, although the WHO would have been *ratione materiae* the most appropriate forum to negotiate an *ad hoc* treaty on the right to health. It should have regulated in detail the most sensitive issues, such as the fair distribution of treatments and vaccines worldwide based on the key assumption of health as a common public good. This would have been in line with Article 2, lect. *k*, of the WHO Constitution, which establishes – among the functions of the Organization – the goal of proposing "conventions, agreements and regulations, and make recommendations with respect to international health matters".

Only with the Declaration of Alma Ata (1979) – which, however, did not take the form of a binding act, such as a treaty or regulation – the WHO affirmed the concept of "primary health care" for all in line with the expansive meaning given to health in the WTO's Preamble.

As was evident in the WTO's "Health for All" strategy that came after the adoption of the Alma Ata Declaration, the Organization did not commit itself to begin a codification process in the human rights sector.

The common practice of the Organization is therefore to exercise its normative authority by mainly relying on soft law instruments, under the form of recommendations, technical guidelines, technical reports, and specific programmes.

Since its establishment, the norm-making role has therefore remained *de facto* limited to the adoption of two treaties (the Framework Convention on Tobacco Control and its Additional Protocol to Eliminate Illicit Trade in

---

79 Fidler first predicted the WHO's reluctance to rely on its treaty-making power and argued that it has a vast "epistemic authority". David P. Fidler, "The Future of the World Health Organization: What Role for International Law", *Vanderbilt Journal of Transnational Law* (1998): 1079.
80 Jose E. Alvarez, *International Organizations as Law-Makers* (Oxford University Press: 2006).
81 Article 23 of the WHO Constitution gives the Assembly the authority "to make recommendations to Members", and Article 62 requires States to report annually on the action undertaken to comply with its recommendations. David P. Fidler, "The Future of the World Health Organization: What Role for International Law?", *Vanderbilt Journal of Transnational Law* 31 (2008): 1079–1126.

Tobacco Products)[82] and two regulations (the Nomenclature Regulations in 1948 and the International Sanitary Regulations (ISRs) in 1951);[83] this was the first global legal regime of surveillance and control of "quarantinable diseases" (which included, *ex* Article 1, "plague, cholera, yellow fever, smallpox, typhus and relapsing fever").[84] The ISRs had the goals of solving the problem of the excessive fragmentation of global health law and systematizing the existing conventional patchwork, since they replaced the previous treaties adopted during the first half of the XX century. The ISRs were superseded in 1969 by the IHR (then amended in 1981 and 2005), which do not focus on the promotion of the right to health but rather on the response and containment of disease outbreaks.[85]

This political choice is in striking contrast to the practice of UN specialized agencies, such as the ILO[86] but presents similarities to the action of other specialized agencies, such as the FAO.[87]

Taylor argues that "in the case of WHO, the extreme conservatism regarding the use of legal institutions appears to reflect a cultural predisposition – a dominant value and guiding philosophy of the organization".[88] This is probably due to a lack of a "normative tradition" and a reluctance of its Member States to rely on hard law instruments.[89] A proposal for a global treaty on HIV/AIDS, for instance, was eventually dropped, and this disease then remained marginalized within the WHO after the establishment of The Joint UN Programme on HIV/AIDS (UNAIDS).

The issue of human cloning is emblematic; although this topic falls within the WHO's mandate for its far-reaching consequences on human health, the proposal for the adoption of an international convention against reproductive

---

82 In this regard, see Ilja Richard Pavone, "Protocol to Eliminate Illicit Trade in Tobacco Products", *Oxford International Organizations, OXIO 399* (2020), https://opil.ouplaw.com/display/10.1093/law-oxio/e399.013.1/law-oxio-e399?rskey=wHIGHP&result=2&prd=OPIL

83 WHA, Resolution WHA4.75 (May 25, 1951), in 35 Official Records of the World Health Organization, at 50 (1952).

84 WHO, Comm. on International Sanitary Regulations, WHO Regulations No. 2: International Sanitary Regulations, at 6, WHO Doc. A4/60 (1951).

85 Ginevra Le Moli, "The Containment Bias of the WHO International Health Regulations", *The British Yearbook of International Law* (2023): 1–41.

86 Jan Johnston, "Law-Making by International Organizations", in Jeffrey L. Dunoff, Mark A. Pollack (eds.), *Interdisciplinary Perspectives on International Law and International Relations. The State of the Art* (Cambridge University Press: 2013), 274–275.

87 FAO, despite an explicit 'treaty making power' envisaged by Art. XIV of its Constitution, has to date adopted few treaties. The most relevant agreements are the International Plant Protection Convention (IPPC) (1951) and the International Treaty on Plant Genetic Resources for Food and Agriculture (2001).

88 Allyn Lise Taylor, "Making the World Health Organization Work: A Legal Framework for Universal Access to the Conditions for Health", *American Journal of Law & Medicine* (1992): 301–343, at 303.

89 In this sense, see Gian Luca Burci, Claude-Henri Vignes, *World Health Organization* (Kluwer Law International: 2004), 155.

cloning made by France and Germany was debated within the GA (not within the WHA). The negotiation led to the approval of the UN Declaration on Human Cloning on 8 May 2005, which banned reproductive cloning.[90]

Against this backdrop, it can be argued that UN specialized agencies tend to rely on soft law instruments instead of hard law rules due to the difficulties related to the negotiation of a treaty or convention, which is a long process that requires diplomatic capacities, especially in sensitive domains, such as health, bioethics, and the environment.

The next chapter is devoted to an analysis of the most important legal instrument adopted within the WHO for the management and containment of infectious diseases, namely, the IHR (2005), and investigates the reasons behind their reform in 2005, their scope, and the obligations that they impose upon States.

6. The International Health Regulations

6.1. Negotiation process

The IHR that replaced the pre-WHO international sanitary conventions among their parties were first adopted by the World Health Assembly in 1951 and have been updated several times. They initially followed what David Fidler called the "classical regime" comprising of an exhaustive list of diseases, rigid maximum control measures, and a relatively passive role for the WHO.[91]

They were overhauled in 2005 after a fast negotiation because of the lessons learned during the 2003 SARS epidemic and the parallel risk of an avian influenza outbreak (although the negotiation process had officially begun in 1995).[92]

Moreover, in general, the reform of the IHR 2005 was a response on the global level to several health emergencies of international concern that started to emerge in the 80s.

The IHR in their original formulation had a limited scope, since they applied only to a small number of diseases, namely, cholera, plague, and yellow fever, which was an inheritance from the past. These diseases had already

---

90 Lect. *b* of the Declaration reads as follows: "Member States are called upon to prohibit all forms of human cloning in as much as they are incompatible with human dignity and the protection of human life".

91 David P. Fidler, "From International Sanitary Conventions to Global Health Security: The New International Health Regulations", *Chinese Journal of International Law* (2005): 325–392, at 328.

92 Revision Process of the International Health Regulations, WHO, www.who.int/ihr/revision process/revision/en/. The revised IHR were enacted by the WHA on 23 May 2005 and entered into force on 15 June 2007; they currently have 196 Parties, including the 194 Member States and the Holy See and Liechtenstein. David P. Fidler, "Revision of the World Health Organization's International Health Regulations", *ASIL Insights* (16 April 2004), https://www.asil.org/insights/volume/8/issue/8/revision-world-health-organizations-international-health-regulations.

been the object of the first international health conference of 1852 and were diseases that historically had a major impact on trade. The lack of flexibility of the IHR and their narrow scope became evident when human immunodeficiency virus/acquired immune deficiency syndrome (HIV/AIDS), one of the most devastating epidemics in world history, first appeared. In June 1981, scientists in the United States reported early clinical evidence of a disease that would become known as AIDS, mainly occurring among the gay community and caused by HIV.[93] As underlined by Gostin, this new disease was not, however, covered under the IHR, and it was not added to the list of diseases that fall within the scope of application of the IHR.[94]

In addition, the Chernobyl nuclear disaster, with severe implications for public health, showed the irrelevance of the IHR when facing the early secrecy by the Soviet authorities after the nuclear reactor explosion.

The new threat posed by various microorganisms used as biological or chemical weapons by terrorist groups (bioterrorism) was also beyond the scope of the IHR. Examples are represented by the Tokyo subway chemical attack with the toxic nerve gas sarin perpetrated in 1995 by the religious group Aum Shinrikyo and the anthrax case following September 11.

The key event that convinced States to resort to the atypical powers under Article 21 of the WHO Constitution was, however, represented by the SARS outbreak in 2003. The epidemic – a severe form of viral pneumonia that is highly contagious, which was diagnosed for the first time in the south of China in February 2003[95] – spread rapidly to over 30 countries (including Canada, Hong Kong, the Russian Federation, and Spain).[96]

This was the first epidemic after HIV/AIDS that constituted a real threat to global health due to its easy person-to-person transmission and its high fatality rate, similar to that of the deadliest infectious diseases, such as smallpox and influenza.

The Chinese authorities in the first phase concealed vital information on the disease outbreak, but following a strong mobilization and pressure by public opinion, they were eventually forced to notify the world of the epidemic in March 2003 and to allow a WHO team to carry out an investigation *in loco* to evaluate the magnitude of the outbreak. A formal alert by the WHO was then launched on 12 March 2003.[97]

93 Robert Gallo, *Virus Hunting: AIDS, Cancer and the Human Retrovirus: A Story of Scientific Discovery* (Basic Books: 1993).
94 Lawrence O. Gostin, "Infectious Disease Law: Revision of the World Health Organization's International Health Regulations", *The Journal of the American Medical Association* (2004): 2623–2627.
95 Some scientists argue, however, that the first clusters of cases date back to November 2002 in the city of Fohan, Guandgong Province.
96 https://www.who.int/health-topics/severe-acute-respiratory-syndrome.
97 https://www.history.com/this-day-in-history/world-health-organization-declares-sars-con tained-worldwide.

Afterwards, the WHO was able to publish daily updating on the course of the disease outbreak through the support of the Global Outbreak Alert and Response Network (GOARN).[98]

The WHO's response, which was based upon travel advice that discouraged trips to the most affected countries in South-East Asia and Canada, and an international collaboration without precedent, allowed the stopping of the epidemic in less than four months.

The SARS outbreak was evidence of the inadequacy of the "classic regime" reflected in the first version of the IHR, and the lack of cooperation by the Chinese government highlighted the fact that the globalized world was facilitating the spread of infectious diseases.

The surveillance mechanism set up by the IHR had not worked properly, since States regularly omitted notifying the WHO of the presence of a disease outbreak in their territory. This was mainly related to the absence of adequate domestic surveillance systems that were unable to detect an outbreak epidemic, and if they were able, it was with severe delay. Furthermore, States are tendentially reluctant to report a new outbreak because they fear negative consequences for their prestige, reputation, and economic losses in terms of trade and tourism.

It was evident that a reinforced cooperation on health issues was necessary and that a single organ should have been in charge of managing these new and emerging global threats to health through the adoption of quick decisions.[99]

In fact, as a product of the regime of horizontal control of diseases outbreaks, the old regulations did not answer properly to the new WHO policy oriented towards a vertical approach to infectious diseases aimed at reducing their incidence within the States with a consequent minor exportation and diffusion.[100] Then, as underlined by Fidler, the old IHR had a too narrow scope limited to the "Asiatic" diseases, which left unresolved the health problems and disease outbreaks of developing countries of sub-Saharan Africa and the question of the prevention of their spread.

The drafters of the new version of the IHR backed the conception that restrictions on trade and mobility should be based on a risk assessment rather than on pre-established maximum measures; that is, this solution seemed scientifically more justifiable and flexible.

Over time, it became evident that States' responses to disease outbreaks and man-made disasters that seriously damaged human health (bioterrorism and nuclear accidents) were handled outside the WHO. States mainly relied on the

---

98 https://extranet.who.int/goarn/.

99 David P. Fidler, "SARS: Political Pathology of the First Post-Westphalian Pathogen", *Journal of Law, Medicine & Ethics* (2003): 485, 486.

100 Dyna Arhin-Tenkorang, Pedro Conceição, "Beyond Communicable Disease Control: Health in the Age of Globalization", in I. Kaul, P. Conceição, K. Le Goulven, R.U. Mendoza (eds.), *Providing Global Public Goods: Managing Globalization* (Oxford University Press: 2003), 484–515; Jan Johnston, "Law-Making by International Organizations", in Jeffrey L. Dunoff, Mark A. Pollack (eds.), *Interdisciplinary Perspectives on International Law and International Relations: The State of the Art* (Cambridge University Press: 2013), 274–275.

technical assistance of other IGOs such as the International Atomic Energy Agency (IAEA) or the World Trade Organization (WTO), subsidiary bodies such as UNAIDS, and informal sources of information (non-governmental organizations (NGOs) and networks).

These concerns led the WHA to call for a substantial revision of the IHR in 1995,[101] although the negotiation process was accelerated as a direct consequence of the SARS outbreak.

6.2. *The all risk approach*

The IHR are grounded on the traditional twin purposes of health diplomacy that aim to protect public health and at the same time avoid excessive interference with trade, specifically, the maximum possible protection against diseases and the minimum interference with international traffic.[102]

The IHR 2005 contain an expanded scope of application compared to the previous version, which was traditionally related to a small number of communicable diseases. In fact, one of the main reasons for revision involved the too narrow scope of the previous regulations, which after the complete eradication of smallpox in 1980, applied to only three infectious diseases, namely, cholera, plague, and yellow fewer.

The IHR pertain to every disease event regardless of nature or origin, marking a shift from a "disease-specific model" to an "all risk approach".[103] Currently, the IHR pertain to any disease ". . . irrespective of origin of source"; this broad terminology ranges from traditional infectious diseases with a human or animal source to pathogenic agents intentionally released by human beings in the atmosphere, which therefore also embraces terrorist attacks with biological or chemical weapons (Art. 1, Para. 5). It is an open-ended approach, since the IHR are related to "any event" (natural or man-made) that might cause a disease outbreak.

As outlined by Gostin, the risks associated with a given disease can thus have origins of persons, animals, vectors, or the environment.[104]

During the negotiation process, States such as the United States strongly supported a direct reference in the IHR to security threats including the intentional release of weapons of mass destruction (WMD).[105]

---

101 Forty-Eight World Health Assembly, Geneva, 1–15 May 1995, WHA 48.7, "Revision and updating of the International Health Regulations".

102 Article 2 states that among the aim of the IHRs is "to prevent, protect against, control and provide a public health response to the international spread of disease in ways that are commensurate with and restricted to public health risks, and which avoid unnecessary interference with international traffic and trade".

103 David P. Fidler, Lawrence O. Gostin, "The New International Health Regulations: An Historic Development for International Law and Public Health", *The Journal of Law, Medicine & Ethics* (2006): 85–94.

104 Lawrence O. Gostin, *Global Health Law* (Harvard University Press: 2014), 184.

105 David P. Fidler, Lawrence O. Gostin, *Biosecurity in the Global Age: Biological Weapons, Public Health, and the Rule of Law* (Stanford University Press: 2007), 138.

In the final version of the IHR, a direct mention of WMD was eventually deleted in favor of more nuanced wording, since Article 7 refers to an "unexpected or unusual public health event". Threats to public health can therefore occur naturally (a zoonosis), can be accidental, or can be caused intentionally. The unintentional release of pathogens raises the issue of the link among health, security, and dual-use research of concern (DURC).

Life science research that is generally intended for the benefit of humankind might be misapplied to do harm; this is the "dual-use dilemma", namely, when research could be beneficial or could harm humanity.[106] Such a benefit might include, for example, the cure for a highly virulent infectious disease or "potential pandemic pathogen", such as avian influenza. A commensurate potential harm might be the creation of a pandemic pathogen.

Dual-use technologies[107] imply a possible misuse of science through the use of modern technologies for the development of bacteriological, chemical, or nuclear weapons that are a serious threat to public health. For example, United States scientist James Conant produced poison gas in World War I and was one of the promoters of the project of the atomic bomb.

One of the most well-known examples of unintentional release of a pathogen agent is the "mousepox case", where two Australian scientists inadvertently produced a lethal mouse virus. The gene for interleukin-4 (IL-4) was inserted into the mousepox virus through genetic engineering techniques. Their goal was to induce infertility in mice – which are a major pest in Australia – that would have acted as an infectious contraceptive for pest control. They discovered instead that the engineered mousepox virus damaged the immune system of exposed mice and killed them. The scientists warned about the possibility of creating similar viruses that are deadly to human beings.[108] Their findings raised criticism due to the possible use by terrorist groups to manufacture biological weapons. Of particular concern was the possibility to create – using the same technique to engineer the mousepox virus – a vaccine-resistant strain of smallpox, which was one of the most devastating disease outbreaks in human history. Although it was officially eradicated in the 1980s,

---

106 Seumas Miller, Michael J. Selgelid, "Ethical and Philosophical Consideration of the Dual-use Dilemma in the Biological Sciences", *Science and Engineering Ethics* (2007): 523–580.

107 According to Regulation (EU) 2021/821 of the European Parliament and of the Council of 20 May 2021 setting up a Union regime for the control of exports, brokering, technical assistance, transit and transfer of dual-use items (recast), the term dual-use items "means items, including software and technology, which can be used for both civil and military purposes, and includes items which can be used for the design, development, production or use of nuclear, chemical or biological weapons or their means of delivery, including all items which can be used for both non-explosive uses and assisting in any way in the manufacture of nuclear weapons or other nuclear explosive devices" (Art. 2, Para. 1).

108 Ronald J. Jackson, Alistair J. Ramsay, Carina D. Christensen, Sandra Beaton, Diana F. Hall, Ian A. Ramshaw, "Expression of Mouse Interleukin-4 by a Recombinant Ectromelia Virus Suppresses Cytolytic Lymphocyte Responses and Overcomes Genetic Resistance to Mousepox", *Journal of Virology* (2001): 1205–1210.

fears remain that former stockpiles – or genetically reconstituted forms of the virus – could be used as a biological weapon.

In response to the mousepox case, a report called Biotechnology Research in an Age of Terrorism – known as the Fink Report – was published in the United States;[109] it was drafted by experts from the academic community, and it therefore largely represented the position of the scientific community to increased fears about bioterrorism. The report recommended that research with a dual-use potentiality should not be prohibited *ex ante* but should be strictly scrutinized by the scientists themselves, who should be fully aware of the threat of bioterrorism.

As observed by some scholars, the IHR 2005 were intended to codify a practice developed by the WHO Secretariat in response to the SARS outbreak of 2003 (that *de facto* disapplied the previous IHR).[110] The goal of the IHR is ". . . to prevent, protect against, control and provide a public health response to the international spread of disease in ways that are commensurate with and restricted to public health risks, and which avoid unnecessary interference with international traffic and trade" (Art. 2).

The IHR do not aim to regulate the domestic response to outbreaks, except for national "core capacities", which are in any case functional to prevent the international spread of a disease outbreak. Specifically, the IHR require States to establish core capacities for surveillance and response not only at their borders (places of entry) but also *throughout* their whole territory (Annex I).

That is, the Director-General cannot – under the IHR – impose lockdowns or mass quarantines during a pandemic, which rest upon the constitutional power of each State, cannot distribute hospital beds, drugs, or vaccines, and cannot decide who does and does not receive primary care.

This point was clearly emphasized by the WHA in Resolution 73.1, affirming that it is "the primary responsibility of governments for adopting and implementing responses to the COVID-19 pandemic that are specific to their national context, as well as for mobilizing the necessary resources to do so".

Nevertheless, the IHR gave extraordinary powers to the Director-General: he has the authority to unilaterally declare a public health emergency of international concern (PHEIC) based also on non-official sources concerning disease outbreaks and against the advice of the Emergency Committee (EC) (which happened in the case of monkeypox in 2022). He must, however, enter into extensive consultations with the State concerned and come to a mutual conclusion within 48 hours on whether a given event constitutes a PHEIC or not (Art. 12, Para. 2, IHR). The willingness of States to provide these extensive powers to a single body is a rarity among UN specialized agencies. However,

---

109   National Research Council, *Biotechnology Research in an Age of Terrorism* (The National Academies Press: 2004).

110   Gianluca Burci, "The Legal Responses to Pandemics. The Strengths and Weaknesses of the International Health Regulations", *Journal of International Humanitarian Legal Studies* (2020): 1–14, at 3.

the "narrative" about these emergency powers must be debunked. After declaring a PHEIC, the DG can only "recommend" measures that although they do have an impact on trade and travel, are non-binding acts.

Furthermore, the faculty of the DG to rely on informal sources of information is strongly limited, and the WHO must reveal to the concerned country the source of any informal or independent information.

6.3. *Main duties upon states*

6.3.1. *Information sharing*

Information sharing is the cornerstone of international disease surveillance and response as witnessed by the precedent of SARS, where China delayed in reporting early cases.[111]

Under Article 6, Paragraph 1 of the IHR, States Parties are required to determine whether the WHO should be notified about a domestic disease outbreak, and it is therefore a "potential" public health emergency with cross-border consequences.

The duty of early notification of disease outbreaks is not a novelty in international health law. For instance, the International Sanitary Convention (1926) established the obligation of "immediate notification" in the presence of "the first recognized case of plague, cholera or yellow fewer found on its territory" (Art. 1, Para. 1) and "the existence of an epidemic of typhus or smallpox" (Art. 1, Para. 3).

Similar procedural obligations have been envisaged in environmental treaties.[112] The duty to notify an environmental emergency that might cause transboundary damage is a general principle of international law.[113]

Under the IHR, States must notify of any disease outbreak arising in their territories within 24 hours; their assessment is not based on a discretional choice by the State but is oriented by the implementation of Annex II.[114]

---

111 https://www.nytimes.com/2003/04/21/world/the-sars-epidemic-epidemic-china-admits-underreporting-its-sars-cases.html.

112 For instance, the Convention on The Control of Transboundary Movements of Hazardous Wastes and their Disposal (1989) affirms that States should disseminate "*information* on the transboundary movement of hazardous wastes and other wastes, in order to improve the environmentally sound management of such wastes and to achieve the prevention of illegal traffic" (Art. 4, Para. 1, lect. h).

113 Daniel G. Partan, "The Duty to Inform in International Environmental Law", *Boston University International Law Journal* (1988): 43–88. Article 8, Paragraph 1, of the Draft Articles on Prevention of Transboundary Harm from Hazardous Activities of 2001 states that "the State of origin shall provide the State likely to be affected with timely notification of the risk and the assessment, and shall transmit to it the available technical and all other relevant information on which the assessment is based".

114 Resolution WHA58.3; Decision instrument for the assessment and notification of events that may constitute a public health emergency of international concern. See https://www.who.int/ihr/revised_annex2_guidance.pdf.

It is a technical procedure based on a standardized algorithm that does not affect the health sovereignty of States.[115] Annex II contains a flowchart that provides guidance to the States Parties in evaluating when a given disease outbreak has reached the "red line" that justifies notification to the WHO's country office within 24 hours. The duty to notify is triggered when at least two of four situational criteria listed in the algorithm are met. The event must have (1) a serious public health impact; (2) it must be unusual or unexpected; and (3) there must be a significant risk of global spread and (4) consequent restrictions to travel and trade.

There is a list of pandemic-prone diseases, such as cholera, pneumonic plague, and yellow fever, whose seriousness is automatically implied.

The duty of notification is therefore not based on a discretional evaluation by the State but is specifically oriented by the application of an *ad hoc* decisional instrument.

Against this backdrop, some scholars have suggested that the criteria contained in Annex II, especially the seriousness of the public health event and its unusual or unexpected nature, are too vague and should be more clearly defined. They also reinforce that a "focus should be placed on keeping the number of missed events to a minimum".[116]

This decisional instrument makes a distinction between a) compulsory notification of events related to a limited number of diseases that appear unusual and unexpected and represent a serious threat to public health and b) compulsory notification of other "events" among two of the four conditions envisaged by Annex II (seriousness of the disease outbreak, unusual or unexpected nature of the event, potential risk of international spread, and potential interference with international trade and travel).

The specific duty of notification is therefore required for any fact that has a potential impact on international public health, including the events originated by unknown causes and those related to a predetermined number of diseases – such as meningitis, yellow fever, and cholera – whose danger and epidemic potential are already well-known.

When the WHO receives such a notification, it has an obligation under *ex* article 10, paragraph 3, IHR to cooperate with the State concerned in carrying out an assessment of the risk of international spread, the interference with international trade and travel, and the appropriateness of response measures.

States Parties – when assessing health events – have two additional important options: the first is to consult with the WHO on the circumstances that

115 Gérard Krause, "Infectious Disease Control Policies and the Role of Governmental and Intergovernmental Organisations", in Alexander Krämer, Mirjam Kretzschmar, Klaus Krickeberg (eds.), *Modern Infectious Disease Epidemiology: Concepts, Methods, Mathematical Models and Public Health* (Springer: 2010), 69–82, 70.

116 Michael Edelstein, David L. Heymann, Johan Giesecke, Julius Weinberg, "Validity of International Health Regulations in Reporting Emerging Infectious Diseases", *Infectious Diseases* 18 (2012): 1115–1120.

have not yet reached the threshold of public health emergency but that might develop in this direction; the other is to ask for related guidance (Art. 8). This consultation process is appropriate when there is insufficient available information to complete the decision instrument assessment or if a State Party seeks advice on appropriate public health investigative or response measures or otherwise wishes to keep the WHO informed.

Under Article 9, Paragraph 2, States Parties must inform the WHO within 24 hours of receipt of evidence of a public health risk outside their border that has the potential to cause an international spread of a disease outbreak as manifested by imported or exported human cases, infected or contaminated vectors, or contaminated goods.

6.3.2. Capacity-building obligations

A health system that works properly and is sufficiently prepared supports an efficient report mechanism. Through the IHR, States have committed themselves to developing "core capacities" within a certain period of time.[117]

Therefore, basic duties upon States Parties, which are the pillar of the mechanism established by the IHR, are "the development, strengthening and maintenance of 'core capacities' to ensure timely surveillance and response" (Arts. 5 and 13 and Annex 1). Such capacities must be developed internally, well beyond the entry points upon which the classic regime was focused.[118]

As to the entry points, Article 20 of the IHR affirms that "States Parties shall designate the airports and ports that shall develop the capacities provided in Annex 1".[119] A similar obligation is envisaged under Article 14 of the Convention on International Civil Aviation of 1944 (Chicago Convention), which affirms that States agree "to take effective measures to prevent the spread of

---

117 Hans Kluge, Jose Maria Martín-Moreno, Nedret Emiroglu, Guenael Rodier, Edward Kelley, Melitta Vujnovic, Govin Permanand, "Strengthening Global Health Security by Embedding the International Health Regulations Requirements into National Health Systems", *BMJ Global Health* (2018): 1–7.

118 For further details, Giulio Bartolini, "Are You Ready for a Pandemic? The International Health Regulations Put to the Test of their Core Capacities Requirements", *EJIL: TALK!* (1 June 2020): https://www.ejiltalk.org/are-you-ready-for-a-pandemic-the-international-health-regulations-put-to-the-test-of-their-core-capacity-requirements/.

119 Annex I, lect. *b*, IHR affirms that States must develop capacities for designated airports, ports and ground crossings "(a) to provide access to (i) an appropriate medical service including diagnostic facilities located so as to allow the prompt assessment and care of ill travelers, and (ii) adequate staff, equipment and premises; (b) to provide access to equipment and personnel for the transport of ill travelers to an appropriate medical facility; (c) to provide trained personnel for the inspection of conveyances; (d) to ensure a safe environment for travelers using point of entry facilities, including potable water supplies, eating establishments, flight catering facilities, public washrooms appropriate solid and liquid waste disposal services and other potential risk areas, by conducting inspection programmes, as appropriate; and (e) to provide as far as practicable a programme and trained personnel for the control of vectors and reservoirs in and near points of entry".

communicable disease through air and travel". According to Annex 9, Standard 8.16 of the Convention, all States are required to "establish a national aviation plan in preparation for an outbreak of a communicable disease posing a public health risk or public health emergency of international concern".

The International Convention for the Control and Management of Ships' Ballast Water and Sediments (2004) is relevant for public health, since it aims at regulating the emptying of ballast waters by vessels in order to prevent, among other things, the diffusion of pathogens that are a danger to human health (Art. 4, Para. 2).

The IHR provide that "a ship of an aircraft shall not be prevented for public health reasons from calling at any point of entry" "however, if the entry point is not equipped for applying health measures under these Regulations, the ship or aircraft may be ordered to proceed at its own risk to the nearest suitable point of entry available to it" (Art. 28, Para. 1).

The State has a specific duty to notify the WHO of such measures and must justify them by providing available scientific evidence (Art. 48, Para. 3).

The idea at the basis of the core capacities is to put in place appropriate health infrastructure at the domestic level that can reinforce the local infrastructure and to have a system of detention and prevention of disease outbreaks at their source before their cross-border spread.[120]

Core capacities include developing both adequate infrastructure in order to detect and assess potential health threats through surveillance systems and laboratories to trace latent health threats with the aim of carrying out a potential risk assessment; ensuring that surveillance systems and laboratories can detect potential threats and understand the nature and potential severity and impact of the event in order to be able to make decisions in public health emergencies; notifying and reporting specific diseases and any potential public health emergency to the WHO through a network of "National IHR Focal Points"; and verifying and responding (countries are expected to be able to implement preliminary control measures immediately and respond appropriately to public health risks and emergencies).

Through Resolution WHA61.2 (2008), the WHA has decided that "States Parties and the Director-General shall report to the Health Assembly on the implementation of the Regulations annually" under Article 54, Paragraph 1, IHR.

Against this backdrop, an IHR Core Capacity Monitoring Framework was developed in 2010 (and then updated in 2013) that suggests to the States Parties a framework of reference of the processes to follow to monitor the development of their essential capacities as required by the IHR at the local,

---

120 Lawrence O. Gostin, Mary C. De Bartolo, Eric A. Friedman, "The International Health Regulations 10 Years on: The Governing Framework for Global Health Security", *The Lancet* (2015): 2222–2226.

intermediate, and domestic levels to facilitate their reporting procedure to the Assembly.

A pivotal problem in relation to the development of the core capacities is that of the absence of a specific commitment by the WHO to finance the improvement of these surveillance capacities.

However, long before the COVID-19 pandemic, research has highlighted the concrete difficulty of developing countries, in particular Sub-Saharan African countries, in meeting their commitment of preparedness under the IHR.[121]

The 2019 Global Health Security Index[122] drew particular attention to the fact that when the pandemic began, the average country preparedness score was 40.2 out of 100. The most prepared States were Canada and the United States in North America, France, Scandinavian countries (Denmark, Finland, and Sweden, except for Norway), Switzerland, and the United Kingdom in Europe, Thailand, South Korea, and Thailand in South-East Asia, and Australia and New Zealand in Oceania.

The "least prepared" countries at the bottom of the ranking were located in Sub-Saharan Africa (Somalia, 16.6 index score and rank 194/195; South Sudan, index score 21.7 and rank 180/195).

The lack of core capacities in developing countries has ancient roots and dates to the heritage of slavery, colonialism, and more recently, liberal reform policies (austerity measures).

Against this backdrop, the WHO highlighted that domestic, regional, and global efforts to reinforce health system and building capacities with the goal of preventing, detecting, and responding to health emergencies "were insufficient" when facing the COVID-19 pandemic.[123]

The COVID-19 pandemic has shown the failure of developing adequate public health capacities to protect the respective populations and to provide timely warning to the WHO and to other States Parties.[124]

The key issue – which is addressed extensively in the next paragraphs – is related to the lack of fulfillment by WHO Member States of their core obligations concerning the protection of the right to health, whose content is deeply analyzed.

The next paragraphs investigate the other measures enacted by the WHO under the form of soft law instruments (recommendations and global strategies).

---

121 Stephen J. Hoffman, "Making the International Health Regulations Matter: Promoting Compliance Through Effective Dispute Resolution", in Simon Rushton, Jeremy Youde eds, *Routledge Handbook of Global Health Security* (Routledge: 2015): 239.

122 https://www.ghsindex.org/.

123 *Report of the Review Committee on the Functioning of the International Health Regulations (2005) During the COVID-19 response, A74/9 Add.1* (5 May 2021), https://cdn.who.int/media/docs/default-source/documents/emergencies/a74_9add1-en.pdf?sfvrsn=d5d22fdf_1&download=true.

124 See Giulio Bartolini, "The Failure of 'Core Capacities' under the WHO International Health Regulations", *The International and Comparative Law Quarterly* 70 (1) (2021): 233–250.

7. Soft law instruments

Recommendations are – alongside conventions – the main standard-setting instruments of IGOs.[125]

As affirmed by Raustiala, international agreements can be negotiated as both binding and non-binding agreements (the author differentiates between *contracts* and *pledges*, where contracts create legal obligations, and pledges establish only moral commitments).[126]

The term "soft law" – coined by Anglo-American doctrine – is generally used to indicate a series of acts, located in a "grey area" of international law, in contrast with the "white area" of hard law. Soft law instruments are not homogenous as to their origin and nature, and although they are void of binding legal effects, they can have a legal relevance in the long term (the only immediate effect is in the field of good faith). The scholars of the "classical school" of international law, however, deny any legal effect to soft law instruments.[127]

Soft law is deemed to establish and delineate objectives to be achieved in the long term rather than in the present, programmes rather than prescriptions, and guidelines rather than strict obligations. Soft law rules are characterized by elasticity, flexibility, and vagueness of the content and scope. For instance, the UNESCO Universal Declaration on Bioethics and Human Rights (2005) aims to "provide a universal framework of principles and procedures to guide States in the formulation of their legislation, policies or other instruments in the field of bioethics (Art. 2, Para. 1).

This terminology is meant to indicate that the instrument or provision in question is not in itself "law", but its importance within the general framework of international legal development is such that particular attention needs to be given to it.[128]

Although an univocal definition does not exist, soft law can be described as "normative provisions contained in non-binding texts".[129]

This phenomenon has been so qualified by some scholars because of the easy and flexible method of law creation;[130] in fact, soft law offers a simpler package to accept by States than hard law.[131]

---

125 See, for instance, the constitutions of the FAO (Art. IV, Para. 2), the ILO (Art. 19, Para. 1), and the International Civil Aviation Organization (ICAO; Art. 54 L). The Constitution of UNESCO assigns to the General Conference the task of proposing international conventions and recommendations (Art. IV.B.4).

126 Kal Raustiala, "Form and Substance in International Agreements", *The American Journal of International Law* (2005): 581–614.

127 Leo Gross, "Problems of International Adjudication and Compliance with International Law. Some Simple Solutions", *American Journal of International Law* (1965): 48–59.

128 Malcolm M. Shaw, *International Law* (Cambridge University Press: 2004), 83–84.

129 Dina Shelton, International Law and "Relative Normativity", in Malcolm Evans (ed.), *International Law* (Oxford University Press: 2014), 141–170.

130 Report of the Secretary General on international legal instruments and mechanism, U.N. Doc. E/CN.17/1996/17/add 1, page 12.

131 For a critical overview, see Jan Klabbers, "The Redundancy of Soft Law", *Nordic Journal of International Law* (1995): 167–182.

Soft law is not included within the traditional sources of international law listed in Article 38 of the Statute of the International Court of Justice (ICJ), namely, treaties, customary law, general principles of law, and judicial decisions and writings.

Soft law encompasses a broad range of acts, resolutions of IGOs (in particular, of the GA), such as the Universal Declaration of Human Rights (UDHR) (1948) and the Declaration of Principles of Friendly Relations Among Nations (1970); declarations adopted as the outcome of international conferences convened by the UN, such as the Stockholm Declaration on Human Environment (1972), the Rio Declaration on Environment and Development (1992), the Agenda 21 (1992), the Millennium Development Goals (2000), the Johannesburg Declaration on Sustainable Development (2002) and the Sustainable Development Goals (2015); the Declaration for Stockholm 50+1 (2022); declarations adopted as the outcome of high-level political meetings, such as the Conference on Security and Cooperation in Europe (CSCE) Helsinki Final Act, which led to the development of the human rights doctrine in Eastern Europe; resolutions dealing with topics that traditionally fall outside States' domestic jurisdiction, such as disarmament, the outer space, the deep seabed, marine protection.

Environmental law is a branch of international law whereas soft law instruments are prevalent.[132]

As previously stated, it is puzzling that the WHO seldom relied on its treaty making power, given that its normative authority is characterized instead by the adoption of soft law instruments.

At the beginning of the HIV/AIDS epidemic in the 1980s, a proposal for a global treaty against HIV/AIDS was eventually dropped.

In more general terms, the decision to enact soft law rules in the field of global health is in line with the stagnation in terms of quantitative and qualitative production of "formal international law" in favor of "informal international lawmaking".[133]

The authority of the WHA to adopt recommendations is granted under Article 23 of the WHO Constitution.[134] Furthermore, Article 62 requires each Member State to "report annually on the action taken with respect to recommendations made to it by the Organization and with respect to conventions, agreements and regulations".

The most important recommendations enacted by the WHA are the International Code of Marketing of Breast-Milk Substitutes (1981)[135] and the

---

132 Handers Eriksen, *International Law* (Cambridge University Press: 2017), 37.
133 Joost Pauvelyn, Ramses A. Wessel, Jan Wouters, "When Structures Become Shackles: Stagnation and Dynamics in International Lawmaking", *European Journal of International Law* (2014): 733–763.
134 Article 23 of the WHO Constitution states that "The Health Assembly shall have authority to make recommendations to Members with respect to any matter within the competence of the Organization".
135 Resolution WHA34.22 of 21 May 1981.

Global Code of Practice on the International Recruitment of Health Personnel (2010).

The Code of 1981 was intended to find a balance between the interests of the producers of milk substitutes and NGOs that opposed the sale of these products in developing countries.[136] It was adopted with the sole dissenting vote of the United States.

8. Global strategies

The adoption of global strategies is a specific feature of the WHO's normative activity.

The Global Strategy on Diet, Physical Activity and Health (2004) was aimed at reducing the diseases related to an inadequate diet or physical activity, such as cancers, heart disease, or obesity.

The Global Strategy for the Prevention and Control of Noncommunicable Diseases (2000), the Action plan for the global strategy for the prevention and control of noncommunicable diseases 2008–2013, and the Global action plan for the prevention and control of noncommunicable diseases 2013–2030[137] are the main pillars of the WHO's activity.

Cardiovascular diseases, cancer, chronic obstructive pulmonary diseases, and diabetes – the most common noncommunicable diseases (NCDs) – are often related to common preventable risk factors associated with an inadequate lifestyle, such as intense tobacco use, an unhealthy diet, and lack of physical activity. According to Paragraph 5, "action to prevent these diseases should, therefore, focus on controlling the risk factors in an integrated manner".[138]

The Global Strategy to Reduce the Harmful Use of Alcohol (2010) was updated by the Global Alcohol Action Plan 2022–2030 ("harmful use of alcohol": according to this wording, a harmful level of use is implied and a "non-harmful" or safe level).[139]

---

136 Sami Shubber, *The International Code of Marketing of Breast-Milk Substitutes: An International Measure to Protect and Promote Breastfeeding* (Nijhoff: 1998).
137 Implementation roadmap 2023–2030 for the global action plan for the prevention and control of NCDs 2013–2030.
138 The three main objectives of the strategy are (Para. 15) "to map the emerging epidemics of noncommunicable diseases and to analyze the latter's social, economic, behavioural, and political determinants with particular reference to poor and disadvantaged populations, in order to provide guidance for policy, legislative and financial measures related to the development of an environment supportive of control; to reduce the level of exposure of individuals and populations to the common risk factors for noncommunicable diseases, namely tobacco consumption, unhealthy diet and physical inactivity, and their determinants; to strengthen health care for people with noncommunicable diseases by developing norms and guidelines for cost-effective interventions, with priority given to cardiovascular diseases, cancer, diabetes and chronic respiratory diseases".
139 WHA, Resolution WHA53.14, "Global Strategy for the Prevention and Control of Noncommunicable Diseases" (2000).

The Comprehensive Mental Health Action Plan 2013–2030 has the goal of ensuring that "all people achieve the highest standard of mental health and well-being".[140]

This was a formal recognition of the importance of mental health with the specific target of a 10% reduction of the suicide rate. The plan is intended to help countries achieve Sustainable Development Goal target 3.4, that is, by 2030, to reduce by one-third premature deaths from NCDs through prevention and treatment and to promote mental health and well-being.

The Global Strategy on Health, Environment and Climate Change (2020)[141] has the goal of providing a possible answer to health risks and challenges associated with environmental degradation and climate change. It has a broad vision of transforming the way of living, working, producing, consuming, and governing of modern society.

It contains a definition of "environmental risks to health" that are defined as "all the environmental physical, chemical, biological and work-related factors external to a person, and all related behaviours" (Para. 4). The document recognizes the strict linkage between health and environment and estimates 13 million deaths each year associated with environmental degradation.[142]

The Global Strategy on Digital Health (2020–2025) is based upon the vision of improving health for everyone and everywhere by accelerating the development and adoption of appropriate, accessible, affordable, scalable, and sustainable person-centric digital health solutions. The main aim of the Strategy is to prevent, detect, and respond to epidemics and pandemics, developing infrastructure and applications that enable countries to use health data to promote health and well-being, and achieving the health-related Sustainable Development Goals and the triple billion targets of the WHO's Thirteenth General Programme of Work, 2019–2023.[143]

The global strategies of the WHO have the function of providing political guidance to the WHO Member States on specific topics. They can be compared, as to their importance, to the plans of action enacted by the FAO, such as the Plan of Action of the World Food Summit (1996).

Part II The right to health and international law

9. The right to health

Part II of this chapter is devoted to the right to health, whose attainment is one of the main goals of the WHO. Despite this – as previously explained –

---

140 The plan is associated with the WHO's Mental Health Gap Action Programmeme (mhGAP), which aims to improve mental health service in developing countries.
141 World Health Organization, *WHO Global Strategy on Health, Environment and Climate Change: The Transformation Needed to Improve Lives and Wellbeing Sustainably Through Healthy Environments* (World Health Organization: 2020).
142 Annette Prüss-Üstün, *Preventing Disease Through Healthy Environments: A Global Assessment of the Burden of Disease from Environmental Risks* (World Health Organization: 2016).
143 https://www.who.int/docs/default-source/documents/gs4dhdaa2a9f352b0445bafbc 79ca799dce4d.pdf.

the WHO failed to codify the right to health through the enactment of a global treaty. Given the absence of a specific treaty, the human right to health is recognized in specific dispositions in human rights treaties of a general, specific, and regional character, whose content is the object of the next paragraphs.

The right to health was widely evoked by scholars, scientists, journalists, and commentators during the COVID-19 pandemic. However, what do we exactly mean by "health"? The concept of health summarizes several values and interests. Against this backdrop, two conceptions of health have been highlighted by Montgomery: the "engineering model" and the "social model".[144] The engineering model is mainly concerned with the well-being of the individual and can be considered a state of complete physical and mental well-being. From the social model perspective, health is determined by multiple factors such as nutrition, environment, social services, and genetic heritage. The difference between these models can, therefore, highlight the distinction between health and health care. The concept of health care was expressed in Resolution 30.43 of WHA of 19 May 1977 entitled "Health for All" (the Preamble states as follows: "considering that health is a basic human right and a worldwide social goal, and that it is essential to the satisfaction of basic human needs and the quality of life").

Health can be considered not only an individual good of each human being but also a public good.[145] It includes aspects of bioethics that can be described as "micro-ethical" rather than "macro-ethical" in scope.[146]

Since 1994, the WHO, in the Declaration on the Promotion of the Rights of Patients in Europe, in light of the developments in health care assistance, has recognized a universal right to health assistance.

The concept of "Global Health Coverage" or "Universal Health Coverage" (UHC) then emerged within the UN in 2015 through the enactment of Resolution 70/1 (2015) ("Transforming our World: the 2030 Agenda for Sustainable Development") that underlined the necessity of an approach to comprehensive health and centered on the individual. Paragraph 26 reads as follows: "To promote physical and mental health and well-being, and to extend life expectancy for all, we must achieve universal health coverage and access to quality health care".[147]

The UN commits itself to accelerating efforts in reducing newborn, child, and maternal mortality by ending all such preventable deaths before 2030 and

---

144 Jonathan Montgomery, *Health Care Law* (Oxford University Press: 2002), 2–4.

145 The theory of public goods originated in economics with the work of Paul Samuelson (Paul Samuelson, "The Pure Theory of Public Expenditures", in *The Review of Economics and Statistics* (MIT Press: 1954), 387–389). A public good can be defined as a good that is non-excludable and non-rivalrous; therefore, no one can be excluded from its use, and the use by an individual does not diminish the availability of the good to others. Examples of public goods include air, water, parks, and national security.

146 Sev S. Fluss, "The Development of National Health Legislation in Europe: The Contribution of International Organizations", *European Journal of Health Law* (1995), cit., 193.

147 For further details, Pia Acconci, "International Actions towards Universal Health Coverage: Soft, but Consistent", *La Comunità internazionale* (2018): 1–20.

to ensuring universal access to sexual and reproductive health care services, including for family planning, information, and education.

A particular engagement is devoted to accelerating the pace of progress made in fighting malaria, HIV/AIDS, tuberculosis, hepatitis, Ebola and other communicable diseases and epidemics, including by addressing growing anti-microbial resistance and the problem of unattended diseases affecting developing countries.

The UN also gives particular attention to the prevention and treatment of NCDs, including behavioral, developmental, and neurological disorders, which constitute a major challenge for sustainable development.

The GA Resolution n. 72/139 (12 December 2017), entitled "Global Health and Foreign Policy: Addressing the Health of the Most Vulnerable for an Inclusive Society", urged

> Member States to respect, protect and promote the right to the enjoyment of the highest attainable standard of physical and mental health, with particular attention provided to the health needs of the most vulnerable, and to consider health in a holistic manner, including in the formulation of foreign policy.
>
> (Para. 3)

The Political Declaration of the High-Level Meeting on Universal Health Coverage of 23 September 2019 ("to achieve universal health coverage by 2030") reaffirmed the right of every human being, without distinction of any kind, "to the enjoyment of the highest attainable standard of physical and mental health" (Para. 1).

Paragraph 5 recognizes that

> universal health coverage is fundamental for achieving the Sustainable Development Goals related not only to health and well-being, but also to eradicate poverty in all its forms and dimensions, ensure quality education, achieve gender equality and women's empowerment, provide decent work and economic growth, reduce inequalities, ensure just, peaceful and inclusive societies and to build and foster partnerships, while reaching the goals and targets included throughout the 2030 Agenda for Sustainable Development is critical for the attainment of healthy lives and wellbeing for all, with a focus on health outcomes throughout the life course.

Historically, the legal reconstruction of the "good" health has privileged the collective dimension of the general interest of society to guarantee a minimum standard of health with a view to preventing the spread of deadly diseases, in particular, infectious diseases.

Furthermore, the right to health has been traditionally included among economic, social, and cultural rights (the second generation rights).[148] These rights imply not only negative duties of non-interference upon States but also a direct intervention by the domestic authorities through the enactment of specific legislation, with the goal of guaranteeing the enjoyment of equal rights to the whole population.[149] Their realization is therefore strictly related to the financial availability of each country.[150]

The language of progressive realization and maximal available resources undercuts the right to health, allowing States to deny even basic levels of health coverage domestically and allowing international assistance for health to remain entirely discretionary.

The interdependence and indivisibility of economic, social, and cultural rights and civil and political rights has never been contested,[151] although several

148 The distinction between civil and political rights, on the one hand, and economic, social, and cultural rights, on the other hand, is at the bottom of the adoption of the two covenants of 1966 (Covenant on Civil and Political Rights and Covenant on Economic, Social and Cultural Rights). Most civil and political rights are translated into a duty of non-interference by the State that can be easily defined with sufficient accuracy and that can find immediate implementation; meanwhile, economic, social, and cultural rights generally imply a specific activity by the domestic governments generally through financing. Their implementation is not therefore immediate but requires a progressive realization that is conditioned by the economic situation and by other factors (such as a specific health policy). This distinction is then relevant as to the treaty-based control mechanisms: the ICCPR has an efficient control procedure (quasi-jurisdictional procedure), while the ICESCR's mechanism is based on periodic reports (*ex* art. 16: "The States Parties to the present Covenant undertake to submit in conformity with this part of the Covenant reports on the measures which they have adopted and the progress made in achieving the observance of the rights recognized herein"). Paul Hunt, Judith Bueno de Mesquita, Joo-Young Lee, Sally-Anne Way, "Implementation of Economic, Social and Cultural Rights", in Scott Sheeran, Sir Nigel Rodley (eds.), *Routledge Handbook of International Human Rights Law* (Routledge: 2013), 545–562.

149 The third generation of rights has recently been developed and mainly addresses vulnerable groups such as the lesbian, gay, bisexual and transgender community, migrants, refugees, and indigenous people. It also includes the right to peace, development, humanitarian assistance, the protection of the environment, and fundamental rights in the field of life sciences (biolaw). Patrick Macklem, "Human Rights in International Law: Three Generations or One?", *London Review of International Law* (2015): 61–92.

150 Article 2, Paragraph 1 of the International Covenant on Economic, Social and Cultural Rights establishes that each State Party "undertakes to take steps, individually and through international assistance and co-operation . . . to the maximum of its available resources, with a view to achieving progressively the full realization of the rights recognized in the Covenant by all appropriate means, including particularly the adoption of legislative measures".

151 Vienna Declaration and Programme of Action, Report of the World Conference on Human Rights. Vienna, Austria: United Nations; 1993. UN document A/CONF.157/23. See Mattew C.R. Craven, *The International Covenant on Economic, Social and Cultural Rights: A Perspective on its Development* (Oxford University Press: 1995).

scholars argue that these adjectives do not really tell us anything about how human rights function or what they conceptually mean.[152]

Furthermore, there is currently widespread agreement that the right to health entails both negative freedoms (informed consent, the right to refuse medical treatment, including life-saving treatments, and the right not to know) and positive freedoms or entitlements (e.g., access to essential medicines, reproductive services and vaccines).[153]

The problem is that there is no clarity about the real content of the right to health, which is influenced by different interpretations and cultural values.

Rooted in theories of social medicine, the right to health in its early formulation encompassed a "holistic vision of patient and population-based health".[154] For instance, the concept of "*solidarité*" – which involves mutual support among members of a given society – is pivotal in Europe[155] and in Asia, but it does not have the same role in North America.[156]

Solidarité is a principle that is central to European health care ethics; the end of World War II determined an expansion of social services.[157] *Solidarité* has its roots in the French Revolution and in the principles of *fraternité* and *mutualité*. In 1748, Montesquieu, in his influential book *L'esprit des lois*, stated,

A few coins given to a naked man in the streets is not enough to fulfil the obligations of the State, which owes to all citizens a livelihood, food, decent clothing and a kind of life that is not harmful to their health.[158]

Solidarité is the object of a growing interest within the bioethical debate, in particular regarding the issues related to the allocation of resources within health systems.[159] It is the core principle of the welfare state, as the foundation of government obligations to provide health services that also allow the most

152 Daniel J. Whelan, *Indivisible Human Rights* (University of Pennsylvania Press: 2010), 1–10.
153 Andrew Bradley, "Positive Rights, Negative Rights and Health Care", *Journal of Medical Ethics* (2010): 838–841.
154 Lawrence O. Gostin, Benjamin M. Meier, Rebekah Thomas, Veronica Magar, Tedros A. Ghebreyesus, "70 Years of Human Rights in Global Health: Drawing on a Contentious Past to Secure a Hopeful Future", *Lancet* (2019): 2731–2735.
155 Ruud Ter Meulen, Ruud Muffels, *Solidarity in Health and Social Care in Europe* (Kluwer Academic Press: 2011).
156 Alicia Ely Yamin, "The Right to Health under International Law and Its Relevance to the United States", *American Journal of Public Health* 95 (7) (2005): 1156–1161.
157 Ben Davies, Julian Savulescu, "Solidarity and Responsibility in Health Care", *Public Health Ethics* (2019): 133–144.
158 Charles L. de Montesquieu, *De l'esprit des lois* (1748), Livre XXIII, Chap. XXIX.
159 Barbara Prainsach, Alena Buyx, *Solidarity. Reflections on an Emerging Concept in Biotehics* (Arts and Humanities Research Council: 2011), https://www.nuffieldbioethics.org/assets/pdfs/Solidarity-report.pdf.

vulnerable groups (the poor, migrants, refugees, disabled persons, and persons affected by rare diseases) achieve a sufficient level of health.

In the Universal Declaration on Bioethics and Human Rights (UNESCO, 2005) the principle of solidarity is expressly recalled in Article 13: "Solidarity among human beings and international cooperation towards that end are to be encouraged". The scarce relevance of solidarity in American bioethics is highlighted by the fact that it is not quoted among the core principles of the Belmont Report (autonomy, beneficence, non-maleficence, and justice).[160]

Solidarity is not present in WHO instruments, such as the IHR, but it is included in the New Anti Pandemic Treaty, which states that "The effective prevention of, preparedness for and response to pandemics requires national, international, multilateral, bilateral and multisectoral collaboration, coordination and cooperation, through global unity, to achieve the common interest of a fairer, more equitable and better prepared world" (Art. 4, Para. 4).[161]

10. Health and human rights

International human rights law – since the adoption of the UN Charter – has given particular attention to the right to health.[162] It emerged as a fundamental human right in the wake of World War II and the general idea according to which medicine was one of the pillars of peace.[163]

World War II and the infamous experiments carried out by both German and Japanese scientists in concentration camps[164] determined a period of optimism, since medicine was deemed a key element of peace among nations.

In 1947, during the Nuremberg Trial, Eleanor Roosevelt summoned a committee to elaborate the Universal Declaration of Human Rights (UDHR) that also mentions health as part of the right to an adequate standard of living (Art. 25). The UDHR, however, does not explicitly formulate a human right to health

---

160 The Belmont Report: Ethical Principles and Guidelines for the Protection of Human Subjects of Research, 30 September 1978.

161 Zero draft of the WHO CA+ for the consideration of the Intergovernmental Negotiating Body at its fourth meeting WHO convention, agreement or other international instrument on pandemic prevention, preparedness and response ("WHO CA+") (1 February 2023), https://apps.who.int/gb/inb/pdf_files/inb4/A_INB4_3-en.pdf.

162 Philip Alston, *The United Nations and Human Rights: A Critical Appraisal* (Oxford University Press: 2020).

163 Pia Acconci, *Tutela della salute e diritto internazionale* (CEDAM: 2011); Jonathan M. Mann, Michael A. Grodin, Sofia Gruskin, George J. Annas (eds.), *Health and Human Rights: A Reader* (Routledge: 1999); Elizabeth Wicks, *Human Rights and Health Care* (Hart Publishing: 2006); Aart Hendriks, "The Right to Health", *European Journal of Health Law* 5 (1994): 187–196; Stefania Negri, "Health, Right to", in Christina Binder, Manfred Nowak, Jane A. Hofbauer, Mag Philipp Janig (eds.), *Elgar Encyclopedia of Human Rights* (Edward Elgar: 2022): 395–405; Brigitte Toebes, *The Right to Health as a Human Right in International Law* (Intersentia: 1999).

164 Derek Pua, Danielle Dybbro, Alistair Rogers, Nicole Dahlstrom, *Unit 731: The Forgotten Asian Auschwitz* (Pacific Atrocities Education: 2018).

but rather enunciates a "right to a standard of living adequate for the health and well-being of himself and of his family" (Art. 25, Para. 1), highlighting access to medical care and other determining factors of health and well-being, such as food, clothing, housing, medical care, and necessary social services.

Article 25, Paragraph 2, also specifies that "motherhood and childhood are entitled to special care and assistance. All children, whether born in or out of wedlock, shall enjoy the same social protection".

The human right to health in its original formulation thus encompassed both individual health services and national health systems, with national health systems including social measures for public health.

The right to health was explicitly affirmed in the Preamble of the Constitution of the World Health Organization in 1948,[165] which recognized for the first time that "health is a state of complete physical, mental and social well-being" and, therefore, not merely the absence of disease or infirmity. Then, it reiterated that "the enjoyment of the highest attainable standard of health is one of the fundamental rights of every human being without distinction of race, religion, political belief, economic or social condition".

In creating a rights-based foundation for global health governance, the WHO Constitution represents the world's most expansive conceptualization of international responsibility for health.

The goal of the WHO is clearly stated in Article 1, namely, "The objective of the World Health Organization (hereinafter called the Organization) shall be the attainment by all peoples of the highest possible level of health".

The right to health as set down in the WHO Constitution was part of the "human rights revolution" after WWII, and the same WHO Constitution can be considered a "Post-Holocaust" document like the Nuremberg Code, the UDHR, the Genocide Convention, and the WMA Declaration of Geneva ("the health and the well-being of my patient should be the first consideration of any physician").[166]

With the adoption of the WHO Constitution, the right to health is "officially" part of the international human rights lexicon.

In Resolution 23.41, the WHA identified "the right to health as a fundamental human right", affirming that "the health aspect of human rights . . . is within the competence of the WHO".[167]

A new international economic order was proclaimed in 1974 through a specific Declaration that called for "the broadest co-operation of all the States

165 For the difference between right to health and right to health care, Pavlos Eleftheriadis, "A Right to Health Care", *Journal of Law, Medicine & Ethics* (2002): 268–285.
166 Johannes Morsink, "World War II and the Universal Declaration", *Human Rights Quarterly* (1993): 357–405.
167 Resolution WHA. 23.41 – Human Rights. N61/86/154(A). 23 February 1973.

members of the international community, based on equity, whereby the prevailing disparities in the world may be banished and prosperity secured for all".[168]

The WHO clearly embraced the "social model" of health, which was plainly outlined in the Declaration of Alma Ata (1978). It provides that

> health, which is a state of complete physical, mental and social well-being and not merely the absence of disease or infirmity, is a fundamental human right and that the attainment of the highest possible level of health is a most important worldwide social goal, whose realization requires the action of many other social and economic sectors in addition to the health sector.

This broad definition of health – grounded in the concept of well-being – raises, however, practical issues. As outlined by Fluss, the declination of health under the lens of well-being is a "philosophical concept"[169] that has scarce practical impact; hence, in most developing countries – plagued by infectious diseases such as HIV/AIDS, malaria, and tuberculosis – the reduction of disease or infirmity is the only priority, and considerations on the concepts of "quality of life" or "life worth living" are not issues in public health debates.

Both Gostin and Lazzarini have expressed concern about this wide definition of the right to health that severely undermines its practical impact. They propose an alternative approach based on "the duty of the State within the limits of its available resources to ensure the conditions necessary for the health of individuals and populations".[170]

This different proposal does not take into account the concept of a minimum standard of health and the distinct responses to health needs that are exclusively on the basis of economic resources. They argue that there are external factors (such as genetics, environmental degradation, urbanization, and over-population) that impact health and are beyond the State's control. Accordingly, countries do have a specific responsibility to guarantee the health of their population but within the specific limit of available resources.

The IHR do not mention the right to health except for the right to health information (Art. 45), unlike the WHO Constitution and the WHO Framework Convention on Tobacco Control, which established that the protection of human health is their main goal.

---

168 Declaration on the Establishment of a New International Economic Order, 3201 (S-VI), 1 May 1974.
169 Sev S. Fluss, "The Development of National Health Legislation in Europe: The Contribution of International Organizations", *European Journal of Health Law* (1995): 193–237.
170 Lawrence O. Gostin, Zita Lazzarini, *Human Rights and Public Health in the AIDS Pandemics* (Oxford University Press: 1997).

In its individual dimension, the right to health presents two distinct aspects. The first is the right to physical and psychological integrity, which implies non-interference by States. This first aspect applies, for instance, to the domain of sexual and reproductive rights. Reproductive rights are defined in the Programme of Action of the International Conference on Population and Development (Cairo, 1994) as "a state of complete physical, mental and social well-being . . . in all matters related to the reproductive system", which "implies that people are able to have a satisfying and safe sex life and that they have the capability to reproduce and the freedom to decide if, when and how often to do so" (Para. 7.2).

Reproductive rights include the right to decide the number, timing, and spacing of children, the right to voluntarily marry and to establish a family, and the right to the highest attainable standard of health. Reproductive rights have been recognized at the international level as a negative right (negative reproductive rights), for instance, in the woman's freedom of choice to decide to have an abortion.[171]

Finding a legal foundation for the positive aspect of this freedom (positive reproductive rights), implying, on the one hand, the duty of the State to prevent and to fight the causes of sterility and, on the other hand, to assist a sterile couple through the techniques of assisted fecundation including surrogate motherhood, is more complicated and has received little attention by academic writers to date.[172]

The right to health was then declined in "the protection of health in the workplace" (Art. 6 UDHR), "the right to a standard of living adequate for health and well-being" (Art. 25 UDHR), and the right to "the highest ascertainable standard of physical and mental health" (Art. 12, Para. 1, ICESCR).

11. The international covenant on economic, cultural, and social rights

The vision behind the early formulation of the right to health as a pillar of peace unraveled along *realpolitik* at the beginning of the Cold War. Due to the contrast between the two superpowers (the United States and the Soviet Union), with one favoring civil liberties and political rights and the other embracing the economic and social dimension of rights, the UN decided that it should have been better to separate the groups of rights into two different treaties.[173]

The process of codification of the UDHR led to the adoption of two distinct conventions in 1966, namely, the International Covenant on Civil and

---

171 In *Dobbs v. Jackson Women's Health Organization* (24 June 2022), the United States Supreme Court overturned the key decision protecting the right to abortion (*Roe v. Wade*).

172 Bartha M. Knoppers, Sonia Le Bris, "Recent Advances in Medically Assisted Conception: Legal, Ethical and Social Issues", *American Journal of Law & Medicine* (1991): 329–361.

173 Maya Hertig Randall, "The History of the Covenants: Looking Back Half a Century and Beyond Get Access Arrow", in Daniel Moeckli (eds.), *The Human Rights Covenants at 50: Their Past, Present, and Future* (Oxford University Press: 2018), 7–30.

Political Rights (ICCPR) and the International Covenant on Economic, Social and Cultural Rights (ICESCR).

The opposition by the United States to economic and social rights resulted "in a narrow definition of the right to health and health determinants" under the 1966 ICESCR.[174]

Article 12 of the ICESCR (1966) recognized the "right to the highest attainable standard of health". Among the specific duties upon States in case of disease outbreak, lect. *c* mentions "the prevention, treatment and control of epidemic, endemic, occupational and other diseases".[175]

Article 12, Paragraph 2 affirms that

[t]he steps to be taken by the States Parties to the present Covenant to achieve the full realization of this right shall include those necessary for . . . (b) the improvement of all aspects of environmental and industrial hygiene; (c) the prevention, treatment and control of epidemic, endemic, occupational and other diseases; (d) the creation of conditions which would assure to all medical service and medical attention in the event of sickness.

According to General Comment Number 14 – the most authoritative interpretation of Article 12 of the Covenant – States have an obligation to control diseases, both individually and through international cooperation, by acting in order to, among other things, "make available relevant technologies, using and improving epidemiological surveillance and data collection on a disaggregated basis, the implementation or enhancement of immunization programmes and other strategies of infectious disease control".[176]

As explained before, the wording "everyone" with reference to the right to health – as enshrined in the ICESCR – applies exclusively to the citizens of a given State; it could also be interpreted as having "extraterritorial scope", implying a narrower "negative" obligation upon States Parties not to nullify or impair the enjoyment of the right to health by individuals outside their territory.

This argument is also supported by the (albeit non-binding) sentiments expressed in the Maastricht Principles on Extraterritorial Obligations of States in the Area of Economic, Social and Cultural Rights.[177]

174 Lawrence O. Gostin, Benjamin M. Meier, Rebekah Thomas, Veronica Magar, Tedros A. Ghebreyesus, "70 Years of Human Rights in Global Health: Drawing on a Contentious Past to Secure a Hopeful Future", *The Lancet* (2018): 2731–2735.

175 Eibe Riedel, "The Right to Health Under the ICESCR. Existing Scope, New Challenges and How to Deal with It", in Andreas von Arnauld, Kerstin von der Decken, Mart Susi (eds.), *The Cambridge Handbook of New Human Rights. Recognition, Novelty, Rhetoric* (Cambridge University Press: 2020), 107–123.

176 Committee on Economic, Cultural and Social Rights (CESCR) General Comment No. 14: The Right to the Highest Attainable Standard of Health (Art. 12).

177 Benjamin Mason Meier, "Global Health Governance and the Contentious Politics of Human Rights: Mainstreaming the Right to Health for Public Health Advancement', *Stanford Journal of International Law* (2010): 1–50.

General Comment Number 14 explains the nature and scope of the "highest attainable standard of health" with a view to avoid the legal loophole represented by the principle of progressive realization that would undermine the fulfillment of State obligations.[178]

That is, progressive realization provides a wide margin of deference to domestic governments that can decide to deny even basic health services. Rather, the General Comment affirms that "progressive realization" implies that "States Parties have a specific and continuing obligation to move as expeditiously and effectively as possible towards the full realization of Article 12" (Para. 31).

The concept of core obligations implies basic and essential health services that are not subject to progressive realization. States Parties have a "core obligation to ensure the satisfaction of, at very least, minimum essential levels of each of the rights enunciated in the Covenant, including essential primary health care" that is, it is a threshold or red line below which States should not go. The concept of minimum core obligations or minimum standard of care has the purpose of avoiding the principle of progressive realization that would undermine the enjoyment of the right to health. However, the exact meaning and scope of the "minimum standard of care" has been widely discussed.[179]

The observations of the CESCR were deepened in the first report of the Special Rapporteur on the Right to Health, which made a clear distinction between freedoms and entitlements.

> Freedoms include the right to be free from discrimination and non-consensual medical treatment. Entitlements include the right to a system of health protection (i.e. health care and the underlying determinants of health), that provides equality of opportunity for people to enjoy the highest attainable standard of health. The right to health is a broad concept that can be broken down into more specific entitlements, such as "the right to essential medicines.
>
> (Para. 19)[180]

Also relevant to the right to health is the right to an adequate standard of living (Art. 11, Para. 1), which includes "food, housing, clothing". Moreover,

---

178 Audrey R. Chapman, Sage Russell, *Core Obligations: Building a Framework for Economic, Social and Cultural Rights* (Intersentia: 2002); Benjamin Mason Meier, Larissa Mori, "The Highest Attainable Standard: Advancing a Collective Human Right to Public Health", *Columbia Human Rights Law Review* 37 (2005): 113–115.

179 Lisa Forman, Gorik Ooms, Audrey Chapman, Eric Friedman, Attiya Waris, Everaldo Lamprea, Moses Mulumba, *BMC International Health and Human Rights* (Springer Nature: 2013).

180 UNHCR, The right of everyone to the enjoyment of the highest attainable standard of physical and mental health, Report of the Special Rapporteur, Paul Hunt, E/CN.4/2004/49, 16 February 2004, paras. 7–56.

Article 11, Paragraph 2 recognizes the "fundamental right of everyone to be free from hunger".

Another relevant disposition is contained in Article 15, Paragraph 1, lect. *b*, which recognizes the right of everyone to enjoy the benefits of scientific progress and its applications. Health can be considered a benefit of scientific progress and its application.

12. Sectorial treaties and right to health

The right to health is also enshrined in sectorial treaties with particular reference to vulnerable groups, such as women, children, and persons with disabilities, and in regional treaties adopted within the context of the European Union (EU), Council of Europe (CoE), African Union (AU), and the Organization of American States (OAS).

12.1. General human rights treaties (at a universal or regional scope)

The Convention on the Elimination of All Forms of Discrimination Against Women (1979) recognizes that

> States Parties shall take all appropriate measures to eliminate discrimination against women in the field of health care in order to ensure, on a basis of equality of men and women, access to health care services, including those related to family planning.
>
> (Art. 12, Para. 1)

Article 24 of the Convention of the Rights of Children (1989) clearly affirms that

> States Parties recognize the right of the child to the enjoyment of the highest attainable standard of health and to facilities for the treatment of illness and rehabilitation of health. States Parties shall strive to ensure that no child is deprived of his or her right of access to such health care services.
>
> (Para. 1)[181]

---

181 Article 24, Paragraph 2 then asserts that "States Parties shall pursue full implementation of this right and, in particular, shall take appropriate measures: (a) to diminish infant and child mortality; (b) to ensure the provision of necessary medical assistance and health care to all children with emphasis on the development of primary health care; (c) to combat disease and malnutrition, including within the framework of primary health care, through, inter alia, the application of readily available technology and through the provision of adequate nutritious foods and clean drinking-water, taking into consideration the dangers and risks of environmental pollution; (d) to ensure appropriate pre-natal and post-natal health care

With reference to persons with disabilities, the UN Declaration on the Rights of Disabled Persons of 1975 (Art. 6) states that "Disabled persons have the right to medical, psychological and functional treatment" and recognizes the same right in the UN Standard Rules on the Equalization of Opportunities for Persons with Disabilities of 1993 (Rule 2, entitled "Medical Care").

The right to health of persons with disabilities is reaffirmed in Article 25 of the Convention on the Rights of Persons with Disabilities (CRPD).The Convention recognizes that persons with disabilities have the right to the enjoyment of the highest attainable standard of health without discrimination on the basis of disability, reiterating the classical formulation of the right to health set out in the ICESCR. Article 25 is the most complete formulation of the right to health in a human rights treaty.[182] "The right to health" or "the right to the highest attainable standard of health" as formulated in the Convention can be interpreted as "a convenient short-hand for the longer formulation", that is, "the right to the enjoyment of the highest attainable standard of physical and mental health". In this regard, States Parties shall take all appropriate measures to ensure access for persons with disabilities to health services that are gender-sensitive, including health-related rehabilitation (Art. 25, Para. 1).

The Convention also establishes a set of duties upon States Parties to ensure that persons with disabilities enjoy "the same range, quality and standard of free or affordable health care and programmes as provided to other persons" (Art. 25, *a*).

The first is the duty to guarantee that States ensure to persons with disabilities not only access to public health care assistance without any discrimination or stigmatization but also requests to health professionals that assure medical assistance of appropriate quality, on the basis of the previous informed consent of the interested person (Art. 25, *d*). Therefore, States have the obligation to avoid any form of discrimination in the health sector due to a condition of disability and must involve persons with disabilities in the decisional process concerning their health therapy through the process for obtaining informed consent.

The principle of the direct involvement of disabled persons in the decision process concerning their health reinforces the principles enshrined both in Article 12 related to the enjoyment of legal capacity by persons with disabilities

---

for mothers; (e) to ensure that all segments of society, in particular parents and children, are informed, have access to education and are supported in the use of basic knowledge of child health and nutrition, the advantages of breastfeeding, hygiene and environmental sanitation and the prevention of accidents; (f) to develop preventive health care, guidance for parents and family planning education and services".

182 Ilja Richard Pavone, "Article 25: Right to Health", in Valentina Della Fina, Giuseppe Palmisano, Rachele Cera (eds.), *The United Nations Convention on the Rights of Persons with Disabilities: A Commentary* (Springer International Publishing: 2017), 471–485.

and in Article 5, which prohibits experiments without the consent of the persons concerned.

Interesting references to diseases are envisaged by international humanitarian law through its rules on the protection of the health of people who are sick, shipwrecked, prisoners of war, and civilians and medical personnel in armed conflict.

The 1949 Geneva Convention I for the Amelioration of the Condition of the Wounded and Sick in Armed Forces in the Field establishes that "Members of armed forces and other persons . . . who are wounded or sick . . . shall not willfully be left without medical assistance and care, nor shall conditions exposing them to contagion or infection be created" (Art. 12).

The 1949 Geneva Convention III on the Treatment of Prisoners of War stipulates, "The Detaining Power shall be bound to take all sanitary measures necessary to ensure the cleanliness and healthfulness of camps and to prevent *epidemics*".

In addition, the 1949 Geneva Convention IV relative to the Protection of Civilian Persons in Time of War states that

> to the fullest extent of means available to it, the Occupying Power has the duty of ensuring and maintaining . . . the medical and hospital establishments and services, public health and hygiene in the occupied territory, with particular reference to the adoption and application of prophylactic and preventive measures necessary to combat the spread of contagious diseases and epidemics. Medical personnel of all categories shall be allowed to carry out their duties.[183]

International labor law also refers to health.[184] With Resolution I of 22 June 2022 on "Occupational Safety and Health",[185] the International Labor Conference amended Paragraph 2 of the ILO Declaration on Fundamental Principles and Rights at Work and included after the words "the elimination of discrimination in respect of employment and occupation" the words "and (e) a safe and healthy working environment".

---

183 See Arts. 13, 15, 25–26, 29–33 of the Geneva Convention on the Treatment of Prisoners (1949); Arts. 38, 56, 76, 81, 85, 91–92 of the Convention on the Treatment of Civilians in Time of War (1949); Art. 11 of the Protocol I related to the Protection of the Victims of International Armed Conflicts (1977); Art. 5, Para. 2, of the Protocol II related to the Protection of the Victims of Non-International Armed Conflicts (1977).

184 ILO Convention No. 187 on occupational safety and health.

185 ILC.110/Resolution I. Resolution on the inclusion of a safe and healthy working environment in the ILO's framework of fundamental principles and rights at work. In the Preamble, the International Labour Conference recognized "the vital importance of occupational safety and health, as compellingly demonstrated by the COVID-19 pandemic and its profound and transformative impact on the world of work".

12.2. Regional level

A high level of health is a common goal for all European Union policies (Art. 9 of the Treaty on the Functioning of the European Union – TFEU) (Lisbon version): "in defining and implementing its policies and activities, the Union shall take into account requirements linked to the promotion of a high level of . . . protection of human health". Article 168 of the TFEU states that "A high level of human health protection shall be ensured in the definition and implementation of all Union policies and activities".[186]

The EU has also recognized health as an individual right in the Charter on Fundamental Rights (Nizza, 2000), which postulates that

> Everyone has the right of access to preventive health care and the right to benefit from medical treatment under the conditions established by national laws and practices. A high level of human health protection shall be ensured in the definition and implementation of all Union policies and activities.[187]

Within the Council of Europe,[188] the European Convention on Human Rights (ECHR) does not mention health, although public health reasons can be a justification for States to derogate the enjoyment of fundamental freedoms, such as the right to a private and family life and freedom of expression.

However, even in the absence of a specific norm, the European Court of Human Rights (ECtHR) has considered health a necessary element of the right to life (Art. 2), requiring States to provide adequate care for HIV-positive patients with severe health problems.[189]

States have a positive obligation to protect mental and physical well-being in many different circumstances. The European Social Charter (1961) refers to "the right to the protection of health" (Art. 11): States must remove as far as possible the causes of ill-health (Art. 11, Para. 1) and should "prevent as far as possible epidemic, endemic and other diseases as well as accidents" (Art. 11, Para. 3).

---

186 "Health" is the exclusive competence of Member States. Article 168, Paragraph 2 states that "Union action, which shall complement national policies, shall be directed towards improving public health, preventing physical and mental illness and diseases, and obviating sources of danger to physical and mental health. Such action shall cover the fight against the major health scourges, by promoting research into their causes, their transmission and their prevention, as well as health information and education, and monitoring, early warning of and combating serious cross-border threats to health". See Tamara K. Hervey, Jean V. Mchale, *European Union Health Law* (Cambridge University Press: 2015).

187 Jean McHale, "Fundamental Rights and Health Care", in Elias Mossialos, Govin Permanand, Rita Baeten, Tamara K. Hervey (eds.), *Health Systems Governance in Europe: The Role of European Union Law and Policy* (Cambridge University Press: 2010), 282–314.

188 For details on the structure and functioning of the Council of Europe and its Court, Rachele Cera, "Consiglio d'Europa", *Enciclopedia Giuridica Treccani – Aggiornamenti*, Vol. XV, (Roma: 2007).

189 *D. v The United Kingdom*, Application No. 30240/96.

The African Charter on Human and Peoples' Rights (Nairobi, 1981) affirms that every individual shall have the right to enjoy the best attainable state of physical and mental health and that States Parties must take all necessary measures "to protect the health of their people and to ensure that they receive medical attention when they are sick" (Art. 16).

The Principles and Guidelines on the Implementation of Economic, Social and Cultural Rights in the African Charter on Human and People's Rights[190] recognizes the right of the individual to "the best attainable state of physical and mental health" (Para. 66). The minimum core obligations of the right to health include the duties "to ensure universal immunisation against major infectious diseases" (Para. 67, lect. *c*) and "to take measures to prevent, treat and control epidemic and endemic diseases" (Para. 67, lect. *d*).

In its Communication concerning the case *Purohit and Anor v Gambia* (2003), the African Commission clearly stated that "the enjoyment of the human right to health as it is widely known is vital to all aspects of a person's life and well-being, and is crucial to the realization of all the other fundamental human rights and freedoms. This right includes the right to health facilities, access to goods and services to be guaranteed to all without discrimination of any kind" (Para. 80).[191]

The American Convention on Human Rights (ACHR) (San José de Costa Rica, 1969) instead fails to recognize an individual right to health (although it was explicitly recalled in the American Declaration on Rights and Duties of Man of 1948 at Art. XI, entitled "Right to the preservation of health and to well-being"). The protection of health is, however, foreseen in specific sectors.

In *Cuscul Piraval et al. v. Guatemala* (23 August 2018), the Inter-American Court of Human Rights clarified the scope of State obligations with reference to HIV-positive persons.[192] The patients had been diagnosed with HIV between 1992 and 2004, but they had not received appropriate medical assistance until 2006 and 2007. The Court recalled that

> medical treatment for people living with HIV requires the availability of sufficient quantities of antiretroviral drugs and other pharmaceutical products for the treatment of opportunistic infections. In this regard, the evidence reveals that 31 of the presumed victims had irregular, inadequate or non-existent access to antiretroviral drugs provided by the State.
>
> (Para. 121)

---

190 African Commission on Human and Peoples' Rights, 2010.
191 *Purohit and Anor v Gambia* (Communication No. 241/2001) [2003] ACHPR 49; (29 May 2003), https://www.achpr.org/public/Document/file/English/achpr33_241_01_eng.pdf.
192 Inter-American Court of Human Rights. *Case of Cuscul Pivaral et al. v. Guatemala*, Judgment of 23 August 2018.

The Court then underlined that "one of the elements of the right to health is that the most vulnerable or marginalized sectors of the population should have access to health care facilities, goods and services, which should be within their geographical and financial reach" (Para. 124).

The Court determined that Guatemala failed to ensure the right to health of the victims (Para. 127) under Article 26 of the Convention; the right to health is "understood as an autonomous right derived from Article 26 of the American Convention" (Para. 73). Then, the Court assessed that Guatemala failed to comply with its duties under Article 4 ('Right to life'), Article 5 ('Right to human treatment') and Article 26 ('Progressive development') of the ACHR (Para. 72). Furthermore, Guatemala violated the principle of non-discrimination since two pregnant women – considering their particular vulnerability – were not provided with adequate health care assistance.

12.3. Biolaw and the right to health

Particular provisions are contained in treaties and declarations belonging to the specific domain of biolaw that although they do not directly refer to health, they may be considered relevant in claims for rights concerning specific medical treatments, specifically at the beginning and end of life.

The Declaration of Geneva of the World Medical Association (WMA) clearly affirms that "the health of my patient will be my first consideration". The WMA Declaration of Helsinki (first version of 1964) states that "it is the duty of the physician in medical research to protect the life, health, privacy, and dignity of the human subject" (Art. 10).

Article 14 of the Universal Declaration on Bioethics and Human Rights (UDBHR) (2005) ("Social responsibility and health")[193] contains a detailed description of the right to health. First, the promotion of health and social development of the population should be a central purpose of governments. The enjoyment of the highest attainable standard of health must be enjoyed "without distinction of race, religion, political belief, economic or social condition" (Art. 14, Para. 2). Developments in science and technology should advance

(a) access to quality health care and essential medicines, especially for the health of women and children, because health is essential to life itself and must be considered to be a social and human good; (b) access to adequate nutrition and water; (c) improvement of living conditions and the environment; (d) elimination of the marginalization and the exclusion

---

193 Cinzia Caporale, Ilja Richard Pavone (eds.), *International Biolaw and Shared Ethical Principles: The Universal Declaration on Bioethics and Human Rights* (Routledge: 2019).

of persons on the basis of any grounds; (e) reduction of poverty and illiteracy.

(Art. 14, Para. 3)

Article 3 of the European Convention on Biomedicine and Human Rights (Oviedo, 1997)[194] is explicitly devoted to the "equitable access to health care". Article 3 affirms that "Parties, taking into account health needs and available resources, shall take appropriate measures with a view to providing, within their jurisdiction, equitable access to health care of appropriate quality".

Paragraph 25 of the Explanatory Report also highlights that access to health care must be equitable. In this context, 'equitable' means first and foremost the absence of unjustified discrimination. Although not synonymous with absolute equality, equitable access implies effectively obtaining a satisfactory degree of care.

Another aspect is the quality of the services provided. Against this backdrop, Article 4 of the Oviedo Convention establishes that "any intervention in the health field including research, must be carried out in accordance with relevant professional obligations and standards".

13. International jurisprudence

The international jurisprudence on the issue of epidemics is quite scarce.

Within the dispute settlement mechanism envisaged by the World Trade Organization (WTO), two key cases deal with disease outbreaks. One is *Brasil – Measures Affecting Imports of Retreated Tyres (Brazilian Tires)*[195] that refers to malaria and other infectious diseases.

Brazil had introduced trade measures banning the importation of retreated tires due to their possible side effects on animal and human health and environmental degradation. In detail, Brazil claimed that the accumulation of these retreated tires was a vector for the transmission of mosquito-borne diseases, such as dengue fever and malaria.

Dengue, in particular, which was considered eradicated, re-emerged in Brazil in the 1990s and soared to the level of an "explosive" outbreak.[196]

The WHO has recognized dengue as "the most important emerging tropical viral disease" and "a major international public health concern".[197] Used

---

194 Council of Europe Convention for the Protection of Human Rights and Dignity of the Human Being with Regard to Biology and Medicine: Convention on Human Rights and Biomedicine, Oviedo, 4 April 1997.

195 WTO, Brazil – Measures Affecting Imports of Retreated Tyres, WT/DS332/AB/R (3 December 2007).

196 World Health Assembly 55, *Dengue Fever and Dengue Haemorrhagic Fever Prevention and Control* (2002), https://apps.who.int/iris/handle/10665/78534.

197 1 World Health Organization, Guidelines for Treatment of Dengue Haemorrhagic Fever in Small Hospitals ix (1999) (Exhibit BRA-14).

tires are in this case the main incubator for the mosquitos that transmit dengue (Brazil has the most cases in the world).

As recognized by the United States Center for Disease Control and Prevention, "infestation may be contained through programmes of surveillance, removal of breeding sites (especially tires), interruption of interstate dispersal of tires, and judicious use of insecticides in breeding sites".[198]

Brazil's restriction on the importation of retreated tires determined a claim by the EU for a violation of GATT.

The WTO's appellate body made a clear reference to infectious diseases:

> at the end of their useful life, tires become waste, the accumulation of which is associated with risks to human, animal, and plant life and health. Specific risks to human life and health include (i) the transmission of dengue, yellow fever and malaria through mosquitoes which use tires as breeding grounds.
>
> (Para. 119)[199]

The Report then reiterated that "in this case the Panel identified the objective of the Import Ban as being the reduction of the exposure to risks arising from the accumulation of waste tires. It assessed the importance of the interests underlying this objective. It found that risks of dengue fever and malaria arise from the accumulation of waste tires and that the objective of protecting human life and health against such diseases is both vital and important in the highest degree" (Para. 179).[200]

The cholera outbreak in Haiti in 2010 was the largest cholera epidemic in recent history.[201] Vibrio cholerae was introduced into Haiti by blue helmets from Nepal. It caused the death of almost 10,000 people and the infection of approximately 800,000, and it led to claims against the UN. In 2016, the UN admitted their responsibility and the former Secretary-General Ban Ki-Moon in his remarks before the General Assembly officially apologized for the negative role of peace keepers in the spread of the cholera outbreak.[202]

---

198 Center for Disease Control and Prevention, Aedes albopictus Infestation – United States, Brazil, Morbidity And Mortality Weekly Report, 8 August 1986 (Exhibit BRA-20).

199 Philippe Sands, *Principles of International Environmental Law* (Cambridge University Press: 2018), 867–869.

200 In another case, namely, *India – Import Prohibition of Agricultural Products* (WTO, India – Measures Concerning the Importation of Certain Agricultural Products (Report of the Appellate Body), 4 June 2015, WT/DS430/AB/R), a dispute arose from the fact that India banned the importation of certain agricultural products from countries that reported cases of H5N1 Influenza (commonly known as Avian Influenza).

201 Melina Garcin, "The Haitian Cholera Victims Against the United Nations", *Zeitschrift fur auslandischesoffentlisches Recht und Volkerrecht* (2015): 671–705.

202 https://www.un.org/press/en/2016/sgsm18323.doc.htm.

14. Conclusions

The introductory chapter of this volume focused first on the WHO and its origins. This chapter explored the reasons underpinning the creation of the WHO, its structure, and its normative power, with a target on the IHR, which are the main international legal instrument that envisages measures for containing the transnational spread of infectious diseases.

Part I of the chapter briefly reconstructed the birth of State cooperation in the field of the containment of infectious diseases. I particularly highlighted the utilitarian end behind the need to cooperate among countries on the control of infectious diseases in the XIX century. I explained that the first health conference convened by France in 1851 witnessed early efforts to create a uniform mechanism of maritime quarantine but only as first line of defense against diseases originating from the Far East. The general idea behind the health conferences that followed was to contain the global spread of infectious diseases from the Far East and avoid at the same time an excessive interference with trade and commerce.

Against this backdrop, I underlined the paradox behind the necessity to protect the West from diseases originating from the East, since the foundations of international law are characterized by conquest, colonization, and exportation of deadly diseases. In fact, the European colonial expansion from the time of Columbus to the XIX century brought as a side effect the spread of zoonotic diseases among native populations in South America, Africa, and Australia and the killing of thousands of natives.

This chapter highlighted – in describing the IHR and previous efforts of health cooperation – that the main structural gap of the global health architecture is represented by the fact that it is mainly centered on the containment of disease outbreaks once they have spread across countries (the "containment bias"). Accordingly, there is a lack of a preventative approach in the IHR, which should deal with the origins of zoonotic diseases and set up mechanisms to avoid the spillover of pathogens from animals to humans.[203]

The overall conclusion is that the IHR – although there are considerable limits as to their content and enforcement – are still the most important legal instrument for the containment of disease outbreaks. Against this backdrop, the ongoing process of reform of the IHR, through the adoption of a new pandemic treaty and an amendment to the IHR, is considered in the next chapter. It is argued that another reform of the IHR – although advisable – is not the most appropriate answer. In fact, the major flaws and weaknesses of

---

203 See Despoina D. Tounta, Panagiotis T. Nastos, Christine Tesseromatis, "Human Activities and Zoonotic Epidemics: A Two-Way Relationship. The Case of the COVID-19 Pandemic", *Global Sustainability* (2022): 1–22; on the close interdependence between human, animal, and environmental health, see also Stefania Negri, Mark Eccleston Turner, "One Health and Pathogen Sharing: Filling the Gap in the International Health Regulations to Strengthen Global Pandemic Preparedness and Response", *International Organizations Law Review* 19 (2022): 188–214.

the IHR – which clearly emerged during the COVID-19 pandemic – need a more structural reform of the WHO. This implies a specific power of the WHO to adopt countermeasures or sanctions against a State that does not fulfill its obligations under the IHR.

Part II of chapter I concentrated on the content and scope of the right to health – whose fulfillment is the main goal of the WHO – in human rights law. I contended that approaching health issues through the lens of human rights is an added value, since it creates a connection with other fundamental rights, such as the protection of vulnerable groups, the right to food, and the right not to be discriminated. At the same time, I underscored the contradiction in terms of the WHO – which has the statutory goal of the promotion of the highest attainable standard of physical and mental health – but has never enacted a specific treaty devoted to health. The Framework Convention on Tobacco Control and its Additional Protocol has the goal of promoting public health but only in the sector of the global tobacco epidemic. The IHR, on their own, do not deal at all with the right to health.

II Is the WHO truly independent? Successes, failures, and perspectives of reform

1. Short overview of WHO's achievements and failures

The WHO, as previously underlined, has a general competence in the health field, ranging from the prevention of infectious diseases and the promotion of the right to health to the management of noncommunicable diseases.

In the first decades of its work, the WHO had an emphasis on communicable disease control and their eradication ("eradication" is defined by the WHO as "the permanent reduction to zero of the worldwide incidence of infection caused by a specific pathogen established in a human or animal population, as a result of deliberate efforts, with no more risk of reintroduction").[1]

This focus led to what has arguably been the WHO's greatest success so far: the smallpox eradication programme. At the end of the 1960s, smallpox was still endemic in developing countries in Sub-Saharan Africa and South-East Asia, although it was wiped out in North America (1952) and Western Africa (1953).

The vaccination campaign, launched in 1957 under the aegis of the Soviet Union,[2] was formally endorsed by the World Health Assembly (WHA) in 1958[3] and suffered in the beginning a series of drawbacks, such as shortages of vaccines, lack of adequate funding and real commitment by the States.[4]

The Global Smallpox Eradication Programme (1959–1967)[5] was intensified and relaunched in 1968 ("Intensification Eradication Programme"), since smallpox was endemic in too many countries. The new programme had the support of both the United States and the Union of Soviet Socialist Republics (USSR), which provided financial, technical, and material assistance.

The new strategy was based upon four pillars, specifically, a consistent increase of funds (the WHA voted for a special budget), a boost of local

---

1 Walter R. Dowdle, "The Principles of Disease Elimination and Eradication", *Bulletin of the World Health Organization* (1998): 22–25.
2 Resolution WHA11.54.
3 Resolution WHA12.54.
4 Donald A. Henderson, Petra Klepac, "Lessons from the Eradication of Smallpox: An Interview with D.A. Henderson", *Philosophical Transactions of the Royal Society B* (2013): 1–7.
5 Sanjoy Bhattacharya, Carlos Eduardo D'Avila Pereira Campani, "Re-assessing the Foundations: Worldwide Smallpox Eradication, 1957–67", *Medical History* (2020): 71–93.

DOI: 10.4324/9781003100645-2

production of high-quality vaccines ("mass vaccination campaigns"), surveillance ("house to house" searches), and containment (detection and isolation of cases).[6]

The programme led to the complete eradication of smallpox in South America in 1971, in Asia in 1975, and in Africa in 1977. Janet Parker, a medical photographer based at the Birmingham University Medical School was the last official victim of Smallpox in 1978.

On 8 May 1980, the 33rd WHA declared the world free of smallpox on the basis of the report of the Global Commission for the Global Certification of Smallpox Eradication, which certified that "smallpox had been eradicated in every country in the world".[7]

Through Resolution WHA34.13, smallpox was then no longer included in the list of diseases covered by the IHR.

In the 1980s, the WHO also launched a specific programme to eradicate the Guinea Worm Disease (known as Dracunculiasis), in partnership with the Carter Center. This disease is caused by the parasite *Dracunculus medinensis* and belongs to the category of neglected tropical diseases (NPT).[8]

Although neither a specific treatment nor a vaccine have yet been discovered, through the Guinea Worm Eradication Programme, the disease has almost been completely eradicated.[9] It dropped from approximately 3.5 million cases in the 1980s to 27 cases reported in 2020 and 15 reported in 2021.[10]

Another successful outcome is represented by the almost complete elimination of poliomyelitis – a serious infectious viral disease that largely affects children under 5 years of age. Effective vaccines against poliomyelitis became available in the mid-1950s (the Koprowsky vaccine) and early 1960s (the safest Sabin vaccine). Mass campaigns were an integral part of early control efforts. Thereafter, polio vaccines were used largely in routine childhood programmes. Resolution WHA 41.28 (1988) to eradicate polio globally[11] led to the development of appropriate strategies to achieve this goal, including mass vaccination campaigns (i.e., national immunization days, sub-national immunization days, and mop-up activities), to attain the highest possible coverage in the shortest possible time.

The Global Polio Eradication Initiative (GPEI) set up in 1988 by the WHO in partnership with UNICEF and the United States Centers for Disease Control and Prevention (CDC) has provided a pivotal support to countries in making significant progress to protect their population from this debilitating

---

6 Marc A. Strassburg, "The Global Eradication of Smallpox", *American Journal of Infection Control* (1982): 53–59.
7 WHO Declaration of Global Eradication of Smallpox, 8 May 1980.
8 https://www.who.int/health-topics/neglected-tropical-diseases.
9 https://www.cartercenter.org/health/guinea_worm/index.html.
10 https://www.cartercenter.org/health/guinea_worm/case-totals.html.
11 Forty-First World Health Assembly, WHA41.28, 13 May 1988, Global eradication of poliomyelitis by the year 2000.

disease. As a result, a decrease by **99.9%** of the global incidence of polio has been registered since the GPEI's foundation.

A complete eradication of wild poliovirus types 2 and 3 (WPV2 and WPV3) was declared in 2015 and 2019, respectively. The WHO African Region was certified as free of wild poliovirus (WPV) in August 2020, although one new case was registered in Malawi in 2022.[12] The year 2021 marked a milestone as efforts towards eradication intensified. In June 2021, a roadmap was launched in order to achieve the goal of a world free from all forms of polioviruses. The GPE Strategy 2022–2026[13] focused on eradicating all poliovirus transmission in endemic countries, such as Afghanistan and Pakistan, where wild poliovirus type 1 (WPV1) persists alongside circulating vaccine-derived poliovirus type 2 (cVDPV2)).

Technological advances in medicine and public health then brought emphasis on noncommunicable disease control. However, a new deadly epidemic appeared in the 1980s: HIV/AIDS. The WHO's response to HIV/AIDS was often depicted as unsuccessful.[14] The WHO's drawbacks and the impossibility of adopting an international instrument dealing with such a novel disease led to a sort of epiphany. The creation by the UN of a separate agency specializing in this disease, UNAIDS, which is a subsidiary body of ECOSOC,[15] was interpreted as an open critique of the WHO, as the management of infectious diseases falls within its core mandate.

UNAIDS was established as the successor of the WHO's Global Programme on AIDS. Its main function is that of coordinating the UN system's response to the HIV/AIDS epidemic within Chapter IX of the UN Charter.[16] The establishment of UNAIDS is an example of the limits of the traditional models of governance in international organizations.

In 2003, the WHO, in cooperation with UNAIDS, launched the "3 by 5" initiative aimed at providing life-prolonging antiretroviral treatments to 3 million people living with HIV/AIDS in low- and middle-income countries in 2005.

The advent of potent antiretroviral therapy in 1996 led to a revolution in the care of patients with HIV/AIDS in the developed world. Although these treatments are not a cure (and a vaccine has not yet been discovered), they

---

12 Certification of Wild Poliovirus Eradication in the African Continent and Sustaining the Gains, Post-Certification, Report of the Secretariat, 25 August 2020, AFR/RC70/7.

13 https://polioeradication.org/gpei-strategy-2022-2026/. The new strategy replaced the previous one ("The Polio Endgame Strategy 2019–2023: Eradication, Integration, Containment and Certification").

14 Bradly Condon, Tapen Sinha, *Global Lessons from the AIDS Pandemic. Economic, Financial, Legal and Political Implications* (Springer: 2008).

15 Resolution 1994/24 of ECOSOC, 26 July 1994, "Joint and co-sponsored United Nations programme on human immunodeficiency virus/acquired immunodeficiency syndrome (HIV/AIDS)".

16 Ilja Richard Pavone, "The HIV/AIDS Pandemic and International Human Rights Law", *LAWASIA Journal* (2009): 96–111, at 100.

have drastically reduced the rates of mortality and morbidity and improved the quality of life of people living with HIV/AIDS.[17]

The 3 by 5 initiative was followed by the development of a set of guidelines entitled "Scaling Up Antiretroviral Therapy in Resource-Limited Settings: Treatment Guidelines for a Public Health Approach".[18] In addition, the WHO has set up a framework for universal access to HIV/AIDS prevention, care, treatment, and support in the health sector by 2010 ("Universal Access by 2010").

2. The epidemiological transition model

The WHO registered a significant change in its policy (from a horizontal to a vertical approach) in the 1970s; this change brought a major focus not only on noncommunicable diseases (NCDs) but also on the promotion of the right to health and the prevention of infectious diseases through vaccination programmes.[19]

The epidemiologist Abdel Omran – in an influential study published in 1971 – theorized that degenerative and man-made diseases would displace pandemics of infection as the primary causes of morbidity and mortality in several industrialized countries.[20]

His theory was centered on the "complex change in patterns of health and disease and on the interactions between these patterns and their demographic, economic and sociologic determinants and consequences". Against this backdrop, he described three stages of transition: i) the age of pestilence and famine; ii) the age of receding pandemics; and iii) the age of degenerative and man-made diseases. Olshansky et al. in 1983 added a further stage: the age of delayed degenerative diseases.[21] Another phase adjoined much later by Martens and Huynen in 2002 was the age of re-emerging infectious diseases.[22]

According to Proposition Two ("Shift in Mortality and Disease Patterns") of the epidemiologic transition model, degenerative and man-made diseases will gradually displace infectious diseases.[23] This led to the general idea at the beginning of the XXI century that the main challenges to public

17 Frank J. Palella Jr., Maria Deloria-Knoll, Joan S. Chmiel, "Survival Benefit of Initiating Antiretroviral Therapy in HIV-Infected Persons in Different CD4+ Cell Strata", *Annals of Internal Medicine* (2003): 620–626.
18 https://www.who.int/3by5/publications/documents/arv_guidelines/en/.
19 Jan De Maeseneer, "Strengthening Primary Care: Addressing the Disparity Between Vertical and Horizontal Investment", *British Journal of General Practice* (2008): 3–4.
20 Abdel R. Omran, "The Epidemiologic Transition: A Theory of the Epidemiology of Population Change", *The Milbank Memorial Fund Quarterly* (1971): 509–538.
21 Jay S. Olshansky, Brian A. Ault, "The Fourth Stage of the Epidemiologic Transition: The Age of Delayed Degenerative Diseases", *The Milbank Quarterly* (1986): 355–391.
22 Pim Martens, Maud Huynen, "A Future Without Health? Health Dimension in Global Scenario Studies", *Bulletin of the World Health Organization* (2003): 896–901.
23 Mohammed H. Wadan, "The Epidemiological Transition", *Eastern Mediterranean Health Journal* (1996): 8–20. https://apps.who.int/iris/handle/10665/118829.

health in industrialized countries (but also with a strong incidence in developing countries) would be mainly represented by NCDs such as tumors, neurodegenerative diseases associated with the process of aging (Alzheimer's, Amyotrophic Lateral Sclerosis, Multiple Sclerosis, and Parkinson's), and severe genetic disorders.[24]

The strong interest in environmental protection in the 1960s and 1970s, the focus on NCDs related to environmental degradation, and the right to a healthy environment facilitated this transition. The Stockholm Declaration on Human Environment adopted in 1972 recognized that "man has the fundamental right to freedom, equality and adequate conditions of life, in an environment of a quality that permits a life of dignity and well-being" (Principle 1).

Instead, contrary to these predictions, the world medical community is facing the emergence of new infectious diseases (SARS, MERS, Zika, and COVID-19), the re-emergence of old infectious diseases (such as Ebola, with recent outbreaks in 2014, 2019, and 2022,[25] and monkeypox, which was endemic in parts of Africa for decades before its spread to high-income countries in 2022), and the persistence of intractable infectious diseases (HIV/AIDS and influenza). The diffusion of these diseases from developing countries to industrialized countries – accelerated by the process of globalization and environmental degradation – has resulted in the emergence of a collective interest in the protection of the health of high-income countries' populations from diseases imported from the South of the world.

Approximately 75% of new human diseases are caused by microbes that originate in animals. These include HIV/AIDS, influenzas (including pandemic

24 On these issues, see GA Resolution 63/237 of 17 March 2009, Recognition of sickle cell anaemia as a public health problem; GA Resolution 64/265 of 22 December 2008, Prevention and control of non-communicable diseases, of 13 May 2010; Political Declaration of the High-level Meeting of the General Assembly on the Prevention and Control of Non-Communicable Diseases of 19 September 2011. Increased life expectancy in Western Europe implies the possibility of artificially prolonging life, and at the same time, it has resulted in a considerable number of cases of neurodegenerative diseases often related to old age. The main issue is that for some terminally ill persons, life is not always the highest attainable value to be protected by all means. The concept of dignity as a central value is pivotal in end of life cases: the EU Charter of Fundamental Rights recognizes that "human dignity is inviolable. It must be respected and protected". Protocol No. 13 to the ECHR affirms that dignity is "inherent" in all human beings. The concept of human dignity is also recognized in Article 1 of the European Convention of Biomedicine, which asserts that "States Parties shall protect the dignity and identity of all human beings". The debate on the legitimacy of active euthanasia and assisted suicide must not be confused with the withdrawal of life-prolonging treatments (or "passive euthanasia"). In the first case, there is a specific act by a doctor or a third person, but in the latter, there is an omission by the physician. Arend Cornelis Hendriks, "End-of-life decisions. Recent jurisprudence of the European Court of Human Rights", *ERA Forum* (2019): 561–570; Carlo Petrini, Walter Ricciardi, "The Convention on Human Rights and Biomedicine Twenty Years Later: A Look at the Past and a Step Towards the Future", *Ann Ist Super Sanità* (2018): 171–173.

25 https://www.theguardian.com/global-development/2022/oct/07/health-workers-among-dead-in-ugandan-ebola-outbreak.

H1N1, H5N1 and H7N9), Severe Acute Respiratory Syndrome (SARS), Middle East Respiratory Syndrome-Coronavirus (MERS-CoV), Ebola, Marburg, monkeypox, and Nipah.[26] Several of these have spread extensively in human populations to cause a global epidemic.

As I discuss in the volume, the current trend of exponential growth of infectious diseases necessitates a focus on the prevention of future disease outbreak. The current application of the IHR, which are only responsive and do not address the root causes of zoonotic diseases, is a significant gap that must be filled. Indeed, the IHR are based on the assumption that disease outbreaks cannot be prevented but only contained and defeated. The new pandemic treaty, which is discussed in the next paragraphs, addresses the issue of prevention in Article 11, Paragraph 4, lect. *e*, which states that each Party shall, in accordance with national law, adopt policies and strategies "for prevention of epidemic-prone diseases, and emerging, growing or evolving public health threats with pandemic potential, notably at the human-animal-environment interface".

3. WHO declarations of PHEIC

The model upon which the WHO and the other UN specialized agencies is based dates back to the XIX century, with a structure grounded on a delimited pattern of authority (on the classic command model of political authority).[27] Except for the EU,[28] which can approve regulations directly binding upon its Member States, and the Security Council, which can adopt enforcement measures under Articles 41 and 42, IGOs generally have limited powers.

During the SARS outbreak in 2003, the then-Director-General Gro Harlem Brundtland decided to declare a health emergency due to the slow response of the WHA and the Executive Board and to warn travelers to avoid certain destinations, including Toronto, Hong Kong, and several provinces of China.[29] She concluded that the WHO should have played a key role in the early phases of a disease outbreak through the collection of information and the conduction of an appropriate risk assessment. As outlined by Burci, in the course of the SARS outbreak, the WHO assumed a specific role of direction rather than simply of coordination.[30] The WHO responded to SARS "with an unprecedented

---

26 For detailed information on the Nipah virus, see https://www.who.int/news-room/fact-sheets/detail/nipah-virus.

27 Niko Krisch, "Liquid Authority in Global Governance", *International Theory* (2017): 1–10.

28 Jan Klabbers, 'Sui Generis? The European Union as an International Organization', in Dennis Patterson, Anna Södersten (eds.), *A Companion to European Union Law and International Law* (Wiley: 2016), 3.

29 World Health Organization, *Update 92: Chronology of Travel Recommendations* (1 July 2003), http://www.who.int/csr/don/2003_07_01/en/index.html.

30 Gianluca Burci, "La Gestion d'une Crise Sanitaire Internationale: Le Cas du SRAS", in Rostane Mehdi, Sandrine Maljean-Dubois (eds.), *La société internationale et les grandes pandémies* (Editions Pedone: 2007), 135, 138.

assertion of emergency powers",[31] resorting to the public shaming of China, recommending travel restrictions, and even issuing an ultimatum to elicit its cooperation.

This practice, which denoted the inefficacy of the previous regime, faced the charges of *ultra vires*.[32]

According to Kamradt-Scott (2015), the emergency measures enacted by the Director-General were justified under Article 28, lect. *i* of the WHO Constitution, which states that the Board "may authorize the Director-General to take the necessary steps to combat epidemics".[33]

The revised version of the IHR that followed then *de facto* "codified" the WHO's behavior during the SARS outbreak.

The IHR officially endowed the DG with the power to declare a PHEIC (Art. 12)[34] and to issue temporary recommendations of urgent measures "to prevent or reduce the international spread of disease and avoid unnecessary interference with international traffic" (Art. 15).[35]

Article 18 of the IHR provides a list of measures that the WHO might recommend, such as screening procedures at airports and seaports, travel bans, placing infected persons in isolation, imposing quarantines and "cordons sanitaires", and contact tracing.

Although defined as "non-binding advice" (Art. 1, IHR), temporary recommendations to avoid certain destinations and to impose lockdowns, social distancing, or quarantines do have an impact on local economies and global travel patterns.

Temporary recommendations automatically expire three months after their issuance unless they are renewed by the DG, who, *inter alia*, declares the end of the emergency (after the advice of the Emergency Committee (EC) and upon request of the concerned State).[36]

A public health emergency of international concern (PHEIC) is defined as "an extraordinary event which is determined to constitute a public health risk to other States through the international spread of disease and to potentially

---

31 Gianluca Burci, Stefania Negri, "Governing the Global Fight Against Pandemics: The WHO, the International Health Regulations, and the Fragmentation of International Law", *International Law and Politics* (2021): 501–504.

32 Christian Kreuder Sonnen, *Emergency Powers of International Organizations* (Oxford University Press: 2019), 155–156.

33 Adam Kamradr-Scott, *Managing Global Health Security: The World Health Organization and Diseases Outbreak Control* (Springer: 2015), 33.

34 Article 12, Paragraph 1 of the IHR states that "The Director-General shall determine, on the basis of the information received, in particular from the State Party within whose territory an event is occurring, whether an event constitutes a public health emergency of international concern in accordance with the criteria and the procedure set out in these Regulations".

35 Mark Eccleston-Turner, Clare Wenham, *Declaring a Public Health Emergency of International Concern: Between International Law and Politics* (Bristol University Press: 2021).

36 Michael Waibel, "The Final Act: Exploring the End of Pandemics", *American Journal of International Law* (2020): 698–707.

require a coordinated international response". It is a final assessment of a health event that might have serious consequences (while States Parties only report an episode that may have a far-reaching impact). A PHEIC is a situation that is serious, sudden, unusual, and unexpected with cross-border implications that requires immediate action. A PHEIC lasts three months, and if not renewed, then it automatically expires. PHEICs have been declared seven times in the time span between 2009 and 2022.

It is innovative in the law of IGOs that one single organ – after being advised by a scientific body, the EC – can adopt a declaration with "potentially wide-ranging consequences".[37] It is an extraordinary power of the DG and a unique case in the law of international organizations, since the declaration of a PHEIC is a unilateral decision adopted without a vote within an assembly and is exclusively based on scientific considerations. It can be compared to the powers of the head of state or government under domestic laws during a state of emergency.[38]

The theory of emergency powers has been framed for domestic governments (when relying on emergency powers, democratic procedures are usually bypassed).[39]

Currently, emergency powers have emerged at the international level, considering that often, security threats such as pandemics, bioterrorism, environmental disasters, and other emergencies are not confined at borders.[40]

Despite these extensive powers provided to the DG, scholars have argued that the new version of the IHR is in reality a surreptitious tool to restrict the DG's autonomy and the WHO's resort to emergency powers;[41] however, the DG must consult a team of independent experts and the concerned State before acting, but he can also decide to act unilaterally as witnessed in the case of monkeypox, which is described in the next paragraphs.

Despite these considerations, the IHR, however, bear a conflict of interest or rather a surreptitious contrast between industrialized and developing countries, which emerged during the negotiation process. Industrialized countries wanted to have access to informal information about possible clusters of infectious diseases and protect themselves from diseases imported from poorer countries, while developing countries wanted to limit the sharing of

37 Christian Kreuder-Sonnen, *Emergency Powers of International Organizations: Between Normalization and Containment* (Oxford University Press: 2019), 152–186.
38 Andraž Zidar, "WHO International Health Regulations and Human Rights: From Allusions to Inclusion", *The International Journal of Human Rights* (2015): 505–526.
39 John Ferejohn, Pasquale Pasquino, "The Law of the Exception: A Typology of Emergency Powers", *International Journal of Constitutional Law* (2004): 210–239.
40 Dominic McGoldrick, "The Interface Between Public Emergency Powers and International Law", *International Journal of Constitutional Law* (2004): 380–429.
41 Adam Kamradt-Scott, "The International Health Regulations (2005): Strengthening Their Effective Implementation and Utilisation", *International Organization Law Review* (2019): 255–256.

information with the West to limit their power to impose excessive trade, travel, and tourism limitations.

In determining whether or not to declare a PHEIC, the DG should assess the appropriate information received by the concerned State, ask the advice of the EC, and carry out a risk assessment; this should imply an evaluation of potential hazards to human health, the risk of international spread, and the interference of such a declaration with international traffic.

Indeed, a unilateral act by an individual organ (represented by the WHO Secretariat and, specifically, by the DG) invites the Member States to adopt specific containment and mitigation measures with the goal of pursuing a common goal, which is the protection of public health.

The declaration of PHEIC has two peculiarities. First, it is not adopted on the basis of political considerations but rather on the basis of scientific evidence in light of the technical expertise of the WHO. In the declaration of a pandemic, it is the main instrument through which the WHO's DG exercises the international public authority (IPA) of international institutions.[42]

Second, the declaration is not discussed and voted within the WHA through a democratic process but through a two-step process that envisages a "green light" by the EC – which is convened on a discretionary basis by the DG – and then, the formal adoption by the DG. The DG has, however, the power to adopt a PHEIC declaration as further clarified in Article 49, which states that "[t]he views of the Emergency Committee shall be forwarded to the Director-General for consideration. The Director-General shall make the final determination on these matters".

Granting one single body the authority to issue such a declaration with significant consequences is an extraordinary feature in the law of international organizations and is an example of "governance by information".[43] That is, emergency authority is placed under the direction of the WHO Secretariat – the administrative body of the organization – which is predominantly composed of medical specialists.[44] The mechanism established under the IHR envisages control *ex ante* – represented by the advice of the EC – and *ex post* through the establishment of IHR Review Committees that periodically

---

42 The concept of IPA of international institutions postulates that acts of international organizations – regardless of their obligatoriness – can be considered an exercise of authority, provided that they can address the behavior of the single governments. In this sense, see Armin von Bogdandy, Philipp Dann, Matthias Goldmann, "Developing the Publicness of Public International Law: Towards a Legal Framework for Global Governance Activities", in Armin von Bogdandy, Rüdiger Wolfrum, Jochen von Bernstorff, Philipp Dann, Matthias Goldmann (eds.), *The Exercise of Public Authority by International Institutions Advancing International Institutional Law* (Springer: 2011), 3–32.
43 Armin von Bogdandy, Pedro A. Villarreal, "International Law on Pandemic Response: A First Stocktaking in Light of the Coronavirus Crisis", *MPIL Research Paper Series, No. 2020–07* (Max Planck Institute for Comparative Public Law and International Law: 2020).
44 J. Benton Heath, "Global Emergency Power in the Age of Ebola", *Harvard International Law Journal* (2016): 1–48, at 21.

evaluate the outcome of the WHO's actions concerning serious disease outbreaks.

The wording of Article 1 of the IHR provides, however, the DG with wide discretionary authority to decide if and when to declare a health emergency.

For instance, in the case of the Ebola outbreak in the Democratic Republic of Congo, the DG declared a PHEIC although the disease had not yet significantly spread, and there was only a significant risk. During the monkeypox outbreak in 2022, the DG declared a PHEIC in the absence of advice from the EC, which did not manage to arrive at a consensus.

There are, however, specific "design" and political limits. The first one – as is widely discussed in the next chapter – is related to the lack of an intermediate alert mechanism, since a PHEIC is often declared when a specific virus is already widely diffused. In this case, the precautionary principle upon which the definition of a PHEIC is grounded is a significant restraint to a prompt response by the international community.

This design weakness is, however, linked to political factors, given that a declaration of PHEIC has wide-reaching consequences for the State where the disease outbreak originated in terms of not only restrictions to travel and trade but also bias and discrimination towards its population.

It seems even legitimate that the concerned country could raise objections and create political pressure to avoid indiscriminate restrictions on trade and travel.

The DG must therefore try to find a delicate balance between risk management through the prevention of a potential epidemic or a pandemic and the necessity to not damage without a rational reason the economic interests of the most affected country or countries.

The declaration of PHEIC allows the WHO to issue "measures that can address travel, trade, quarantine, screening, [and] treatment" and to determine best practices.[45]

These exceptional competences of the DG that grant him/her a rapid decision-making power during an epidemic or pandemic are a truly atypical feature in the landscape of the UN specialized agencies.[46]

This suggests an enormous trust in a technical organization with strong expertise in the health field.

The WHO recommendations and technical guidelines addressed to Member States enjoy a legitimacy and high level of compliance insofar as States perceive the real independency of the organization.

The decision to declare or not a PHEIC or a pandemic is not a matter related to a democratic consensus but rather is dependent on scientific

---

45 IHR Procedures concerning public health emergencies of international concern (PHEIC), World Health Organization, https://www.who.int/ihr/procedures/pheic/en/.

46 David Fidler, "From International Sanitary Conventions to Global Health Security: The New International Health Regulations", *The Chinese Journal of International Law* 4 (2005): 325–392.

considerations. Nevertheless, beyond the epidemiological exercise, the DG's authority demands strong political leadership since the decision to declare a PHEIC has significant repercussions beyond the health sphere.

Epistemic authority refers to authority based on epistemic elements, such as knowledge and science. The general idea is that scientific knowledge should address policy-making, which, in turn, would be translated into proper, generally recognized legal instruments, such as conventions, resolutions, and declarations.

As previously discussed, a PHEIC declaration and the emergency recommendations that follow have a negative impact on the affected country in terms of restrictions to trade and travel by other countries.

The technical nature of this decision-making process has, however, raised criticisms as it is in opposition with the constructivist approach according to which scientific knowledge and particularly the assessment of an epidemiological risk, is socially determined.[47]

The first element of the technocratic decision-making process is represented by the fact that the basis of the decision to declare or not a PHEIC or a pandemic is grounded in the scientific advice provided by the EC.

In the next section, we see how this played out in the cases of the H1N1 influenza, the resurgence of wild polio, Ebola 2014–2016, MERS, Zika, Ebola in 2019, COVID-19, and monkeypox.

4. Declarations of PHEIC: The WHO's practice

4.1. *The H1N1 influenza pandemic (2009–2010)*

On 25 April 2009, for the first time since the reform of the IHR, the WHO DG issued a declaration of PHEIC with reference to unusual cases of A (H1N1) influenza ("Swine Flu") registered in Mexico and the United States.

This influenza – although originating in Mexico – was initially labelled as Swine Flu. The categorization of "Mexico Flu" considering the memories of previous influenza pandemics (the Spanish Flu, the Asian Flu, and the Hong Kong Flu) would have provoked excessive damage to the local economy.

However, the reference to pigs determined a chain of consequences, including precautionary measures, that by far exceeded the WHO recommendations. The Egyptian government, for instance, decided to cull the whole population of pigs in the country as a pre-emptive measure, despite the absence of any official case of human infection. Trade bans on the import of live pigs, pork, and pork products were then imposed by countries such as China, Indonesia, the Philippines, and the Russian Federation.

The Joint FAO/WHO/OIE Statement on influenza A (H1N1) and the safety of pork (6 May 2009) affirmed that "pork and pork products, handled

---

47 Alonzo Plough, Sheldon Krimski, "The Emergence of Risk Communication Studies: Social and Political Context", *Science, Technology & Human Values* (1987): 7–9.

in accordance with good hygienic practices recommended by the WHO, the Codex Alimentarius Commission and the OIE, will not be a source of infection".[48]

On 11 June 2009, the DG then proclaimed the maximum level of alert (level 6) by calling the A (H1N1) influenza a pandemic.[49] This decision was not based upon the severity of the disease but rather upon its worldwide spread since it was diffused among 70 countries.

In this case, the WHO was accused of having overestimated the severity of the disease outbreak and of undue influence by the pharmaceutical sector.[50]

Three inquiries were then carried out to evaluate the effective independency of the WHO's actions, and a lack of evidence of inappropriate conduct was concluded.[51]

Accusations of conflict of interest towards the members of the EC (whose nominatives were not made public by the then-DG), who did not act on the basis of scientific evidence but rather on pressure of the pharmaceutical industry, were raised.[52]

The case of H1N1 is generally considered a "crying wolf" case, that is, a situation that registered an excessive reaction by the Organization.[53]

4.2. The resurgence of wild polio (2014-)

On 5 May 2014, the DG declared for the second time a PHEIC under the IHR because of the spread of poliovirus throughout several regions in Africa and the Middle East. Temporary recommendations then followed.[54] The choice to declare a PHEIC could appear to be not logical at all, since few cases had been reported, and the diffusion of polio lasted several years.[55]

In reality, the DG chose to declare a PHEIC as certain cases of a resurgence of wild polio in Afghanistan, Nigeria, and Pakistan were putting at risk the eradication of the disease at the global level; initiatives against polio had a strong impulse in 1988 with the launch of the Global Eradication

48 https://www.woah.org/en/joint-fao-who-oie-statement-on-influenza-ah1n1-and-the-safety-of-pork/.
49 https://apps.who.int/mediacentre/influenzaAH1N1_presstranscript_20090611.pdf?ua=1.
50 Shawn Smallmann, "Who Do You Trust? Doubt and Conspiracy Theories in the 2009 Influenza Pandemic", *International & Global Studies* (2015): 1–24.
51 Deborah Cohen, Philip Carter, "WHO and the Pandemic Flu Conspiracies", *British Medical Journal* (2010): 1274–1279.
52 Paul Flynn, *The Handling of the H1N1 Pandemic: More Transparency Needed* (Council of Europe Parliamentary Assembly: 2010).
53 Rory Watson, "WHO is Accused of "Crying Wolf" Over Swine Flu Pandemic", *British Medical Journal* (2010): 1094.
54 Temporary Recommendations to Reduce International Spread of Poliovirus; http://polioeradication.org/polio-today/polio-now/public-health-emergency-status/.
55 Lawrence O. Gostin, Rebecca Katz, "The International Health Regulations: The Governing Framework for Global Health Security", *The Milbank Quarterly* (2016): 264–313, at 274.

Polio Initiative (GPEI).[56] The wide spread of the virus was due to the ever-lasting military conflicts in these zones, to political and economic instability that severely limited access to health services, and probably to anti-vaccination sentiments among the population linked to political and religious concerns.[57]

The EC summoned in the case of polio advised temporary recommendations to reduce the risk that the virus could spread from endemic countries to other weaker States.[58]

It recommended, first, that all residents and long-term visitors receive a dose of the oral polio vaccine (OPV) or the inactivated poliovirus vaccine prior to international travel.

It also recommended that travelers are provided with an International Certificate of Vaccination or that they record their polio vaccination to use as proof of vaccination.

In the Statement of the Thirty-first Polio IHR Emergency Committee of 11 March 2022, the Committee unanimously agreed that the risk of international spread of poliovirus remains a PHEIC for several reasons.[59] An almost complete eradication of wild polio (WPV) was not yet reached; in Pakistan, no new cases have been registered since January 2021, but four were recorded in Afghanistan in 2021, and one was recorded in Mozambique in 2022.

The EC was particularly concerned by a case of WPV1 that was signaled in Malawi, since the members of the Committee were unaware of the means

---

56 https://polioeradication.org/.
57 As recounted by Lawrence O. Gostin (2014), in 2011, the Pakistani physician Shakil Afridi was hired by the CIA to gather DNA samples to confirm the presence of Osama Bin Laden in Pakistan, with the goal of killing him. To accomplish his mission, he put in place a fake programme of vaccines against Hepatitis B in the city of Abbottabad. This hoax fueled a wide diffidence towards the vaccine campaigns and seriously damaged the programmes of the global eradication of polio. After the murder of Bin Laden, the Taliban prohibited anti-polio vaccines in several zones of Pakistan under their control and attacked the health personnel in charge of immunizing the population. Afterwards, the Pakistani government dropped out the eradication programmes and ordered the health personnel of several humanitarian organizations to leave the country; the UN also temporarily retired their staff of polio eradication in 2012. In May 2014, the Obama administration formally declared that the United States ceased its use of vaccine campaigns for espionage purposes in August 2013, without formally apologizing for having violated the consolidated practice of a strict separation between humanitarian assistance and military and intelligence operations. The negative effects have been evident; most of the cases of polio reported in 2014 were registered in Pakistan, and cases reported in Afghanistan, Syria, and Iraq were strictly related to those that originated in Pakistan, highlighting the deep connection among terrorism, political instability, and public health. See Lawrence O. Gostin, "Global Eradication: Espionage, Disinformation and the Politics of Vaccination", *The Milbank Quarterly* (2014): 413–414.
58 WHO, Guidance for Implementation of the IHR Temporary Recommendations under the IHR (2005) to reduce the International Spread of Polio, 16 May 2014.
59 https://www.who.int/news/item/11-03-2022-statement-of-the-thirty-first-polioihr-emergency-committee.

of transmission from Pakistan to Africa in time and place. Furthermore, they added that the humanitarian crisis in Afghanistan (where the Taliban returned to power in 2021) had a negative impact on eradication efforts and that a large pool of unvaccinated "zero dose" children in remote areas constitutes a major risk of re-introduction of WPV1.[60] Finally, they underlined that the COVID-19 pandemic may have unpredictable adverse impacts on polio surveillance and immunization activities.

4.3. The case of MERS

The Middle East Respiratory Syndrome-Coronavirus (MERS-CoV) – a zoonotic disease transmitted to humans from dromedaries – was identified for the first time in Saudi Arabia in September 2011 and has since then reached 27 States.

In this case, the DG had summoned an EC, which gathered 10 times before September 2015, and the last two times occurred during a wide spread of the virus from Saudi Arabia to South Korea, which caused a wide-ranging epidemic.[61]

In line with the advice of the EC, the DG decided – despite wide criticism – to avoid proceeding with the declaration of PHEIC. In particular, the EC recommended only carefully monitoring the situation and reinforcing the prevention and control of the disease.

Most of the reported cases were related to hospital wards, and in the absence of a wide man-to-man diffusion of the disease, the EC concluded that the conditions to declare a PHEIC were not met.

In other global health emergencies, such as the cholera outbreak in Haiti, the Fukushima nuclear disaster in Japan, and the use of chemical weapons in Syria, the DG has not even summoned the EC.

4.4. The case of Ebola 2014–2016

The Ebola outbreak in Western Africa in 2014–2016 was one of the deadliest waves of Ebola Virus Disease (EVD) since the first case was officially reported in 1976. The official data report 28,646 total cases (among which 28,616 were in Guinea, Liberia, and Sierra Leone) and 11,323 total deaths (among which 11,310 occurred in Guinea, Liberia, and Sierra Leone), while in earlier outbreaks, only 2,387 cases and 1,590 deaths were registered.[62]

This was not the first outbreak of Ebola in sub-Saharan Africa (since 1976, when the first case was registered, epidemic clusters have been periodically reported in several countries of the region).

60 https://polioeradication.org/where-we-work/afghanistan/.
61 WHO Statement on the Ninth Meeting of the IHR Emergency Committee regarding MERS-CoV, 17 June 2015, WHO Statement on the Tenth Meeting of the IHR Emergency Committee regarding MERS, 3 September 2015.
62 WHO, Ebola Disease Virus, Fact Sheet 103, WHO Ebola Situation Report.

Successes, failures, and perspectives of WHO reform 71

However, beyond the numbers, the epidemic represents the worst debacle in the recent history of the WHO, whose leadership during the SARS outbreak was heavily challenged and scaled back showing contradictions and limits, since the WHO failed to provide an effective operational response.[63]

On 20 July 2014, a Liberian citizen affected by EVD had traveled on a plane to Lagos, Nigeria, spreading for the first time the virus in a new country through air transportation. This event raised serious concern among world public opinion.

The EC summoned on 6 and 7 August 2014 concluded by unanimity on 8 August 2014 that EVD had reached the threshold for being qualified as a PHEIC. Indeed, the Ebola outbreak in West Africa constituted an "extraordinary event" and a public health hazard to other States.[64]

Following the EC's advice, the same day, the DG declared the Ebola outbreak in West Africa a PHEIC.

The possible consequences of further international spread were considered particularly serious in view of the virulence of the virus, the intensive community and health facility transmission patterns, and the weak health systems in the currently affected and most at-risk countries. A coordinated international response was deemed essential to stop and reverse the international spread of Ebola.

Several initiatives addressed to the containment of the epidemic (of a both normative and operative character) were then undertaken.

With reference *in primis* to the actions of cooperation during the emergency, the WHO played important roles of direction and support of international, regional, and domestic efforts against the epidemic. Although the action of the Organization has been evaluated as overall ineffective, the central role of the WHO in the technical direction and operative support to the governments and to the other subjects in the implementation of the necessary activities to fight against the epidemic were explicitly recognized in the same Resolution 2177/2014 (although this Resolution was adopted in response to the incapacity of the WHO to adequately contain the disease).[65]

As far as the WHO's activities were addressed to the containment of the Ebola epidemic, the Organization has carried out, on the one hand, operative

---

63 Clare Wenham, "What We Have Learnt About the World Health Organization from the Ebola outbreak", *Philosophical Transactions of the Royal Society B* (2017): 1–5.

64 Statement on the 1st meeting of the IHR Emergency Committee on the 2014 Ebola outbreak in West Africa, 8 August 2014.

65 Actually, as I underline in chapter VI, after the adoption of Resolution 2177 by the Security Council (SC) and the institution of the UN Mission for Ebola Emergency Response (UNMEER) on the initiative of the UN Secretary-General, the roles of coordinator of the subjects involved in tackling the epidemic and of the delivery of humanitarian aid were undertaken by the same UNMEER. In this phase, the WHO continued to cooperate and carry out the activities requested by the SC under the direction of UNMEER until July 2015, when – because it reached its goals – UNMEER ceased its activities, and the WHO newly assumed the role of coordinator of the activity of international response to the Ebola epidemic starting from the 1st of August of the same year. For further details on UNMEER, Robert Frau, "Law as an Antidote? Assessing the Potential of International Health Law Based on the Ebola-Outbreak 2014", *Goettingen Journal of International Law* 7 (2016), 225–272, at 253.

initiatives[66] and, on the other hand, normative activities implementing the norms of the IHR.

With reference to the normative activities of the WHO, after early notification by Liberia, Sierra Leone, and Guinea of a growing number of cases (at that time, 932 deaths and 1,700 people infected), the DG officially launched the "red alarm" declaring a PHEIC.

The EC recommended to the most hit countries to, among other things, carry out accurate control and screening of the passengers directed towards international destinations, but a strong opposition emerged by LMICs against the imposition of travel and trade bans due to the lack of any scientific proof of their efficacy to prevent the further spread of the disease at the international level.

On 28 August 2014, the WHO issued a roadmap for an up-scaled response to the Ebola outbreak, which envisaged temporal strategies and goals but failed to generate a coordinated response.[67]

Due to the inadequacy of the WHO to manage the health crisis under an operational point of view, the SC took over leadership and adopted on 18 September 2014 Resolution 2177/2014, which was the first time in its history that it explicitly qualified an infectious disease as a threat to peace and security.[68]

On 19 September 2014, the UN Secretary-General officially created the UN Mission for Ebola Emergency Response (UNMEER), the first UN mission related to a health emergency, following the adoption by the GA of Resolution 69/1.[69] The establishment of UNMEER represents the breaking point of the international response to Ebola: the promised funds were effectively gathered, and new programmes started to be launched.

Eventually, on 29 March 2016, the EC concluded that "the Ebola situation in West Africa no longer constitutes a public health emergency of international

---

66 The operative initiatives undertaken by the Organization in relation to the Ebola epidemic included i) the management of the health, technical, financial, and logistic aid, ii) the control of the infection, iii) the correct transmission of data concerning the epidemic, and iv) the collaboration between the countries of origin and the neighboring States. Furthermore, for the purpose of allowing the realization of these activities, the WHO sent its experts and consultants to the countries directly hit by the contagion; it also elaborated action plans to assist the States in the revision and implementation of their own domestic plans and to coordinate international support and its implementation, it invited the States and air and naval companies to lift the restrictions on the limits to the circulation of people coming from the countries directly hit by the contagion, and it actively did something itself for the development of a vaccine, which was then produced in 2016 (https://news.un.org/en/story/2016/12/548442-final-trial-results-confirm-ebola-vaccine-provides-high-protection-un-health).

67 https://www.who.int/vietnam/news/detail/28-08-2014-who-issues-roadmap-for-scaled-up-response-to-the-ebola-outbreak.

68 SC/RES/2177 (2014). For further analysis of this resolution, see chapter VI of this book.

69 Resolution A/RES/69/1, 19 September 2014.

concern".[70] Consequently, the DG officially declared the end of the state of emergency and also terminated, in line with what is envisaged under Article 15 of the IHR, the validity of the temporary recommendations, which required the States to immediately eliminate every restriction to trade and travel in relation to the most affected countries.

The Ebola outbreak brought serious socioeconomic consequences to the most hit States that had recovered after a long period of civil wars and political instability, and their services and health infrastructure were extremely limited and not able to face a crisis of this proportion.

At the economic level, the World Bank estimated for the three countries an economic loss of approximately 1.6 billion dollars in 2015 and a steady increase of the unemployment rate,[71] despite the limited spread of the disease to LMICs (only 36 cases outside Guinea, Liberia, and Sierra Leone: 1 case in Italy, 8 cases in Mali (with 6 deaths), 20 cases in Nigeria (with 8 deaths), 1 case in Senegal, 1 case in Spain, 1 case in the United Kingdom, and 4 cases in the United States (with 1 death)).[72]

4.5. The case of Zika

Early reports of this infectious disease date back to 1947 in the Zika forest in Uganda. Zika is a viral disease, and the main vector responsible for its transmission is the *Aedes aegypti* mosquito, although sexual intercourse is also a method of transmission.[73] The first case of infection was reported in the North of Brazil in May 2015.[74]

At the same time, Brazil, French Polynesia, and several other countries hit by the Zika virus registered an anomalous and significant rise of cases with serious neurological disorders.

The National Focal Points of South America notified that cases of Zika were confirmed in the lab at the Pan American Health Organization (PAHO), which in December 2015, gave the official epidemiological alert.[75]

Zika is very rarely lethal, and it causes mild symptoms, such as fever, rash, and headaches. The mild nature of Zika was noted in contrast to other

---

70 WHO, Statement on the 9th Meeting of the IHR Emergency Committee regarding the Ebola Outbreak in West Africa, 29 March 2016.
71 World Bank, The Economic Impact of Ebola on Sub-Saharan Africa: Updated Estimates for 2015, January 2015.
72 WHO Ebola Situation Report – 30 March 2016.
73 https://www.cdc.gov/zika/index.html.
74 Rachel Lowe, Christovam Barcellos, Patrícia Brasil, Oswaldo G. Cruz, Nildimar Alves Honório, Hannah Kuper, Marilia Sá Carvalho, "The Zika Virus Epidemic in Brazil: From Discovery to Future Implications", *International Journal of Environmental Research and Public Health* (2018): 1–18.
75 WHO and PAHO, Epidemiological Alert – Neurological Syndrome, Congenital Malformations, and Zika Virus Infection: Implications for Public Health in the Americas, 1 December 2015.

Aedes-transmitted viral infections such as dengue, which can cause severe complications such as haemorrhagic shock and death, or chikungunya, which is associated with prolonged and often severe arthralgias and arthritis, or Japanese encephalitis, which is linked to high case fatality rates and frequent neurological disabilities in survivors.[76]

The major source of concern was instead related to the suspected association of the Zika virus with clusters of microcephaly and other neurological disorders. Furthermore, mother-to-child transmission of the virus is a source of certain birth defects.

In response to the epidemic, on 1 February 2016, the DG summoned an EC to evaluate whether the threshold to declare a PHEIC was reached.

The same day, on the basis of unanimous advice by the EC, the outbreak of Zika in Brazil (2016) was declared a PHEIC.[77] The decision was not based on the seriousness of the disease itself in terms of morbidity and mortality but rather on the strict connection with cases of microcephaly and Guillain-Barré Syndrome (GBS).[78] The DG indicated that "I am now declaring that the recent cluster of microcephaly cases and other neurological disorders reported in Brazil, following a similar cluster in French Polynesia in 2014, constitutes a Public Health Emergency of International Concern".[79] In this case, the application of the precautionary principle has thus far not yielded a negative outcome, although the WHO's course of action was criticized. Against this backdrop, Gostin and Katz outlined that – under a legal point of view – the wording of the PHEIC created confusion: neither microcephaly nor GBS are infectious diseases but are neurological congenital disorders that are therefore not hazards that could cross borders under Annex 2 of the IHR; instead, the Zika virus and the vector of the *Aedes aegypti* mosquito instead have the potential of international transmission.[80]

There was a lack of scientific evidence, at least in the first phase, on the linkage between the Zika virus and neurological and fetal complications; in effect, as admitted by the same EC, the declaration in this case was not adopted on the basis of what they knew at the present moment but rather on what was not yet known.[81]

---

76 Ignatius Wellington Fong, "Chikungunya Virus and Zika Virus Expansion: An Imitation of Dengue Virus", *Emerging Zoonoses* (2017): 101–130.
77 WHO statement on the first meeting of the International Health Regulations (2005) (IHR 2005) Emergency Committee on Zika virus and observed increase in neurological disorders and neonatal malformations.
78 https://www.nhs.uk/conditions/guillain-barre-syndrome/.
79 WHO, Director-General Summarizes the Outcome of the Emergency Committee Regarding Clusters of Microcephaly and Guillain-Barré Syndrome, 1 February 2016.
80 Lawrence O. Gostin, Robert Katz, The International Health Regulations: The Governing Framework for Global Health Security", *The Milbank Quarterly* (2016): 264–313, at 275.
81 David L. Heymann, Abraham Hodgson, Amadou Alpha Sall, David O. Freedman, Erin Staples, Fernando Althabe, Kalpana Baruah, Ghazala Mahmud, Nyoman Kandun, Pedro F.C. Vasconcelos, Silvia Bino, "Zika Virus and Microcephaly: Why is this Situation a PHEIC?", *The Lancet* (10 February 2016): 719–721.

The same members of the EC declared that

> our advice to declare a PHEIC was not made on the basis of what is
> currently known about Zika virus infection . . . Our advice to declare a
> PHEIC was rather made on the basis of what is not known about the
> clusters of microcephaly, Guillain-Barré Syndrome, and possibly other
> neurological defects . . . that are associated in time and place with out-
> breaks of Zika infection.[82]

However, keeping in mind the precedent of Ebola, it was clear that the WHO
decided to act in a different manner since the "wait and see approach" had previously failed. It is possible to assert that it would have been too hazardous for the
WHO to wait to obtain more scientific evidence before reacting. If the WHO
had failed to consider the initial reports of an upsurge of Zika cases and microcephaly and then afterwards, the certainty of a link between the two diseases had
been established, then this would have had a negative effect on the reputation
of the Organization, which was already undermined by the Ebola outbreak.[83]

In the months following the declaration, several scientific studies effectively
confirmed the suggested relation between the Zika virus and the aforementioned neurological complications.

As consequence of this new evidence, during its third meeting held on
14 June 2016, the EC confirmed that the Zika virus was a PHEIC,[84] and it
reiterated the invitation, already expressed during the previous meetings, to
reinforce the activities of surveillance, control of the vector of contagion, and
communication of risk.

In operative terms, the response of the WHO and the PAHO started well
before the declaration of PHEIC. In particular, 2 weeks after the declaration
on 14 February 2016, the WHO launched the Strategic Response Framework
and Joint Operations Plan, January-June 2016, then updated by the Zika Strategic Response Plan, revised for July 2016-December 2017, to provide guidance for the international response to the infection related to the Zika virus
and its complications and consequences.

The plan provides the basis for coordination and collaboration between the
WHO and its partners so that the capacity of preparation and answer to the
disease outbreak is supported as much as possible.

---

82 Fifth meeting of the Emergency Committee under the International Health Regulations
   (2005) regarding microcephaly, other neurological disorders and Zika virus.
83 Pedro Villareal, "The WHO's Institutional and Legal Role in Communicable Disease Epidemics: From Pandemic Influenza to Zika", *Völkerrechtsblog* (2016), https://voelkerrechtsblog.
   org/the-whos-institutional-and-legal-role-in-communicable-disease-epidemics-from-pan
   demic-influenza-to-zika/.
84 WHO, Statement on the Third Meeting of the International Health Regulations (2005)
   (IHR 2005) Emergency Committee on Zika Virus and Observed Increase in Neurological
   Disorders and Neonatal Malformations, 14 June 2016.

The plan focuses on the prevention and management of the medical complications caused by the Zika virus, addressing pregnant women, their families, and their community and offering appropriate counselling on health and reproductive health and the management of risk arising from mosquitos.

Travel warnings were issued by a significant number of countries, and the outbreak led to a significant reduction in tourism, including calls to cancel the Olympics in Rio de Janeiro.[85]

The WHO – through the involvement of several partners – gained appropriate financing for the Contingency Fund for Emergencies (CFE) in the period between 8 February and 30 June 2016 to support the national governments and communities to prevent and manage the complications and to mitigate the economic and social consequences of infections from the Zika virus.[86]

In May 2016, the UN Secretary-General established a Zika Multi Partner Trust Fund (MPTF) with the goal of generating, managing, and ensuring the effective use of the necessary resources to reach the goals of the Zika Strategic Response Framework.[87]

On 18 November 2016, the EC gathered for the fifth and last time, and it reached the conclusion that the Zika virus and the consequences associated with it remain a significant and lasting challenge to public health, which requires intense long-term action to properly manage the global response to the disease outbreak. It reached the conclusion that the Zika virus no longer constituted a PHEIC, but it enacted further temporary recommendations.[88]

What characterizes the Zika epidemic, unlike other health emergencies, are the long-term consequences that it has provoked and continues to provoke: "The spread of Zika virus will have long-term health consequences for families, communities and countries whose health systems will be challenged to care for children born with these complications for years to come".[89]

4.6. The Ebola outbreak in the Democratic Republic of Congo (2019–2020)

On 8 May 2018, a new Ebola outbreak was declared by local authorities in the Democratic Republic of the Congo.[90]

A first disease outbreak took place in the "province de l'Equateur", which lies in the northwest part of the country. The situation became worse as a

85 Eduardo Massad, Francisco Antonio Bezerra Coutinho, Annelies Wilder-Smith, "Is Zika a Substantial Risk for Visitors to the Rio de Janeiro Olympic Games?", *Lancet* 388 (2016): 25.
86 https://www.who.int/emergencies/funding/contingency-fund/CFE_Impact_2017.pdf.
87 https://news.un.org/en/story/2016/05/528612-un-launches-multi-partner-trust-fund-zika-virus-response.
88 https://www.who.int/news/item/18-11-2016-fifth-meeting-of-the-emergency-committee-under-the-international-health-regulations-(2005)-regarding-microcephaly-other-neurolo gical-disorders-and-zika-virus.
89 WHO, Zika Strategic Response Plan, Revised for July 2016 – December 2017, cit., 5.
90 https://www.who.int/news/item/08-05-2018-new-ebola-outbreak-declared-in-demo cratic-republic-of-the-congo.

second outbreak was registered in the North Kivu province, this time in the northeast of the country, which is located at the border between Uganda and Rwanda, highly increasing the probability of cross-border transmission.

The political instability of the country and armed conflict triggered the spread of the disease outbreak. A first meeting of the EC was summoned on 17 October 2018; in its statement, the EC expressed serious concern about ongoing armed conflicts and the rise of new cases without known links, but it advised against a declaration of PHEIC "at this time".[91]

The Declaration of PHEIC was eventually issued on 17 July 2019.[92] Unlike the Ebola crisis of 2014–2016 in Western Africa, this was not the first time that a cluster of Ebola appeared in Congo.[93]

4.7. *The COVID-19 outbreak*

On 30 January 2020, following the advice of the EC, the DG eventually declared COVID-19 a PHEIC. The reasons for the extreme delay in the adoption of the declaration (since information on the disease started to flow at the end of December 2019) are deeply analyzed in the next chapter. More than three years after the "red alarm" by the WHO and the pandemic declaration of March 2020, the WHO DG determined on 5 May 2023, acting upon advice from the EC, "that COVID-19 is now an established and ongoing health issue which no longer constitutes a public health emergency of international concern (PHEIC)".[94] The EC, in its report to the DG, highlighted decisive factors in the downgrading of COVID-19, such as the decreasing trend in COVID-19 deaths, the decline in COVID-19-related hospitalizations and intensive care unit admissions, and the high levels of population immunity to SARS-CoV-2. The EC contended that COVID-19 no longer represented a PHEIC since it no longer met the requirement of being "an unusual or unexpected event", as defined in Article 1 IHR (2005).[95]

91 WHO, Statement on the October 2018 meeting of the IHR Emergency Committee on the Ebola virus disease outbreak in the Democratic Republic of the Congo, 17 October 2018.

92 Ebola outbreak in the Democratic Republic of the Congo declared a Public Health Emergency of International Concern, https://www.who.int/news/item/17-07-2019-ebola-outbreak-in-the-democratic-republic-of-the-congo-declared-a-public-health-emergency-of-international-concern.

93 Lawrence O. Gostin, Alexandra Phelan, Alex Godwin Coutinho, Mark Eccleston-Turner, Ngozi Erondu, Oyebanji Filani, Tom Inglesby, Rebecca Katz, Allan Maleche, Jennifer B. Nuzzo, Oyewale Tomori, Matthew Kavanagh, "Ebola in the Democratic Republic of the Congo: Time to Sound a Global Alert?", *The Lancet* (2019): 617–620.

94 Statement on the fifteenth meeting of the IHR (2005) Emergency Committee on the COVID-19 pandemic, 5 May 2023.

95 Pedro A. Villareal, "We're in this for the Long Haul: The End of the Public Health Emergency of International Concern Due to COVID-19", *EJIL Talk* (8 May 2023), https://www.ejiltalk.org/were-in-this-for-the-long-haul-the-end-of-the-public-health-emergency-of-international-concern-due-to-covid-19/.

Notably, however, the DG, although declaring an end to the health emergency, issued temporary recommendations to WHO Member States to avoid a resurgence of the virus, such as an updating of respiratory pathogen pandemic preparedness plans.[96]

The downgrading of COVID-19 does not mean that it is no longer an existing problem. The WHO DG has therefore highlighted the necessity of implementing sustainable long-term public health strategies and launched the 2023–2025 COVID-19 Strategic Preparedness and Response Plan,[97] which has the goal of guiding countries in transitioning to long-term management of COVID-19. Then, he recommended to WHO Member States to "continue to lift COVID-19 international travel related health measures" and "not require any proof of vaccination against COVID-19 as a prerequisite for international travel".

4.8. The monkeypox outbreak

Monkeypox is an infectious disease of a zoonotic source – endemic in certain areas of West and Central Africa – hosted by African rodents and non-human primates. Two early cases were registered in 1958 in colonies of monkeys (Asian monkeys, *M. fascicularis*) in a research lab in Copenhagen. The exact source of this disease, however, remains unknown. The first case in a human being was recorded in1970.[98] It is a neglected disease that was mainly "relegated" to sub-Saharan Africa; it gained the attention of the international community since experiencing an unprecedented spread in Western Europe and other regions, especially among men who have sex with men (MSM).

The strategy to contain the disease outbreak in Western countries, such as Canada, the United Kingdom, and the United States, is based on the administration of smallpox vaccines – which are also efficient against monkeypox – to the individuals who have had close contact with an infected person (so-called "ring vaccination").[99]

Given that initial cases had no epidemiological links to areas historically affected by the disease, such a scenario suggests – in the words of the WHO – that "undetected transmission might have been ongoing for some time in those countries" and that "monkeypox virus activity has been neglected and not well controlled for years in countries in the WHO African Region".

On 23 June 2022, a first meeting of the EC was convened by the DG. After an updating of the epidemiological situation, the EC decided by consensus that the threshold to declare a PHEIC was not yet reached. However,

---

96 Strengthening pandemic preparedness planning for respiratory pathogens: policy brief, 27 April 2022.

97 file:///C:/Users/cnr%20ethics/Downloads/WHO-WHE-SPP-2023.1-eng%20(2).pdf.

98 Scott Parker, R. Mark Buller, "A Review of Experimental and Natural Infections of Animals with Monkeypox Virus Between 1958 and 2012", *Future Virology* (2013): 129–157.

99 Max Koslov, "Can Vaccines Contain the Global Monkeypox Outbreaks?", *Nature* (2022): 444–445.

it recognized the emergency nature of the disease outbreak, requiring joint collaboration and mutual assistance under Article 44 IHR.

A second meeting was held on 23 July 2022 when the epidemiological situation registered 14,533 cases (5 deaths in total) from 72 countries within all six WHO Regions, hitting mainly the gay and bisexual community, as it was clear that the means of transmission was mainly through sexual intercourse.

The EC noted an increased number of countries reporting early cases of monkeypox outside Africa and a surge in the number of cases in several West and Central African countries.

The EC was, however, highly divided on whether the conditions to declare a PHEIC were met or not, and it failed to provide advice to the DG.

The minority (six members) who were in favor of declaring a PHEIC argued that the way of transmission of the virus and the fact that it mainly hit the homosexual community reminded them of the early stages of the HIV/AIDS epidemic in the 1980s. In light of the memories of HIV/AIDS, they therefore considered the official alarm by the WHO as a window of opportunity for containing the global spread of the virus and avoiding it becoming endemic outside sub-Saharan Africa. They therefore considered that the conditions to declare a PHEIC were met (it is an extraordinary event, of significant risk of international spread, and requires a coordinated response).

Nine members instead took the view that the overall epidemiological situation had not substantially changed since the first meeting of the EC, that the greatest burden of the outbreak has been concentrated in 12 countries in Europe and the Americas with no evidence of an exponential increase in the number of cases, and that the most affected communities of homosexual, bisexual, and other MSM could be protected with targeted measures. They also claimed that a possible side effect of a PHEIC declaration would be growing stigma and discrimination against the LBGTQ community. Against this backdrop, it is highly questionable that a scientific body, which should justify its assessment exclusively on an epidemiological basis, relied on political considerations related to the protection of human rights that are of course relevant but are not within its field of competence.

The DG, however, decided to autonomously declare monkeypox as a PHEIC on 23 July 2022, also without the specific support of the EC. His unilateral decision was taken on the basis of the precautionary approach;[100] that is, the lack of scientific certainty on the disease mortality and its exact levels of diffusions were not obstacles to the adoption of a PHEIC declaration.[101] Notably, in

---

100 Donato Greco, "What Does the Monkeypox Outbreak Tell Us About Global Health Governance? Critical Remarks on the New WHO Declaration of Public Health Emergency of International Concern", *EJIL Talk* (10 August 2022), https://www.ejiltalk.org/what-does-the-monkeypox-outbreak-tell-us-about-global-health-governance-critical-remarks-on-the-new-who-declaration-of-public-health-emergency-of-international-concern/.

101 On 11 May 2023, following the advice of the EC (Fifth Meeting of the International Health Regulations (2005) (IHR) Emergency Committee on the Multi-Country Outbreak of mpox), the WHO DG declared that the monkeypox outbreak was no longer a global health emergency.

the previous case of COVID-19, the DG was highly criticized for his extreme delay in acting. It is within the discretionary powers of the DG to declare a PHEIC against or in absence of the advice of the EC, although in the previous cases, the declaration followed the EC's deliberation. In the present case, due to the deadlock within the EC, which was unable to decide in favor or against a declaration of PHEIC, the DG exercised his discretionary powers as envisaged by the IHR.

Monkeypox – which has been circulating for decades in sub-Saharan Africa – showed once again that the perceived level of threat of a disease outbreak largely depends on how greatly it affects Western countries. It seems clear that the international community shows a concrete interest in these neglected diseases and makes investments in vaccines and treatments only when the populations of high-income countries are in danger of being hit by infectious diseases imported from the poorest countries of the world.

Another issue is related to the pattern of a delayed PHEIC declaration, which raises once again the lack of an intermediate alert system. It is true that it is not possible to declare every infectious disease a PHEIC, but the extreme delay in declaring a PHEIC allowed monkeypox to spread globally.

After this analysis of the declarations of PHEIC enacted by the DG, which are the main instrument to launch the red alarm in case of severe disease outbreak, in the next Paragraph, I underline the main institutional limits of the WHO in the management of epidemics and pandemics. Against this backdrop, notably, the declaration of PHEIC and the temporary recommendations that follow are non-binding acts belonging to the domain of soft law.

5. The WHO's lack of enforcement powers

Despite the wide discretional powers of the DG, namely, the authority to declare a PHEIC and to issue temporary recommendations, the normative dimension of the WHO's reaction to disease outbreaks is not accompanied by a sufficient operational direction or action in the field.

This also raises the issue of the lack of enforcement powers in case of breach or non-compliance with its acts – which is, *inter alia*, a common feature of UN specialized agencies.

The lack of compliance with the IHR is a "chronic" pathology of the WHO.[102] However, it was "an explicit choice of design",[103] since the WHO's

---

https://www.who.int/news/item/11-05-2023-fifth-meeting-of-the-international-health-regulations-(2005)-(ihr)-emergency-committee-on-the-multi-country-outbreak-of-monkey-pox-(mpox).

102   The term "pathologic" derives from the work of Michael N. Barnett and Marta Finnemore, "The Politics, Power and Pathologies of International Organizations", *International Organization* (1999): 699–732.

103   Pedro A. Villareal, "COVID-19 Symposium: "Can They Really Do That?" States' Obligations Under the International Health Regulations in Light of COVID-19 (Part II)", *Opinio Juris* (2020), http://opiniojuris.org/2020/03/31/covid-19-symposium-can-they-really-do-that-states-obligations-under-the-international-health-regulations-in-light-of-covid-19-part-ii/.

authority should have mainly relied on the level of trust of the Member States in its technical expertise and on the general idea that countries would voluntarily comply with its rules, whereas during the COVID-19 pandemic, it shirked this particular role of leader.

One of the core issues debated after the "hot phase" of the COVID-19 pandemic in 2020–2022 before the post-pandemic scenario – which was already widely discussed after the Ebola outbreak in 2014–2016 – involves the impossibility to adopt sanctions or countermeasures in case of a lack of compliance with the IHR's obligations or temporary recommendations. It is reasonable to maintain that the lack of compliance with the duties envisaged by the IHR has become a "pathology" of the global health architecture and undermines the WHO's credibility.[104] As witnessed by the practice of States, there is a reluctance to provide adequate information and to promptly notify the WHO of disease outbreaks and a tendency to adopt more restrictive measures on travel and trade than those recommended by the WHO.[105]

The IHR are not "minimal safeguards" but rather specific limits within which States operate; the WHO is therefore in charge of recommending specific measures to avoid the spread of certain infectious diseases.

States are provided by the IHR with a wide margin of latitude regarding how to respond to a declaration of PHEIC and to the recommendations issued by the DG. Article 1 IHR states that the recommendations constitute "non-binding advice". Equally, Article 3, Paragraph 4 IHR reaffirms that States Parties "have the sovereign right to legislate and to implement legislation in pursuance of their health policies". However, this sovereign right cannot be exercised without limits. According to the wording of Article 3, Paragraph 4, States must exercise it "in accordance with the Charter of the United Nations and the principles of international law" and "[i]n doing so they should uphold the purpose of these [IHR]".

It is up to the WHO to decide if and whether to adopt measures that severely limit trade and travel.

Article 43 provides the possibility for Member States to enact additional measures for the containment of a given disease outbreak through a formula that is very similar to the "equivalent protection" envisaged by international human rights law.[106]

However, States policies to contain a disease outbreak cannot arbitrarily limit the movement of people and goods. Article 43 of the IHR further reflects the necessity to balance State sovereignty and the need to not interfere in an indiscriminate manner with travel and trade.

---

104 *Supra*, footnote 102 at 699.
105 Raphael Lencucha, Shashika Bandara, "Trust, Risk, and the Challenge of Information Sharing During a Health Emergency", *Globalization and Health* (2021): 17–21.
106 Elisa Ravasi, *Cover Human Rights Protection by the ECtHR and the ECJ. Human Rights Protection by the ECtHR and the ECJ. A Comparative Analysis in Light of the Equivalency Doctrine* (Brill/Nijhoff: 2017).

For example, on the one hand, Article 43 makes clear that the IHR "shall not preclude States Parties from implementing health measures . . . in response to . . . a PHEIC, which . . . achieve the same or greater level of health protection than WHO recommendations".

On the other hand, it provides that "[s]uch measures shall not be more restrictive of international traffic and not more invasive or intrusive to persons than reasonably available alternatives that would achieve the appropriate level of health protection".

The problem of the enforcement of the IHR and the temporary recommendations was first raised as a consequence of the 2009 bird flu epidemic (the H1N1 virus): the report that followed highlighted that "the most important structural shortcoming of the IHR is the lack of enforceable sanctions".[107] The assessment of States' response to the Ebola outbreak called for the possibility to investigate "options for *sanctions* for inappropriate and unjustified actions under the Regulations".[108] Therefore, the Panel had explicitly invited the Revision Committee to explore the prospect of calling to the attention of the Security Council issues related to a systematic violation of the IHR.

In its response of 2016, the EC has nonetheless affirmed that the IHR are based on the concepts of collaboration and cooperation rather than repression.[109] It has, however, maintained that in the case of global health risk arising from the incapacity or lack of will of a State to tackle a serious disease outbreak, the DG could bring the issue to the attention of the Secretary General who might involve the Security Council (p. 82).

Alternatively, the EC has recalled the solution procedure for disputes envisaged under Article 56 of the IHR to which States can refer in case of disagreement on the adequacy of the public health measures adopted in response to a health risk or health emergency of international concern. Article 56, Paragraph 1 IHR asserts that

> in an event of dispute between two or more States concerning the interpretation or application of these Regulations, the States Parties concerned shall seek in the first instance to settle the dispute through negotiation, peaceful means, good offices, mediation, conciliation.

In the case of failure of these means, the dispute might be referred to the DG (Art. 56, Para. 2) or as a last resort, to arbitration (Art. 56, Para. 3).

Article 56, Paragraph 5 affirms that "in the event of a dispute between WHO and one or more States Parties concerning the interpretation or

---

107 WHO, Implementation of the International Health Regulations (2005). Report of the Review Committee on the Functioning of the International Health Regulations (2005) in relation to Pandemic (H1N1) 2009, doc. A64/10 of 5 May 2011, p. 13, para. 24.

108 The WHO Report of the Ebola Interim Assessment Panel (2015), Para. 19.

109 Report of the Review Committee on the Role of the International Health Regulations (2005) in the Ebola Outbreak and Response, p. 81.

application of these Regulations, the matter shall be submitted to the Health Assembly".

Article 75 of the WHO Constitution is also relevant since it affirms that

any question or dispute concerning the interpretation or application of this Constitution which is not settled by negotiation or by the Health Assembly shall be referred to the International Court of Justice in conformity with the Statute of the Court.

In *Armed Activities on the Territory of the Congo*, the International Court of Justice (ICJ) recognized the validity of Article 75 of the WHO Constitution. The ICJ stated as follows: "The Court observes that the DRC has been a party to the WHO Constitution since 24 February 1961 and Rwanda since 7 November 1962 and that both are thus members of that Organization. The Court further notes that Article 75 of the WHO Constitution provides for the Court's jurisdiction, under the conditions laid down therein, over 'any question or dispute concerning the interpretation or application' of that instrument" (Para. 99).

China has never issued a declaration that recognizes the compulsory jurisdiction of the Court. Therefore, China cannot be brought before the ICJ for a violation of its obligations under the WHO Constitution, namely, Article 63, which provides as follows: "Each Member shall communicate promptly to the Organization important laws, regulations, official reports and statistics pertaining to health which have been published in the State concerned".[110] China allegedly withheld early reports of human-to-human infections of COVID-19, leading the WHO to believe that human-to-human transmission was not possible.

6. How to improve the global health architecture

6.1. The call for reform

The multiple failures of the global health architecture in the management of the COVID-19 pandemic raised the issue of reform of the IHR. The slow response in containing the disease outbreak in its early stages, the lack of transparency and information sharing by the Chinese government, the absence of enforcement mechanisms by the WHO, the phenomenon of vaccine nationalism, and the unfair distribution of COVID-19 vaccines and treatments, demonstrated the inadequacy and flaws of the IHR.

The world would have been safe from COVID-19 if the WHO had the possibility to declare a PHEIC in December 2019 or the power to impose a precautionary lockdown in Wuhan to wait for a strict evaluation of the severity

---

110 Linlin Sun, "China's Perception of State Sovereignty in International Dispute Settlement", in Niels M. Blokker, Daniëlla Dam-de Jong, Vid Prislan (eds.), *Furthering the Frontiers of International Law: Sovereignty, Human Rights, Sustainable Development Liber Amicorum Nico Schrijver* (Brill: 2021), 414–439.

of the disease outbreak or its extinction. Unfortunately, the legal framework provided by the IHR is "toothless",[111] since the WHO is too dependent upon the goodwill of its Member States.

The response to the collapse of the early warning mechanism envisaged by the IHR facing the COVID-19 pandemic can take two forms: to push for the implementation of the IHR or to reform the whole architecture.

The IHR are based on the idealistic assumption according to which a series of factors, such as the epistemic authority of the DG and the compliance pull of his/her declarations and recommendations, do not require compulsory mechanisms or sanctions since States will fulfill the WHO's technical guidance in good faith.[112]

According to the functionalist view of international institutions, States should engage themselves in ensuring the implementation of the recommendations issued by the bodies of IGOs.[113] States are interdependent in several sectors and therefore need to cooperate among one another permanently and not sporadically.[114]

Against this backdrop, the systemic weakness that caused the failure of the structure set up by the IHR during the COVID-19 pandemic was not related to its content (although there is an absence of adequate attention to the issue of the prevention of disease outbreaks) but to the lack of implementation ("implementation gap").

The shortfall of adequate core health capacities not only in the "Third World" but also in high-income countries (such as the United States and EU countries) – whose development is one of the key obligations under the IHR – was one of the main causes of the disease's rapid spread.[115]

It is therefore necessary to improve the compliance system by establishing monitoring mechanisms with compulsory external oversight, which should be more stringent than the weak mechanisms that the WHO currently has in place.

Current monitoring devices rely on self-assessment by Member States (rather than external oversight) and are voluntary in nature. The WHO focuses on the States' will to act in good faith and to genuinely cooperate. Therefore, the WHO does not have the power to carry out an independent investigation on a territory of a Member State without its explicit consent.

111 Oona Hathaway, Alasdair Philips-Robins, "COVID-19 and International Law Series: Reforming the World Health Organization", *Just Security* (11 December 2020).
112 On the concept of "compliance pull", see Thomas M. Franck, *The Power of Legitimacy Among Nations* (Oxford University Press: 1990).
113 Pedro Villarreal, "The 2019–2020 Novel Coronavirus Outbreak and the Importance of Good Faith for International Law", *Völkerrechtsblog* (28 January 2020), https://voelker rechtsblog.org/the-2019-2020-novel-coronavirus-outbreak-and-the-importance-of-good-faith-for-international-law/.
114 In this sense, see Jan Klabbers, "The Emergence of Functionalism and International Institutional Law: Colonial Inspiration", *European Journal of International Law* (2014): 645–675.
115 Myungsei Sohn, Dasol Ro, Dae Hyup Koh, Sookhyun Lee, So Yoon Kim, "The Problems of International Health Regulations of Responding to COVID-19 and Improvement Measures to Improve Its Effectiveness", *Journal of Global Health and Science* (2021): 1–7.

A further weakness within the reporting obligations under the IHR is the absence of a specific organ that is in charge of overseeing implementation. We can find examples of such centralized oversight of reporting in other treaties. For example, under the Convention on the Trade on Endangered Species (CITES), the well-known wildlife treaty that deals with the trade of endangered species, a standing committee oversees that periodic reports have been submitted on time and issues a report that includes detailed recommendations regarding ways to improve implementation.[116]

Similarly, under the Single Convention on Narcotic Drugs (1961), after States submit their reports, the International Narcotics Control Board (INCB) may require additional studies and information.[117] The INCB then publishes its findings regarding the implementation status and recommendations for improvements. The Board has also the right to publish a report without the explicit consent of the concerned State.

In contrast, such powers are currently not expressly granted to the WHO Secretariat under the IHR.

The delay in the adoption of a Declaration of PHEIC with reference to COVID-19 suggests that the binary alarm system does not work properly. The key issue is therefore how to improve the alarm system envisaged by the IHR, although after any epidemic, a call for reform is systematically raised.

An article by David Durrheim et al. suggests a three-tiered model, based on three levels of alarm (each level should be based on specific epidemiological criteria and actions plans).[118]

Level 1 is raised when an outbreak in a given country is a disease with potential cross-border implications. Public health efforts on a local level must be undertaken to prevent its global transmission. Level 2 implies a spread on a regional level (multiple countries have experiences of a given disease outbreak with a limited spread), and level 3 involves ongoing transmission and serious clusters in multiple countries.

6.2. *The new pandemic treaty*

The Independent Panel for Pandemic Preparedness & Response in its two reports[119] clearly stated that the COVID-19 pandemic heightened awareness

---

116 https://cites.org/eng/disc/sc.php.
117 https://www.incb.org/.
118 David N. Durrheim, Lawrence O. Gostin, Keymanthri Moodley, "When Does a Major Outbreak Become a Public Health Emergency of International Concern", *Lancet* 20 (2020): 887.
119 The first report "COVID-19: Make it the Last Pandemic" was presented to the WHA in May 2021 (https://theindependentpanel.org/wp-content/uploads/2021/05/COVID-19-Make-it-the-Last-Pandemic_final.pdf). It was then followed by a second report: "Losing time: End this pandemic and secure the future Progress six months after the report of the Independent Panel for Pandemic Preparedness and Response" (November 2021) (https://theindependentpanel.org/wp-content/uploads/2021/11/COVID-19-Losing-Time_Final.pdf).

of the need to reform the global health architecture. It called for a radical reform of the WHO through the adoption of a binding treaty complementary to the IHR. It drew a parallel with the Chernobyl nuclear power plant accident in 1986, which triggered a reform of international nuclear law. Specifically two treaties, one on Early Notification of a Nuclear Accident, the other on Assistance in the Case of a Nuclear Accident or Radiological Emergency, were then adopted under the aegis of the International Atomic Energy Agency (IAEA).

The call for a new pandemic treaty gained momentum in Spring 2021,[120] and it has been championed by the WHO's DG, the EU,[121] the United States, and several countries from Africa, Asia, and South America. Concerns have instead been expressed by Brazil, China, and the Russian Federation, which pushed back on the adoption of a binding act, given that it implies a strong erosion of health sovereignty.

On 31 May 2021, the WHA decided to start a debate on the adoption of a new international treaty on pandemics. Negotiations began at an extraordinary meeting of the WHA at the end of 2021.[122]

The call for the adoption of an international treaty on pandemics, however, dates back to the G7 leaders statement of 19 February 2021.[123] In their statement of 25 February 2021 on COVID-19 and health, the members of the European Council strongly reiterated their support for the idea of a new pandemic treaty, affirming that "we are committed to advancing global health security, including by strengthening the World Health Organization and working towards an international treaty on pandemics within its framework" (Para. 10).[124]

---

120 "This new treaty should be based on a reshaping of principles and a spirit of collective solidarity according to principles of equity, inclusivity and transparency, having as a practical goal the increase of the capacities of both prevention and response to pandemic emergencies". WHO, *Director-General's Closing Remarks at the World Health Assembly* (31 May 2021), https://www.who.int/director-general/speeches/detail/director-general-s-closing-remarks-at-the-world-health-assembly-31-may-2021).

121 See Council of the European Union, *EU Supports Start of WHO Process for Establishment of Pandemic Treaty: Council Decision* (20 May 2021), https://www.consilium.europa.eu/en/press/press-releases/2021/05/20/eu-supports-start-of-who-process-for-establishment-of-pandemic-treaty-council-decision/.

122 Ronald Labonté, Mary Wiktorowicz, Corinne Packer, Arne Ruckert, Kumanan Wilson, Sam Halabi, "A Pandemic Treaty, Revised International Health Regulations, or Both?", *Globalization and Health* (2021): 1–4; Jorge Viñuales, Suerie Moon, Ginevra Le Moli, Gian Luca Burci, "A Global Pandemic Treaty Should Aim for Deep Prevention", *The Lancet* 397 (2021): 1791–1792; Lawrence O. Gostin, Benjamin Mason Meier, Barbara Stocking, "Developing an Innovative Pandemic Treaty to Advance Global Health Security", *The Journal of Law, Medicine & Ethics* (2021): 503–508.

123 https://www.consilium.europa.eu/en/press/press-releases/2021/02/19/g7-february-leaders-statement/.

124 https://www.consilium.europa.eu/en/press/press-releases/2021/02/25/statement-of-the-members-of-the-european-council-on-covid-19-and-health-25-february-2021/.

A special session of the WHA (29 November – 1 December 2021) was convened upon request of the DG.[125] The spread of the Omicron variant – the latest SARS-CoV-2 coronavirus variant of concern after Delta – was an accelerator in the negotiation process.

By consensus, the WHA decided on 1 December 2021[126] to provide a specific mandate to an Intergovernmental Negotiating Body (IBN) to start the drafting of a "convention, agreement or other international instrument on pandemic prevention, preparedness and response". According to Article 19 of the WHO, a solution had already been employed with the adoption of the WHO Framework Convention on Tobacco Control and its additional protocol. The first meeting of the IBN was held on 24 February 2022.[127] On 3 March 2022, the European Council provided its authorization – through a decision – to start negotiations on the new pandemic treaty.[128]

> This new treaty should be based on a reshaping of principles and a spirit
> of collective solidarity according to principles of equity, inclusivity and

125 Special session of the World Health Assembly to developing a WHO convention, agreement or other international instrument on pandemic preparedness and response, WHA74(16), Agenda item 17.3, 31 May 2021.
126 The World Together: Establishment of an intergovernmental negotiating body to strengthen pandemic prevention, preparedness and response, SSA2(5), 1 December 2021. The Second Session of the WHA decided "to establish, in accordance with Rule 41 of its Rules of Procedure, an intergovernmental negotiating body open to all Member States and Associate Members (the "INB") to draft and negotiate a WHO convention, agreement or other international instrument on pandemic prevention, preparedness and response, with a view to adoption under Article 19, or under other provisions of the WHO Constitution as may be deemed appropriate by the INB" (Art. 1). The decision of 1 December 2021 was preceded by a first draft of 28 November 2021 ("The World Together: Establishment of an intergovernmental negotiating body to strengthen pandemic prevention, preparedness and response", Draft Decision, SSA2/CONF./1Rev.1).
127 In its introductory speech, the WHO's DG stated, "While we are operating under an ambitious timeline, we need to take the lessons learned from the COVID-19 pandemic and use them to build back better. The aim should be a world better prepared to prevent pandemic threats and respond to them when they do occur, in at least five ways: first, by building national, regional and global capacities for preparing and responding to pandemics and other global health emergencies, based on a whole-of-government and whole-of-society approach; second, by establishing global access and benefit sharing for all pathogens, and determining a global policy for the equitable production and distribution of countermeasures; third, by establishing robust systems and tools for pandemic preparedness and response; fourth, by building a long-term plan for sustainable financing, so that support for global health threat management and response systems is shared by all; and fifth, by empowering WHO to fulfil its mandate as the directing and coordinating authority on international health work, including for pandemic preparedness and response"; https://www.who.int/director-general/speeches/detail/who-director-general-s-opening-remarks-at-first-meeting-of-the-intergovernmental-negotiating-body-to-draft-and-negotiate-a-who-convention-agreement-or-other-international-instrument-on-pandemic-prevention-preparedness-and-response-24-february-2022.
128 https://www.consilium.europa.eu/en/press/press-releases/2022/03/03/council-gives-green-light-to-start-negotiations-on-international-pandemic-treaty/.

transparency, having as a practical goal the increase of the capacities of both prevention and response to pandemic emergencies.[129]

The WHA therefore decided to adopt a treaty and not to amend the IHR; the new instrument is, however, intended as complementary to rather than substitutive of the IHR.[130]

6.3. Advantages

The adoption of a binding act in the form of a treaty was eventually supported by the head of the WHO, the European Union, and a number of countries, including Germany, France, and South Africa. The United States did not find the idea alluring, but it formally endorsed the suggestion of a new treaty.

The instrument is rooted in three key axes that involve the enhancement of the "sharing of information", the "sharing of pathogens", and the "sharing of technologies".

The treaty has the purpose of addressing – *inter alia* – three key issues. One is the equitable access to vaccines, treatments, and diagnostic (which is the main goal of the COVID-19 Act Accelerator). Against this backdrop, there is already a model represented by the Pandemic Influenza Preparedness (PIP) Framework, whose main goals are to improve the sharing of influenza viruses and increase the fair and equitable access to vaccines for developing countries.[131] The PIP Framework applies to H511 and other influenza viruses that have a pandemic potential and not to seasonal influenza.

The second issue encompasses the origin of COVID-19, the deep roots of the resurgence of zoonotic diseases in recent decades, and the prevention of future disease outbreaks. One of the main drawbacks of the IHR is the lack of a reflection on the interrelation of zoonotic spillover between wildlife trade and farmed animals; this governance gap is related to the absence of a legal framework based on the precautionary principle aimed at the prevention of the spillover of zoonotic diseases. It is worth recalling, however, that the IHR already envisage a reporting procedure on possible animal-born illnesses with a potential global spread and give particular attention to outbreak surveillance,

129 WHO, *Director-General's Closing Remarks at the World Health Assembly* (31 May 2021), https://www.who.int/director-general/speeches/detail/director-general-s-closing-remarks-at-the-world-health-assembly-31-may-2021.

130 Silvia Behrendt, Amrei Müller, "Why the Rush? A Call for Critical Reflection on the Legal and Human Rights Implications of a Potential New International Treaty on Pandemics", *EJIL Talk – Blog of the European Journal of International Law* (29 July 2021), https://www.ejiltalk.org/why-the-rush-a-call-for-critical-reflection-on-the-legal-and-human-rights-implications-of-a-potential-new-international-treaty-on-pandemics/. For further consideration, also with respect to the pandemic treaty and the global health agenda, see Lawrence O Gostin, Benjamin Mason Meier, Barbara Stocking, Developing an Innovative Pandemic Treaty to Advance Global Health Security, *Journal of Law, Medicine & Ethics* (2021): 503–508.

131 https://www.who.int/initiatives/pandemic-influenza-preparedness-framework.

containment, and response. Consequently, inter-regime linkages, as the adequate interplay among wildlife law, animal law, and health law, are of paramount importance to avoid future pandemics and to achieve an appropriate balance between environmental exploitation and sustainable development.[132] The notion of "deep prevention" promoted by eminent scholars[133] should be the pillar of the new pandemic treaty or of any type of regulation in the field of global health of the drivers of disease outbreaks – in particular those that trigger a zoonotic infection.

Against this backdrop, Paragraph 8 of the Preamble of the WHO Pandemic Accord clearly reaffirms[134]

> the importance of multisectoral collaboration at national, regional, and international levels to safeguard human health, detect and prevent health threats at the animal and human interface, zoonotic spill-over and mutations, and to sustainably balance and optimize the health of people, animals and ecosystems, in a One Health approach.

This would require a greater collaboration among the WHO, the World Organization for Animal Health (OIE), the Food and Agriculture Organization (FAO), the United Nations Environment Programme (UNEP), the Convention on International Trade in Endangered Species of Wild Fauna and Flora (CITES), and the Convention on Biodiversity to address zoonotic spillover.

Against this backdrop, the precautionary principle should be applied in the presence of any outbreak causing respiratory infections, implying that human-to-human transmission occurs unless specific evidence indicates otherwise. This is exactly what happened with the monkeypox outbreak, where the DG declared a PHEIC despite a scientific dispute on whether the virus had reached the threshold to be classified as a health emergency of global concern.

This would imply a change of paradigm, since the IHR do not focus on disease prevention but rather on disease management. The IHR are based on the assumption that the prevention of disease outbreaks is not a matter that falls within their field of competence and that outbreaks are natural events.

Other necessary reforms are related to the possibility of carrying out investigations *in loco* also without the consent of the State concerned. This is of paramount importance since it would allow the WHO to promptly evaluate whether there is a potential disease cluster and to launch a timely alarm.

---

132 "Inter-regime linkages" is a term coined by Young to address the "interplay among distinguishable, institutional arrangements". See Oran R. Young, "Institutional Linkages in International Society: Polar Perspectives", *Global Governance* 2 (1996): 1.

133 Jorge Viñuales, Suerie Moon, Ginevra Le Moli and Gian Luca Burci, "A Global Pandemic Treaty Should Aim for Deep Prevention", *The Lancet* 397 (2021): 1791–1792.

134 Negotiating Text of the WHO convention, agreement or other international instrument on pandemic prevention, preparedness and response – WHO Pandemic Agreement. Advanced unedited version – 16 October 2023, Doc A/INB/7/x.

The issue of appropriate funding is then crucial ("financing gap"); in this regard, two initiatives have been launched by the WHO Working Group on Sustainable Financing and the G20 High Level Independent Panel on Financing the Global Commons for Pandemic Preparedness and Response.

The main constraints to the adoption of a pandemic treaty concern the lasting contrast between industrialized and developing countries (including China).

Western countries want to reinforce early warning mechanisms, since they have a concrete interest in avoiding the spread of zoonotic diseases that originate in developing countries (in particular, South-East Asia).

Developed countries are in favor of open reporting and collection of data, appropriate information and statistics on cases, and genomic sequences from pathogens.

The key issue is whether China – which bears veto power within the Security Council – is really committed to a strengthened mechanism based on transparency and appropriate sanctions in case of non-compliance. The cases of SARS and COVID-19 and the under-reporting of cases and rates of infections and mortality have shown the tendency of the Chinese government to not act in good faith and to "cheat" concerning the real diffusion of disease outbreaks in its territory.

Developing countries, on their own, are willing to have equitable access to vaccines and treatments. The open questions are the scale of ambition, the political will of the WHO Member States, and how much funding they are willing to invest.

To work properly and to really prevent a new pandemic, a deep reform of the global health architecture implies a shift of authority from the national to the international level.[135]

Such a utopian scenario suggests wide emergency powers of an IGO alone and enforcement capacities. The WHO would therefore have direct access to epidemiological data on disease outbreaks and the possibility of deciding to impose local lockdowns or to directly distribute vaccines or treatments.

6.4. Drawbacks and other options

Although it might seem as the most obvious outcome to the COVID-19 outbreak to reinforce the global health system in the post-pandemic scenario, a new pandemic treaty is not an easy task.

---

135 In this sense, see Christian Kreuder-Sonnen, "The WHO After Corona: Discretionary Powers for the Next Pandemic?", *Verfassungsblog on Matters Constitutional* (2020), https://verfassungsblog.de/the-who-after-corona-discretionary-powers-for-the-next-pandemic/.

First, the negotiation of a treaty requires time and a real commitment by the States to limit their sovereignty and to invest funding in a specific sector. Even after its adoption, its real impact is strictly dependent upon the level of signatures and ratifications. There is the positive example of the Paris Agreement that was ratified by 193 States (with the only exceptions represented by Eritrea, Libya, Iran, and Yemen). However, recent decades have shown a crisis of multilateralism, strong difficulty in the adoption of new treaties, multilateral stress, and a decline in international cooperation.[136]

At the current juncture, multilateralism and the international legal order are facing a deep crisis due to the rise of populism, the surge of nationalism, and "authoritarian international law".[137] The war in Ukraine (2022), in full disregard of international law, showed once again the fallacy of the global security architecture and the decline of liberal democracies. After the push of international law-making in the 1990s with the adoption of the global environmental treaties, international cooperation has consistently declined.[138]

The rise of emerging economies (BRICS) and the axis between China (promoting a "New World Order") and the Russian Federation (promoting a "Post-Western World Order") are factors that hinder a resurgence of multilateralism; in 2016, these States promoted a Joint Declaration on the Promotion of International Law, which countered the criticism levelled against these countries as a consequence of Russia's annexation of the Crimean Peninsula and China's territorial ambitions in the South China and East China Seas, with particular reference to Taiwan. Against this backdrop, they advocated an international law of coexistence rather than of cooperation. As outlined by Wolfrum, the "law of cooperation" contrasts with the "law of coexistence".[139] Russia's aggression against Ukraine was, however, a clear sign of a deep rift between the Western world, which was united in condemning Moscow and adopting sanctions against Russia, and the Putin regime.

As observed by some scholars, COVID-19 raised the so-called "patriotism" paradox: recalling the interests of their own citizens first, populist governments tend to reinforce their national sovereignty through active disengagement from global treaty regimes and international organizations.[140]

Despite uncertainties behind the new binding treaty, notably, there is already a global framework on disease response, as represented by the IHR. It

136 Jutta Brunnée, Challenging International Law: What is New? *Opinio Juris* (2018) http://opiniojuris.org/2018/11/13/challenging-international-law-whats-new/.

137 Tom Ginsburg, "Authoritarian International Law", *American Journal of International Law* (2020): 221–260.

138 Rafael Domingo, "The Crisis of International Law", *Vanderbilt Journal of Transnational Law* (2009): 1543–1593.

139 Rüdiger Wolfrum, *Cooperation, International Law of Max Planck Encyclopedia of Public International Law* (Oxford University Press: 2010).

140 Peter G. Danchin, Jeremy Farrall, Shruti Rana, Imogen Saunders, "The Pandemic Paradox in International Law", *American Journal of International Law* (2020): 598–607.

already mandates States to report on disease outbreaks and to share information in an appropriate manner.

A more practical solution could be to reinforce the existing tool through the adoption of an additional protocol to the IHR. This should clearly state the duty to pass on, as quickly as possible, information about a hazardous risk discovered in one country that could have potential cross-border implications. A similar obligation is envisaged in the 1986 Convention on Early Notification of a Nuclear Accident enacted after the Chernobyl disaster.[141] This requires notification

> in the event of any accident involving facilities or activities of a State Party or of persons or legal entities under its jurisdiction or control, from which a release of radioactive material occurs or is likely to occur and which has resulted or may result in an international transboundary release that could be of radiological safety significance for another State.
>
> (Art. 1)

The Convention requires States Parties to report the accident's time, location, nature, and other data essential for assessing the situation (Art. 2). Notification must be made to affected States directly or through the IAEA and to the IAEA itself. In the field of environmental law, Principle 19 of the Rio Declaration on Environment and Development similarly states a duty of cooperation through "preventive notification about activities that might have a transfrontier impact".[142]

Against this backdrop, the United States made a proposal to amend the IHR at the 75h WHA,[143] which envisaged, *inter alia*, the establishment of a Universal Health Periodic Review mechanism to reinforce the surveillance system.[144]

The United States government in particular advanced an amendment to Article 12 IHR to considerably widen the margin of appreciation of the DG in deciding whether to exercise or not its executive powers. According to this

141 https://www.iaea.org/topics/nuclear-safety-conventions/convention-early-notification-nuclear-accident.
142 Principle 19 of the Rio Declaration states that "States shall provide prior and timely notification and relevant information to potentially affected States on activities that may have a significant adverse transboundary environmental effect and shall consult with those States at an early stage and in good faith".
143 https://apps.who.int/gb/ebwha/pdf_files/WHA75/A75_18-en.pdf; see also Silvia Behrendt, Amrei Müller, "The Far-Reaching US Proposals to Amend the International Health Regulations at the Upcoming 75th World Health Assembly: A Call for Attention", *EJIL Talk* (18 May 2022), https://www.ejiltalk.org/the-far-reaching-us-proposals-to-amend-the-international-health-regulations-at-the-upcoming-75th-world-health-assembly-a-call-for-attention/.
144 Pedro A. Villareal, "The Law of the WHO and COVID-19 Pandemic Reformism", *German Yearbook of International Law* (2022): 11–40.

amendment, the DG would no longer need to engage in previous consultations with the State concerned and find an agreement but could decide autonomously to issue a new category of alarm, namely, an intermediate public health
alert that requires "heightened international awareness" (Art. 12, Para. 6).
In addition, the United States proposal would empower the six WHO
Regional Directors to declare a "public health emergency of regional concern"
(PHERC) (Art. 12, Para. 7).

7. Conclusions

This chapter mainly focused on the practice of the WHO through a reconstruction of the declarations of PHEIC enacted since the reform of the IHR
in 2005. Against this backdrop, I highlighted the novelty of the declaration of
PHEIC with reference to monkeypox, where the DG decided to act even in
the absence of advice by the EC.

This conspicuous practice of the WHO in managing disease outbreaks has,
however, revealed shortcomings and weaknesses of the whole global health
architecture, under the profile of prevention of disease outbreaks and lack of
equity in the distribution of vaccines and treatments.

A large part of the chapter was devoted to the new pandemic treaty, which
is aimed at addressing the main shortcomings of the IHR. The treaty –
modelled as a framework convention – similar to the UN Framework Convention on Climate Change – establishes key principles that should govern disease
outbreaks.

The objectives are clearly stated in Article 2 of the WHO Pandemic Agreement (advanced version of 16 October 2023)

> The objective of the WHO Pandemic Agreement, guided by equity, the
> right to health and the principles and approaches set out therein, is to
> prevent, prepare for and respond to pandemics, with the aims to com-
> prehensively and effectively address systemic gaps and challenges that
> exist in these areas, at national, regional and international levels.

The accord incorporates principles and wording of international environmental law. Article 3, Paragraph 2 establishes for instance that

> States have, in accordance with the Charter of the United Nations and
> the principles of international law, the sovereign right to legislate and to
> implement legislation in pursuance of their health policies.

It resembles the wording of Principle 2 of the Rio Declaration on Environment and Development (1992), which affirms that

> States have, in accordance with the Charter of the United Nations and
> the principles of international law, the sovereign right to exploit their
> own resources pursuant to their own environmental and developmental

policies, and the responsibility to ensure that activities *within their juris-diction or control do not cause damage to the environment of other States or of areas beyond the limits of national jurisdiction.*

Article 3, Paragraph 1, also recalls the principle of equity (which is contained in Principle 5 of the Rio Declaration). It recognizes that "Equity includes the unhindered, fair, equitable and timely access to safe, effective, quality and affordable pandemic-related products and services, information, pandemic-related technologies and social protection", therefore, the previous pandemic of COVID-19 – "no one is safe until everyone is safe". This implies that developed countries – which hold more resources related to pandemics (including vaccines, treatments, and manufacturing capacity) – have a differentiated responsibility with reference to global pandemic prevention, preparedness, response, and recovery. Therefore, they should provide specific support to developing countries, especially those that "(i) are particularly vulnerable to adverse effects of pandemics; (ii) do not have adequate capacities to respond to pandemics; and (iii) potentially bear a disproportionately high burden".

Article 4 is devoted to "prevention" and establishes in Paragraph 4, *a*, (ii), that each State Party shall, in accordance with its capabilities: "conduct risk assessment of pathogens (presenting significant risks) and vector-borne diseases to prevent spill-over in human and animal population and cause serious diseases".

The One Health concept is eventually codified in Article 5, which clearly states in Paragraph 3 that

> the Parties commit to identify and address the drivers of pandemics and the emergence and reemergence of disease at the human-animal-environment interface by identification and integration of interventions into relevant pandemic prevention, preparedness plans, and, where appropriate, according to national legislation and capacity, through strengthening synergies with other relevant instruments.

Despite these novelties, some scholars have questioned the real added value of a framework convention – with no enforcement mechanism – establishing general principles in a sector that requires a prompt reaction by the States facing disease outbreaks.[145] There is also a risk of overlapping with the parallel amendment process of the IHR.[146]

---

145 Clare Wenham, Mark Eccleston-Turner, Maike Voss, "The Futility of the Pandemic Treaty: Caught Between Globalism and Statism", *International Affairs* (2022): 1–16.
146 Report of the Review Committee regarding amendments to the International Health Regulations (2005). Report by the Director-General, A/WGIHR/2/5, 6 February 2023.

The main challenges related to a new pandemic are related first to the pre-vention phase, which should be reinforced not only through the One Health approach but through more incisive measures such as a global ban of wet markets. Another core issue is the prompt reaction by the WHO – which implies transparency in communicating and sharing data (and genetic sequencing) about new disease outbreaks by the affected State – and the possibility of adopting an intermediate alarm. This should be a sort of "yellow light" launched well before a given disease outbreak has started to spread globally.

One of the most contentious issues, however, remains the equitable access to treatments and vaccines for developing countries during a pandemic. This implies a real commitment and goodwill by wealthier countries to promote sustainable and equitably distributed production and transfers of technology and know-how.

III The COVID-19 pandemic and the global and domestic responses

What went wrong?

1. Introduction

The COVID-19 pandemic has raised unprecedented challenges for the global health framework, and its long-term consequences are not yet predictable. The legal and institutional regime aimed at preventing and controlling the spread of infectious diseases, grounded on the IHR and the WHO Director-General's discretionary powers, has also been severely tested.

The pandemic questioned the role and the impartiality of the WHO in managing health emergencies and at the same time highlighted the design weaknesses of the IHR as an adequate tool to coordinate a valid international response to disease outbreaks.

The WHO Director-General has been broadly criticised for his apparent ineffectiveness amidst the COVID-19 pandemic.[1] A trigger of factors (both institutional and political) led to the uncontrolled spread of the disease with three levels of responsibility (the WHO, China, and the Member States).

This chapter claims that the question is not if the WHO failed – this is a matter of fact as shown by the decisions to negotiate a new pandemic treaty and to amend the IHR[2] – but why and how.

More specifically, the chapter evaluates what went wrong and what can be done to strengthen global health governance by evaluating whether the new pandemic treaty is the most adequate solution to avert new disease outbreaks.

There is a mismatch between what one would expect an intergovernmental organization (IGO) such as the WHO should do to prevent the global spread of a disease outbreak and what it can do in the realms of "realpolitik". The globalist approach to infectious diseases, recalling principles that include equity, solidarity, and considering health as a common concern of humankind,

---

1 Pia Acconci, "The Responses of International Organizations to the Health Emergency due To the Covid-19. A First Impression", *Rivista di diritto internazionale* (2020): 415–452.
2 Pedro A. Villarreal, "Lawmaking at the WHO: Amendments to the International Health Regulations and a New Pandemic Treaty After COVID-19", *SWP Comment* (2023): 1–7.

DOI: 10.4324/9781003100645-3

collapsed before the nationalist reaction of States to the pandemic.[3] Through a "nation-state first" approach, governments across the world focused mainly on their populations and their immediate short-term needs (such as the necessity to obtain vaccine doses in advance).

In the reconstruction of the early phases of the disease outbreak, when investigating what mistakes occurred, one must first evaluate whether it was a specific problem of the WHO or if another stakeholder could have successfully responded to the pandemic. The key issue is that in general terms, IGOs have limited normative powers, except for the Security Council (which can adopt enforcement measures under Chapter VII of the UN Charter) and *sui generis* organizations such as the European Union.[4]

The WHO can only recommend measures, cannot adopt countermeasures or sanctions in case of a lack of compliance, and is highly dependent on the good faith of its Member States to provide information and data.[5] Furthermore, it does not have the power to carry out investigations on the grounds and verification of data without the State's consent, in contrast to the model of other IGOs such as the International Atomic Energy Agency (IAEA).[6]

Hence, the WHO is heavily dependent on information and data provided by its Member States. Without their cooperation and their goodwill in the collection and reporting of data, the mechanism of disease warning is simply nonfunctional. It can be assumed, then, that sharing such information is a common interest. However, this is not so straightforward: during the SARS outbreak in 2003, the WHO Member States had already shown a certain reluctance to provide correct and transparent information because they feared retaliation.

With reference to the early stages of the COVID-19 outbreak, it was never clarified whether the human-to-human transmission was limited to hospitals and clinics (between health staff and patients), occurred in close quarters or in families, or spread more easily among wider communities.

It is argued that the Chinese government has specific responsibility for having concealed information on the real extent of the disease outbreak and on its origin, which is exactly what happened with the SARS's precedent.

3 Eric Otenyo, *Covid-19 and Vaccine Nationalism Managing the Politics of Global Pandemics* (Elsevier: 2023), 3.
4 Jan Klabbers, "Sui Generis? The European Union as an International Organization", in Dennis Patterson, Anna Södersten (eds.), *A Companion to European Union Law and International Law* (Wiley: 2016), 3.
5 As explained in the previous chapter, the WHO has "treaty making power" in Articles 21–22 of its Constitution, but in practice, it has seldom relied on this power.
6 Through its safeguard activities, the IAEA can verify that States comply with their commitment to use nuclear programs for peaceful purposes. The inspection capabilities of the IAEA have been incorporated into an Additional Protocol (Additional protocol for verification of nuclear safeguards, 1997). The IAEA can carry out *ad hoc* inspections, routine inspections, special inspections, and safeguard visits. For further details, see IAEA Report, The International Legal Framework for Nuclear Security, (IAEA International Law Series No. 4: 2011).

China's lack of transparency and good faith in providing information on the real spread of the virus to the WHO, considering that reliable sources argue that the virus was circulating in the country since November 2019,[7] were key factors in the global spread of the disease. China's decision to leave asymptomatic patients off their coronavirus infection tally sparked debate. Good faith – which is a general principle of international law – is pivotal in the IHR's architecture, since the whole mechanism is based on reliable data provided by States Parties.

To further worsen the situation, the former United States President Trump had openly criticized the WHO for its pandemic response – as it was considered too deferential towards China – and outlined the US's grievances about the WHO' s handling of the disease outbreak and its presumed ties to China.[8]

The WHO Member States, for their part, were unwilling to cooperate – acting prevalently in a random order. There are lingering issues that still need answers. Furthermore, the national health systems were often unequipped to face a pandemic of this magnitude and scrambled to craft an appropriate response. The pandemic could have been contained in its early phases if the WHO Member States would have invested in their core public health capacities and rigorously complied with their duties under the IHR.

2. The levels of responsibility for the spread of COVID-19

a) The WHO

The WHO failed in its early response for several reasons related to its structure and functioning (one of these is the lack of a real early warning mechanism before a disease outbreak reaches the red line of a global health emergency).

The WHO was in fact unable to fulfil its own institutional mandate, that is, to prevent the spread of diseases, because of a flawed decision-making process.

The WHO was accused of failure for not seeking information on the novel coronavirus from other sources given China's reluctance to be fully transparent, for not challenging the fragmented data initially provided by the Chinese government, and more generally, for being too deferential towards Xi Jinping's regime.[9]

Then, the WHO responded with extreme delay on the basis of a wait-and-see approach, and it provided imprudent advice to its Member States by inviting them to not put in place travel bans even after China had already adopted stringent measures to tackle the disease.[10]

---

7 David L. Heymann, Nahoko Shindo, "COVID-19: What is Next for Public Health?", *The Lancet* (22 February 2020): 542 ss.

8 "Coronavirus: What are President Trump's Charges against the WHO?", https://www.bbc.com/news/world-us-canada-52294623.

9 Gian Luca Burci, "The Legal Response to Pandemics. The Strengths and Weaknesses of the International Health Regulations", *Journal of International Humanitarian Legal Studies* (2020): 1–14.

10 WHO, Updated WHO Advice for International Traffic in Relation to the Outbreak of the Novel Coronavirus 2019-nCoV (24 January 2020). See also, Donato Greco, "Diritto internazionale e salute pubblica: l'Organizzazione mondiale della sanità alla prova della pandemia di Covid-19", *La Comunità Internazionale* (2020): 203–239.

Furthermore, the WHO Director-General was blamed by former United States President Trump of having too many ties with the Chinese government.[11] That is, the Director-General's impartiality and independence, which is the basis of the WHO's International Public Authority (IPA) as a technocratic institution, were heavily questioned.

The policy of appeasement towards China is evident in all the official communications by the WHO in January and February 2020, where China was represented as a virtuous example of how to defeat a disease outbreak. However, this policy was probably a specific choice in order to avoid any diplomatic tension with the Chinese government and to obtain its collaboration.

b) China

The Chinese government carries the main burden for the spread of the disease. There is much debate around the good faith of the Chinese local and central authorities at the beginning of the disease outbreak. It is highly probable that – from November 2019 until mid-January 2020 – they concealed and suppressed information about the initial spillover and evidence of human-to-human transmission.[12]

On 16 December 2019, a patient – who was employed at the Huanan Seafood Wholesale Market – was admitted to a local hospital (Wuhan Central), presenting with fever and infection in his lungs. Despite treatment with both antibiotics and anti-flu medication, his condition never improved, and he eventually died.[13]

On 27 December 2019, a specific notification was made by a local lab test to hospitals in Wuhan that the disease was caused by a new strain of coronavirus with 87% of genetic similarity to SARS-CoV, the virus that causes SARS.[14] This chain of events followed a similar path as the 2002–2003 SARS outbreak but with very serious consequences.

China's responsibility has a double dimension (ethical and legal). The first is related to a lack of respect of its moral duty of prevention in the transmission of zoonotic diseases, which is strictly related to weak regulations concerning wet markets, food safety, and animal welfare. Article 2 of the IHR clearly states that "the purpose and scope of these Regulations are to *prevent*, protect against, control and provide a public health response to the international

---

11 Javier C. Hernández, "Trump Slammed the W.H.O. Over Coronavirus. He's Not Alone", *The New York Times* (8 April 2020), https://www.nytimes.com/2020/04/08/world/asia/trump-who-coronavirus-china.html.

12 Matthew Henderson et al., *Coronavirus Compensation? Assessing China's Potential Culpability and Avenues of Legal Response* (Henry Jackson Society: 2020), 14, www.henryjacksonsociety.org/wp content/uploads/2020/04/Coronavirus-Compensation.pdf.

13 Jeremy Page et al. "How It All Started: China's Early Coronavirus Missteps", *The Wall Street Journal* (6 March 2020), www.wsj.com/articles/how-it-all-started-chinas-early-coronavirus-missteps-11583508932.

14 Gerry Shih et al. "Early Missteps and State Secrecy in China Probably Allowed the Coronavirus to Spread Farther and Faster", *The Washington Post* (1 February 2020), www.washingtonpost.com/world/2020/02/01/early-missteps-state-secrecy-china-likely-allowed-coronavirus-spread-farther-faster/.

spread of disease", although the IHR do not envisage a concrete obligation to prevent pathogen spillover or to adopt specific measures in this regard. To date, international law does not envisage a specific obligation to prevent zoonotic spillover through the adoption of specific measures at a domestic level, which should avoid the contagion. The IHR are based on the assumption that epidemics and pandemics are natural events and cannot therefore be prevented but only contained and extinguished.

Against this backdrop, it can be argued that China violated first its due diligence obligations related to the "no-harm principle"; this is one of the core principles of international environmental law according to which States must ensure that activities carried out within their jurisdiction do not cause significant cross-boundary damage.[15]

This principle does not require States to actually prevent or halt the harm from taking place but rather to attempt to do so or to minimise the risk thereof to the best of their abilities.[16]

Wet markets, from which the spillover likely originated – although not explicitly banned by Chinese wildlife law – are a phenomenon largely tolerated and unregulated by the Chinese government. This raises the issue of the "implementation gap" of environmental law[17] since the CITES already prohibits the trade of endangered species, such as the pangolin, which is highly probable of being the potential intermediate host of SARS-Cov-2.[18]

For example, China's market for shark fins – which is traditionally considered a symbol of wealth and a delicacy – reflects its lack of attention to the problems related to environmental degradation and the respect for animal welfare.[19]

15 Philippe Sands, Jacqueline Peel, *Principles of International Environmental Law*, 3rd ed. (Cambridge University Press: 2012), 239. As stated by the International Court of Justice (ICJ) in its advisory opinion on "the Legality of the Threat of Nuclear Weapons", "The existence of the general obligation of States to ensure that activities within their jurisdiction and control respect the environment of other States or of areas beyond national control is now part of the corpus of international law relating to the environment" (Para. 29).
16 Draft articles on Prevention of Transboundary Harm from Hazardous Activities, with commentaries 2001.
17 On the gap in environmental law between legislative expectations and actual outcomes, see Daniel A. Farber, "The Implementation Gap in Environmental Law", *Journal of Korean Law* (2016): 3–32.
18 Ping Liu, Jing-Zhe Jiang, Xiu-Feng Wan, Yan Hua, Linmiao Li, Jiabin Zhou, Xiaohu Wang, Fanghui Hou, Jing Chen, Jiejian Zou, Jinping Chen, "Correction: Are Pangolins the Intermediate Host of the 2019 Novel Coronavirus (SARS-CoV-2)?", *PLOS Pathogens* 17 (6) (2021).
19 Despite significant legal developments, many pelagic sharks' existence is being threatened and facing significant decline, as depicted by the well-known documentary of Louie Psihoyos "Racing Extinction". Sharks, skates, and rays belong to the class *Chondrichthyes* and along with other species of fish are experiencing a rapid decline because of overfishing and unsustainable fishing across the world, including illegal, unregulated and unreported fishing (IUU), deliberate or accidental catches, bottom trawling, and destruction of reproductive habitats. The growing demand for shark fins in Asian countries for fin soup, a delicacy of Chinese cuisine, has boosted the market for shark finning, which risks the extinction of several sharks. Jessica Spiegel, "Even Jaws Deserves to Keep His Fins: Outlawing Shark Finning Throughout Global Waters", *Boston College International and Comparative Law Review* (2001): 409–438; Ilja

Second, the Chinese government was not sufficiently transparent in communicating reliable data to the WHO on the real flow of the new coronavirus that spread (when exactly?) in the wet market in Wuhan before it had exported many cases to the rest of the world. This concerns the underreporting of the early stages of the disease outbreak and the attempts to downplay the pandemic threat.

In fact, the WHO's response to COVID-19 was greatly hampered by China's limited communication and official denials until January 2020 and according to some scholars, by a clear political strategy to avoid calling out the country.[20]

Furthermore, the pandemic has shown how the political interests of single States have an impact on the action of international institutions and strongly hinder their response. That is, the geopolitical weight of a given country and the risk of contagion in high-income countries are key factors in deciding whether or not to declare a PHEIC. The case of monkeypox – a neglected disease in sub-Saharan Africa for decades – clearly showed that the international community reacts to a disease outbreak only when it potentially affects the health of the citizens of high-income countries.

As is well-known, China chose a "zero COVID-19" policy with severe restrictions to civil and political rights, including the right to free movement, lockdowns, contact tracing, forced hospitalization and isolation, and border closures.[21]

One of the key features of Xi Jinping's policy was the refusal to import foreign mRNA vaccines and at the same time promoting China's own, less effective Sinovac and Sinopharm vaccines.

This policy implied poor vaccination rates, a low immunization rate among the population, and an upsurge of COVID-19 between the end of 2022 and the beginning of 2023, as the Chinese government decided to lift the zero COVID-19 policy.

c) *The member states*

The WHO Member States, for their part, were woefully unprepared to deal with the coronavirus crisis and scrambled to craft an appropriate response.

The pandemic could have been contained in its early phases if the WHO Member States would have invested in their core public health capacities and rigorously complied with their obligations under the IHR.

The IHR establish a set of core capacities, which – if achieved – should ensure both a country's adequate preparedness when facing health emergencies and the capacity to provide a response.

Richard Pavone, "Race to Extinction: Shark Conservation Under International and European Law and its Limits", *Ocean and Coastal Law Journal* (2018): 45–86.

20 Hinnerk Feldwisch-Drentrup, "How WHO Became China's Coronavirus Accomplice", *Foreign Policy* (2 April 2020), https://foreignpolicy.com/2020/04/02/china-coronavirus-who-health-soft-power/.

21 Smriti Mallapaty, "China is Relaxing Its Zero-COVID Policy – Here's What Scientists Think. Researchers Say the Rule Changes Will Lead to a Rise in Infections that Could Overwhelm Hospitals", *Nature* 612 (9 December 2022), 383–384.

These core capacities include, for instance, the obligation of designating or establishing a National Focal Point (NFP) and authorities with the required attributes and capacities to fulfil their responsibilities under the IHR (Art. 4) and the duty of developing, strengthening, and maintaining the capacity required to detect, assess, notify, and report events.[22] This means developing, strengthening, and maintaining the capacity to promptly and effectively respond to public health risks and public health emergencies of international concern.

As stated in a report by the Director-General,

> The COVID-19 pandemic has revealed significant gaps in pandemic preparedness in countries across the world, including in the areas of: surveillance, health systems, equipment and training, essential public health functions and the role of national IHR focal points, emergency legislation, risk communication and coordination.
>
> (Para. 16)[23]

The lack of effectiveness in curbing the spread of the disease was mainly related to i) the extreme delay by the WHO in sounding the alarm, ii) the absence of political cooperation, and iii) a shortfall in the implementation of the IHR.

Government unpreparedness in facing a serious disease outbreak was already revealed during the Ebola outbreak in Western Africa in 2014, when it became evident that the real problem was not associated with a structural weakness of the content of the IHR but rather by the absence of adequate implementation.[24]

The time-worn methods of tackling an infectious disease – wide testing on patients, contact tracing, isolation, and quarantine – allowed the most prepared countries, such as New Zealand, South Korea, Vietnam, and Thailand – to successfully contain the disease outbreak in its early stages.

More generally, most of the WHO Member States acted on a unilateral basis by mainly closing frontiers and imposing lockdowns on their own population to thus produce a fragmented, "zero-sum" response globally. Most of them had no previous experience in dealing with an infectious disease outbreak of this scale.

---

22 Article 5, annex 1A (Core capacity requirements for surveillance and response) and annex 1B (Core capacity requirements for designated airports, ports and ground crossings).

23 Strengthening preparedness for health emergencies: implementation of the International Health Regulations (2005) Interim progress report of the Review Committee on the Functioning of the International Health Regulations (2005) during the COVID-19 Response, EB148/19, 12 January 2021.

24 Ayelet Berman, "Closing the Compliance Gap: From Soft to Hard Monitoring Mechanism Under the International Health Regulations", *Washington University Global Studies Law Review* (2021): 593–610.

The COVID-19 pandemic has clearly demonstrated – even if considering the virtuous examples of disease management, such as New Zealand and Singapore – that a country cannot effectively protect its own citizens only on the basis of simple unilateral measures at the frontiers and the isolation and screening of travellers at the entry points.[25]

However, States do not have to wait for a green light from the WHO to activate their pandemic plans, as plainly shown by the case of Vietnam, which is a demonstration of success in keeping the disease's transmission rates under control.[26] Well before the declaration of PHEIC by the WHO – as soon as the first cases of "severe pneumonia with unknown aetiology" in Wuhan were detected – the Vietnamese government carried out a first risk assessment and enacted precautionary measures.

Three key elements of the Vietnamese policy (swift decision-making, effective public health messaging, and aggressive contact tracing) allowed the country to have one of the lowest rates of transmission of the virus worldwide.[27]

Some argue that the United States government, like its Chinese counterpart, was aware since January 2020 of the existence of the virus and its potential lethality through intelligence briefings.[28]

The United States declared a public health emergency on 31 January 2020, concomitantly blocking travel from China.[29] Inexplicably, the United States Administration downplayed the coronavirus pandemic that caused a higher death rate per capita in the United States compared to other countries.[30] The United Kingdom and the United States were nevertheless entirely reactive rather than proactive in the measures that they took.

The United Kingdom's slow reaction in the early phases of the COVID-19 pandemic was related to the British tradition of the liberal State and *laissez-faire*. Britain was much slower to introduce major regulations and chose, in an early stage, a policy based on "herd immunity".

25 Michael G. Baker, Nick Wilson, Andrew Anglemyer, "Successful Elimination of Covid-19 Transmission in New Zealand", *The New England Journal of Medicine* (2020): e56 (1)–e56 (3).

26 https://news.un.org/en/story/2020/08/1070852.

27 Emma Willoughby, "An Ideal Public Health Model? Vietnam's State-Led, Preventative, Low-Cost Response to COVID-19", *Brookings* (2021), https://www.brookings.edu/blog/order-from-chaos/2021/06/29/an-ideal-public-health-model-vietnams-state-led-preventative-low-cost-response-to-covid-19/.

28 Shane Harris, Greg Miller, Josh Dawsey, Ellen Nakashima, "U.S. Intelligence Reports from January and February Warned about a Likely Pandemic", *The Washington Post* (20 March 2020), https://www.washingtonpost.com/national-security/us-intelligence-reports-from-january-and-february-warned-about-a-likely-pandemic/2020/03/20/299d8cda-6ad5-11ea-b5f1-a5a804158597_story.html.

29 https://trumpwhitehouse.archives.gov/presidential-actions/proclamation-declaring-national-emergency-concerning-novel-coronavirus-disease-covid-19-outbreak/. The state of emergency with reference to COVID-19 ended on 11 May 2023 (https://www.hhs.gov/coronavirus/covid-19-public-health-emergency/index.html).

30 https://www.worldometers.info/coronavirus/country/us/.

With the beginning of the vaccination program, the government then moved from the "contain" stage to the "delay" stage, which involved the lifting of most of the regulations and limitations in order to allow the population to reinforce their immune system by catching the disease.

The scarce political cooperation and solidarity are, in fact, one of the main features of the global response to the novel coronavirus, which is in sharp contrast to the precedent of the Ebola outbreak in Western Africa in 2014.[31]

This was mentioned by the UN in its resolution of 2 April 2020 ("Global Solidarity to Fight the Coronavirus Disease 2019 – COVID-19").[32] It recognized that COVID-19 "requires a global response based on unity, solidarity and renewed multilateral cooperation" (Preamble) and asked for "intensified international cooperation to contain, mitigate and defeat the pandemic, including by exchanging information, scientific knowledge and best practices and by applying the relevant guidelines recommended by the World Health Organization" (Para. 5).

Likewise, on 19 May 2020, a similar resolution was adopted by the 73rd World Health Assembly, which called for "a spirit of collaboration at all levels" (Para. 1).

Uncoordinated travel and trade restrictions and more generally, the perception that States can effectively protect themselves from a pandemic in isolation or competing with other countries for limited resources are counterproductive. Actions undertaken on such premises have seriously destabilized the existing multilateral regime and its institutions with long-term adverse consequences.

In a presumed era of global health governance,[33] the paradox is that there are more similarities than differences with the past in the behaviour of States.

3. The "Mission Creep" of the WHO

The missed cooperation during the Covid-19 pandemic, associated with the loss of credibility of the WHO, called into question the whole global health governance architecture in times of strong unilateralism and weak international law.

After the announcement of the United States withdrawal from the WHO by the former United States presidency (then reversed by the decision of President Biden to re-join it), some commentators argued that the WHO should be disbanded considering its limited value and questioned its practical utility.[34]

---

31 Michael McKenzie, "Between Politics and Policy: International Cooperation Beyond COVID-19", *E-International Relations* (2020): 1–10.
32 Resolution A/RES/74/270, 2 April 2020.
33 On the architecture of global governance, see Sophie Harman, *Global Health Governance* (Routledge: 2012).
34 Editorial Board, "How WHO Lost Its Way", *Wall Street Journal* (15 May 2020), https://www.wsj.com/articles/how-who-lost-its-way-11589583282.

The Wall Street Journal's Editorial Board (WSJ) criticized the whole framework upon which the WHO was founded and called for a radical change. In detail, it maintained the need to replace the WHO with a new, more efficient, and less bureaucratic entity equivalent to Interpol. This type of "light organization" or "pseudo-organization", shaped on the model of the Organization for Security and Co-Operation in Europe (OSCE) or G8/G20, would be able to coordinate in an efficient manner a response to future disease outbreaks, the WSJ argues.

The "original sin" of the WHO – according to the WSJ – related to the fact that it had embraced a holistic approach to the right to health – as proclaimed in the WHO Constitution (which entrusted the WHO with the too ambitious goal of promoting "the attainment by all peoples of the highest possible level of health").[35] The WHO implied a progressive widening of its agenda by also discussing the fight against NCDs and improving domestic health systems (that is, the WHO, in addition to the traditional vertical approach to infectious diseases, focused also on a horizontal approach aimed at promoting the right to health and reinforcing domestic health systems).

This "mission creep" – which has its roots in the Alma Ata Declaration – would divert resources and attention from the primary goal represented by the fight against infectious diseases.

This view – which was considered a "historical misdiagnosis" of the flaws of the WHO[36] – is in effect, rather simplistic since it does not take into account the necessity to reinforce the "core health capacities" during epidemics or pandemics. Specifically, an adequate response to transboundary and emerging diseases cannot be limited to measures such as a rapid alarm, the closing of borders, and trade and travel restrictions but requires stronger domestic health systems and the strengthening of the human right to health. The focus on the prevention of the root causes of infectious diseases in developing countries marked, *inter alia*, a shift from the "classic regime" of disease control to a more structured mechanism of global health governance.

Of course, the reply to the proposal of complete extinction of the WHO is negative, given that multilateralism is the only instrument to avoid the nationalist drift of international law and a return to the Westphalian order. The invasion of Ukraine by the Russian Federation in 2022 and the deadlock within the Security Council showed once again that international law is facing a period of regression due to the rise of authoritarian regimes.[37]

Against this backdrop, the COVID-19 pandemic did not witness the re-emergence of the concept of borders "but perhaps a doubling down on its

---

35 Roger Bate, Katen Porter, "Curing the International Health System", *AEI* (1 September 2009), https://www.aei.org/articles/curing-the-international-health-system/.

36 Jose E. Alvarez, "The WHO in the Age of the Coronavirus", *The American Journal of International Law* (2020): 578–587, at 580.

37 Larry Diamons, "Democratic Regression in Comparative Perspective: Scope, Methods, and Causes", *Democratization* (2020): 22–42.

role as [a] semi-porous membrane designed to both exclude, detain, and privilege".[38]

The WHO's highly criticized response to COVID-19 intersected with the geopolitical dispute between China and the United States in 2020 on the leadership of the world order.

The main contention of the former United States Administration was that the WHO – and particularly, the Director-General – had become too deferential towards China and, therefore, an outright advocate of the Chinese's attempt to cover up the disease outbreak in its early stages.[39]

The WHO's relationship with China has certainly assumed a new form compared to the past since previous Director-Generals did not hesitate to criticize China openly. Margaret Chan, former WHO Director-General from 2007 to 2017 for two terms, although she was of Hong Kong nationality and was elected due to Chinese support, showed great independence from her homeland. She successfully managed Avian Influenza and the SARS outbreaks without showing any deference towards the Chinese government.[40]

4. In search of the WHO's responsibilities

4.1. Background

As already mentioned, something went wrong with the early warning mechanism. Furthermore, the correctness of the first technical guidance provided to the Member States to mitigate and contain the virus was arguably wrong. The technical guidance on travel and trade at the dawn of the disease outbreak did not recommend travel restrictions or any specific health measures for travellers.[41]

It has been argued that the first cases were earlier than initially thought[42] – tracing back to November 2019 – and that the Chinese authorities tried to play down the severity of the novel coronavirus.[43]

---

38 Frédéric Mégret, "COVID-19 Symposium: Returning "Home"–Nationalist International Law in the Time of the Coronavirus", *Opinio Juris* (2020), http://opiniojuris.org/2020/03/30/covid-19-symposium-returning-home-nationalist-international-law-in-the-time-of-the-coronavirus/.

39 "Coronavirus: What are President Trump's Charges Against the WHO?", https://www.bbc.com/news/world-us-canada-52294623.

40 Kimmy Chung, "Beijing Never Pressured Me in Office, Former WHO Chief Margaret Chan Says", *South China Morning Post* (7 July 2021), https://www.scmp.com/news/hong-kong/politics/article/2101770/beijing-never-pressured-me-office-former-who-chief-margaret. Miriam Shuchman, "Improving Global Health – Margaret Chan at the WHO", *The New England Journal of Medicine* (2007): 654–656.

41 "WHO Advice for International Travel and Trade in Relation to the Outbreak of Pneumonia Caused by a New Coronavirus in China" (10 January 2020), https://www.who.int/news-room/articles-detail/who-advice-for-international-travel-and-trade-in-relation-to-the-out break-of-pneumonia-caused-by-a-new-coronavirus-in-china/.

42 https://www.scmp.com/news/china/society/article/3074991/coronavirus-chinas-first-confirmed-covid-19-case-traced-back.

43 Edward Wong, Julian E. Barnes, Zolan Kanno-Youngs, "Local Officials in China Hid Coronavirus Dangers From Beijing, U.S. Agencies Find", *The New York Times* (19 August 2020), https://www.nytimes.com/2020/08/19/world/asia/china-coronavirus-beijing-trump.html.

On 31 December 2019, the WHO China Country Office was informed of cases of pneumonia of unknown aetiology (unknown cause) detected in Wuhan City, Hubei Province of China.[44]

It is worth recalling that under Articles 6 and 7 of the IHR, States Parties have a duty of timely notification and information sharing. States are required, under Article 6, Paragraph 2, particularly after notifying the WHO of an event that may constitute a public health emergency of international concern (PHEIC), to "communicate to WHO timely, accurate and sufficiently detailed public health information available to it . . ., where possible including . . . [the] number of cases and deaths".

Article 63 of the WHO Constitution then affirms that "Each Member shall communicate promptly to the Organization . . . . *official reports* and *statistics* pertaining to health which have been published in the State concerned".

Early reports of infections in health care personnel and accurate data concerning the number of asymptomatic individuals, which are a crucial element in ascertaining the real flow of COVID-19, were allegedly concealed. The new coronavirus had supposedly been identified and the SARS-CoV-2 genome had been mapped by Chinese scientists weeks before the government officially declared the health emergency.[45]

The WHO can use informal sources (newspapers, rumours, NGOs, and the internet) to obtain any information on a disease cluster (hint of a health event), and then, it can request the affected State to provide detailed information (Art. 9). If a State does not comply with its obligations, then the WHO can publish this information on the web ("naming and shaming") against the will of the country. In the case of China, this mechanism did not work, probably due to the high level of media control by the Chinese Communist Party.

The Taiwan Centre for Disease Control (Taiwan CDC) had acquired knowledge through online sources of at least seven cases of atypical pneumonia in Wuhan.[46]

Taiwan – which has only the status of an observer within the WHO[47] – informed the Organization on 31 December 2019 regarding the IHR focal

44 https://www.who.int/docs/default-source/coronaviruse/situation-reports/20200121-sitrep-1-2019-ncov.pdf.

45 Chris Buckley, David D. Kirkpatrick, Amy Qin, Javier C. Hernández, "25 Days That Changed the World: How Covid-19 Slipped China's Grasp", *The New York Times* (30 December 2020), https://www.nytimes.com/2020/12/30/world/asia/china-coronavirus.html.

46 "The Facts Regarding Taiwan's Email to Alert WHO to Possible Danger of COVID-19", *Taiwan Centers for Disease Control*, https://www.cdc.gov.tw/En/Bulletin/Detail/PAD-lbwDHeN_bLa-viBOuw?typeid=158.

47 Since the UN voted to recognize the People's Republic as the sole representative of China in 1971 and the World Health Assembly followed suit in 1972, Taiwan has not had full member status in the WHO, but it is involved in the Organization's work. Matthias Hartwig, "The Relationship between the People's Republic of China and Taiwan from the perspective of international law: How many Chinas exist in international law?" *Questions of International Law. Zoom-in* (2023): 23–43.

point about this "atypical pneumonia" similar to SARS and requested further advice from the WHO.[48]

Then, Taiwan firmly assumed human-to-human transmission of the novel coronavirus, although no evidence was found or information was provided by the Chinese government. Therefore, the Taiwanese government chose the precautionary principle and set up reinforced controls at the borders and quarantine measures as if human-to-human transmission was *de facto* occurring.

One of the key arguments of former United States President Trump in accusing the WHO was that Director-General Ghebreyesus voluntarily ignored the early alarm by Taiwan. In effect, the Taiwanese government had complained about the lack of an official answer to its inquiry.

However, it is worth recalling that the WHO informed the Global Outbreak Alert and Response Network (GOARN) about unknown viral pneumonia in the city of Wuhan on 2 January 2020.[49]

On 9 January 2020, the pneumonia outbreak was identified by the Chinese authorities as a novel coronavirus, and the WHO summoned a first teleconference involving global expert networks.[50] On 10 January 2020, the first novel coronavirus genome sequence was made publicly available,[51] and the same day, the WHO stated that "from the currently available information, preliminary investigation suggests that there is no significant human-to-human transmission, and no infections among health care workers have occurred".[52] Therefore, at the beginning of the disease outbreak, the WHO maintained that human-to-human transmission of the novel coronavirus was not at a level that would justify the adoption of more incisive measures such as restrictions to international traffic.

On 14 January 2020, the WHO tweeted that there was "no clear evidence" that the coronavirus could spread between people,[53] reporting the conclusions of the preliminary investigation by the Chinese authorities. This tweet, which was proved wrong by the rapid spread of the new coronavirus, is a symbol of the WHO's excessive reliance on information provided by the Chinese authorities, which admitted human-to-human transmission only on 20 January 2020.[54]

48 https://www.cdc.gov.tw/En/Bulletin/Detail/PAD-lbwDHeN_bLa-viBOuw?typeid=158.
49 Global Outbreak Alert and Response Network, https://extranet.who.int/goarn/.
50 World Health Organization, "WHO Statement Regarding Cluster of Pneumonia Cases in Wuhan, China" (9 January 2020), https://www.who.int/china/news/detail/09-01-2020-who-statement-regarding-cluster-of-pneumonia-cases-in-wuhan-china.
51 Edward Holmes, "Initial Genome Release of Novel Coronavirus 2020" (14 January 2020), http://virological.org/t/initial-genome-release-of-novel-coronavirus/319; the sequence has also been deposited on GenBank, https://www.ncbi.nlm.nih.gov/nuccore/MN908947.
52 *Supra*, footnote 50.
53 https://twitter.com/who/status/1217043229427761152?s=21.
54 Lily Kuo, "China Confirms Human-to-Human Transmission of Coronavirus", *The Guardian* (21 January 2020), https://www.theguardian.com/world/2020/jan/20/coronavirus-spreads-to-beijing-as-china-confirms-new-cases.

4.2. The meetings of the Emergency Committee of 22–23 January 2020 and the decision not to declare a PHEIC

On 22 January 2020, the Director-General summoned a first meeting of the Emergency Committee (EC) to debate the novel coronavirus. It has never been clarified why it took three weeks to convene the EC after the early notification of 31 December 2019. During these meetings, the EC was briefed about early cases by China, Japan, the Republic of Korea, and Thailand.

One critical issue raised division among WHO Members: it was clear at that time that the virus could spread from person to person, but the exact way that the virus was transmitted was not yet fully comprehensible.

A declaration of PHEIC would have entailed a risk of strong restrictions on trade and flights to and from China, although this is not a direct effect of the declaration of PHEIC but a possible reaction by the States to this act, and, as is well-known, the WHO's policy is to avoid excessive restrictions on flights and trade.[55]

On 23 January 2020, a new meeting was convened according to additional data provided by the Chinese authorities, which confirmed that human-to-human transmission was occurring and a preliminary R0 estimate of 1.4–2.5, although the extent of human-to-human transmission was not yet clear.

The EC recognised human-to-human transmission of COVID-19 and recommended airport exit screening. The members of the EC decided, however, that the conditions to declare a PHEIC were not yet fully met.[56]

The conclusions of the meeting were made available after the previous charges of a lack of transparency.[57] The majority decided that it was too early to declare a PHEIC because of the limited number of cases abroad and in consideration of the efforts made by the Chinese government.

It can be assumed that there was a political motivation to not damage China with the adoption of a PHEIC with its evident political and economic consequences (i.e., trade and flight limitations).

Indeed, the Director-General (DG), following the advice of the EC stated "for the moment, WHO does not recommend any broader restrictions on travel or trade. We recommend exit screening at airports as part of a comprehensive set of containment measures".[58]

55 Barbara von Tigerstrom, Kumanan Wilson, "COVID-19 Travel Restrictions and the International Health Regulations (2005)", *The British Medical Journal of Global Health* (2020): 1–4.
56 Statement on the first meeting of the International Health Regulations (2005) Emergency Committee regarding the outbreak of novel coronavirus (2019-nCoV), https://www.who.int/news/item/23-01-2020-statement-on-the-meeting-of-the-international-health-regulations-(2005)-emergency-committee-regarding-the-outbreak-of-novel-coronavirus-(2019-ncov).
57 Mark Eccleston-Turner, "Transparency in IHR Emergency Committee Decision Making: The Case for Reform", *BMJ Global Health* (2019): 1–3.
58 *WHO Director-General's Statement on the Advice of the IHR Emergency Committee on Novel Coronavirus*, https://www.who.int/director-general/speeches/detail/who-director-general-s-statement-on-the-advice-of-the-ihr-emergency-committee-on-novel-coronavirus.

The EC also advised the People's Republic of China to continue to pursue what they considered a policy of transparency and sharing of data. It seems that the EC's members considered China a reliable partner that was acting in good faith.

The DG's decision to not declare a PHEIC was made despite confirmed cases among health care workers in China (the same day quarantine was declared in Wuhan) and outside China and specific warnings from Hong Kong and Taiwan of growing cases of unknown pneumonia, arguing that they were transmitted from human-to-human.

In the next few days, Australia, Canada, and France registered the first cases of patients infected by the new coronavirus.

Notably, the EC is only an advisory body, and the DG can decide to declare a PHEIC against its advice (and the will of the concerned State). However, in the WHO's practice, the DG has so far always endorsed – without raising any issue – the EC's advice,[59] except for the monkeypox outbreak.[60]

4.3. What went wrong?

a) The role of the Emergency Committee

When the EC is summoned by the DG and meets at the strategic health operations centre (SHOC), one should expect the greatest expertise available to get the advice of the highest quality on how to deal with a potential epidemic or pandemic. On 22 January 2020, the EC was requested to make a pivotal decision on whether or not to advise the DG to declare a PHEIC. After the reports presented by China, Japan, and Thailand, where the first cases were confirmed, the debate focused on a very challenging issue.[61] Human-to-human transmission was by now ascertained, but it was not yet clear how easily the virus could spread.

The key question was whether the human-to-human transmission was relegated to a determined area, within families, or just between patients and physicians or nurses; in this case, the disease outbreak could have been contained

59 Gian Luca Burci, "The Outbreak of Covid-19 Coronavirus: Are the International Health Regulations Fit for Purpose?" *EJIL: Talk!* (27 February 2020), ejiltalk.org/the-outbreak-of-covid-19-coronavirus-are-the-international-health-regulations-fit-for-purpose/.
60 Kai Kupferschmidt, "WHO Chief Declares Monkeypox an International Emergency After Expert Panel Fails to Reach Consensus. Narrow Majority on Emergency Committee Voted Against Ringing WHO's Loudest Alarm Bell", *Science* (23 July 2022), https://www.science.org/content/article/declaring-monkeypox-an-international-emergency-who-chief-rejects-expert-panels-advice.
61 On 13 January 2020, Thailand reported to the WHO a similar case of "unknown pneumonia". On 16 January 2020, Japan informed the WHO of a confirmed case of the novel coronavirus, referred to as 2019-nCoV. On 20 January 2020, the Republic of Korea reported its first case of a novel coronavirus, https://www.vertic.org/wp-content/uploads/2020/06/FS15A_IHR_COVID19_EN_MAY_2020.pdf.

without giving the global alarm and the negative impact on the economy of the State of origin that this entails.

In light of the division within the EC on the necessity to declare a PHEIC, a new meeting was convened a day later on 23 January 2020. The main duty of the DG is to convoke the EC but not necessarily to follow its advice since he has the power to override this organ; but, in the WHO's practice, the DG has never declared a PHEIC against the recommendations issued by the EC, which is a scientific body that acts exclusively on an epidemiological basis. Therefore, it would be politically improper to act against scientific advice, and this is the reason why the DG usually acts only after he has obtained unanimity or at least the majority (except for monkeypox, as previously explained).

If one looks retrospectively at the composition of the EC, members and advisers, they were experts from countries that do not have close ties with China, such as the United States, France, South Korea, Canada, Japan, Netherlands, Australia, Senegal, Saudi Arabia, Sweden, and New Zealand. Since China expressed its objection to declaring an emergency during the first meeting on 22 January 2020, it is evident that some of the EC members supported its position (their advice is confidential).

However, EC members have a personal responsibility to disclose personal, financial, or professional connections that might constitute a conflict of interest.

Presuming the good faith of the EC's members, one might therefore argue that the delay in declaring a PHEIC was an issue of both incapacity and scarcity of epidemiological data from China since the EC had been unable to evaluate the seriousness of the SARS-CoV-2 outbreak.

In more general terms, the role and composition of the EC leave deeper issues unresolved: under the point of view of democracy, it is questionable that a strict group of public health experts – appointed and chosen by the DG – can have a so crucial role in the determination of a PHEIC with its far-reaching consequences on the political and economic levels. On this point, one might, however, argue that in the end, the EC offers non-binding advice, and the consequences of this advice are non-binding recommendations by the DG.

On 30 January 2020, the DG – in a tweet – explicitly congratulated "the speed with which China detected the outbreak, isolated the virus and sequenced the genome and shared it with WHO and the world are very impressive. So is China's commitment to transparency and to supporting other countries".[62]

The crucial issue is whether the EC members were effectively independent of any pressure from the Chinese government,[63] which exerted considerable diplomatic coercion on other countries.

---

62 https://twitter.com/who/status/1222968207524450308.
63 Julian Borger, "Caught in a Superpower Struggle: The Inside Story of the WHO's Response to Coronavirus", *The Guardian* (18 April 2020), https://www.theguardian.com/world/2020/apr/18/caught-in-a-superpower-struggle-the-inside-story-of-the-whos-response-to-coronavirus.

Concerns were expressed during the precedent disease outbreaks, and doubts have been reinforced by the hesitancy of the majority of the EC's members to advise whether or not to declare a PHEIC.

One might suspect that they were influenced by political factors rather than relying exclusively on scientific considerations. Taiwan claimed that – despite its early warning – it was never invited to participate in the three emergency committee meetings summoned in January 2020 due to Chinese obstruction.[64]

In effect, the declaration of PHEIC has severe economic and political implications through the restriction of international trade and travel. The designation of PHEIC implies the failure of a given State to contain a disease outbreak, and a wrong decision might have serious consequences on the WHO's legitimacy. This is why early notification of first cases and correct information from an affected country are crucial in the DG's decision.

As is well-known, the WHO has traditionally been hesitant to recommend travel bans for both scientific and economic reasons. From the first point of view, the objection raised is that travel bans do not efficiently hinder the movement of people; most importantly, the economic implication of travel bans and their negative effect on tourism cannot be underestimated.

On 28 January 2020, the WHO's DG declared, "we appreciate the seriousness with which China is taking this outbreak, especially the commitment from top leadership, and the transparency they have demonstrated, including sharing data and genetic sequence of the virus".

Despite criticism directed at the DG for his policy of appeasement towards Xi Jinping's government, such diplomatic flattery could also be considered the counterbalance for ensuring Chinese cooperation with information and allowing the WHO to visit sites. In light of the obstructionism by Beijing, the WHO's praise of China was probably a political choice to avoid a stalemate of cooperation with China. Rather, public condemnation of China would have been counter-productive and would have implied negative consequences at the diplomatic level.

The DG decided not to recommend any travel restrictions to and from China, although the lockdown had already been imposed in Wuhan. This policy of appeasement unleashed the wrath of former United States President Trump who throughout 2020, blamed the WHO for being inefficient.

However, the recommendations are not binding, and States have the possibility to enact stricter domestic measures (Art. 43 IHR); in this case, they have only an obligation to communicate their actions to the WHO, according to a classic mechanism in global governance known as "comply or explain", which must be based on scientific evidence.

---

64 Wen-Chen Chang, "Taiwan's Fight Against COVID-19: Constitutionalism, Laws, and the Global Pandemic", *Verfassungsblog* (2020), https://verfassungsblog.de/taiwans-fight-against-covid-19-constitutionalism-laws-and-the-global-pandemic/.

These recommendations were updated during the 3rd Meeting of the Emergency Committee (1st May 2020),[65] and States were invited to implement

appropriate travel measures and analyze their effects on international transmission of COVID-19, with consideration of the balance between benefits and unintended consequences, including entry and exit screening, education of travellers on responsible travel behaviour, case finding, contact tracing, isolation, and quarantine, by incorporating evidence on the potential role of pre-symptomatic and asymptomatic transmission.

China's influence within the WHO is not, however, related to substantial financial contributions to the Organization.

WHO's subservience to major funding States is an issue that dates to the 1970s and is an element of the weakness of the Organization. The WHO's budget is based on Assessed Contributions (AC) and Voluntary Contributions (VC) (specific voluntary contributions) that amount to 80% of the budget,[66] which is often earmarked according to donors' priorities.

As outlined by Taylor and Habibi, the biennial budget of the WHO is well below $5 billion, which is half of the annual budget of the United States Centers for Disease Control and Prevention (CDC).[67]

The rest are assessed contributions, the dues that a Member State pays, which are calculated according to two indicators: wealth and population. The high level of dependence on VC has limited the WHO's activity, which makes it highly responsive to its main funding States and thus jeopardises its independence.[68]

However, China is the third-highest donor with 75,796K and provides a very small voluntary contribution (10,184K).[69] Despite this, China's strong influence on the WHO is evident. China is an important stakeholder within the WHO since it represents the health demands of middle- and low-income countries. The People's Republic of China is the only representative (1971) within the WHO, and it will continue to support the "One China" principle, which recognizes the government in Beijing as the legitimate Chinese government.

---

65 https://www.who.int/news-room/detail/01-05-2020-statement-on-the-third-meeting-of-the-international-health-regulations-(2005)-emergency-committee-regarding-the-outbreak-of-coronavirus-disease-(covid-19).

66 https://www.who.int/about/funding.

67 Allyn L. Taylor, Roojin Habibi, "The Collapse of Global Cooperation Under the WHO International Health Regulations at the Outset of COVID-19: Sculpting the Future of Global Health Governance", *ASIL Insights* (5 June 2020), https://www.asil.org/insights/volume/24/issue/15/collapse-global-cooperation-under-who-international-health-regulations.

68 On 24 May 2022, the Seventy-fifth World Health Assembly decided through a "landmark decision on sustainable financing for WHO" to increase the portion of the budget financed by the Member States from 16% to 50% by 2028 to reinforce the leadership and independence of the Organization (https://www.who.int/news/item/24-05-2022-daily-update-24-may-2022).

69 https://open.who.int/2018–19/contributors/contributor?name=China.

The DG's delayed response to COVID-19 stands in stark contrast to the management of the 2003 SARS outbreak in China. In this case, the former DG openly criticized China. The Report of the WHO-China Joint Mission followed in its recommendations the decision of the Chinese authorities to exclude asymptomatic individuals as a vehicle of transmission: "the proportion of truly asymptomatic infection is unclear but appears to be relatively rare and does not appear *to be a major driver of transmission*".[70]

It is a fact that the first technical guidance addressed to States was blatantly wrong: the Global Surveillance for human infection with the novel coronavirus (2019-nCoV) (31 January 2020) did not include asymptomatic individuals as possible carriers of the new coronavirus and therefore did not recommend to carry out the test on this category of patients.[71]

The guidelines indicated the elements of a suspect case of an individual infected with COVID-19: a patient with a severe acute respiratory infection (fever, cough, and requiring hospital admission), with no other aetiology that fully explains the clinical presentation and a history of travel to or residence in China during the 14 days before symptom onset. The updated version of 27 February 2020 reassessed the WHO's recommendations to the Member States.[72] The suspect case included a patient with acute respiratory illness (fever and at least one sign/symptom of respiratory disease, e.g., cough, shortness of breath) and a history of travel to or residence in a location reporting community transmission of COVID-19 disease during the 14 days before symptom onset; a patient with any acute respiratory illness that has been in contact with a confirmed or probable COVID-19 case in the last 14 days before symptom onset; a patient with severe acute respiratory illness (fever and at least one sign/symptom of respiratory disease, e.g., cough, shortness of breath; requiring hospitalization) *in the absence of an alternative diagnosis that fully explains the clinical presentation.*

b) Design flaw

Undue political pressure from China or simple incapacity are potential explanations for the extreme delay of the WHO in "ringing the bell". Another explanation is related to a structural problem of the IHR, that is, a design flaw.

A PHEIC is declared only when an event is already sufficiently acute and it has started to spread internationally. It is not an early warning but a formal alert, and in the case of COVID-19, it was provided when the virus was already diffused worldwide (except for Antarctica and Greenland). The IHR

---

70 https://www.who.int/docs/default-source/coronaviruse/who-china-joint-mission-on-covid-19-final-report.pdf.
71 https://apps.who.int/iris/bitstream/handle/10665/330857/WHO-2019-nCoV-Surveil lanceGuidance-2020.3-eng.pdf?sequence=1&isAllowed=y.
72 https://apps.who.int/iris/bitstream/handle/10665/331231/WHO-2019-nCoV-Surveil lanceGuidance-2020.4-eng.pdf?sequence=1&isAllowed=y.

therefore only allow for a binary decision: a PHEIC is declared or not. The structural weakness is thus related to the lack of an intermediate alert system.

In the Declaration of 30 January 2020, the DG showed awareness about this problem, hoping that the "WHO should continue to explore the advisability of creating an intermediate level of alert between the binary possibilities of PHEIC or no PHEIC, in a way that does *not require reopening negotiations* on the text of the IHR (2005)".

The DG recommended developing a New Alert and Response Notice (WARN) system that should provide adequate information to the WHO Member States of the actions required to tackle an event that has not yet reached the threshold of a PHEIC, but it may nonetheless require a coordinated response. It should take the form of a notice containing a WHO risk assessment to be shared among the Member States, and it should detail the specific public health actions that are recommended to prevent cross-border transmission. Given that the WHO has provided recommendations even in the absence of a declaration of PHEIC,[73] the added legal value of this WARN system is not clear.

The need for reform was then reiterated in a WHO Interim Report, which proposed an intermediate level of alert, a type of "yellow light" as an initial warning signal (Para. 32).[74]

This type of proposal is not a novelty, since it was already recommended in a previous document on the response to the Ebola outbreak in Western Africa (although it was never endorsed by the WHO Member States).[75] The Panel recommended

> the possibility of an intermediate level that would alert and engage the wider international community at an earlier stage in a health crisis. This could facilitate preparedness, preventive action, and dedication of resources, which could avert an escalation of the situation.

This type of reform, which could be called a "traffic light mechanism"[76] or "tiered alert system",[77] to be functional should bypass the risk-based approach upon which the assessment of the DG is conducted. This would imply overtaking the classic reluctance of the WHO and the EC to impose travel and trade restrictions before a risk assessment is carried out since they are usually considered ineffective and counterproductive.

73 https://www.who.int/news/item/05-02-2015-who-statement-on-the-eighth-meeting-of-the-ihr-emergency-committee-regarding-mers-cov.

74 https://www.who.int/publications/m/item/interim-progress-report-on-the-functioning-of-the-ihr-2005-during-the-covid-19-response.

75 https://www.who.int/csr/resources/publications/ebola/report-by-panel.pdf?ua=1.

76 Gian Luca Burci, "The Legal Response to Pandemics. The Strengths and Weaknesses of the International Health Regulations", *Journal of International Humanitarian Studies* (2020): 204–217.

77 https://theindependentpanel.org/mainreport/.

Even though the various proposals envision different tiers – ranging from only a yellow light before a PHEIC to a flowchart with five levels of alarm[78] – they all have the goal of encouraging the early reporting of and response to potentially serious disease outbreaks. Despite the wide range of possibilities, the first problem is, however, how to concretize a potential reform. The easiest solution could imply the negotiation and adoption of an additional protocol amending the IHR or at least an Annex II and introducing a more nuanced alarm mechanism. Otherwise, a technical note could provide a specific flowchart to both the EC and the DG based on a multi-tiered declaration approach; that is, the DG could be able to recommend specific measures to its Member States even before the formal declaration of a PHEIC. The necessity to replace the all-or-nothing nature of PHEIC declarations is not new in the academic debate, but due to the worldwide diffusion of the COVID-19 pandemic, it has become crucial. Such reform could relaunch the IHR and increase the role of the WHO in managing future pandemics, but the normative power of a PHEIC declaration should not be overestimated since it is not a binding act but rather an instrument of governance through information. States do not wait for a red light from the WHO to react to potential epidemics or pandemics but in view of their source of information, can decide to proceed earlier if they want. This was witnessed in the early stages of COVID-19 when Vietnam and Taiwan decided to adopt stringent measures well before the end of January.

Accordingly, as underlined by some scholars, a reform of the PHEIC's mechanism would not solve the core issues of the alert and response system behind the IHR, which mainly does have a political dimension.[79] States are reluctant to act in good faith and to share information in case of a disease outbreak, tend not to comply with the DG's temporary recommendations, and have not developed adequate core capacities to respond to disease outbreaks.

5. The declaration of PHEIC of 30 January 2020 and the measures recommended

A PHEIC was eventually declared on 30 January 2020[80] when there was undeniable evidence of community spread since the virus was rampant in Wuhan (and then became widely diffused around the rest of the world). The declaration was adopted when the world community was already under alarm. Italy had already blocked flights from China, and the United States very soon

---

78 https://institut-fuer-globale-gesundheit.de/wp content/uploads/2020/01/Final_Proposal_Scorecard_IGGB_310120.pdf.

79 Clare Wenham, Matthew Kavanagh, Alexandra Phelan, Simon Rushton, Maike Voss, Sam Halabi, Mark Eccleston-Turner, Mara Pillinger, "Problems With Traffic Light Approaches to Public Health Emergencies of International Concern", *Lancet* (2021): 1856–1858.

80 Statement on the second meeting of the International Health Regulations (2005) Emergency Committee regarding the outbreak of novel coronavirus (2019-nCoV).

did thereafter. When the PHEIC was finally declared, nearly 10,000 cases of patients affected by COVID-19 were confirmed, including 83 cases from States outside China. On the same day, the United States confirmed the first case of a patient hit with the new coronavirus,[81] and the Philippines registered the first death outside China due to the virus. This was a patient who arrived from Wuhan on 21 January 2020 – two days before a lockdown was declared in the city.

The first element of the Declaration is the praise of China:

> The Committee welcomed the leadership and political commitment of the very highest levels of the Chinese government, their *commitment to transparency*, and the efforts made to investigate and contain the current outbreak. China quickly identified the virus and shared its sequence so that other countries could diagnose it quickly and protect themselves, which has resulted in the rapid development of diagnostic tools.

"The measures China has taken are good not only for that country but also for the rest of the world". Then again,

> the Committee emphasized that the declaration of a PHEIC should be seen in the spirit of support and appreciation for China, its people, and the actions China has taken on the frontlines of this outbreak, with transparency, and, it is to be hoped, with success.

In its temporary recommendations, the DG predicted further exportation of cases and asked all countries to be prepared for containment, including active surveillance, early detection, isolation, and case management, and contact tracing.

The DG recommended isolation of suspected cases, quarantine, and contact tracing, stating that the most severe restrictions – such as lockdowns and massive quarantines – should be decided at the national level. Therefore, the DG never claimed to recommend the constitutionally and politically very sensitive question of lockdowns. This approach displayed particular attention to human rights by the WHO.

Surveillance, contact tracing, isolation, and quarantine were the backbone of the outbreak response.[82]

In the first moments, however, the WHO advised Member States not to consider asymptomatic persons as a possible vehicle for transmission of COVID-19.

---

81 "CDC Confirms Person-to-Person Spread of New Coronavirus in the United States", *Center for Disease Control and Prevention* (30 January 2020), www.cdc.gov/media/releases/2020/p0130-coronavirus-spread.html.

82 Looking back at a year that changed the world. *WHO's Response to COVID-19* (22 January 2021), https://www.who.int/publications/m/item/looking-back-at-a-year-that-changed-the-world-who-s-response-to-covid-19.

Moreover, the first technical guidelines did not include asymptomatic individuals among the suspected cases and therefore did not recommend domestic authorities to carry out tests on this category of persons.[83]

The main criterion to carry out a test on a patient was represented by a "severe acute respiratory infection". In addition, the Report of the WHO-China Joint Mission on Coronavirus Disease 2019 (COVID-19) traced in its recommendations the decision of Chinese authorities – in the first phases of the outbreak – to exclude asymptomatic persons as a possible vehicle of transmission, arguing that "the proportion of truly asymptomatic infection is unclear but appears to be relatively rare and does not appear to be a major driver of transmission".[84]

This position has been refuted by the same data reported by China since April 2020, according to which most COVID-19 patients would be without symptoms.[85] The PHEIC was confirmed in the EC's following meeting. In the Statement on the tenth meeting of 19 January 2022, the EC highlighted the defiance represented by the high transmission levels of the SARS CoV-2 Omicron Variant Of Concern (VOC).[86] The DG determined that "the COVID-19 pandemic continues to constitute a PHEIC" and issued temporary recommendations. First, States were invited to "continue to use evidence-informed public health and social measures, therapeutics, diagnostics, and vaccines for COVID-19, and to share response experiences with WHO".

The DG recommended that States slacken policies based on isolation and quarantine through the introduction of testing; specifically, through a risk-based approach, States should find an appropriate balance between the risks of transmission of the Omicron variant among the population and the continuation of key functions.

In the Technical Document "Enhancing response to Omicron SARS-CoV-2 variant",[87] the WHO affirmed that "based on the currently available evidence, the overall risk related to Omicron remains very high".

Particular attention was then devoted to the recommendation on the issue of the roll-out of COVID-19 vaccines; the DG pushed for the goal of having "at least 70% of all countries' populations vaccinated by the start of July 2022 and integrate COVID-19 vaccination into routine health services". These aspirations remained highly unrealised; as outlined in a media briefing on 29 June 2022,

83 *Global Surveillance for Human Infection With Novel Coronavirus (2019-nCoV): Interim Guidance* (31 January 2020), https://apps.who.int/iris/handle/10665/330857.
84 https://www.who.int/docs/default-source/coronaviruse/who-china-joint-mission-on-covid-19-final-report.pdf.
85 Michael Day, "Covid-19: Four Fifths of Cases are Asymptomatic, China Figures Indicate", *British Medical Journal* (2 April 2020), https://www.bmj.com/content/bmj/369/bmj.m1375.full.pdf
86 https://www.who.int/news/item/19-01-2022-statement-on-the-tenth-meeting-of-the-international-health-regulations-(2005)-emergency-committee-regarding-the-coronavirus-disease-(covid-19)-pandemic. Omicron (B.1.1.529) was classified as a SARS-CoV-2 Variant of Concern in a statement of 26 November 2021.
87 https://www.who.int/publications/m/item/enhancing-readiness-for-omicron-(b.1.1.529)-technical-brief-and-priority-actions-for-member-states.

the DG affirmed that "hundreds of millions of people, including tens of millions of health workers and older people in lower-income countries, remain unvaccinated, which means they are more vulnerable to future waves of the virus".[88]

The persisting gaps in vaccination rates across multiple countries were highlighted by the WHO DG in his declaration of 5 May 2023, although he stated that COVID-19 no longer constitutes a PHEIC and formally declared the end of the state of emergency.

6. The declaration of the pandemic of COVID-19 as a trigger for domestic pandemic plans

On 11 March 2020, the Director-General issued a formal declaration that classified COVID-19 as a pandemic.[89] On 23 March 2020, he then emphasised that the world was facing a pandemic with exponential growth and recommended not limiting the response of States to defensive measures, such as social distancing measures, but to complement them with aggressive and targeted tactics, which are 1) testing every suspected case, 2) isolating and 3) caring for every confirmed case, and 4) tracing and 5) quarantining every close contact[90] (such invitation was then reiterated in the subsequent press statement of 27 March 2020).[91]

In the press statement of 22 April 2020, a sixth pillar was added related to the engagement and empowerment of the population of each country. The DG underlined that the full participation of persons was essential in the fight against the coronavirus.

This declaration represents the highest level of alert and triggers a set of political and legal consequences. The pandemic declaration, unlike the PHEIC, is not envisaged in the IHR but by technical guidelines, precisely by the Pandemic Influenza Preparedness and Response (2010),[92] the WHO Pandemic Influenza Risk Management (2017),[93] and Article 15, Paragraph 2, of the new pandemic treaty.[94]

88 https://www.who.int/director-general/speeches/detail/who-director-general-s-opening-remarks-at-the-media-briefing–29-june-2022.
89 Domenico Cucinotta, Maurizio Vanelli, "WHO Declares COVID-19 a Pandemic", *Acta Biomed* (2020): 157–160.
90 WHO Director-General's opening remarks at the media briefing on COVID-19–23 March 2020.
91 WHO Director-General's opening remarks at the media briefing on COVID-19–27 March 2020.
92 Pandemic influenza preparedness and response: a WHO guidance document, https://apps.who.int/iris/handle/10665/44123. On the lack of a definition of a pandemic under international law, Pedro A. Villareal, "Pandemics: Building a Legal Concept for the Future", *Washington University Global Studies Law Review* (2021): 611–626.
93 *Pandemic Influenza Risk Management: A WHO Guide to Inform and Harmonize National and International Pandemic Preparedness and Response*, https://apps.who.int/iris/handle/10665/259893.
94 Article 15, Paragraph 2, of the Zero draft of the WHO CA+ states that "Recognizing the central role of WHO as the directing and coordinating authority on international health work, and mindful of the need for coordination with regional organizations, entities in the United Nations system and other intergovernmental organizations, the WHO Director-General shall, in accordance with terms set out herein, declare pandemics".

According to these guidelines, an influenza pandemic is a virus to which most humans have little or no existing immunity that "acquires the ability to cause sustained human-to-human transmission leading to community-wide outbreaks. Such a virus has the potential to spread rapidly worldwide, causing a pandemic".[95]

The main criterion taken as a reference by the WHO to declare a pandemic is the degree of diffusion of a given virus on a global scale and not its level of mortality, although the specific threshold to determine a "high" spread is vague.[96] Other criteria are the facility of contagion, rapid spread, minimum immunity among the population, and a high infectious rate.

The first document highlights the intermediate steps before declaring a pandemic, and the DG is the only body in charge of coordinating the measures that States must adopt.

The first is the alert phase. The DG has the power, in the case of a serious disease outbreak, as previously underlined, to declare a health emergency; this does not necessarily imply that a pandemic declaration will follow if the contagion is limited. The second is the pandemic phase: when containment measures have collapsed, and the disease spreads among States.

The pandemic means the passage from containment measures – which have failed – to mitigation measures to dilute over time the spread of the virus and to allow the health systems to properly prepare themselves for the recurring waves of cases.

The power of the WHO DG to declare a pandemic is not envisaged either by the WHO Constitution or the IHR but by the Guidelines of 2010, which establish that "the designation of the global pandemic phase will be made by the Director-General of the WHO".

The legal vacuum in the IHR that neither defines a pandemic nor formally provides the DG with the power to declare a pandemic has generated confusion.[97]

Some governments, for instance, in declaring a state of emergency, have referred to the declaration of a pandemic rather than to the declaration of PHEIC.

Moreover, a pandemic declaration does not have any specific legal consequence but is an exercise of international public authority by the DG.[98]

95 World Health Organization, Pandemic Influenza Risk Management (2017) (WHO/WHE/IHM/GIP/2017.1), at 26.
96 The lack of the element of the "seriousness" of the disease has raised concern; see Peter Doshi, "The Elusive Definition of Pandemic Influenza", *Bullettin of the World Health Organization* (2011): 532–538.
97 For a glimpse of this debate, see Pedro A. Villarreal, *Pandemias y derecho: una perspectiva de gobernanza global* (Universidad Nacional Autónoma de México, Instituto de Investigationes Jurídicas: 2019), 29–32.
98 Pedro A. Villarreal, "Pandemic Declarations of the World Health Organization as an Exercise of International Public Authority: The Possible Legal Answers to Frictions Between Legitimacies" *Göttingen Journal of International Law* 7 (2016): 125–126.

A Report of 23 May 2022 noticed that response measures by States Parties, including travel and trade restrictions and joint efforts to develop adequate treatments and vaccines, were triggered after the pandemic declaration and not after the PHEIC declaration.[99]

States perceived the pandemic declaration as the highest level of alert and response.

Therefore, even if devoid of binding legal force, these declarations (and the included recommendations) have a remarkable epistemic legitimacy well beyond the mere distinction between hard and soft law. It is a case of "governance through information";[100] that is, the WHO, in providing adequate information to its Member States, orientates their domestic policies in the field of health.

The decision to classify COVID-19 as a pandemic, which means a most serious level compared to previous disease outbreaks, such as Ebola in Western Africa (2014) and Zika (2016), had, however, clear political implications.

The DG wanted to catalyse the attention of the international community to have a coordinated response and to obtain additional resources and funding.

On 13 March 2020, the WHO launched a new financing initiative, the COVID-19 Solidarity Response Fund, which allowed private stakeholders, firms, and institutions to donate funds devoted to the fight against COVID-19.[101]

The Fund – in line with the actions envisaged by the COVID-19 Strategic Preparedness and Response Plan – had the goals of reinforcing the health system of all countries, in particular, those more vulnerable and with a major risk of transmission, identifying new cases, blocking the transmission chain of the virus, and taking care of patients.[102]

The WHO's DG, with the pandemic declaration, also wanted to denounce the alarming levels of inaction by the Member States that had determined a wide spread of the virus in their territory; he therefore resorted to his public authority.

Certainly, the WHO cannot publicly criticize a Member State, but it is evident that some countries underestimated the threat of COVID-19 and

---

99 *Director-General's Report to Member States at the 75th World Health Assembly* (23 May 2022), https://www.who.int/director-general/speeches/detail/who-director-general-s-opening-address-at-the-75th-world-health-assembly–23-may-2022.

100 In general, on the role of information in the context of international institutions, see Armin von Bogdandy, Matthias Goldmann, Ingo Venzke, "From Public International to International Public Law: Translating World Public Opinion into International Public Authority", *European Journal of International Law* (2017): 115–145.

101 https://www.who.int/news-room/detail/13-03-2020-who-un-foundation-and-partners-launch-first-of-its-kind-covid-19-solidarity-response-fund.

102 The new COVID-19 Strategic Preparedness and Response Plan (SPRP 2021). | COVID-19: Critical preparedness, readiness and response of 24 February 2021.

adopted – at least in the early phase – measures that revealed themselves to be too weak.

Consider, for example, the case of the United Kingdom, which initially declared that it would have adopted a strategy based on gradual restrictions to reach what is defined as herd immunity. This strategy was not functional since a patient can get the pandemic virus twice – even if vaccinated.

The DG underlined that the measures of social distancing, self-isolation, and quarantine are the main strategies to combat the spread of the virus since many individuals are contagious and without symptoms (pre-symptomatic and asymptomatic transmission of COVID-19).[103]

A pandemic declaration means that the domestic authorities can no longer contain the spread of the disease and must adopt mitigation strategies to diminish the contagion among the population.

From the operative point of view, the declaration is a "call to action" and has legal consequences. A pandemic declaration, as previously stated, informs the States that Phase 6 has begun. According to the pandemic phase descriptions, Phase 6 implies community-level outbreaks in different WHO regions. Notably, the duty upon States to activate domestic plans against pandemics is not directly envisaged by the IHR but by the technical guidelines of the Pandemic Influenza Preparedness and Response.

7. Concluding remarks

Considering the criticism levelled at the WHO for its management of new centuries' disease outbreaks and in particular, the COVID-19 pandemic, this chapter contains a reflection on what effectively went wrong.

As highlighted by some scholars,[104] the *lack of political cooperation* was the main feature of the global response to the novel coronavirus disease, although the optimal solution would have implied actions that go beyond pure self-interest. The free-riding strategy of several States during the "hot phase" of the pandemic frustrated early efforts to contain the worldwide spread of the virus.

Therefore, I contend that the WHO's faults are mainly due to its design flaw and the lack of enforcement powers upon the Member States unwilling to cooperate rather than on a presumed complicity with the Chinese government.

Benvenisti argues that the WHO's founders crafted the Organization on the basis of two wrong assumptions. The first is that States would have a genuine interest in cooperating in the prevention and containment of the spread

---

103 Miriam Casey-Bryars, John Griffin, Conor McAloon, Andrew Byrne, Jamie Madden1, David Mc Evoy, Áine Collins, Kevin Hunt, Ann Barber, Francis Butler, Elizabeth Ann Lane, Kirsty O'Brien, Patrick Wall, Kieran Walsh, "Presymptomatic Transmission of SARS-CoV-2 Infection: A Secondary Analysis Using Published Data", *BMJ Open* (2021): 1–9.

104 For instance, see Eyal Benvenisti, "The WHO-Destined to Fail? Political Cooperation and the COVID-19 Pandemic", *American Journal of International Law* (2020): 588–597.

of infectious diseases.[105] As shown by the history of global health law, States usually pursue their own interests and tend to conceal disease outbreaks. As outlined by Worsnop, States are unwilling to report correct data about a disease outbreak rather than being incapable of doing it since they fear retaliation by the other States, such as the imposition of trade and travel barriers.[106]

The second assumption is that they believed that the WHO – through a science-based approach – would influence State behaviour and that countries would spontaneously follow its instructions in case of disease outbreak. In effect, this vision is clearly outlined in the WHO's Constitution since the Executive Board has the authority "to take emergency measures within the functions and financial resources of the Organization to deal with events requiring immediate action".

That is, the WHO's founders gave too much weight to the *coordination* phase, claiming that in the name of science and considering the WHO's epistemic authority as a science-based organization, States would blindly implement its recommendations and technical guidance. It is a utopian vision since the WHO was created by industrialized countries with United States leadership and a specific utilitarian view: avoiding the spread of infectious diseases coming from developing countries (through access to appropriate information) and imposing travel and trade bans. Accordingly, the West wanted to protect itself from the pathogens of Africa and South-East Asia, and the United States in particular had the aim of demonstrating their intention to eradicate disease and poverty considered to be the fuel of Communism.[107]

The WHO's efforts to gain momentum among its Member States have been hindered by competing political and economic interests, given that industrialized and developing countries have different needs. As shown by another issue – global warming – States are fully aware of the way forward on climate change (namely, the "decarbonization" of their economies),[108] but they hesitate to fully cooperate. They instead have a "compulsion to repeat" a given behaviour even if it damages the environment; there are, of course, conflicting interests (protection of the environment versus the right to economic development).

---

105 Joseph Grieco, *Cooperation Among Nations* (Cornell University Press: 1990). The issue of elements behind States' will to cooperate has been object of a vast array of studies; see, among others, Stephen Krasmer, *International Regimes* (Cornell University Press: 1983); Robert Keohane, *After Hegemony* (Princeton University Press: 1984).

106 Catherine Z. Worsnop, "Concealing Disease: Trade and Travel Barriers and Timeliness of Outbreak Reporting", *International Studies Perspectives* (2019): 344–372.

107 Elizabeth Fee, Marcu Cueto, Theodore M. Brown, "At the Roots of the World Health Organization's Challenges: Politics and Regionalization", *American Journal of Public Health* (2016): 1912–1917.

108 David G. Victor, "Deep Decarbonization: A Realistic Way Forward on Climate Change", *Yale Environment 360* (2020), https://e360.yale.edu/features/deep-decarbonization-a-realistic-way-forward-on-climate-change.

However, some countries have instead an incentive to cheat on the real flow of their CO2 emissions.[109]

The difficulty of full cooperation in the environmental sector was indicated by the impossibility of the Security Council to adopt a thematic resolution on the interrelation among climate change, security, and conflicts.

As highlighted by some scholars, the solution to prevent and manage pandemics such as COVID-19 requires that all actors choose specific actions beyond their pure self-interest and decide voluntarily to engage in a given behaviour dictated by the WHO.[110] Nevertheless, the free-riding strategy of most States – as demonstrated by vaccine nationalism – has frustrated multilateral efforts to contain the pandemic.

In the case of a global pandemic, States, as already discussed in this book, tend to react on a unilateral basis and on the presumption of protecting their domestic interests (and their citizens) first. To this aim, they tend to underestimate data on disease outbreaks, are wary of notifying the global community about disease outbreaks due to fear of retaliation, and adopt defensive measures, such as closing borders.

Pressure by domestic stakeholders to steer domestic responses reinforces unilateralism.

In more general terms, one can argue that it was not only one specific problem of the WHO in addressing the COVID-19 pandemic properly; it is difficult to predict that another IGO would have better managed the disease outbreak. All IGOs in times of global crises are highly constrained by a lack of enforcement powers, excessive bureaucracy, and States' sovereignty, showing a discrepancy between their ambitions and realpolitik.[111]

With particular reference to infectious diseases, the WHO has faced serious problems in guaranteeing the appropriate coordination of States' responses to recent disease outbreaks (in particular, Ebola in Western Africa and COVID-19). The lack of leadership of the WHO in managing infectious diseases with a wide diffusion, the repeated calls for reform of the IHR after every declaration of PHEIC, and the criticism that has followed are all signals of the weakness of the WHO. The "original sin" is that the WHO is not adequately equipped for the challenges it faces. Recalling international relations theories, one might assume that it is not rationally designed to fit its specific purposes.

109 Jilles van den Beukel, "Why It's So Difficult to Reduce CO2 Emissions", *energypost.eu* (4 February 2016), https://energypost.eu/difficult-reduce-co2-emissions/.
110 Patrick Mellacher, "Cooperation in the Age of COVID-19: Evidence from Public Goods Games", *ARXIV.ORG* (18 November 2020), https://arxiv.org/ftp/arxiv/papers/2011/2011.09189.pdf.
111 On this topic, see, *inter alia*, Giulio M. Gallarotti, "The Limits of International Organization: Systematic Failure in the Management of International Relations", *International Organization* (1991): 183–220.

IV The origins of COVID-19, pandemic risk, and the limits of environmental law

1. Disease spillover and environmental degradation

In the last decade, most declarations of health emergencies by the WHO have been correlated with zoonoses. A study by the Royal Society B has crossed data on 142 zoonoses caused by wild animals included within the category of the most threatened species listed in the *IUCN Red List of Threatened Species*.[1] Research has highlighted that important natural reservoirs of many infectious diseases are represented by both wild animals (non-human primates (NHPs) and bats) and farmed animals (pigs and chicken). Against this background, poaching and the illegal trade of wild animals, on the one hand, and the destruction and degradation of habitats, on the other hand, have been identified as major risk factors in animal transmitted diseases.

As the world is facing a steady increase in zoonotic diseases in recent decades (SARS, MERS, Ebola, Wild Polio, and monkeypox), the origin of COVID-19 raises the issue of how we can prevent future pandemics. Against this backdrop, this chapter aims to underline the impact of habitat destruction and deforestation on the way that human beings interact with ecosystems, animals, and microbes.

In particular, it highlights what went wrong under the lens of environmental governance rules in preventing the spread of the current pandemic, and it analyzes the potential role of environmental law, particularly the wildlife trade regime, in averting future disease outbreaks after the COVID-19 experience.

This chapter demonstrates that environmental law – although not adequately focused on disease prevention compared to other sectors of international law – such as health law, can and must play a pivotal role in avoiding upcoming epidemics and pandemics. It illustrates that the current gaps of environmental law, particularly wildlife law, beget infectious disease outbreaks.

This chapter is based on the assumption that current wildlife law is not sufficiently equipped to treat infectious diseases and must necessarily be complemented by a linkage with other regimes, such as animal law and health law. Environmental

---

1 Christine K. Johnson et al., 'Global Shifts in Mammalian Population Trends Reveal Key Predictors of Virus Spillover Risk', *Proceedings of the Royal Society B* (8 April 2020), https://royalsocietypublishing.org/doi/10.1098/rspb.2019.2736.

DOI: 10.4324/9781003100645-4

law, it is argued, is weakened by a series of tenets concerning the relationship between humankind and nature. A critique of the state-of-the-art of international environmental law and zoonotic diseases leaves no doubt that a preventative approach must be adopted to address human vulnerability to infectious diseases.[2]

To this aim, I analyze the origins of SARS-CoV-2 and argue that the spillover (most likely in the wet market in Wuhan) was due to strictly interrelated reasons: first, habitat destruction, deforestation, and environmental degradation brings humans in direct contact with wild species otherwise relegated to tropical forests; second, the slaughtering and trading of wild species in wet markets is in complete disregard of animal welfare standards. This chapter contends that a global ban of wet markets is the best solution that would also mark a shift from anthropocentrism to an ecosystemic approach in line with the One Health concept.

2. The origins of COVID-19 and the limits of environmental law

Any disease agent that transfers from an animal source to humans is considered a zoonosis; 80% of emerging contagious diseases – such as Ebola, HIV/AIDS, SARS-CoV, MERS-CoV, COVID-19, and monkeypox – have a zoonotic source. Among them, 70% of zoonotic diseases originate from animals that usually live in tropical rainforests and have no close contact with human beings.[3] As previously outlined, zoonotic diseases are strictly related to the encroachment of wildlife habitats.[4]

The transmission (spillover) of a given disease can occur in a direct manner through high-risk activities such as hunting, farming, and butchering wildlife (e.g., HIV/AIDS and the "hunter's theory"), in an indirect manner from wildlife through wet markets, or from livestock through slaughterhouses.

Long after the COVID-19 pandemic emerged, the exact origin of the coronavirus still remains a subject of intense scientific debate. In this framework, the origin intersects the issue of the plausible transmission of the novel coronavirus (SARS-CoV-2) from animal to human in the wet market of Wuhan, probably through the pangolin[5] or the raccoon dog[6] ("intermediate host").

2 Patricia L. Farnese, "The Prevention Imperative: International Health and Environmental Governance Responses to Emerging Zoonotic Diseases", *Transnational Environmental Law* (2014): 285–309.
3 Nicolas De Sadeleer, Jacques Gofroid, "The Story Behind COVID-19: Animal Diseases at the Crossroads of Wildlife, Livestock and Human Health", *European Journal of Risk Regulation* 11 (2020): 210–227, at 221.
4 Bryony A. Jones et al., "Zoonosis Emergence Linked to Agricultural Intensification and Environmental Change", *Royal Society* 110 (21) (2013): 8399–8404.
5 Matthew C. Wong, Sara J. Javornik Cregeen, Nadim J. Ajami, Joseph F. Petrosino, "Evidence of Recombination in Coronaviruses Implicating Pangolin Origins of nCoV-2019", *bioRxiv* (2020): 1–9; Tommy Tsan-Yuk Lam et al., "Identifying SARS-CoV-2-Related Coronaviruses in Malayan Pangolins", *Nature* (2020): 282–285.
6 Smriti Mallapaty, "COVID-Origins Study Links Raccoon Dogs to Wuhan Market: What Scientists Think", *Nature* (2023): 771–773.

Bats are arguably reservoir hosts for SARS-CoV-2, whose natural cycle of infection takes place in a jungle habitat and involves monkeys and mosquitoes in tropical areas of China,[7] while the intermediate host – the Chinese Pangolin – may have facilitated transfer to humans. Chinese Pangolins are nocturnal mammals that are slaughtered for their meat, which is considered a delicacy, and for their scales, which are used as traditional medicine in South-East Asia. The wild meat of pangolins is usually sold in wet markets, which could have served as a possible ground zero for the virus.

In the scientific community, most agree that COVID-19 was the result of a natural spillover in the wet market of Wuhan, which was the pandemic epicenter,[8] and evidence clearly supports pangolin as an intermediate host.[9] A report in Science magazine confirms that the early epicenter of the COVID-19 pandemic was the seafood wholesale market in Wuhan.[10] In wet markets, wild animals often at risk of extinction are traded live and slaughtered on site, in full disregard of animal welfare standards. This strict contact between human beings and wild animals facilitates spillover, the process through which emerging infectious diseases that originate in wild animals are transmitted to human beings.

The already quoted work of Worobey et al. published in Science in 2022 clearly confirms that most of the human infections centered around the Huanan Seafood Wholesale Market, and through its analyses, it showed that the emergence of SARS-CoV-2 occurred through the live wildlife trade in China[11]

According to theories from political ecology, the dominant position of the natural spillover in the wet market of Wuhan (the "apolitical ecology perspective") following the chain of natural/animal and then cultural/human does

---

7 Alice Latinne, Ben Hu, Kevin J. Olival, Guangjian Zhu, Libiao Zhang, Hongying Li, Aleksei A. Chmura, Hume E. Field, Carlos Zambrana-Torrelio, Jonathan H. Epstein, Bei Li, Wei Zhang, Lin-Fa Wang, Zheng-Li Shi, Peter Daszak, "Origin and Cross-Species Transmission of Bat Coronaviruses in China", *Nature Communications* (2020): 1–15.

8 Jonathan E. Pekar, Andrew Magee, Edyth Parker, Niema Moshiri, Joel O. Werheim, "The Molecular Epidemiology of Multiple Zoonotic Origins of SARS-CoV-2", *Science* (2022): 960–966.

9 The Report of the WHO-China Joint Mission on the Novel Coronavirus denotes the zoonotic source of the virus. "Early Cases Identified in Wuhan are Believed to have Acquired Infection From a Zoonotic Source as Many Reported Visiting or Working in the Huanan Wholesale Seafood Market", *Report of the WHO-China Joint Mission on Coronavirus Disease 2019 (COVID-19)* (16–24 February 2020), at 1–40, at 10, https://www.who.int/docs/default-source/coronaviruse/who-china-joint-mission-on-covid-19-final-report.pdf. Another report by the WHO on the origins of COVID-19 highlights four scenarios: direct zoonotic transmission to humans (spillover); introduction through an intermediate host followed by spillover ("to be a likely to very likely pathway"); introduction through the (cold) food chain; and introduction through a laboratory incident (a very remote possibility). WHO-convened Global Study of Origins of SARS-CoV-2. Joint WHO-China Study, 14 January–10 February 2021, Joint Report.

10 Michael Worobey et al., "The Huanan Seafood Wholesale Market in Wuhan was the Early Epicenter of the COVID-19 Pandemic", *Science* (2022): 951–959.

11 *Supra*, footnote 10.

not represent, however, a full picture of the issue, but eventually tends to criminalize the Chinese culture.[12]

It could be argued that the emergence of the COVID-19 pandemic can be traced back to a certain way of how human societies relate to and alter their environment rather than to Chinese customs. Therefore, the major interactions between humans and animals, the growing contiguity of human settlements to natural reserves (including their steady decrease), and the raising of livestock in factory farms are all factors that have drastically increased the risk of zoonotic diseases.[13] In fact, human activities that alter the human environment – as affirmed by Wallace –[14] are the source of the novel coronavirus and of rising zoonotic diseases.

To date, environmental law has not managed to provide an answer to all of these issues related to the steady spread of infectious diseases and does not address in an appropriate manner – from the point of view of disease prevention – the interrelation between emerging zoonotic diseases and habitat degradation.[15]

In fact, explicit references to health in environmental treaties are scarce, except for the UNECE Protocol on Water and Health.[16] The most important biodiversity-related international agreement is the Convention on Biological Diversity (CBD), which aims toward "the conservation of biological diversity, the sustainable use of its components and the fair and equitable participation in the benefits derived from the use of genetic resources" (Preamble).[17]

12 Viktor Humpert, "A Political Ecology Perspective on the Origins of the COVID-19 Pandemic", (2021) https://degrowth.org/2021/05/18/a-political-ecology-perspective-on-the-origins-of-thecovid-19-pandemic/

13 Bryony A. Jones et al., "Zoonosis Emergence Linked to Agricultural Intensification and Environmental Change", *Proceedings of the National Academy of Sciences of the United States of America* (2013): 8399–8404.

14 Rob Wallace, *Dead Epidemiologists: On the Origins of COVID-19* (Monthly Review Press: 2020).

15 Patricia L. Farnese, "The Prevention Imperative: International Health and Environmental Governance Responses to Emerging Zoonotic Diseases", *Transnational Environmental Law* 3 (2) (2014): 285–309.

16 The Protocol on Water and Health to the 1992 Convention on the Protection and Use of Transboundary Watercourses and International Lakes was adopted in London on 17 June 1999 and entered into force on 9 August 2005. According to Article 1, "The objective of this Protocol is to promote at all appropriate levels, nationally as well as in transboundary and international contexts, the protection of human health and well-being, both individual and collective, within a framework of sustainable development, through improving water management, including the protection of water ecosystems, and through preventing, controlling and reducing water-related disease".

17 Under the CBD, conservation and sustainable use of natural resources are regarded as the main drivers of biodiversity policies. Article 6 of the CBD ("General Measures for Conservation and Sustainable Use"), states that "Each Contracting Party shall, in accordance with its particular conditions and capabilities: (a) Develop national strategies, plans or programmes for the conservation and sustainable use of biological diversity or adapt for this purpose existing strategies, plans or programmes which shall reflect, inter alia, the measures set out in this Convention relevant to the Contracting Party concerned; and (b) Integrate, as far as possible and as appropriate, the conservation and sustainable use of biological diversity into relevant sectoral or cross-sectoral plans, programmes and policies". On the CBD, see Elise Morgera, Jona Razzaque (eds.), *Biodiversity and Nature Protection Law* (Edward Elgar: 2017).

Despite its significant impact on the development of biodiversity law, the CBD has never taken into consideration zoonotic diseases and their linkage with biodiversity loss.

The Secretariat of the CBD has, however, acknowledged the strict inter-relation between wildlife consumption and the increase of zoonoses. The Technical Information on Biodiversity and Pandemics[18] reads as follows: "The hunting, trading, butchering and preparation of wildlife for consumption has led to a significant proportion of known zoonoses, emerging infectious dis-eases and pandemics such as Ebola virus disease, HIV/AIDS, Monkeypox, SARS and COVID-19" (Para. 15).

A reference to health is contained in the Cartagena Protocol on Biosafety (2000),[19] which is aimed at addressing some of the impacts of health and envi-ronment on modern biotechnology. The Protocol regulates the international transport and release of genetically modified organisms (GMOs) to protect natural biological diversity. It states in Article 1 that

> In accordance with the precautionary approach . . . the objective of this Protocol is to contribute to ensuring an adequate level of protection in the field of the safe transfer, handling and use of living modified organ-isms resulting from modern biotechnology that may have adverse effects on the conservation and sustainable use of biological diversity, taking also into account *risks to human health*, and specifically focusing on transboundary movements.

The Nagoya Protocol on Access and Benefit Sharing (2010) specifically recognizes in its Preamble the relevance of the IHR and "the importance of ensuring access to human pathogens for public health preparedness and response purposes".[20] Notably, Article 8(*b*) is relevant to disease outbreaks, stipulating that Parties shall

---

18 Note by the Executive Secretary, *CBD/SBSTTA-SBI-SS/2/INF/1* (2 December 2020), https://www.cbd.int/doc/c/2abd/08b3/123a81e9d2b3b9d6eb0dd9b8/sbstta-sbi-ss-02-inf-01-en.pdf.

19 The Cartagena Protocol on Biosafety to the Convention on Biological Diversity was adopted in Montreal on 29 January 2000 and entered into force on 11 September 2003.

20 The Nagoya Protocol on Access to Genetic Resources and the Fair and Equitable Sharing of Benefits Arising from their Utilization to the Convention on Biological Diversity was signed on 29 October 2010 and entered into force on 12 October 2014. The scope of the Protocol is stated in Article 3: "This Protocol shall apply to genetic resources within the scope of Article 15 of the Convention and to the benefits arising from the utilization of such resources. This Protocol shall also apply to traditional knowledge associated with genetic resources within the scope of the Convention and to the benefits arising from the utilization of such knowl-edge". See Claire Lajaunie, Serge Morand, "Nagoya Protocol and Infectious Diseases: Hin-drance or Opportunity?", *Frontiers in Public Health* (2020), https://www.frontiersin.org/articles/10.3389/fpubh.2020.00238/full; Ilja Richard Pavone, "Access & Benefit Sharing in the Nagoya Protocol: Implementation Progress and Gaps", *Anuário brasileiro de direito internacional* (2018): 129–154.

pay due regard to cases of present or imminent emergencies that threaten or damage human, animal or plant health, as determined nationally or internationally. Parties may take into consideration the need for expeditious access to genetic resources and expeditious fair and equitable sharing of benefits arising out of the use of such genetic resources.

3. The gaps of environmental law

The COVID-19 pandemic shed light on the limits of environmental law by drawing attention to the deep disconnection between human beings and nature and the way that we interact with the environment that surrounds us. The lack of an ecosystemic approach that recognizes the direct linkage among human health, animal health, and the protection of the environment is the main structural limit that must be reassessed.

In the next paragraphs, I analyze the gaps in wildlife law, since the illegal trade of most endangered species that can host dangerous pathogens in wet markets facilitates the spillover of zoonotic diseases. I also examine the gaps in forest law, since deforestation has led to the progressive retreat of the traditional buffer zones that keep animals and their pathogens separated from human beings.

3.1. Wildlife law

According to most scientists, enhanced predation of wildlife is leading several threatened species to the brink of extinction.[21] With Resolution 2136/2014 on the Democratic Republic of the Congo (30 January 2014), the Security Council identified illegal poaching as a source of illegal funding for international terrorism.[22]

The two pillars of the international regime on the protection of wildlife – which should avoid the extinction of most threatened species – are represented by multilateral environmental agreements (MEA): one is the Convention on

---

21 Richard Leakey, Roger Lewin, *The Sixth Extinction: Patterns of Life and the Future of Humankind* (Doubleday: 1995).

22 In the Preamble, the Security Council recognized "the linkage between the illegal exploitation of natural resources, including poaching and illegal trafficking of wildlife, illicit trade in such resources, and the proliferation and trafficking of arms as one of the major factors fuelling and exacerbating conflicts in the Great Lakes region of Africa". Then, the Security Council urged States to adopt specific financial and travel measures against "individuals or entities supporting armed groups in the DRC through illicit trade of natural resources, including gold or wildlife as well as wildlife products" (Para. 4, lect. g). Although illegal poaching itself was not expressly qualified as a "threat to peace and security", its consequences on regional security were, however, taken into consideration. For further details, see Anne Peters, "Novel Practice of the Security Council: Wildlife Poaching and Trafficking as a Threat to the Peace", *EJIL Talk* (12 February 2014), https://www.ejiltalk.org/novel-practice-of-the-security-council-wildlife-poaching-and-trafficking-as-a-threat-to-the-peace/.

International Trade in Endangered Species of Wild Fauna and Flora (CITES, Washington, 1973),[23] and the other is the Convention on the Conservation of Migratory Species of Wild Animals (CMS, Bonn, 1979).[24]

The UN Framework for the Immediate Socio-economic Response to COVID-19 (April 2020)[25] has underlined the key role of these agreements in tackling the COVID-19 pandemic (Para. 28).

In this framework, the Chinese Pangolin (*Manis pentadactyla*) is protected by CITES, and the international trade of this species is prohibited under this treaty.[26]

Appendix I of CITES provides protective measures to mitigate the potential negative impacts of illegal trade on the most threatened species. Exporters must fulfill restrictive conditions to export species listed in Appendix I. First, competent national authorities must provide a grant that verifies that the export will not be detrimental to the conservation of the species in question, that the live specimens were not obtained in violation of domestic laws, and that no risk of injury, damage to health, or cruel treatment during shipment has been guaranteed. Second, an exporter must present an export permit to the customs department of the recipient country. Finally, importation of species listed in Appendix I is also conditional upon a finding that the import will not be detrimental to the survival of the species, that minimum standards of housing and care are satisfied, and that the specimen will not be used for "primarily commercial purposes".

23 In general, on CITES, see Simon Lyster, *International Wildlife Law. An Analysis of International Treaties concerned with the Conservation of Wildlife* (Cambridge University Press: 2012).
24 Thomas G. Kelch, *Globalization and Animal Law: Comparative Law, International Law and International Trade* (Wolters Kluwer: 2011), 222.
25 https://unsdg.un.org/sites/default/files/2020–04/UN-framework-for-the-immediate-socio-economic-response-to-COVID-19.pdf.
26 The pangolin was originally included in Appendix II, https://cites.org/eng/app/index.php, namely, "the lists of species that are not necessarily now threatened with extinction but that may become so unless trade is closely controlled". Appendix I encompasses "all species threatened with extinction which are or may be affected by trade". Trade in Appendix I-species may be authorized only in "exceptional circumstances" (Art. II (1) CITES). Appendix II lists less endangered species and allows under exceptional circumstances their international trade. At the 17th Meeting of COP 17 in Johannesburg in 2016, Bangladesh proposed to transfer all 8 species of pangolins to Appendix I of CITES. https://cites.org/sites/default/files/eng/cop/17/prop/060216/E-CoP17-Prop-08.pdf. The eight species are: *Manis crassicaudata, Manis culionensis, Manis gigantean, Manis javanica, Manis pentadactyla, Manis temminckii, Manis tetradactyla,* and *Manis tricuspis.* The proposal for amendment was eventually approved by a two-thirds majority as envisaged under Article XV, Paragraph 1, lect. *b.* Article XV, Paragraph 2, lect. *b* states that "Amendments shall be adopted by a two-thirds majority of Parties present and voting. For these purposes 'Parties present and voting' means Parties present and casting an affirmative or negative vote. Parties abstaining from voting shall not be counted among the two-thirds required for adopting an amendment". *Amendment to Appendices I and II of the Convention Adopted by the Conference of the Parties at Its 17th Meeting, Johannesburg (South Africa)* (24 September–4 October 2016), https://cites.org/sites/default/files/notif/E-Notif-2016–063.pdf.

However, the illegal trade of the pangolin species has not diminished: as shown by a report from the Wildlife Justice Commission issued in February 2020,[27] despite the upgrade of pangolin to Appendix I of CITES, there was a rapid growth in the industrial scale of illegal trafficking of pangolin scales in the period of 2016–2019.

In a press statement issued on 22 April 2020,[28] the United Nations Office on Drugs and Crime (UNODC) clearly affirmed that pangolins are

the most trafficked mammal in the world, with seizures of illegal cargo originating in Africa and intended for Asian markets having increased tenfold since 2014. Between 2014 and 2018, the equivalent of 370,000 pangolins were seized globally, suggesting that millions have been trafficked and killed.[29]

Furthermore, the horseshoe bat – a virus reservoir – is not listed under CITES (and the raccoon dog, one of the plausible intermediate hosts, is not listed). CITES' listing mechanism does not take into account the potential risk of transmission of disease from animal to human beings of a given species, and the inclusion of an animal in Appendixes I, II, or III is exclusively based on its vulnerability to extinction.

The UNODC Executive Director Ghada Waly expressly stated that

Wildlife crime endangers the health of our planet – and our own health. Pangolins offer no threat to humans in their own habitat, but allowing them to be trafficked, slaughtered and sold in illicit markets along with other wild species greatly increases the risk of transmission of viruses and other pathogens. For the sake of preserving biodiversity and preventing the next public health emergency, the illegal wildlife trade must stop.[30]

CITES, is not, however, the most appropriate legal instrument to prevent zoonoses for several reasons. First, it is not preventative, because it does not address the root causes of habitat destruction or illegal trade. Second, it does not list species on health grounds or on their potentiality to transmit infectious diseases to human beings.[31] Third, it does not consider animal welfare issues.

27 https://www.prnewswire.com/in/news-releases/the-trafficking-of-pangolin-scales-must-be-tackled-as-a-transnational-organised-crime-says-new-report-from-the-wildlife-justice-commission-839709132.html.
28 UNODC, "Wildlife Trafficking Harms Animals and Human Health: The Case of Pangolins".
29 https://www.unodc.org/unodc/press/releases/2020/April/wildlife-trafficking-harms-animals-and-human-health_-the-case-of-pangolins.html.
30 https://www.unodc.org/documents/press/releases/Pangolins_WCR2020_press_release.pdf.
31 Stefan Borsky, Hannah Hennighausen, Andrea Leiter, Keith Williges, "CITES and the Zoonotic Disease Content in International Wildlife Trade", *Environmental and Resource Economics* (2020): 1001–1017.

Currently, wildlife law has a single species approach (special protection is afforded to species threatened with extinction), and its rules address populations (or ecosystems) to be conserved and does not treat individual conditions or suffering. Welfare issues deserve some attention only from the moment in which wild animals are caught by humans and are extracted from the wild (and this is the case of the gear entanglement of whales).[32]

There is another issue related to the structural limits of CITES, since it only applies to the import and export of endangered species and does not cover domestic trade. That is, CITES does not apply to internal trade with a transboundary dimension and currently, does not cover the domestic Chinese trade of endangered species, meaning that it operates primarily at the borders. Trade is defined as "export, re-export, import and introduction from the sea" (Art. 1, lect. *c*). The entire trade control system of CITES was not able to effectively prevent the domestic trafficking of pangolins and to avert the transmission of SARS-CoV-2 from animals to humans. The main issue is therefore a correct implementation of environmental treaties at the domestic level. In light of the business behind wet markets, it is plausible to argue that the Chinese government has not adopted incisive legislative measures aimed at fighting the illegal trade of pangolin but rather has tolerated such practice.[33] The same pangolin is protected under Chinese law and particularly, by the CITES implementation law. Article VIII of CITES explicitly states that the Parties shall "take appropriate measures to enforce the provisions of the present Convention and to prohibit trade in specimens in violation thereof"; it should also include criminal sanctions on both the trade and illegal detention/custody of species protected under CITES.

Therefore, one might assume that China has violated its treaty obligations, and here originates the core issue on the implementation gap of environmental law and in the specific case of wildlife law. The Chinese legislation, well before the disease outbreak, already envisaged that wild animals traded in wet markets should be subjected to appropriate supervision and control by local authorities concerning the respect for food safety rules.

3.2. *Forest law*

Tropical rainforests are a reservoir of biological diversity and sinks for the absorption of CO2. The FAO Global Forest Resources Assessment 2020

---

32 The WOAH (*World Organization for Animal Health*) has approved a specific code (*Terrestrial Animal Code*), and the WTO has enacted the well-known "Agreement on Sanitary and Phytosanitary Measures", whose goal is "to restrict the use of unjustified sanitary and phytosanitary measures for the purpose of trade protection".

33 On 24 February 2020, the Chinese government announced the Decision on Completely Prohibiting the Illegal Wildlife Trade, Eliminating the Bad Habit of Indiscriminately Eating Wild Animals, and Truly Ensuring the Health and Safety of the People (the text in Chinese can be found here, https://perma.cc/5LQV-AEB5); see Amanda Whitfort, "COVID-19 and Wildlife Farming in China: Legislating to Protect Wild Animal Health and Welfare in the Wake of a Global Pandemic", *Journal of Environmental Law* (2021): 57–84.

showed that – despite legal efforts – deforestation continues globally at a rate of 10 million hectares a year.[34]

Furthermore, deforestation has direct and indirect effects on human health since global warming promotes the habitat of insect disease vectors – such as mosquitos – that cause malaria global warming, and desertification.

A survey on large-scale deforestation in West and Central Africa carried out from 2001 to 2014 highlighted that the spillover of the Ebola virus was directly related to the destruction of natural habitats and forest clearance.[35]

Deforestation particularly plays a pivotal role in the emergence and re-emergence of infectious diseases originating from wild animals, since it exposes individuals to microbes or disease vectors otherwise confined to tropical rainforests. Specifically, in tropical areas, forest harvesting has been related to an increase in contagious diseases such as malaria, dengue fever, and yellow fever.[36]

Climate change thus further promotes disease spillover, since it provides vulnerable conditions for diverse infectious diseases born by water, air, and food.[37]

Deforestation, global warming, and contagious diseases are therefore intertwined, since tropical rainforests act as both carbon sinks and a barrier against microbes.

Moreover, natural environmental disasters can facilitate the spread of diseases but with a minor impact. The theory that the diffusion of contagious diseases is significantly affected by climatic cycles such as the El Niño-Southern Oscillation has been advanced by several scientists in the context of cholera outbreaks.[38]

As outlined by Fidler, human history is characterized by the interaction with pathogenic microbes related to the alteration of the environment.[39]

---

34 http://www.fao.org/forest-resources-assessment/2020. However, the deforestation rate diminished to 20% compared to the previous period of 2010–2015 in line with the establishment of the Aichi Biodiversity Targets, even if this low reduction is strongly related to the decline in forest expansion. Positive examples of reforestation and a halt to forest harvesting are represented by the cases of Côte d'Ivoire, Ghana (from 2018 to 2019, the rate of forest loss was reduced by around 50% in both countries), and Indonesia.

35 Jesús Olivero, John E. Fa, Raimundo Real, Ana L. Márquez, Miguel A. Farfán, J. Mario Vargas, David Gaveau, Mohammad A. Salim, Douglas Park, Jamison Suter, Shona King, Siv Aina Leendertz, Douglas Sheil, Robert Nasi, "Recent Loss of Closed Forests is Associated with Ebola Virus Disease Outbreaks", *Scientific Reports* (2017): 1–9.

36 https://www.nationalgeographic.com/science/article/deforestation-leading-to-more-infectious-diseases-in-humans.

37 Asim Anwar, Sajid Anwar, Muhammad Ayub, Faisal Nawaz, Shabir Hyder, Noman Khan, Imran Malik, "Climate Change and Infectious Diseases: Evidence from Highly Vulnerable Countries", *Iranian Journal of Public Health* 48 (12) (2019): 2187–2195.

38 Rita R. Colwell, "Global Climate and Infectious Disease: The Cholera Paradigm", *Science* 274 (1996): 2025–2031.

39 David P. Fidler, "Microbialpolitik: Infectious Diseases and International Relations", *American University International Law Review* (1998): 1–53, at 23.

Environmental policies to address forest depletion and deforestation are based on the creation of protected areas, restoration, and combating desertification. Actions to promote sustainable resource and habitat management are grounded on the responsibilization of local communities.

At the Earth Summit of 1992 (Rio Conference – UNCED),[40] which marked the beginning of the process of "environmental globalism"[41] with the adoption of the two landmark conventions on biological diversity and climate change, States failed to agree on a binding treaty on tropical forests alone.

Developing countries from Latin America and South-East Asia, in particular Brazil and Malaysia, leveled strong opposition. Environmental nationalism was the reply of developing countries belonging to the "megadiversity countries" to pressures from the industrialized world.[42]

In general, developing countries were reluctant to agree on a trade-off between economic development and the environment – which is at the core of the concept of sustainable development – imposed by developed countries unless they bestow substantial financial aid.

Concern for deforestation and the encroachment of natural habitats was raised at UNCED due to the failure of previous global efforts. Against this background, the Tropical Forest Action Plan (TFAP, 1985) and the International Tropical Timber Organization (ITTO, 1986) had a limited impact on deforestation's rates. The Statement on Forest Principles (SFP)[43] alongside Chapter 11 of Agenda 21 devoted to deforestation (Combating Deforestation) should have served as building blocks for the adoption of a binding treaty on forests. Despite these initiatives, a binding treaty on forests – which

---

40 United Nations Conference on Environment and Development (UNCED). The outcome of the Conference was represented by two binding treaties (Convention on Biological Diversity and the United Nations Framework Convention on Climate Change), a declaration (the Declaration on Environment and Development, or Rio Declaration), a programme of action (Agenda 21) and a statement (The Non-Legally Binding Authoritative Statement of Principles for a Global Consensus on the Management, Conservation and Sustainable Development of all Types of Forests). See Patricia Birnie, Alan Boyle, Catherine Redgwell, *International Law & the Environment* (Oxford University Press: 2008), 50–53; Malgosia Fitzmaurice, S. Maljean-Dubois, Stefania Negri (eds), *Environmental Protection and Sustainable Development from Rio to Rio+20* (Brill/Martinus Nijhoff Publishers: 2014).

41 In this sense, see Sergio Marchisio, Giovanni Cordini, Paolo Fois, *Diritto ambientale. Profili internazionali europei e comparati* (Giappichelli: 2017).

42 Andrew Huller, "The Politics of Amazonian Deforestation", *Journal of Latin American Studies* (1991): 197–215.

43 The Non-Legally Binding Authoritative Statement of Principles for a Global Consensus on the Management, Conservation and Sustainable Development of All Types of Forests. Preamble, lect. (b) states, "The guiding objective of these principles is to contribute to the management, conservation and sustainable development of forests and to provide for their multiple and complementary functions and uses".

should recognize the link between a loss of biodiversity and emerging diseases – is still elusive.[44]

The need to balance environmental protection, economic development, and traditional uses (such as hunting) is, however, evident from lect. (*c*) of the Preamble of the SFP:

> Forestry issues and opportunities should be examined in a holistic and balanced manner within the *overall context of environment and development*, taking into consideration the multiple functions and uses of forests, *including traditional uses*, and the likely economic and social stress when these uses are constrained or restricted, as well as the potential for development that sustainable forest management can offer.

Among the core principles, it is clearly recognized that States have

> in accordance with the Charter of the United Nations and the principles of international law, *the sovereign right to exploit their own resources pursuant to their own environmental policies* and have the responsibility to ensure that activities within their jurisdiction or control do not cause damage to the environment of other States or of areas beyond the limits of national jurisdiction.
>
> (Art. 1, lect. *a*)[45]

The SFP does not mention the threat of infectious diseases, although one might not consider public health among the "significant adverse impacts" subjected to environmental impact assessment (principle 8 *h*).

The Aichi Biodiversity Targets, which were promoted by the CBD and consist of 20 specific targets to address and mitigate biodiversity loss across the globe, provide little guidance for the problems related to deforestation and emerging infectious diseases. Against this backdrop, Target Number 5 envisaged that "by 2020, the rate of loss of all natural habitats, including forests, is at least halved and, where feasible, brought close to zero, and degradation and

---

44 Jeff Tollefson, "Why Deforestation and Extinctions Make Pandemics More Likely", *Nature* (7 August 2020): 175–176.
45 The same wording is present in Article 3 of the CBD: "States have, in accordance with the Charter of the United Nations and the principles of international law, the sovereign right to exploit their own resources pursuant to their own environmental policies, and the responsibility to ensure that activities within their jurisdiction or control do not cause damage to the environment of other States or of areas beyond the limits of national jurisdiction".

fragmentation are significantly reduced". As highlighted in the Global Biodiversity Outlook (2020),

> The recent rate of deforestation is lower than that of the previous decade, but only by about one third, and deforestation may be accelerating again in some areas. Loss, degradation and fragmentation of habitats remains high in forest and other biomes, especially in the most biodiversity-rich ecosystems in tropical regions. Wilderness areas and global wetlands continue to decline. Fragmentation of rivers remains a critical threat to freshwater biodiversity.[46]

The Glasgow Leaders' Declaration on Forests and Land Use (2022)[47] fails to mention the relationship between deforestation and the spillover of infectious diseases. The Declaration's signatories include megadiverse countries such as Brazil, the Democratic Republic of the Congo, and Indonesia; they have committed to work collectively to halt and reverse forest loss and land degradation by 2030 while delivering sustainable development and promoting an inclusive rural transformation. This Declaration, however, recognizes the crucial role of tackling forest loss and land degradation in order to address climate change, biodiversity decline, and sustainable development. In particular, States committed to "conserve forests and other terrestrial ecosystems and accelerate their restoration" (Para. 1).

After examining the root causes of zoonotic diseases, in the next paragraphs, I focus my attention on the problem of wet markets and outline possible solutions (such as a global ban).

4. The problem of wet markets and the lack of a global ban

For centuries, human beings have exploited wildlife for food, skin, and trade. The over-exploitation of some species of wildlife has brought them to the brink of extinction. The unsustainable use of most endangered animals is damaging to their survival and has strong consequence on the environment and human health.[48] The sustainable use of biodiversity is one of the key pillars of the CBD. This principle also encompasses the sustainable use of wildlife since they are a source of sustenance for several indigenous peoples and local communities (IPLCs) and a food delicacy for local populations especially in South-East Asia.

The principle of sustainable use of biodiversity does not question, however, meat consumption and, therefore, wet markets. As previously stated,

---

46 https://www.cbd.int/gbo/.
47 26th UN Climate Change Conference of the Parties (COP26) in Glasgow on 31 October – 13 November 2021.
48 The most endangered species are included in the IUCN Red List of Threatened Species, https://www.iucnredlist.org/resources/summary-statistics.

environmental law – in addition to animal law – are grounded on the logic of the priority of human beings over animals and the fact that humans are morally superior to animals. The prohibition of such markets is thus an issue that is part of the margin of appreciation that each State enjoys, although there are global guidelines and standards that deal with such a topic.[49]

The key problem is related to the lack of a binding treaty that would explicitly ban the wet markets themselves or the trade, breeding, or consumption of some wild species based on public health reasons.

A global ban on the wildlife trade only for food consumption (which would allow trade for other uses, such as traditional medicine, animal research, zoo animals, and pets) would be a concrete policy option.[50] This has already been indirectly envisaged in the WHO recommendations to reduce the risk of transmission of emerging pathogens from animals to humans in live animal markets or animal product markets (26 March 2020; the WHO also recommends avoiding the consumption of raw or undercooked animal products).[51]

Against this backdrop, the European Union, within the context of the negotiation of a new pandemic treaty, has supported the idea of a specific ban on wet markets and envisages incentives for countries to report new viruses or variants.[52]

A global ban of wildlife markets is not, however, without criticism for being over-simplistic. Some scholars have argued that wildlife-oriented solutions are not enough to prevent future pandemics, since they do not provide a full narrative of the problem.[53] A ban or blanket prohibition would only divert the attention away from the real issue represented by the asymmetric relationship between human beings and the environment. Second, many zoonotic diseases have spread in farm animals and not in wildlife markets, such as the H1N1 influenza pandemic, North American pig farms, and mad cow disease. Third, illegal trade would be boosted, which implies reinforcing the verification mechanism in CITES.

Paradoxically, indirect protection can have a major impact in terms of improvement of both animal welfare and conservation; the problem lies in the fact that current wildlife law fails to provide a response to the problem of wet markets and the domestic illegal trade of wildlife.

---

49 See, for instance, the WHO global strategy for food safety. Reducing public health risks associated with the sale of live wild animals of mammalian species in traditional food markets – infection prevention and control (2022).

50 In this sense, see A. Alonso Aguirre, Richard Catherina, Hailey Frye, Louise Shelley, "Illicit Wildlife Trade, Wet Markets, and COVID-19: Preventing Future Pandemics", *World Medical and Health Policy* (2020): 256–265.

51 https://apps.who.int/iris/handle/10665/332217.

52 https://www.euractiv.com/section/global-europe/news/eu-wants-pandemic-treaty-to-ban-wet-markets-reward-virus-detection/.

53 Evan A. Eskew, Colin J. Carlson, "Overselling Wildlife Trade Bans will not Bolster Conservation or Pandemic Preparedness", *The Lancet Planetary Health* 4 (6) (2020): 215–216.

Against this backdrop, the WHO, the World Organization for Animal Health (founded as OIE) and the United Nations Environment Programme (UNEP) exhorted Member States to temporarily suspend the sales of wild mammals at food markets.[54] However, the WHO, in recognizing the role of wet markets in providing local communities with safe and nutritious food, has not supported the policy of a global ban but rather a simple moratorium.

The WHO, OIE and UNEP, in applying the precautionary principle, called on

> all national competent authorities to *suspend* the *trade* in live caught wild animals of mammalian species for food or breeding and *close sections of food markets selling live caught wild animals* of mammalian species *as an emergency measure* unless demonstrable effective regulations and adequate risk assessment are in place.
>
> (Recommendation 1)

These emergency measures should have a temporary nature to allow domestic authorities to conduct a risk assessment[55] of each market "to identify critical areas and practices that contribute to the transmission of zoonotic pathogens".

These provisional rules should verify whether wild animals are illegally caught and introduced to wildlife farms and whether required food safety, hygiene, and environmental standards are respected.

Recommendation 2 calls upon States to improve "standards of hygiene and sanitation in traditional food markets to reduce the risk of transmission of zoonotic diseases and person-to person transmission of disease".

This can be particularly challenging in low- and middle-income countries and remote regions, where such markets are important in food distribution systems and are part of cultural traditions, as resources to detect and monitor infectious diseases are often scarce.

The WHO introduced the concept of *Healthy Food Markets*[56] and set the target of improving standards of hygiene and sanitation with a view of avoiding future disease outbreaks related to the lack of compliance with basic food safety requirements.

In this regard, guidelines that establish minimum hygienic requirements have already been enacted within the context of FAO: these are the General Principles for Food Hygiene contained in the Codex Alimentarius,[57] which are

---

54 Reducing public health risks associated with the sale of live wild animals of mammalian species in traditional food markets. Interim guidance, 12 April 2021.

55 An environmental risk assessment evaluates the quantitative and qualitative characteristics of the environment to highlight the risk to the environment and human health due to the potential presence or use of specific pollutants.

56 WHO, *A Guide to Healthy Food Markets* (2006), https://www.who.int/foodsafety/publications/capacity/healthymarket_guide.pdf.

57 Tom Heilandt, "Codex Alimentarius: Safe, Good Food for Everyone – Everywhere", in Cinzia Caporale, Ilja Richard Pavone, Maria Pia Ragionieri (eds.), *International Food Law* (Wolter Kluwers: 2021), 91–111.

based on two concepts: Good Hygienic Practices (GHP) for specific foods and the Hazard Analysis Critical Control Point (HACCP) system. "Food hygiene" has been defined by the Codex as "all conditions and measures necessary to ensure the safety and suitability of food at all stages of the food chain". GHP can therefore be considered "all practices regarding the conditions and measures necessary to ensure the safety and suitability of food at all stages of the food chain".

However, as I have clarified in this chapter, the interaction between humans and wild animals creates a major risk of transmission of zoonotic diseases. Therefore, in the next section, I argue that a global ban of wet markets could be the more practical solution to prevent a new pandemic, although as shown by the political ecology work, wet markets are only the tip of an iceberg and have their roots in the encroachment of the environment and in capitalistic society.

5. A global ban of wet markets and the One Health approach

The prohibition of wet markets, although not in line with the WHO's position and highly problematic for its conflict with local traditions, is consistent with an emerging principle in international environmental law, which has not yet been codified in any treaty or convention, namely, the *One Health Concept*. As is well-known, this concept aims to reconcile human health, environmental protection, and animal welfare.[58] The One Health paradigm was developed in the aftermath of the 2003 outbreak of SARS and in due course by the diffusion of the highly pathogenic avian influenza H5N1.[59] The series of strategic goals known as the "Manhattan Principles", drafted by the Wildlife Conservation Society in 2004, plainly acknowledge the strict interrelation between human and animal health and the threats of zoonotic diseases to food supply and the economy.[60]

The One Health paradigm acts as a "boundary object",[61] which is defined as a multi-interpretable concept that is "both plastic enough to adapt to the local needs and the constraints of the several parties employing them, yet robust enough to maintain a common identity across sites".[62]

58 Arne Ruckert, Kate Zinszer, Christina Zarowsky, Ronald Labonté, Hélène Carabin, "What Role for One Health in the COVID-19 Pandemic?" *Canadian Journal of Public Health* 111 (2020): 641–644.

59 John S. Mackenzie, Martyn Jeggo, "The One Health Approach – Why is It So Important?", *Tropical Medicine and Infectious Disease* (2019): 88–92.

60 Wildlife Conservation Society One World-One Health: Building Interdisciplinary Bridges. http://www.oneworldonehealth.org/sept2004/owoh_sept04.html.

61 Aline Lebeuf, "Making Sense of One Health: Cooperating at the Human-Animal-Ecosystem Health Interface", *Health and Environment Reports, No. 7* (April 2011), https://www.ifri.org/sites/default/files/atoms/files/ifrihereport7alineleboeuf.pdf.

62 Susan Leigh Star, James R. Griesemer, "Institutional Ecology, Translations' and Boundary Objects: Amateurs and Professionals in Berkeley's Museum of Vertebrate Zoology", *Social Studies of Science* (1989): 387–420.

The Global Biodiversity Outlook 5 recognizes the prevention role of One Health stating that "the risk of future pandemics could be reduced through a more integrated, cross-sectoral and inclusive One Health approach that builds the health and resilience of people and the planet".[63]

The One Health Joint Plan of Action (2022–2026) clearly indicates that "Environmental degradation caused by human activities poses several health threats that are invariably complex and rooted in how humans interact with and use the environment".[64]

Currently, however, international action towards its codification remains primarily aspirational and is relegated to the realm of doctrinal debate. The only treaty based on this principle is the WTO Agreement on the Application of Sanitary and Phytosanitary Measures (1995) (SPS Agreement), which recognizes the right of States Parties to "to take sanitary and phytosanitary measures necessary for the protection of human, animal or plant life or health" (Art. 2).

UNEP, however, adopted on 7 March 2022 a resolution grounded on the One Health concept,[65] which established for the first time animal welfare's role in sustainability.

The adoption of this resolution is a milestone, since it underlines the necessity of a holistic approach to global health that recognizes the nexus among animal welfare, sustainable development, and human health. Such interdependence is recognized in the Preamble, which reads as follows: "acknowledging that animal welfare can contribute to addressing environmental challenges, promoting the One Health approach and achieving the Sustainable Development Goals"; "Noting that the health and welfare of animals, sustainable development and the environment are connected to human health and well-being".[66]

The WHO CA+ first recognizes in the Preamble that "most emerging infectious diseases originate in animals, including wildlife and domesticated animals, then spill over to people" (Para. 23) and then reaffirms the importance of a One Health approach and the need for "synergies between multisectoral and cross-sectoral collaboration at the national, regional, and international levels to safeguard human health, detect and prevent health threats at the animal and human interface, in particular zoonotic spill-over and mutations,

---

63 Secretariat of the Convention on Biological Diversity (2020) Global Biodiversity Outlook 5. Montreal (2020), https://www.cbd.int/gbo/gbo5/publication/gbo-5-en.pdf.

64 FAO, UNEP, WHO, and WOAH. "One Health Joint Plan of Action (2022–2026)", *Working Together for the Health of Humans, Animals, Plants and the Environment, Rome* (2022), https://www.woah.org/app/uploads/2022/04/one-health-joint-plan-of-action-final.pdf.

65 Resolution adopted by the United Nations Environment Assembly on 2 March 2022, "5/4. Animal welfare–environment–sustainable development nexus".

66 On the necessity to recognize a major role of animal welfare in biodiversity law and wildlife law, see Guillaume Futhazar, "Biodiversity, Species Protection, and Animal Welfare Under International Law", in Anne Peters (ed.), *Studies in Global Animal Law* (Springer Open: 2020), 95–108.

and to sustainably balance and optimize the health of people, animals and ecosystems" (Para. 26).

Article 18, Paragraph 3 of the WHO CA+ is quite relevant, since it affirms that

> the Parties will identify and integrate into relevant pandemic prevention and preparedness plans interventions that address the drivers of the emergence and re-emergence of disease at the human animal-environment interface, including but not limited to climate change, land use change, wildlife trade, desertification and antimicrobial resistance.

As underlined by some scholars, in addition to the lack of binding norms, there is also a shortage of an adequate ethical reflection, since environmental law has and continues to have an anthropocentric setting.[67]

The conflict of values among human health, animal welfare, and environmental protection raises practical dilemmas. A zoonotic disease control strategy can imply serious conflicts of interest between public health institutions, on the one hand, and the agri-food industry, on the other hand, and with cultural traditions such as wet markets. It is worth recalling that One Health strategies can imply the culling of healthy animals, and there is thus not yet a balance of values since human health always prevails over animal welfare.

This is exactly what happened in Denmark, where the government decided to cull millions of minks, which are raised for their pelts, after a mutated version of COVID-19 was discovered in this species (it was probably transmitted to the animals by an infected operator). This event has raised a debate on the necessity to ban the fur industry.[68]

This situation has once again revealed the prevalence of the economic interests of human beings (in the specific case of mink breeders) over animal welfare and the fact that animal law does not question the human exploitation of animals. However, the existing interpretations of the One Health concept neither in legal documents nor in the doctrinal debate address in an appropriate manner the current moral dilemmas.[69]

6. Conclusions

The COVID-19 pandemic has put a spotlight on the necessity to address the biodiversity crisis along with the climate crisis, the necessity to protect

---

67 Joost van Herten, Bernice Bovenkerk, Marcel Verweij, "One Health as a Moral Dilemma: Towards a Socially Responsible Zoonotic Disease Control", *Zoonoses and Public Health* (2019): 26–34.
68 Kitty Block, Sara Amundson, "Now is the Time for Countries Across the World to Ban Fur", *A Human World* (2021), https://blog.humanesociety.org/2021/06/now-is-the-time-for-countries-across-the-world-to-ban-fur.html.
69 Benjamin Capps, "One Health Ethics", *Bioethics* (2020): 348–355.

animal welfare, and the need for substantial changes in global environmental policies.[70]

Although the COVID-19 pandemic cannot be considered a "food safety issue" *strictu sensu*, its origin is directly related to the food chain, the lack of respect for animal welfare standards, and environmental degradation.

Despite growing societal concerns for animals, incremental legal reforms, and new advances in moral and political philosophy, our relationship with animals remains inherently hostile by far. Whether it is concentrated animal feeding operations (CAFOs), live animal markets, or habitat destruction, we keep animals in conditions of systemic and ongoing exploitation. In countries around the world, the demand for animal meat rises as the world population increases. Animal welfare concerns are also gaining more attention as consumers perceive the links among animal health, animal welfare, and human well-being. The challenge is how to combine the unavoidable increase in food animal production while simultaneously ensuring high animal welfare standards and protecting food security.

The ongoing pandemic has put a spotlight on the interface between the health of humans and animals and the protection of the environment.

The problem is how to reach the vision behind the common target agreed by world governments for 2050, "Living in Harmony with Nature", given the lack of both a strong environmental and health governance. A "solution scan" drafted by a team of scientists and zoologists[71] has advanced the proposal to reinforce the One Health approach in its normative dimension.[72] The practical issue lies, however, in the difficulty to conciliate different moral views and to adopt a shared and globally accepted definition of One Health. Furthermore, some environmentalists might criticize this approach: formally linking human health to the encroachment of natural habitats could be considered the outcome of an anthropocentric view.

A practical solution to solve the moral dilemma of the conflicting interests between humans and animals could be to adopt as a philosophical

---

70 United Nations Decade on Biodiversity, "Government Pandemic Spending Measures Continue to Harm Biodiversity. UN Biodiversity Convention Discusses Biodiversity, One Health and Response to COVID-19" (15 December 2020), https://www.cbd.int/doc/press/2020/pr-2020-12-15-sbstta-sbi-en.pdf.

71 Silviu Petrovan, David C. Aldridge, Harriet Bartlett, Andrew Bladon, Hollie Booth, Steven Broad, Donald M. Broom, Neil D. Burgess, Sarah Cleaveland, Andrew A. Cunningham, "Post COVID-19: A Solution Scan of Options for Preventing Future Zoonotic Epidemics", *Biological Reviews of the Cambridge Philosophical Society* (2021): 2694–2715. The solution scan started as a collaboration between the Biosecurity Research Initiative at St. Catharine's College (Cambridge University) and the Conservation Evidence headed by the Department of Zoology (Cambridge University).

72 In this sense, see Katharina Braun, "COVID-19, People, and Other Animals. The 'One Health' Approach in Light of COVID-19", *Völkerrechtsblog* (12 November 2020), https://voelkerrechtsblog.org/covid-19-people-and-other-animals/.

underpinning of any future reform of environmental treaties the principle of "two factor egalitarianism" developed by VanDeVeer.[73]

Van DeVeer suggests that – with the goal of promoting overall utility – a hierarchy between the interests of human and animals should be made. According to him, peripheral interest of humans do not prevail as a matter of principle over basic interests of animals. Only in the case of a clash between basic interests, those of humans shall prevail, since they are beings with more complex psychological capacities and therefore deserve a greater moral weight.

After having agreed on its ethical basis, future reforms could act as the fixture between the three elements of One Health (human health, environmental protection, and animal welfare).[74] A potential treaty or additional protocol to CITES based on the One Health paradigm should envisage a global ban of wet markets to avert future pandemics (although the WHO, as already underlined, did not back this option but rather recommended a moratorium). A global ban would be the outcome of the request of global animal welfare standards and would indeed reinforce both animal law and environmental law. The problem is that the WHO Pandemic Agreement (version of 16 October 2023) refers only to the duty "to strengthen animal disease preventive measures and monitor and mitigate environmental factors associated with the risk of zoonotic disease spill-over and spill-back" (Art. 4, Para, 4, *e*), and it neither mentions wet markets nor prohibits them.

A wet market global ban has met strong resistance from developing countries as it contrasts with the respect for their cultural traditions, since wet markets are a consolidated custom. Once again, there is a sharp contrast between animal welfare and cultural or religious traditions, as raised with reference to the issue of ritual slaughtering, and the economic factor, since wet markets are a source of financial gain.[75]

However, a global ban could easily be achieved through an additional protocol to CITES that should fix stricter regulation of the domestic trade of endangered species. Large-scale trafficking of wildlife should be addressed at the same level of transnational organized crime, and CITES should be provided additional powers to investigate illegal trade at the domestic level, which is the main gap of this treaty.

The narrow scope of CITES – and particularly, its limited focus on the international trade of endangered species – has raised a debate on a potential

---

73 Donald VanDeVeer, "Interspecific Justice", *Inquiry: An Interdisciplinary Journal of Philosophy* (1979): 55–79.
74 Alexandra L. Phelan, Lawrence O. Gostin, "Law as a Fixture Between the One Health Interfaces of Emerging Diseases", *Transactions of The Royal Society of Tropical Medicine and Hygiene* 111 (6) (2017): 241–243.
75 On ritual slaughtering, see Anne Peters, "Religious Slaughter and Animal Welfare Revisited: CJEU, Liga van Moskeeën en islamitische Organisaties Provincie Antwerpen (2018)", *Derecho Animal* (2019): 27–39.

amendment to address health risks.[76] One suggestion might be to draft a new appendix that strictly regulates trade not only of endangered species but also of the species whose illegal trade might put human or animal health at risk through the transmission of zoonosis (a zoonosis protocol). An amendment to CITES could include a new appendix listing species at a high risk of propagating zoonotic diseases aside from the level of threat or conservation status.

More generally, the most appropriate option to avert future pandemics may be inter-regime linkage ("interregime linkages", a term coined by Young to address the "interplay among distinguishable, institutional arrangements").[77] Against this backdrop, a reinforcement not only of environmental law and health law but also of global animal law would be helpful.[78]

Since the legal regime of the WHO is not sealed or self-contained, it must be supported by other norms of international law, such as human rights law, environmental law, humanitarian law, and trade law.[79] A theoretical division of tasks within international law – based on the concept of inter-regime linkage – might be the following: environmental law should address the root causes of zoonotic diseases, while health law and human rights law should direct in an appropriate manner the management and containment of a disease outbreak.

Radical solutions – such as the closure of all wet markets – are necessary and cannot be postponed. This does not mean, however, diverting attention away from the causes of the rapid spread of zoonotic diseases, which are connected to factors such as environmental degradation, habitat destruction, and deforestation, or failing to search for an appropriate answer through environmental law.

---

76 Dan Ashe, John Scanlon, "A Crucial Step Towards Preventing Wild-Life Related Pandemics", *Scientific American* (2020), https://www.scientificamerican.com/article/a-crucial-step-toward-preventing-wildlife-related-pandemics/.

77 Oran R. Young, "Institutional Linkages in International Society: Polar Perspectives", *Global Governance* (1996): 1 et seq.

78 In this sense, Anne Peters, "COVID-19 Shows the Need for a Global Animal Law", *Derecho Animal (Forum of Animal Law Studies)* (2020): 86–97.

79 In general, on self-contained regimes, see Bruno Simma, Dirk Pulkowski, "Of Planets and the Universe: Self-Contained Regimes in International Law", *Netherlands Yearbook of International Law* (2006): 483–529.

V COVID-19 vaccines, the end of the pandemic, and unsettled issues[*]

Part I The COVID-19 pandemic, vaccine nationalism, and the distributive dilemma

1. Introduction

Edward Jenner – an XVIII-century British physician – is usually ascribed to having developed the first vaccine in history.[1] He deserves credit for having invented a rudimentary version of a smallpox vaccine – triggering an immune reaction in a human body – through the inoculation of a sample of an animal virus affected by smallpox.

The formalin-inactivated vaccine (IPV) discovered by Jonas Salk in 1953 and the live-attenuated vaccines (OPV) developed by Albert Sabin in 1956 have been the outcome of experiments that began in 1935 and were an important breakthrough in the almost complete eradication of polio.

In 1952, the United States reported over 21,000 cases of paralytic poliomyelitis – which is caused by the poliovirus. The introduction of the inactivated polio vaccine in 1955 determined a slight decrease in cases (from 2,562 in 1960 to only 162 cases from 1980 to 1999).

Vaccination has provided a significant contribution to the improvement of global health. Two major infectious diseases, namely, smallpox and rinderpest, were globally eradicated through the use of vaccines by the World Health Organization (WHO) in 1980[2] and 2011, respectively.[3]

---

[*] An original version of Chapter V, *Part I The COVID-19 pandemic, vaccine nationalism, and the distributive dilemma,* was published in *The Revue Belge de Droit International* (2022); while Part II *Mandatory COVID-19 vaccinations and human rights in Europe: how to find a delicate balance,* was published in *Ordine Internazionale e Diritti Umani (OIDU)* (2023).

1 Andrea A. Rusnock, "Historical Context and the Roots of Jenner's Discovery", *Human Vaccines & Immunotherapeutics* 12 (2016): 2025.

2 https://www.who.int/health-topics/smallpox#tab=tab_1.

3 https://www.oie.int/en/for-the-media/press-releases/detail/article/eradication-isnt-the-end-of-the-rinderpest-story/.

DOI: 10.4324/9781003100645-5

The development of a vaccine is a lengthy process that usually takes several years and different stages (preclinical, studies on animals, clinics, and then, large-scale vaccine production and licensing).[4]

The celerity with which COVID-19 vaccines have been devised was notably faster compared to other vaccines. Their discovery raised the challenge of how to make these vaccines rapidly, fairly, and equitably accessible to the whole world's population. Against this backdrop, the wider issue correlated with vaccine nationalism answers to a "me-first" logic.[5]

This has raised a distributive dilemma and the problem of timely access to affordable medicines, since the COVID-19 pandemic has generated a global demand for such vaccines that has by far exceeded supply[6] and as a consequence, a world vaccination imbalance.

In this context, governments have been under time pressure to procure vaccines quickly and safely and to provide them to their inhabitants to exit the state of affairs represented by restrictive measures, lockdowns, and limitations of civil liberties that had devastating social and economic impacts. Through advance purchase agreements (APAs) – that is, contracts between a given country and a vaccine manufacturer – most governments have guaranteed access to a predetermined set of doses and prioritized access at a given price (that is different for each country and is not often disclosed).

APAs have proliferated due to the lack of corrective measures at the international level in the drug market. This legal vacuum in the WTO system has determines an unfair distribution of vaccine doses, with a few countries such as Israel and the United Kingdom that managed to immunize most of their population in few months as the early vaccines were delivered, while other countries in the South of the world struggled to receive a few doses. Intellectual property rights and a lack of manufacturing capacity have been additional barriers that have impeded timely access to vaccines in developing countries.

The COVID-19 vaccine race highlighted a fracture in the call for universal and equitable access to COVID-19 vaccination by the UN and its specialized agencies between multilateral initiatives towards this goal (such as COVAX), on the one hand, and national isolationism, on the other hand.

Although there has been a wide doctrinal debate on whether vaccines should have been considered a "common good",[7] wealthy countries, despite facing growing pressure to make sure lower-income nations get fair access to vaccines,

4 Meagan E. Deming, Nelson L. Michael, Merlin Robb, Myron S. Cohen, Kathleen M. Neuzil, "Accelerating Development of SARS-CoV-2 Vaccines – The Role for Controlled Human Infection Models", *New England Journal of Medicine* (2020): 383–390.

5 David P. Fidler, "Vaccine Nationalism's Politics", *Science* (2021): 749.

6 Alan O. Sykes, "Short Supply Conditions and the Law of International Trade: Economic Lessons from the Pandemic", *American Journal of International Law* 114 (2020): 647–656.

7 Muhammad Yunus, Cam Donaldson, Jean-Luc Perron, "COVID-19 Vaccines A Global Common Good", *helancet.com/healthy-longevity* 1 (October 2020), https://www.thelancet.com/action/showPdf?pii=S2666–7568%2820%2930003–9.

decided to act exclusively on the basis of their own domestic interests. Part I of this chapter analyzes the main political and legal issues that determined the lack of a global roll out of COVID-19 vaccines and argues that intellectual property rights are not the only obstacle to fair and equal vaccine distribution. It is particularly highlighted that the absence of a legal framework addressing vaccine distribution has been the main driver of the rise of vaccine nationalism.

2. The distributive dilemma and vaccine nationalism

The discovery of the first COVID-19 vaccines by pharmaceutical companies such as AstraZeneca,[8] Pfizer (Pfizer-BioNTech COVID-19 Vaccine), Moderna[9] (Moderna COVID-19 vaccine), Johnson & Johnson, and the Russian Sputnik has raised several bioethical dilemmas about distributive justice.[10]

Vaccine nationalism emerged as a key feature of these new phases following the production and distribution of the first COVID-19 vaccines, since governments decided to act on the basis of their own domestic interests, giving priority to the protection of the health of their own populations. Vaccine nationalism refers to the policy of wealthier countries (with the capacity to afford it) having secured in advance large quantities of vaccine doses through bilateral agreements with pharmaceutical companies, which determines an unfair distribution.[11]

APAs assure priority access to the medical product; therefore, countries that cannot afford to purchase doses of a vaccine or of a treatment at the price established could face difficulties in obtaining access when the vaccines are first placed on the market.

The vaccination uptake that has allowed high-income countries to begin a program of immunization of the most vulnerable groups of their populations depended, therefore, on the country's willingness to engage in a direct negotiation with a given pharmaceutical company and its financial ability to afford the doses.[12]

---

8 The AstraZeneca vaccine (Viral vector vaccine, AZD1222) was produced by the University of Oxford and has an average efficacy of 70%; data show only light symptoms in participants treated with AZD1222. https://www.astrazeneca.com/media-centre/press-releases/2020/azd1222hlr.html.
9 The Moderna RNA vaccine was developed in Cambridge, Massachusetts. It has a coverage of 94%.
10 Vaccine manufacturers received in 2020 approximately $10 billion in public and non-profit funding.
11 APAs are bilateral agreements struck in advance between a vaccine manufacturer, on the one hand, and a given government or IGO, on the other hand. Through these contracts, a State commits itself to buy from a multinational firm a given dose of an unfinished product at a given price. Some developed States had already secured in 2020 more than 2 billion doses of potential future COVID-19 vaccine through bilateral agreements (advance purchase agreements). In 2021, the richer countries – which cover approximately 13% of the world's population – purchased most of the vaccine doses produced by pharmaceutical companies. Alexandra L. Phelan, Mark Eccleston-Turner, Michelle Rourke, Allan Maleche, Chenguang Wang, "Legal Agreements: Barriers and Enablers to Global Equitable COVID-19 Vaccine Access", *The Lancet* (2021): 800–802.
12 As of 25 March 2021, approximately 29.3 million people in the United Kingdom had received the first dose of the AstraZeneca vaccine (https://coronavirus.data.gov.uk/details/vaccinations).

Most APAs concerning the COVID-19 vaccines in 2021 were garnered by AstraZeneca, Johnson & Johnson, Moderna, and Pfizer. For instance, 41 APAs have been signed in order to secure doses of the AstraZeneca AZD1222, for a total of doses ordered of 128,931,951.[13]

Israel was the first country able to vaccinate most of its population against COVID-19. As of 15 March 2021, most of Israel's population had already been fully vaccinated, and 60% had received the first dose,[14] which is a success compared to the 32% of the United States population fully vaccinated as of 3 May 2021.[15]

Despite multilateral initiatives towards fair and equitable access to treatments and vaccines against COVID-19, a shift from the rhetoric of cooperation and global public goods (GPGs) to the realistic view of international relations clearly emerged during the COVID-19 pandemic.

The EU through the European Commission endorsed the APA mechanism on the basis of both a specific agreement with its Member States[16] and its vaccination strategy.[17]

The Commission was specifically mandated to negotiate APAs with manufacturers on behalf of its Member States (Art. 1 of Annex I).[18] According to Article 2 of Annex I,

> it is the Participating Member States, and not the Commission, that shall acquire vaccine doses from the manufacturers on the basis of the APAs unless otherwise agreed. All relevant vaccination policies shall, therefore, remain matters for the Participating Member States.

The paradox of the EU's acceptance of the APA mechanism lies in the fact that Annex I of the agreement ("Initial Considerations") explicitly refers to

13 https://ihsmarkit.com/research-analysis/covid19-vaccines-apa-tracker-preorders-price.html.
14 Bruce Rosen, Sarah Dine, Nadav Davidovitch, "Lessons in COVID-19 Vaccination From Israel", *Health Affairs Blog* (18 March 2021), https://www.healthaffairs.org/do/10.1377/hblog20210315.476220/full/.
15 https://www.npr.org/sections/health-shots/2021/01/28/960901166/how-is-the-covid-19-vaccination-campaign-going-in-your-state?t=1620146972566.
16 Commission Decision on approving the agreement with Member States on procuring Covid-19 vaccines on behalf of the Member States and related procedures, Brussels, 18.6.2020 C(2020) 4192 final. For details, see Juliana Rodriguez Rodrigo, "A Few Thoughts on the Advance Purchase Agreement of COVID-19 Vaccine Between the European Commission and AstraZeneca", *Eurojus* (2021): 31–50.
17 Communication from the Commission. EU Strategy for COVID-19 vaccines, Brussels, 17.6.2020 COM(2020) 245 final.
18 The EU sealed deals with six companies (Astra Zeneca, Janssen P. NV, CureVac, Sanofi-GSK, BioNTech-Pfizer, and Moderna), for up to 2.3 billion vaccine doses (https://www.consilium.europa.eu/en/infographics/covid-19-vaccines/). The APA negotiated between the EU and AstraZeneca was published on 29 January 2021. file:///C:/Users/cnr%20eth ics/Downloads/Vaccines__contract_between_European_Commission_and_AstraZeneca_ now_published.pdf. Germany acquired 30 million additional vaccine doses through a separate agreement with BioTech.

COVID-19 vaccines as a GPG – which should therefore be freely available – and contains a pledge by the EU to provide access to vaccines to low- and middle-income countries "in sufficient quantity and at low prices".

The indiscriminate proliferation of APAs implied a delay in the delivery of vaccine doses that gave rise to an increase of tensions among governments over the procurement of COVID-19 jabs.

In March 2021, the Italian government blocked the shipment of vaccine doses produced by AstraZeneca in Italian facilities destined to Australia.[19] Despite charges of vaccine protectionism, the decision by the former Italian Prime Minister Draghi followed a specific policy envisaged by the European Commission. According to the EU exports control regulation,[20] a vaccine manufacturer that is based in an EU country must obtain specific authorization from the national government where their COVID-19 jabs are produced before exporting them out of European territory.

In addition, Article XI, Paragraph 2(a) of the General Agreement on Tariffs and Trade (GATT) envisages the possibility of temporary export prohibitions or restrictions for the purpose of addressing "critical shortages of foodstuffs or other *products essential* to the exporting [country]".

Beyond the vaccine dispute, APAs have raised ethical concerns as to their fairness, given that low-income countries cannot afford such an agreement and cannot therefore secure priority access for their populations to a given drug or vaccine.

This phenomenon is not new as the same thing happened when an effective antiretroviral treatment became available for HIV/AIDS and during the 2009 H1N1 pandemic. In these situations, the same sort of vaccine nationalism emerged with high-income countries dominating the global delivery of the vaccines, which hindered any attempt of a global roll out of the H1N1 vaccine.[21] Richer countries – such as the United States – administered large proportions of the H1N1 vaccine to their own populations before the vaccine was given to LMICs.[22]

This led to speculations on a lack of transparency in the WHO's actions and to charges of privileged access for a few industrialized countries to A (H1N1) influenza vaccines.[23]

19 https://www.esteri.it/mae/it/sala_stampa/archivionotizie/comunicati/richiesta-di-autor izzazione-all-esportazione-di-vaccini-anti-covid-19-da-parte-di-astrazeneca.html.

20 Commission Implementing Regulation (EU) 2021/111 of 29 January 2021 making the exportation of certain products subject to the production of an export authorization.

21 Ana Santos Rutschman, "The Reemergence of Vaccine Nationalism", *Saint Louis University School of Law, Legal Studies Research Paper Series, No. 2020–16* (2020).

22 David P. Fidler, "Negotiating Equitable Access to Influenza Vaccines: Global Health Diplomacy and the Controversies Surrounding Avian Influenza H5N1 and Pandemic Influenza H1N1", *PLoS Medicine* (2010), https://journals.plos.org/plosmedicine/article?id=10.1371/journal. pmed.1000247.

23 David P. Fidler, "International Law and Equitable Access to Vaccines and Antivirals in the Context of 2009-H1N1 Influenza", in Institute of Medicines (eds.), *The Domestic and*

APAs are, however, also used as a tool to foster fair and equitable access to vaccines for LMICs within advanced market commitments (AMCs). AMCs are a specific mechanism designed to expedite the development of priority new vaccines and to guarantee their availability to LMICs.[24] APAs are, in fact, used by global health organizations and public-private partnerships (such as GAVI – the Vaccine Alliance) to secure vaccines for LMICs. Through private donations, childhood pneumococcal vaccines and Ebola vaccines have been guaranteed to LMICs.

The COVID-19 pandemic, however, highlighted a legal vacuum. A global deal agreed by all States on the equal distribution of COVID-19 vaccines or treatments in case of epidemic or pandemic – based on the model of the Pandemic Influenza Preparedness Framework – was never established before the WHO CA+.

3. The necessity of a global roll out of COVID-19 vaccines

The main issue related to the distribution of vaccines is therefore that COVID-19 is a global phenomenon, and the unilateral policy to provide vaccine doses only to a small group of the world's population hinders a global recovery.[25]

The WHO Director-General affirmed this: "[t]he world is on the brink of catastrophic moral failure – which will be paid with lives and livelihoods in the world's poorest countries".[26]

In effect, it makes no sense – in the current globalized world – to establish COVID-19-free areas or COVID-19-free States if neighboring countries still continue to have high rates of infection. It seems obvious that vaccine nationalism is counterproductive in defeating the pandemic, since according to the WHO, at least 70% of the global population should be vaccinated in order to reach herd immunity.[27]

The priority allocation stages for vaccine roll out envisage at stage one to cover 3% of the population (people on the front lines such as health care and social workers); stage two should target 20% of the population (people over 65 years old and high-risk), and eventually stage 3 should be addressed to 20% + of the population (further priority groups).[28]

International Impacts of the 2009-H1N1 Influenza A Pandemic Global Challenges, Global Solutions (The National Academies Press: 2010).

24 https://www.who.int/immunization/programmes_systems/financing/analyses/Brief_17_AMC.pdf?ua=1.

25 Senuri De Silva, "The Effect of Vaccine Nationalism and the Global Right to Health", *leidenlawblog* (4 February 2021), https://leidenlawblog.nl/articles/the-effect-of-vaccine-nationalism-and-the-global-right-to-health.

26 https://news.un.org/en/story/2021/01/1082362.

27 WHO 'Coronavirus disease (COVID-19): Herd immunity, lockdowns and COVID-19'. https://www.who.int/news-room/q-a-detail/herd-immunity-lockdowns-and-covid-19.

28 *WHO SAGE Values Framework for the Allocation and Prioritization of COVID-19 Vaccination* (14 September 2020), https://apps.who.int/iris/handle/10665/334299.

There is the serious risk that COVID-19 – similar to most communicable diseases such as HIV/AIDS, malaria, and tuberculosis – will become in the long term a "disease of under-development", now that COVID-19 no longer constitutes a PHEIC.

Considerations of global solidarity are therefore necessary; in fact, States should have a genuine interest in cooperating to reach a fair and equitable distribution of the new vaccines, at least in guaranteeing the widest possible coverage.

An unfair distribution would have strong repercussions in terms of travel and trade, a recession of the world economy, and migration pressure.

Attention has turned to the expansion of production capacities in order to foster a wide roll out of vaccines and to efficiently distribute them to poorer countries and the most vulnerable groups.

Scaling up production to provide global coverage is, however, a difficult challenge that requires the necessity of designing an equitable and efficient global plan for fair and equitable vaccine allocation.[29]

A global vaccination policy against COVID-19 has several dimensions that need to be analyzed: development and production at a large scale, affordable pricing, a wider allocation, and deployment.[30]

To date, several factors have hampered a fair distribution of COVID-19 vaccines and a full implementation of the previously mentioned dimensions.

As explained earlier, the first factor is a domestic choice of vaccine policy; governments of richer countries purchased and hoarded supplies of COVID-19 vaccines exclusively for their own population.

There are then legal issues since vaccine-producer countries and brand-name pharmaceutical companies rely on intellectual property protections; this means high prices and the fact that the COVID-19 vaccines are too expensive for low-income countries. The considerable cost of medicines and vaccines – although it is differentiated among countries[31] – is a factor that hinders the access to essential health care treatments of populations of poorer countries.

Against this backdrop, Oxford/AstraZeneca (AZ) and Johnson & Johnson[32] have chosen to partially waive to the profits of their vaccines. AstraZen-

---

29 Wei Wang, Qianhui Wu, Juan Yang, Kaige Dong, Xinghui Chen, Xufang Bai, Xinhua Chen, Zhiyuan Chen, Cécile Viboud, Marco Ajelli, Hongjie Yu, "Global, Regional, and National Estimates of Target Population Sizes for Covid-19 Vaccination: Descriptive Study", *The BMJ* (15 December 2020), https://www.bmj.com/content/371/bmj.m4704.

30 Olivier J. Wouters, Kenneth C. Shadlen, Maximilian Salcher-Konrad, Andrew J. Pollard, Heidi J. Larson, Yot Teerawattananon, Mark Jit, "Challenges in Ensuring Global Access to COVID-19 Vaccines: Production, Affordability, Allocation, and Deployment", *The Lancet* (12 February 2021): 1023–1034.

31 Ower Dyer, "Covid-19: Countries are Learning What Others Paid for Vaccines", *The BMJ* (2021): 372.

32 https://www.jnj.com/our-company/johnson-johnson-announces-agreement-in-principle-with-gavi-to-supply-janssens-covid-19-vaccine-candidate-to-lower-income-countries-in-2021.

eca and Oxford University signed a specific deal where they committed to sell their vaccines at a no-profit price.[33]

Pfizer and Moderna have taken the opposite approach. This also explains the difference in costs. The Pfizer vaccine costs approximately $19 for each dose, and the Moderna vaccine costs around $25, while the AstraZeneca vaccine costs approximately $4. However, even the cheaper AZ vaccine is beyond the reach of LMICs.[34]

There are also logistical problems since these vaccines must be kept at very low temperatures, and their supply to tropical regions is highly problematic. This suggests technical questions given that developed countries – beyond the patent issue – do not have enough technical and manufacturing facilities that would allow them to produce generic versions of the vaccines by themselves.

4. Overview of patent law

4.1. The TRIPS agreement

Several biotech and pharmaceutical companies worldwide have rushed to come up with a vaccine to defeat the novel coronavirus. The vaccines discovered and produced have become a gold mine for the inventors.

The United States pharmaceutical company Pfizer expected for 2021 an increase of $15 billion of additional income due to the sale of the vaccine developed and produced with the German BioNtech.[35]

The first vaccines (the Pfizer/BioNTech vaccine) were distributed in the United Kingdom in December 2020.[36]

The COVID-19 vaccines (an effective treatment) are private intellectual property (IP) and are subject to patent rights protection as a "pharmaceutical product".[37]

Patent law favors the first in time: it grants to the inventor a temporary monopoly for the exploitation of a useful invention. The legal framework governing intellectual property rights (IPRs) and pharmaceutical products is represented by the TRIPS Agreement (Multilateral Agreement on Intellectual

33 "AstraZeneca: Won't Profit From COVID-19 Vaccine in Pandemic", https://apnews.com/article/virus-outbreak-europe-medication-a1ec6915874850dfd38b062f08d04629.

34 Belgium's Secretary of State for Budget, Eva De Bleeker, *Inadvertently Revealed the EU's Negotiated Prices for Every Major Vaccine on Twitter on 17 December 2020 (The Tweet was Then Deleted)*, https://www.hln.be/binnenland/zoveel-gaan-we-betalen-voor-de-coronavaccins-staatssecretaris-zet-confidentiele-prijzen-per-ongeluk-online~a3dceef4/180355293/.

35 https://s21.q4cdn.com/317678438/files/doc_financials/2020/q4/Q4-2020-PFE-Earnings-Release.pdf.

36 https://www.bbc.com/news/uk-55227325.

37 Karen Durell, "Vaccines and IP Rights: A Multifaceted Relationship", *Methods in Molecular Biology* (2016): 791–811; Holger Hestermeyer, *Human Rights and the WTO. The Case of Patents and Access to Medicines* (Oxford University Press: 2007).

Property, WTO, 1995).[38] TRIPS guarantees an exclusive right of exploitation (monopoly) to the patent holder, although this might lead to high prices (Art. 28).[39] Part II of TRIPS requires States to confer patent rights, that is, exclusive rights of exploitation, for 20 years with respect to "new" inventions involving an "inventive step" that "are capable of industrial application".

Without the profits envisaged by patent monopolies, research in the field of treatments and vaccines for human and animal diseases would stall.[40] Patent protection promotes innovation by providing financial incentives to research and development (R&D). All medical discoveries of the last century including vaccines, HIV and Hepatitis C treatments, and cancer drugs are due to R&D.

The monopoly regime, however, inflates prices for IP-protected products, and it creates problems for LMICs that cannot afford medicines, drugs, and vaccines at the market price.

The price of patented drugs for HIV is a *vexata quaestio*. For example, the cost of HIV medications is very high. Thirty tablets of etravirine (Intelence), efavirenz (Sustiva), lamivudine/zidovudine (Combivir), and rilpivirine (Edurant) have an average cost of $1,000.[41]

Only Western countries – due to governmental subsidies – can afford such drugs. Consequently, HIV/AIDS has become a chronic disease for patients of industrialized countries and a deadly disease for HIV-positive people in LMICs.

A domestic or regional authority (in the EU, the European Patent Office)[42] grants patent rights. Therefore, a patented product cannot be produced, sold, imported, or exported in jurisdictions covered by a patent unless it receives specific leave from the patent-holder. Despite the necessity of patent protection to advance research and development, the current IP system triggers further concerns about equitable access to vaccines on the ground of public health considering the exceptional situation caused by COVID-19.

Potential issues around manufacturing, exporting, and importing generic versions of a patented COVID-19 vaccine or treatment may arise. The first issue regards access by developing countries to affordable COVID-19 vaccines

38 Ping Xiong, *An International Law Perspective on the Protection of Human Rights in the TRIPS Agreement. An Interpretation of the TRIPS Agreement in Relation to the Right to Health* (Brill: 2012).

39 Article 28 reads as follows: "1. A patent shall confer on its owner the following exclusive rights: (a) where the subject matter of a patent is a product, to prevent third parties not having the owner's consent from the acts of: making, using, offering for sale, selling, or importing for these purposes that product; (b) where the subject matter of a patent is a process, to prevent third parties not having the owner's consent from the act of using the process, and from the acts of: using, offering for sale, selling, or importing for these purposes at least the product obtained directly by that process. 2. Patent owners shall also have the right to assign, or transfer by succession, the patent and to conclude licensing contracts".

40 Roger Collier, "Drug patents: The Evergreening Problem", *Canadian Medical Association Journal* (2013): E385–E386.

41 https://www.healthline.com/health/hiv-aids/cost-of-treatment.

42 www.epo.org.

or treatments. The second is whether a State would be eligible to import generic versions of a patented vaccine or treatment in case of insufficient manufacturing capacity.

The current IP legal architecture is at the center of a global cross-cutting debate on how to guarantee fair, equitable, and fast access to effective treatments and/or vaccines against COVID-19 and the interrelatedness between the right to health and patent rights.[43] The clash between patent law and human rights has already been raised as HIV/AIDS retroviral treatment is highly effective against the virus.[44] South Africa's intellectual property challenge for affordable access to AIDS drugs spawned a heated debate with particular reference to the most vulnerable groups of the South.[45]

The TRIPS Agreement has, however, reconciled commercial interests and human rights by providing some "flexibilities". Under certain circumstances, a domestic law may authorize another producer to manufacture generic versions of patented products without the leave of the rights holder (compulsory licenses) (Art. 31) ("TRIPS Flexibilities").[46] However, this process is not automatic, since a State must enter into consultation and negotiation with the patent owner. The circumstances under which a compulsory license may be granted include situations of "national emergency or other situations of extreme urgency".

Moreover, "any such use shall be authorized *predominantly* for the supply of the domestic market of the Member authorizing such use" (Art. 31, *f*). This has resulted in an impediment to developing countries that – in light of a chronic lack of adequate facilities – cannot produce by themselves medicines and vaccines.

4.2. *Patent rights vs. public health*

In light of the well-known controversy between South Africa and some pharmaceutical companies on the import from India of generic anti-retroviral drugs for the treatment of HIV, the international community felt inclined to

---

43 Aisling McMahon, "Global Equitable Access to Vaccines, Medicines and Diagnostics for COVID-19: The Role of Patents as Private Governance", *Journal of Medical Ethics* (2021): 1–7.

44 Debora Halbert, "Moralized Discourses: South Africa's Intellectual Property Fight for Access to AIDS Drugs", *Seattle Journal for Social Justice* 1 (2) (2002): 257–295; William W. Fisher, Cyrill P. Rigamonti, "The South Africa AIDS Controversy. A Case Study in Patent Law and Policy", *The Law and Business of Patents: Harvard Law School* (2005): 1–56.

45 For a more detailed understanding of these issues, see Nerina Boschiero, "Intellectual Property Rights and Public Health: An Impediment to Access to Medicines and Health Technology Innovation?" in Laura Pineschi (ed.), *La tutela della salute nel diritto internazionale ed europeo tra interessi globali e interessi particolari, XXI Convegno Parma 9–10 giugno 2016* (Editoriale Scientifica: 2017), 259–294; Raffaele Cadin, "E' più immorale, e antigiuridico secondo il diritto internazionale, copiare un brevetto o negare l'accesso ai farmaci essenziali ai malati di AIDS nei Paesi poveri?", *Rivista della cooperazione giuridica internazionale* (2004): 42–66.

46 Aditi Bagchi, "Compulsory Licensing and the Duty of Good Faith in TRIPS", *Stanford Law Review* 55 (2003): 1529–1556.

reconcile patent rights and human rights.[47] The constitutionality of the South African legislation, which allowed access to generic versions of HIV/AIDS treatment, was challenged in March 2001 by 39 pharmaceutical industries before the High Court in Pretoria. They claimed that this legislation violated their IP rights and argued that it arbitrarily expanded the government's power to issue compulsory licenses and to import generic versions of HIV/AIDS treatments from India. The companies eventually dropped the legal action in April 2001 after a wave of global outrage, as they feared excessive damage to their reputation.[48]

In response to these events, the Doha Declaration on TRIPS and Public Health, adopted on 14 November 2001, acknowledged the need to balance patent protection with a compulsory licensing system. It has provided a wide interpretation of the flexibilities in Article 31 of the TRIPS Agreement, envisaging a mechanism of patent protection and compulsory licensing system.[49]

It states that it is up to each country to determine what is an "emergency situation" (public health crises, such as HIV/AIDS, in the past have been considered emergency situations).

On the one hand, WTO Members pledged "that intellectual property protection is important for the development of new medicines. We also recognize the concerns about its effects on prices" (Para. 3).

On the other hand, they affirmed that

> we agree that the TRIPS Agreement does not and should not prevent members from taking measures to protect public health. Accordingly, while reiterating our commitment to the TRIPS Agreement, we affirm that the Agreement can and should be interpreted and implemented in a manner supportive of WTO members' right to protect public health and, in particular, to promote access to medicines for all.
>
> (Para. 4)

A Protocol amending the Trips Agreement (6 December 2005)[50] introduced Article 31*bis* that envisages a waiver for Article 31(*f*) for countries lacking domestic manufacturing capabilities to import generic drugs produced in other countries (the "eligible importing Members" are those classified as "developing or least developed"). Article 31*bis* represents a quite significant

47 Pat Sidley, "Drug Companies Sue South African Government Over Generics", *The British Medical Journal* (2001): 447.
48 Lissett Ferreira, "Access to Affordable HIV/AIDS Drugs: The Human Rights Obligations of Multinational Pharmaceutical Corporations Obligations of Multinational Pharmaceutical Corporations", *Fordham Law Review* (2002): 1133–1179.
49 https://www.wto.org/english/thewto_e/minist_e/min01_e/mindecl_trips_e.htm.
50 WTO Treaty Series No. 34, WT/Let/508, WT/L/641. The amendment entered into force on 23 January 2017.

reform in WTO law.[51] States Parties can now grant special compulsory licenses exclusively for the production and export of affordable generic medicines to other members that cannot domestically produce the needed medicines in sufficient quantity.[52]

However, this legal mechanism is still unaffordable for most LMICs due to the condition of required "adequate remuneration" to the patentholder (Art. 31*bis*, Para. 2) and to the fact that they must rely on a foreign manufacturer.[53]

The key issue is that the compulsory licensing outlined in the TRIPS Agreement – that allows overcoming the patent system to a certain degree – is not adequate enough to ensure a global rollout of COVID-19 vaccines especially in LMICs.

LMICs are dependent on the importation of doses of vaccines from manufacturers located in foreign countries, such as Brazil, China, India, and South Africa.

In addition to lifting the legal restrictions, there is also the issue related to the lack of adequate know-how by manufacturers located in emerging economies or developing countries. Therefore, a commitment for technology transfer from high-income economies is required to improve the capacities of local manufacturers and to provide a solution to the production bottleneck. This concentration of vaccine manufacturing capacity within a few countries has strongly hindered a global roll out of vaccines.[54]

That is, the TRIPS Agreement does not address the problem of the structural conditions of LMICs, and it has not led to a sufficient increase in domestic pharmaceutical manufacturing capacities.

4.3. States' obligations and global solidarity

The waiver foreseen by the TRIPS agreement can be justified under the human rights obligation to guarantee the right to health to everyone. Indeed, WTO

---

51 Reto Hilty, "Legal Remedies Against Abuse, Misuse, and Other Forms of Inappropriate Conduct of IP Right Holders", in Reto Hilty, Kung-Chung Liu (eds.), *Compulsory Licensing. Practical Experiences and Ways Forward* (Springer: 2015), 377–396.

52 Article 31*bis*, Paragraph 1 affirms that "The obligations of an exporting Member under Article 31(f) shall not apply with respect to the grant by it of a compulsory licence to the extent necessary for the purposes of production of a pharmaceutical product(s) and its export to an eligible importing Member(s)".

53 Article 31*bis*, Paragraph 2 states that "Where a compulsory licence is granted by an exporting Member under the system set out in this Article and the Annex to this Agreement, adequate remuneration pursuant to Article 31(h) shall be paid in that Member taking into account the economic value to the importing Member of the use that has been authorized in the exporting Member". The decision to issue a compulsory licence and the determination of the total amount of the remuneration must be subject to judicial or other independent review (Paras. (*i*) and (*j*)). Anthony Taubman, "Rethinking TRIPS: 'Adequate Remuneration' for Nonvoluntary Patent Licensing", *Journal of International Economic Law* 11 (2005): 927–970.

54 W. Nicholson Price II, Arti K. Rai, Timo Minssen, "Knowledge Transfer for Large-Scale Vaccine Manufacturing", *Science* (2020): 912–914.

Members are also Parties to the ICESCR that establishes specific duties upon States that must be taken into consideration.

Under Article 1, Paragraph 2 of the ICESCR, "in no case may people be deprived of its own means of subsistence". The extreme delay in vaccine supply in developing countries was a trigger for extreme poverty and poor health conditions; it has definitively impeded the realization of the highest attainable standard of physical and mental health as recognized in the WHO Constitution, human rights treaties, and domestic constitutions.

Against this backdrop, the Committee on Economic, Social and Cultural Rights has affirmed in its General Comment Number 14 that immunization is a component of States' obligations to protect *their populations* against epidemic diseases (Para. 44).

This is consistent with the common interpretation of Article 12 of the ICESCR, according to which the State's obligation to protect the right to health is primarily addressed to their own inhabitants.[55]

This vision was then confirmed by the International Court of Justice (ICJ) in its advisory opinion on the Legal Consequences of the Construction of a Wall in the Occupied Palestinian Territory, arguing that "the International Covenant on Economic, Social and Cultural Rights contains no provision on its scope of application. This may be explicable by the fact that the Covenant guarantees rights *which are essential territorial*".[56]

Traditionally, States bear a human rights duty only within their jurisdiction or areas within their control.

This interpretation – which therefore excludes an extraterritorial obligation with reference to the right to health – is confirmed by democratic considerations, since national or supranational authorities (such as the EU) must respond directly to their own populations.

This is an obstacle in the presence of transnational threats such as epidemics, pandemics, environmental damage, or natural disasters.[57]

Therefore, States do not have a direct obligation to guarantee the right to health beyond their national borders towards populations living in other countries.

Even so, in light of the transnational dimension of the COVID-19 pandemic, do States have a specific obligation to procure vaccines for their own populations, on the one hand, and contribute to a global vaccine roll out, on the other hand?

---

55 *Supra*, note 6, at 651.
56 ICJ, "Advisory Opinion, Legal Consequences of the Construction of a Wall in the Occupied Palestinian Territory, 9 July 2004", *ICJ Reports* (2004): 136, para. 112.
57 For a critique of the traditional State-centered conception of human rights, see generally, Tilmann Altwicker, "Transnationalizing Rights: International Human Rights Law in Cross-Border Contexts", *European Journal of International Law* (2018): 581–606.

There is a separation of obligations owed by States towards their citizens and a general duty towards persons in territories beyond their control – which is extra-territorial obligation – to not impede the enjoyment of the right to health.

How can these obligations be understood in the context of a pandemic characterized by scarce resources and time pressure? Can APAs be considered an impediment to the enjoyment of the right to health in LMICs? Of course not, since States owe first a specific obligation to protect the health of their own citizens.

However, States – including vaccine-producer countries – have at least a specific duty to *cooperate* in order to adopt every necessary measure to prevent, treat, and control epidemics. In this vein, unlike the International Covenant on Civil and Political Rights (ICCPR) and the European Convention on Human Rights (ECHR), the ICESCR make several references to international cooperation and assistance.[58] As previously explained, a global pandemic cannot be defeated by vaccine nationalism, and genuine cooperation among States must be the cornerstone of an international response.

In the Statement on universal affordable vaccination for COVID-19, international cooperation and intellectual property, the Committee on Economic, Social and Cultural Rights emphasized that

> States have a duty of international cooperation and assistance to ensure access to vaccines for COVID-19 wherever needed, including by using their voting rights as members of different international institutions or organizations, including regional integration organizations such as the European Union.
>
> (Para. 3)[59]

States therefore have a duty to cooperate under Article 2, Paragraph 1 of the ICESCR in relation to Article 12, Paragraph 2 (*c*) and (*d*), that is, "the prevention, treatment, and control of epidemic, endemic, occupation and other diseases" and "the creation of conditions which would assure to all medical service and medical attention in the event of sickness". Article 2, Paragraph 1 of the ICESCR, the "umbrella clause of the Covenant",[60] obliges States Parties

> to take steps, individually and through international assistance and co-operation, especially economic and technical, to the maximum of its available resources, with a view to achieving progressively the full

---

58 Elif Askin, "Extraterritorial Human Rights Obligations of States in the Event of Disease Outbreaks", in Leonie Vierck, Pedro A. Villareal, A. Katarina Weilert (eds.), *The Governance of Disease Outbreaks. International Health Law: Lessons from the Ebola Crisis and Beyond* (Nomos: 2018), 175–212, at 191.

59 Committee on Economic, Social and Cultural Rights. Statement on universal affordable vaccination for COVID-19, international cooperation and intellectual property, E/C.12/2021/1, 12 March 2021.

60 Daniel J. Whelan, "The Two Covenants and the Evolution of Human Rights", in Anja Mihr, Mark Gibney (eds.), *The SAGE Handbook of Human Rights*, Vol. I (SAGE: 2014), 123–144, at 132.

realization of the rights recognized in the present Covenant by all appropriate means, including particularly the adoption of legislative measures.

General Comment Number 14 emphasizes that "the existing gross inequality in the health status of the people, particularly between developed and developing countries, as well as within countries, is politically, socially, and economically unacceptable and is, therefore, of *common concern to all countries*" (Para. 38).

Furthermore, General Comment Number 14 affirms that "States have a joint and individual responsibility, in accordance with the Charter of the United Nations and relevant resolutions . . . *to cooperate* in providing disaster relief and humanitarian assistance in times of emergency . . . Each State should contribute to this task *to the maximum of its capacities* . . . Moreover, given that some diseases are easily transmissible beyond the frontiers of a State, the international community has *a collective responsibility* to address this problem. The economically developed States parties have a special responsibility and interest to assist the poorer developing States in this regard" (Para. 40).

Against this backdrop, the UN Charter recognizes a general obligation to cooperate among Member States (Art. 56) with the goal of achieving specific purposes, such as promoting

a. higher standards of living, full employment, and conditions of economic and social progress and development; b. solutions of international economic, social, *health*, and related problems; and international cultural and educational cooperation; and c. universal respect for, and observance of, human rights and fundamental freedoms for all without distinction as to race, sex, language, or religion.

In addition, States have pledged to respect, protect, and fulfill the right to development. Under Article 1 of the Declaration on the Right to Development (1986), States should not take measures or actions that impede or prevent individuals and peoples from contributing, enjoying, and participating in their "economic, social, cultural or political development, in which all human rights and fundamental freedoms can be fully realized".

The right to development is also taken into consideration by international trade law; the Preamble to the WTO Agreement refers to "expanding the production of and trade in goods and services, while allowing for the optimal use of the world's resources in accordance with the objective of sustainable development".

In the Statement on the coronavirus disease (COVID-19) pandemic and economic, social and cultural rights, the Committee on Economic, Social and Cultural Rights[61] made clear reference to equity in health:

States parties are under an obligation to devote their maximum available resources to the full realization of all economic, social and cultural

61 Statement by the Committee on Economic, Social and Cultural Rights, 17 April 2020.

rights, including the right to health. . . . States must make every effort to mobilize the necessary resources to combat COVID-19 in the most *equitable* manner.

(Para. 14)

5. COVID-19 vaccines and benefit sharing

Equity in the development and distribution of medicines and vaccines against COVID-19 should be the object of a more structured debate. The COVID-19 pandemic has disproportionately affected those who are already disadvantaged and will continue to be disadvantaged, both within and between countries.[62]

Since health inequalities have been considered by the Committee on Economic, Social, and Cultural Rights as a common concern to all countries, they can therefore be considered in the same way as climate change and the loss of biodiversity.

In this vein, it is worth recalling that the right to health is also complemented by the right of everyone "to enjoy the benefits of scientific progress and its applications" (Art. 15, Para. 1, *b*).

Developing countries may not have access to COVID-19 vaccines without an adequate governance framework, and it should be a common concern of all States to vaccinate most of the world population to stop the spread of the pandemic.

The new pandemic treaty recognizes "equity" as one of its core principles, stating that

> effective pandemic prevention, preparedness, response and recovery cannot be achieved without political will and commitments in addressing the structural challenges in inequitable access to fair, equitable and timely access to affordable, safe and efficacious pandemic-related products and services, essential health services, information and social support, as well as tackling the inequities in terms of technology, health workforce, infrastructure and financing, among other aspects.

(Art. 4, Para. 4)

A strong commitment to equity is envisaged in Article 10, lect. *h*, which affirms that the WHO should have access to 20% of "pandemic-related products" (including vaccines) in order to fairly distribute them to priority populations identified in national health plans. Ten percent of these pandemic-related products shall be provided to the WHO in the form of donations, and the other 10% are to be provided at "affordable prices".

---

62 See Nuffield Council on Bioethics, "Fair and Equitable Access to COVID-19 Treatments and Vaccines", *Rapid Policy Briefing* (29 May 2020), https://www.nuffieldbioethics.org/assets/pdfs/Fair-and-equitable-access-to-COVID-19-treatments-and-vaccines.pdf.

5.1. Fair and equitable access to COVID-19 vaccines

5.1.1. The target of global health coverage

The availability of essential drugs at affordable prices and on a non-discriminatory basis is one of the components of the right to health as fleshed out in General Comment Number 14 (Para. 12, *a*).[63]

A 2006 report by the Special Rapporteur on the Right to Health, Paul Hunt, raised the issue of the "human right to medicines".[64]

> Medical care in the event of sickness and the prevention, treatment and control of diseases depend to a great extent on timely access to quality medicines. Despite progress made, an estimated 2 billion people still lack access to essential medicines. There remains an intrinsic link between poverty and the realization of the right to health, where developing nations have the greatest need and the least access to medicines.
>
> (Para. 48)

Since half of the global population is not covered by essential health services, the UN has set a specific target of global health coverage. States committed themselves under the 2030 Agenda for Sustainable Development Goals "to promote physical and mental health and well-being, and to extend life expectancy for all, we must achieve universal health coverage and access to quality health care" (Para. 26).[65]

Among the 17 United Nations Sustainable Development Goals, Goal 3 concerns "health and well- being". In detail, Target 3.8 aims to "achieve universal health coverage, including financial risk protection, access to quality essential health care services and access to safe, effective, quality and affordable essential medicines and vaccines for all".

The UN Human Rights Council emphasized on several occasions the interrelation between extreme poverty and right to health and recalled the notion of global health coverage.[66]

---

63 The WHO Action Program on Essential Drugs and Vaccines (WHA 37.32, 17 May 1984).
64 UNGA, "Report of the Special Rapporteur on the Right of Everyone to the Enjoyment of the Highest Standard of Physical and Mental Health, Paul Hunt", UN doc. A/61/338 (13 September 2006), Para. 37.
65 Resolution adopted by the General Assembly on 25 September 2015 (A/70/L.1). Transforming our world: the 2030 Agenda for Sustainable Development.
66 Human Rights Council, "Access to Medicines in the Context of the Right of Everyone to the Enjoyment of the Highest Attainable Standard of Physical and Mental rights", Resolution 32/15, Doc. A/HRC/32/L/Rev. 1 (1 July 2016); Human Rights Council, "Promoting the Right of Everyone to the Enjoyment of the Highest Attainable Standard of Physical and Mental Health Through Enhancing Capacity-Building in Public Health", Resolution 32/16, Doc A/HRC/32/L.23/Rev. 1 (1 July 2016).

Resolution 32/15 calls upon States

> to promote access to medicines for all, including through the use, to the full, of the provisions of the Agreement on Trade-Related Aspects of Intellectual Property Rights, which provide flexibility for that purpose, recognizing that the protection of intellectual property is important for the development of new medicines, as well as the concerns about its effects on prices.

Resolution 32/15 then acknowledges the need of *universal health coverage*, implying that

> all people have access without discrimination to . . . quality medicines and *vaccines*, while ensuring that the use of these services does not expose users to financial hardships, with a special emphasis on the poor, vulnerable, and marginalized segments of the population.

With Resolution n. 72/139 (12 December 2017) entitled "Global Health and Foreign Policy", the General Assembly established two fundamental principles. On the one hand, it affirmed the necessity of guaranteeing the health of persons belonging to the most vulnerable sectors of society to reach a more inclusive society. It therefore recognized that the health of the most vulnerable persons is both an element and a condition of a more inclusive society.

On the other hand, it highlighted the importance of "a specific emphasis on the . . . vulnerable and marginalized segments of the population" (Art. 6), which is the foundation of a strategy aimed at guaranteeing global health coverage.

According to the Political Declaration of the AG High-Level Meeting on Universal Health Coverage (2019), the concept of universal health coverage "implies that all people have access, without discrimination, to nationally determined sets of the needed promotive, preventive, curative, rehabilitative and palliative essential health services, and essential, safe, affordable, effective and quality medicines and *vaccines*" (Preamble, 8).[67]

Equal access to vaccines is therefore a general principle of international law recognized in several soft law instruments but not yet codified in any treaty or binding act adopted by an intergovernmental organization (IGO). It is therefore a pledge and not an obligation by States to guarantee fair and equitable access to affordable medicines and vaccines to populations of poorer countries.

---

67 Political Declaration of the High-level Meeting on Universal Health Coverage, "Universal Health Coverage: Moving Together to Build a Healthier World" (23 September 2019), https://www.un.org/pga/73/wp-content/uploads/sites/53/2019/07/FINAL-draft-UHC-Political-Declaration.pdf.

5.1.2. COVID-19 vaccines as a common public good?

Despite the UN rhetoric on global health coverage, the key question is whether vaccine-producer countries have a real obligation under general international law to provide vaccines and treatments against COVID-19 to poorer countries. As previously discussed, under the ICESCR, States have a simple obligation to cooperate and not hinder the enjoyment of the right to health of other populations. However, their duties with reference to access to treatments and vaccines are mostly related to their own citizens.

Against this backdrop, one could hypothesize that – within the common interest of the eradication of infectious diseases, specifically, COVID-19 and the necessity to guarantee global health coverage – vaccines and/or treatments against this disease might be considered a GPG. The concept of GPG first appeared in the scholarly debate in the 1970s, and there is much literature on the matter.[68] The term "good" refers to a product, not to a normative attribute.[69]

According to economic theory, a public good has several distinct characteristics: non-excludability (no one can be excluded from the good's use, even a State that has not contributed to its production or financing) and non-rivalry (its availability is not excluded by the good's consumption).[70] A classic example of a GPG is represented by fresh air. Furthermore, it must be accessible to several countries, to a wide spectrum of their population, and to present and future generations.

Private goods are, however, excludable and rival. These goods can therefore be provided by private actors, such as the case of the lighthouse that serves all sailors, or by the State. In the latter case, the State – in the fields of national defense, education, and civil and environmental protection – guarantees their creation and maintenance.

Public health cannot be considered a public good; the state of health of a person or of a population of a given country is a private good, since the main beneficiaries are the single person of the population of a country. Furthermore, the goods and services that are necessary to guarantee and sustain health, such as adequate nutrition, housing, treatment, and health services, are competitive and exclusive goods.

State interventions of health policy that have the goal of improving public health and generating positive externalities on the global level can instead be qualified as GPGs for health.

---

68 Marcur Olson, *The Logic of Collective Action: Public Goods and the Theory of Groups* (Harvard University Press: 1965).

69 Gregory Schaffer, "International Law and Global Public Goods in a Legal Pluralist World", *The European Journal of International Law* (2012): 669–693.

70 Paul A. Samuelson, "The Pure Theory of Public Expenditure", *Review of Economics and Statistics* (1954): 387–389; Lincoln C. Chen, Tim G. Evans, Richard A. Cash, "Health as a Global Public Good", in Inge Kaul, Isabelle Grunberg, Marc Stern (eds.), *Global Public Goods: International Cooperation in the 21st Century* (Oxford: 2003), 284–304.

Examples are health policies for the prevention and containment of infectious diseases with a high risk of global spread (such as HIV/AIDS, tuberculosis, and poliomyelitis) or policies that control the cross-border circulation of particular elements or risk factors, such as tobacco, drugs, and living modified organisms (LMOs) resulting from modern biotechnology.[71]

If one can conceive health as a GPG – as the product of global public politics – then States should genuinely cooperate. On the international level, the situation is more complex. There is no global government that can act as a referee or judge of the global interest of the international community or as a legitimate agent for the production and protection of GPGs. There is instead political pluralism, organized at the horizontal level in the society of States and in a vertical sense through the complex interaction between States and IGOs and between States and transnational private actors.

The structural limits of international law in organizing collective action for the protection of GPGs have emerged within the context of climate change. Despite the indisputable impact of global warming on human health and the environment, States have failed to act in a coordinated manner. Despite multilateral efforts already undertaken to reduce the emissions of the main greenhouse gases (GHGs; carbon dioxide, methane, nitrous oxide, and fluorinated gases such as HFCs, PFCs, and SF6) which have led to a series of international conferences and negotiations, progress towards a low-carbon economy has not been made, and CO2 emissions have not yet drastically diminished.[72] The scarce practical impact of the Kyoto Protocol and the Paris Agreement on Climate Change has demonstrated the tendency of a few States to free-ride.[73]

The concept of GPG is, however, "an ideal type", since both conditions (non-rivalry and non-excludability) are not easy to obtain. Most are impure public goods.[74] International law does not yet recognize the category of GPG, such as the common heritage of humankind (the seabed, the human genome, and outer space) or common concerns (climate change and the loss of biodiversity).[75]

---

71 In this regard, see the Cartagena Protocol on Biosafety to the Convention on Biological Diversity, https://bch.cbd.int/protocol/.

72 In 2020, the COVID-19 pandemic resulted in the largest ever decline in global emissions.

73 Ilja Richard Pavone, "The Paris Agreement and the Trump Administration: Road to Nowhere?", *Journal of International Studies* (2018): 34–49. Despite the large acceptance of the Paris Agreement, the former Trump administration chose a free-riding strategy and decided to withdraw from the treaty. However, on 19 February 2021, the United States under the Biden administration, officially re-entered the Paris Agreement after the deposit of the instrument of acceptance of the Agreement on 20 January 2021. See C.N.10.2021.TREATIESXXVII.7.d. of 20 January 2021. See also Renee Cho, "The U.S. Is Back in the Paris Agreement. Now What?" (2021), https://blogs.ei.columbia.edu/2021/02/04/u-s-rejoins-paris-agreement/.

74 In this regard, see Daniel Bodansky, "What's in a Concept? Global Public Goods, International Law and Legitimacy", *The European Journal of International Law* (2012): 651–688.

75 Thomas Cottier, *The Prospects of Common Concern of Humankind in International Law* (Cambridge University Press: 2021).

Despite the structural difficulties met by international law while aiming for collective action for the production and protection of common goods, some progress has been made in the elaboration of notions that reflect the idea of common goods. One example is the category of *erga omnes* obligations, as ushered in by the renowned *dictum* in the *Barcelona Traction* case.[76] The ICJ has highlighted the concept of *erga omnes* obligations, that is, a duty owed towards the international community.[77] This category was then codified in the Draft articles on Responsibility of States for Internationally Wrongful Acts (Art. 48, Para. 1, lect. *b*) that introduced the notion of "obligations owed to the international community as a whole".[78]

The legal category of *erga omnes* obligations – familiar to the lexicon of international law – can no doubt be equivalent to GPGs that reach the same goal of protecting health in its dimension of a public good.[79]

COVID-19 vaccines could be considered a hybrid GPG since most pharmaceutical companies have received public or mixed funding. The United States government and the Coalition for Epidemic Preparedness Innovations (CEPI) have largely funded the research and development of COVID-19 vaccines by the five main pharmaceutical companies (they have distributed between $957 million and $2.1 billion in funding commitments).[80] This contradicts arguments that IP rights are a sort of reward for the investments made by the biotech sector in R&D.

GPGs raise, however, an issue of global governance; even if it is assumed that COVID-19 vaccines are a GPG, then who decides – given the limited doses available – the recipients of the vaccines? Who should be vaccinated first, with the aim of mitigating the impact of the pandemic? Should people of the age group between 20–30 years be prioritized as they are the major spreaders? Or should the most vulnerable groups of the world's population have precedence, such as the elderly, patients affected by rare diseases, migrants, and disabled persons?

Against this backdrop, the WHO has undertaken several initiatives, specifically, the UN General Assembly and multilateral fora such as G7, with the goal

76 ICJ, "Case concerning the Barcelona Traction, Light and Power Company, Limited (New Application: 1962) (Belgio c. Spagna), Judgment of 5 February 1970", *ICJ Reports* (1970), p. 3 ss. The category of *erga omnes* obligations has since been reiterated in other cases. See ICJ, "Case concerning United States Diplomatic and Consular Staff in Tehran (United States v. Iran), Judgment of 24 May 1980", *ICJ Reports* (1980), p. 3 ss; ICJ, "Legal Consequences of the Construction of a Wall in the Occupied Palestinian Territory, Advisory Opinion, 9 July 2004", *ICJ Reports* (2004), 136 ss.
77 Bruce Jenks, "The United Nations and Global Public Goods: Historical Contributions and Future Challenges", in Gilles Carbonnier (ed.), *International Development Policy: Aid, Emerging Economies and Global Policies* (Palgrave Macmillan: 2012), 31–47.
78 James Crawford, "The ILC's Articles on Responsibility of States for Internationally Wrongful Acts: A Retrospect", *American Journal of International Law* (2002): 874–890.
79 Giorgio Gaja, "Obligations and Rights 'Erga Omnes' in International Law: Second Edition, Report for the Insitut de droit international: Annuaire de l'Institut de droit international (2005)".
80 See Kavya Sekar, "Domestic Funding for COVID-19 Vaccines: An Overview", *Congressional Research Service: Insights* (29 March 2020), https://crsreports.congress.gov/product/pdf/IN/IN11556.

of guaranteeing fair and equitable access to COVID-19 vaccines and treatments. These initiatives have often relied on GPG rhetoric, without offering concrete alternatives to the IP mechanism.

6. Specific declarations on fair and equitable access

6.1. Global level

6.1.1. WHO

During the 73rd World Health Assembly (WHA) Assembly (18–19 May 2020), a resolution on COVID-19 was adopted through consensus and with the support of 140 countries.[81]

The WHA called particularly for the "universal, timely and equitable access to, and fair distribution of, all quality, safe, efficacious and affordable essential health technologies and *products* . . . that are required in the response to the COVID-19 pandemic as a *global priority*".

Against this backdrop, the WHA expressly recalled the flexibilities within the Doha Declaration on the TRIPS Agreement and Public Health, although it made no explicit reference to the use of compulsory licenses.[82]

However, the WHA did not declare COVID-19 vaccines as GPGs; the WHO Resolution declared only "*extensive immunization* against Covid-19" as a GPG without specifically mentioning the role of vaccines (which are essential to immunization) (Para. 6).[83]

Vaccines and immunization are not the same thing, but they are directly related. Immunization describes the effect,[84] while vaccines describe the action.[85]

Against this backdrop, Costa Rica made a concrete proposal to the WHO:[86] the Solidarity Call to Action put forward a voluntary licensing mechanism of

---

81 WHA Resolution 'COVID-19 Response', *WHA 73.1* (19 May 2020), https://apps.who. int/gb/ebwha/pdf_files/WHA73/A73_CONF1Rev1-en.pdf. Pedro A. Villareal, "Pandemic Intrigue in Geneva: COVID-19 and the 73rd World Health Assembly", *EJIL Talk* (22 May 2020), https://www.ejiltalk.org/pandemic-intrigue-in-geneva-covid-19-and-the-73rd-world-health-assembly/.

82 WHA 73 United States of America Explanation of Position "COVID-19 Response" Resolution Written Statement.

83 Paragraph 6 of the Resolution reads, "WHO recognizes the role of extensive immunization against COVID-19 as a global public good for health in preventing, containing and stopping transmission to bring the pandemic to an end, once safe, quality, efficacious, effective, accessible and affordable vaccines are available".

84 Immunization is the process whereby a person is made immune or resistant to an infectious disease, typically by the administration of a vaccine. https://www.cdc.gov/vaccines/vac-gen/imz-basics.htm.

85 Vaccination employs vaccines to stimulate the body's own immune system to protect the person against subsequent infection or disease. https://www.who.int/health-topics/vaccines-and-immunization#tab=tab_1.

86 Costa Rica Open Letter to World Health Organization (March 2020), https://www.keionline.org/wp-content/uploads/President-MoH-Costa-Rica-Dr-Tedros-WHO24March2020.pdf.

COVID-19 treatments once available.[87] The Solidarity Call to Action invited patent holders to voluntarily share knowledge, intellectual property, and data necessary to combat COVID-19.[88] That is, the government of Costa Rica proposed the creation of a global pooling mechanism with the aim of facilitating access to and the use of IP for the technologies that are necessary to detect, prevent, control, and treat the pandemic. It further proposed that the global IP pooling mechanism "should provide free access or licensing on reasonable and affordable terms, in every member country". A patent pooling mechanism had already been debated in response to previous disease outbreaks (SARS, H5N1 influenza, and H1N1 influenza).

Costa Rica's proposal was inspired by the Medicines Patent Pool's system (MPP). MPP is a UN-backed public health organization that aims to increase access to and facilitate the development of life-saving medicines and vaccines for LMICs.[89] The WHO had already inquired into the possibility of patent pools in the context of the SARS epidemic in 2002 and SARS-CoV (1) in 2003.[90]

On 12 November 2020, a group of 18 pharmaceutical companies that represent a significant portion of the world's generic pharmaceutical manufacturers committed to cooperate with MPP in order to accelerate and guarantee access to significant doses of new COVID-19 treatments for LMICs.[91] Despite this generic pledge, manufacturers, however, decided not to practically support such an initiative, and MPP was therefore doomed to failure.

6.1.2. United Nations

The General Assembly (GA) has acknowledged on several occasions the importance of global cooperation in tackling the COVID-19 pandemic. In 2020, it filled the vacuum left by the deadlock within the Security Council due to the dispute between the United States and China on the source of COVID-19 and the disregard of the former Trump administration towards multilateralism. Resolution 74/270 (2020) on global solidarity to fight the coronavirus

---

87 Making the response to COVID-19 a public common good. Solidarity Call to Action.

88 For more details, see "Making the Response to COVID-19 a Public Common Good: Solidarity Call to Action" (1 June 2020), https://www.who.int/initiatives/covid-19-technology-access-pool/solidarity-call-to-action/docs/default-source/coronaviruse/solidarity-call-to-action/solidarity-call-to-action-01-june-2020. See also Muhammad Zaheer Abbas, "Treatment of the Novel COVID-19: Why Costa Rica's Proposal for the Creation of a Global Pooling Mechanism Deserves Serious Consideration?" *Journal of Law and the Biosciences* (2020): 1–10.

89 https://medicinespatentpool.org/.

90 James H. Simon, Erica Claassen, Carmen Correa, Albert D. Osterhaus: "Managing Severe Acute Respiratory Syndrome (SARS) Intellectual Property Rights: The Possible Role of Patent Pooling", *Bulletin of the WHO* (September 2005), 707–710.

91 Open Pledge from Global Manufacturers of Generic Medicines Against COVID-19, https://medicinespatentpool.org/partners/mpp_global_manufacturers_open_pledge/.

disease 2019 (COVID-19)[92] recognized in the Preamble that the COVID-19 pandemic requires "a global response based on unity, *solidarity* and renewed multilateral cooperation".

This resolution took the form of a declaration of principles, and it was the first act adopted by the GA urging unity and global cooperation.

Although it did not expressly mention treatments or vaccines against COVID-19, it underlined core principles that should underpin the global response, such as support for the role of the UN and multilateralism, respect for human rights, the condemnation of racism and xenophobia, and attention to the most vulnerable groups.

On 20 April 2020, a specific resolution on access to treatments and vaccines against COVID-19 was adopted. It is an action-oriented resolution, which was put forward by Mexico, cosponsored by 179 countries, and adopted by consensus.[93] The Resolution is entitled "international cooperation to ensure global access to medicines, vaccines and medical equipment to face COVID-19".[94]

The reference to international cooperation in this resolution, the recognition by all UN Member States of the necessity of multilateral action to fight the pandemic, and the key role of IGOs were considered "a sign of good health of international cooperation".[95]

The first preambular paragraph recognizes that the pandemic "requires a global response based on unity, solidarity, and multilateral cooperation".

In Operative Paragraph (OP) 1, the AG reaffirms the coordinating role of both the UN and the WHO in addressing the COVID-19 pandemic. The United States, while deciding not to vote against the resolution, openly expressed its concern to the express reference to the WHO in OP1.[96]

The resolution then establishes the necessity to set up a multilateral mechanism to ensure "fair, transparent, equitable, efficient and timely access to and distribution of . . . COVID-19 vaccines, with a view to making them available to all those in need, in particular in developing countries" (OP 2).

The problem is that an efficient multilateral mechanism based on the principles of equity and solidarity – except for COVAX – was never set up, and

92 Resolution n. 74/270, 2 April 2020, "Global Solidarity to Fight the Coronavirus Disease 2019(COVID-19)", https://undocs.org/pdf?symbol=en/A/RES/74/270. The Resolution was promoted by a heterogeneous group of States (Ghana, Indonesia, Liechtenstein, Norway, Singapore and Switzerland) and was adopted through the 'Covid-19-silence procedure' foreseen by UNGA Decision n. 74/544.

93 Pablo Arrocha Olabuenaga, Juan Ramón de la Fuente, "Mexico's Initiative to Ensure Global Access to Medicines, Vaccines and Medical Equipment to Face COVID19", *JustSecurity.org* (29 April 2020).

94 Resolution n. A/74/L.56, 8 April 2020.

95 Raymundo T. Treves, "The Health of International Cooperation and UNGA Resolution 74/274", *Questions of International Law, Zoom-out* 70 (2020): 21–36, at 30.

96 USA, Explanation of Position on Res A/74/274 (20 April 2020).

domestic egoism in the roll out of COVID-19 vaccines prevailed, as indicated by the proliferation of APAs.

Then, the GA encouraged Member States in coordination with the private sector to develop, manufacture and distribute COVID-19 vaccines following the key principles of "efficacy, safety, *equity, accessibility, and affordability*" (OP 3).

The GA recognized the goal of guaranteeing global access to medicines, vaccines, and medical equipment that were needed to face COVID-19 (Art. 5).

The principle of equity was then recalled by the UN Secretary-General on 17 February 2021 where he emphasized that vaccine equity was "the biggest moral test".[97]

Considering the roll out of COVID-19 vaccines, he envisaged the creation of an Emergency Task Force among G20 countries to develop a global immunization plan, and he recognized a role of the Security Council to guarantee the availability of vaccine doses in countries characterized by instability and insecurity.

A similar position was taken at a regional level by the Parliamentary Assembly of the Council of Europe with Resolution 2361 (2021),[98] which stated that "an equitable deployment of COVID-19 vaccines is also needed to ensure the efficacy of the vaccine. If not widely enough distributed in a severely hit area of a country, vaccines become ineffective at stemming the tide of the pandemic" (Para. 4).

It asked Member States to ensure high quality trials that are sound, conducted in an ethical manner and in line with the relevant provisions of the European Convention on Human Rights and Biomedicine, and progressively include children, pregnant women, and nursing mothers (Para. 7.1.1).

The Assembly then quoted the principle of equitable access to health care affirmed in Article 3 of the Biomedicine Convention in framing national vaccine allocation plans, which should guarantee that "Covid-19 vaccines are available to the population regardless of gender, race, religion, legal or socioeconomic status, ability to pay, location and other factors that often contribute to inequities within the population" (Para. 7.1.2).[99] States should then develop strategies for the equitable distribution of COVID-19 vaccines both within member States (Para. 7.1.2.), "taking into account that the supply will

97 https://reliefweb.int/report/world/secretary-general-calls-vaccine-equity-biggest-moral-test-global-community-security.
98 Resolution 2361 (2021) Covid-19 vaccines: ethical, legal and practical considerations, 27 January 2021.
99 Article 3 of the Biomedicine Convention states that "Parties, taking into account health needs and available resources, shall take appropriate measures with a view to providing, within their jurisdiction, equitable access to health care of appropriate quality".

initially be low, and prepare for how to expand vaccination programmes when the supply expands" (Para. 7.2.2).

7. The COVAX initiative

The UN and the WHO clearly maintain that all countries – regardless of their developmental or economic status – should have access to available treatments and vaccines against COVID-19.

The overarching principles – which should guide the global roll out of COVID-19 vaccines – as highlighted by the WHO during the COVID-19 pandemic and reiterated in the WHO CA+, are solidarity, accountability, transparency, responsiveness to public health needs, equity and fairness, affordability, collaboration, and regulatory and procurement efficiency.[100]

The WHO Solidarity Call to Action ("Making the response to COVID-19 a public common good") of 1 June 2020 invited patent holders to voluntarily place patented products necessary for COVID-19 (once available) in the MPP[101] so that they were available on a non-exclusive basis for licensing in every country and be affordable and accessible, especially in LMICs.

The WHO, the Global Alliance for Vaccines (GAVI), and the Coalition for Epidemic Preparedness Innovations (CEPI) then shaped a global framework, namely, the Access to COVID-19 Tools (ACT) Accelerator, which was intended as a global collaboration to accelerate development, production, and equitable access to COVID-19 tests, treatments, and vaccines (a pooling of financial and scientific resources).[102] The ACT Accelerator was built on the public-private partnership (PPP) model, which permeates global health governance.[103]

Within this framework, COVAX – one of the pillars of the ACT Accelerator – was established as "a global risk-sharing mechanism for pooled procurement and equitable distribution of coronavirus vaccines".[104] It facilitates the equitable access and distribution of COVID-19 vaccines (with a prioritization of

---

100   WHO Concept for fair access and equitable allocation of COVID-19 health products. Final working version. 9 September 2020, file:///C:/Users/cnr%20ethics/Downloads/who-covid19-vaccine-allocation-final-working-version-9sept.pdf.

101   It negotiates voluntary licenses with originator companies to allow generic manufacturers to make generic drugs for HIV, tuberculosis, and hepatitis C.

102   Pia Acconci, "L'effettività delle azioni internazionali per l'immunizzazione planetaria anti COVID-19 tra interessi collettivi e unilaterali", *Eurojus* (2021): 51–68, at 55.

103   On the growing role of public-private partnerships in the fight against epidemics and pandemics, Jelena von Achenbach, "The Global Distribution of COVID-19 Vaccines by the Public-Private Partnership COVAX from a Public-Law Perspective", *Leiden Journal of International Law* (2023): 1–25; Katerini Tagmatarchi Storeng, Antoine de Bengy Puyvallée, Felix Stein, "COVAX and the Rise of the 'Super Public Private Partnership' for Global Health", *Global Public Health* (2021): 1–17.

104   https://www.gavi.org/covax-facility.

people most at risk and vulnerable groups) at a given price.[105] It was established with the aim of creating incentives towards R&D and minimizing and overcoming the problem of APAs and vaccine nationalism.

COVAX developed a diversified portfolio of vaccines and negotiated with different pharmaceutical companies with different scientific technologies, delivery times, and prices. The system envisions the possibility for high-income, self-financing countries to purchase vaccines from COVAX at an estimated average price of $11 per dose; a different price (an average price between $1 and $2 per dose) was established for LMICs.

COVAX was conceived as a "risk-sharing mechanism": it has diminished the risk for drug companies that have invested a considerable amount of funds in R&D without being sure about future demand. At the same time, it reduces the prospect that LMICs will not have access to sufficient doses of COVID-19 vaccines.

The ACT Accelerator and COVAX were established in order to guarantee a fair and equal distribution of COVID-19 vaccines and treatments without discrimination.[106]

COVAX has distributed vaccines in LMICs according to a blueprint, specifically, the WHO "Fair Allocation Framework", with the goal of covering 20% of the most vulnerable people in LMICs.

This public-private partnership is certainly an innovative setting and is very much in the logic of global governance. The Biden administration pledged $4 billion to COVAX, marking a sharp departure from Trump's free-riding strategy,[107] and designated 10% of vaccines produced in the United States to LMICs.[108]

The EU, for its part, is one of the leading contributors to COVAX with over €2.2 billion, including another €900 million pledged by Germany.[109]

105 In total, 64 higher income economies have signed the commitment agreement to COVAX (not the EU due to charges of a lack of transparency and conflict of interest). Moreover, 92 LMICs are eligible for support to procure vaccines through the GAVI COVAX Advance Market Commitment (AMC), a financing instrument aimed at supporting the procurement of vaccines for these countries.

106 Armin Von Bodgdandy, Pedro A. Villareal, "The Role of International Law in Vaccinating Against Covid-19: Appraising the Covax Inixiative", *MPIL Research Paper Series, No. 2020-46* (2020): 1–24, <file:///C:/Users/cnr%20ethics/Downloads/SSRN-id3733454.pdf>.

107 *Fact Sheet: President Biden to Take Action on Global Health through Support of COVAX and Calling for Health Security Financing* (18 February 2021), https://www.whitehouse.gov/briefing-room/statements-releases/2021/02/18/fact-sheet-president-biden-to-take-action-on-global-health-through-support-of-covax-and-calling-for-health-security-financing/.

108 https://www.whitehouse.gov/briefing-room/speeches-remarks/2021/05/04/remarks-by-president-biden-on-the-covid-19-response-and-the-vaccination-program/.

109 https://ec.europa.eu/commission/presscorner/detail/en/IP_21_690. See also Ann Danaiya Usher, "Uncertainties over EU COVID-19 Vaccine Sharing Scheme. Legal Hurdles and Political Questions Remain Over a European Commission Mechanism for Donating COVID-19 Vaccines to Other Nations", *The Lancet* (2021): 1197.

A shift towards multilateralism as a consequence of the election of United States President Joe Biden in place of Donald J. Trump was evident in the wording of the final statement of the G7 of February 2020.

A new alliance between the United States and the EU to defeat the pandemic through multilateralism was the key element of the G7 summit of February 2021. There is a clear reference to the necessity to work "with, and together to strengthen, the World Health Organization (WHO), and supporting its leading and coordinating role".

G7 leaders decided to increase support for COVAX in 2021 and committed US \$4.3 billion to ensure fair and equitable access to tests, treatments, and vaccines.[110]

However, the unilateral policies of developed countries have transformed this device that is an instrument for a global vaccine roll out addressed exclusively to low-income countries ("financed states"). The group of 91 recipient countries have been selected on the basis of their Gross Domestic Product. The first round of allocation of COVID-19 vaccines began at the end of February 2021, and the first recipients were Ghana, Côte d'Ivoire, Angola, Rwanda, Sudan, Sierra Leone, and Tajikistan.[111]

Despite its achievements, the COVAX initiative has had several shortcomings. COVAX, initially heralded as the global solution to the global delivery of COVID-19 vaccines and treatments, was in practice slightly successful on the procurement side due to a temporal delay in the acquisition of vaccine doses for LMICs. Although the first shipments of vaccines addressed to LMICs began at the end of February 2021, by mid-March 2021, the United Kingdom had already immunized one-third of its population.

There are several reasons (political and foundational) behind the partial failure of COVAX.

The political one is that most high-income countries have chosen to bypass the COVAX portfolio and enter into unilateral deals with pharmaceutical companies to purchase in advance a large amount of COVID-19 vaccines doses.

In addition, the system was originally conceived as reliant on the goodwill and good faith of high-income countries to fund COVAX's advance market commitment to purchase vaccine doses intended for LMICs. That is, the COVAX facility has not challenged the current IP mechanism or proposed to waive IP and to improve technology transfer towards LMICs.

Facing the wide spread of the pandemic and its deadly variants, a group of States beyond COVAX began a global mobilization requesting a derogation from the current legal framework of the rigid defense of IP of the multinationals that own the IPRs related to the vaccines against COVID-19. Accordingly,

---

110 *G7 Leaders' Statement* (19 February 2021), http://www.governo.it/sites/governo.it/files/G7LeadersStatement_20210219.pdf.

111 https://www.gavi.org/covax-vaccine-roll-out.

on 2 October 2020, India and South Africa submitted a formal proposal to the WTO asking for a temporary waiver of IP on COVID-19 vaccines.[112]

They specifically pointed out that the flexibilities already envisaged by the TRIPS agreement are part of a complex and lengthy process, requiring each country to apply individually. The key problem is thus related to the remuneration that is due to the pharmaceutical company, which is, however, unaffordable for most countries. This mechanism should have therefore been shortened and simplified.

They then underlined that most pharmaceutical companies received a considerable amount of public resources. AstraZeneca and Moderna have effectively received funds from governments,[113] while the Pfizer-BioNTech vaccine was instead entirely privately funded.

The decisive point was the decision to reject their proposal to derogate from IP rights protection with the votes of all Western countries, including the United States (in the first phase) and the EU along with the support of the former Brazilian President Bolsonaro. The United States eventually decided to back the proposal to lift temporarily patent protections for coronavirus vaccines,[114] but despite this support, they found strong opposition by Germany.

Therefore, some countries decided to shield pharmaceutical companies' IP rights from a potential loss of profit, although they provided public funding for R&D.

Navigating this divide was Okonjo-Iweala, Director-General of the WTO, who proposed a compromise "in which we can license manufacturing to countries so that you can have adequate supplies while still making sure that intellectual property issues are taken care of".[115]

Such a move had already been taken with the AstraZeneca vaccine, and an emergency use authorization was provided to the Serum Institute of India (SII) to manufacture a generic version of the AZ vaccine.[116] The Biden administration backed the solution of the WTO.[117]

---

112 Waiver from Certain Provisions of the TRIPS Agreement for the Prevention, Containment and Treatment of Covid-19 Communication from India and South Africa, https://docs.wto.org/dol2fe/Pages/SS/directdoc.aspx?filename=q:/IP/C/W669.pdf&Open=True.

113 https://www.forbes.com/sites/judystone/2020/12/03/the-peoples-vaccine-modernas-coronavirus-vaccine-was-largely-funded-by-taxpayer-dollars/?sh=2f3103656303.

114 https://www.bbc.com/news/world-us-canada-57004302.

115 Jonathan Josephs, "New WTO Boss Warns Against Vaccine Nationalism", *BBC News* (16 February 2021), https://www.bbc.com/news/business-56079088.

116 https://www.astrazeneca.com/media-centre/press-releases/2021/serum-institute-of-india-obtains-emergency-use-authorisation-in-india-for-astrazenecas-covid-19-vaccine.html.

117 David Brunnstrom, Michael Martina, "Exclusive: Quad Nations Meeting to Announce Financing to Boost India Vaccine Output – U.S. Official", *Reuters* (9 March 2021), https://www.reuters.com/article/us-health-coronavirus-vaccines-quad-excl/exclusive-quad-nations-meeting-to-announce-financing-to-boost-india-vaccine-output-u-s-official-idUSK-BN2B12QM.

8. Some remarks on the lessons learned by vaccine nationalism

COVAX was the largest, widest vaccine roll out in history, with a global participation amounting to 191 countries. COVAX – despite criticism – managed to allocate over a billion vaccines to over 140 countries.

COVAX was initially conceived as the global solution for a coordinated distribution of COVID-19 vaccines among both richer and poorer countries, but it eventually followed a charity logic by distancing itself from the narrative of common public goods echoed by the EU and the UN and its specialized agencies

Vaccine nationalism, however, is a clear signal of the failure of international law to shift from a law of coexistence to a law of international cooperation. The lack of a fair and equitable distribution of COVID-19 vaccines – allowing few countries to vaccinate their own populations first and leaving LMICs behind – has shown, first, that international cooperation has floundered in the age of the COVID-19 pandemic, and health inequalities have been hampered. Criteria such as better management of the pandemic, as shown by the cases of Australia, New Zealand, Thailand, and Vietnam, and major vulnerabilities, as represented by LMICs, did not provide preferential access to COVID-19 vaccines.

The problem is that the global landscape has switched from the rhetoric of GPGs to a reality based on nationalism and statism.

Vaccine nationalism was a missed opportunity to enhance global cooperation in the health sector. Despite the lack of an international agreement on equitable access to COVID-19 vaccines or treatments, it is worth recalling that the previously mentioned Goal 3 of the Sustainable Development Goals/ UN Agenda 2030 explicitly requires States to guarantee safe, effective, quality, and affordable vaccines.

Since the situation arising out the COVID-19 pandemic is exceptional, one solution that COVAX failed to address could have been to treat all COVID-19-related products (vaccines, treatments, and medical equipment) as GPGs: this would have implied the absence of IP restrictions on their use and the qualification of vaccines as an open source tool.[118] Although it does not challenge IP protection, the WHO CA+ recognizes in the Preamble, at Paragraph 49, "the need to establish a future pandemic prevention, preparedness and response mechanism that *is not based on a charity model*".

As long as the supply of vaccines remained constrained, the majority of LMICs were not able to start the type of mass vaccination programmes that gathered pace in the developed world. The lack of a global roll out has widened the risk of further mutations of the virus, potentially undermining the effectiveness of existing vaccines.

---

118 For further details, Nerina Boschiero, "Covid-19 Vaccines as Global Common Goods: An Integrated Approach of Ethical, Economic Policy and Intellectual Property Management" *Global Jurist* 22(2) (2022): 177–230.

Beyond IP, another unaddressed issue that hampered the scaling up of vaccine supply was the complexity of ramping up vaccine manufacturing capacity.

The issue of the unfair distribution of COVID-19 vaccines has, however, provided important lessons to the international community. For example, the problems related to a global roll out of a vaccine in the presence of an epidemic and pandemic should be addressed in peace time and not during an emergency situation.

In light of the lessons of the previous H1N1 pandemic, the international community should have set up a global plan to scale up vaccine production, well before COVID-19 vaccines were developed, in order to transfer sufficient know how, expertise, and manufacturing capacity to LMICs.[119]

Part II Mandatory COVID-19 vaccinations and human rights in Europe: How to find a delicate balance?

9. Vaccine hesitancy

Vaccinations are considered among the greatest medical achievements of modern medicine. The discovery of the COVID-19 vaccines and the roll out of mass vaccination campaigns (including booster doses and vaccines for minors) have allowed developed countries to slowly come back to normal life by immunizing most of their populations and entering a post-pandemic scenario.[120]

The development of a vaccine is a lengthy process that usually takes several years and different stages (preclinical, studies on animals, clinics, and then large-scale vaccine production and licensing).

The speed with which COVID-19 vaccines were devised was notably faster compared to other vaccines. Their discovery first raised the challenge of how to make these vaccines rapidly, fairly, and equitably accessible to the whole world's population. Against this backdrop, there is the wider issue correlated with vaccine nationalism[121] – which was deeply discussed in Part I of this chapter – that created a distributive dilemma and the problem of timely access to affordable medicines, since the COVID-19 pandemic has generated a global demand for such vaccines that has by far exceeded supply and as a consequence, the world's vaccination imbalance.[122]

119 Against this backdrop, the EU and the United States set up a joint COVID-19 Manufacturing and Supply Chain Taskforce to deepen "cooperation and resolve issues around expanding vaccine and therapeutics production capacity" (Para. 3). United States–European Commission Joint Statement: Launch of the joint COVID-19 Manufacturing and Supply Chain Taskforce Brussels, 22 September 2021, file:///C:/Users/cnr%20ethics/Downloads/United_States_European_Commission_Joint_Statement__Launch_of_the_joint_COVID-19_Manufacturing_and_Supply_Chain_Taskforce.pdf.
120 The first safe and effective vaccine against COVID-19 was authorized by the European Commission through a conditional marketing authorization in December 2021 (https://ec.europa.eu/commission/presscorner/detail/en/ip_20_2466).
121 David P. Fidler, "Vaccine Nationalism's Politics", *Science* (2021): 749.
122 *Supra*, note 6.

The COVID-19 vaccine race highlighted a fracture between the call for universal and equitable access to COVID-19 vaccination by the UN and its specialized agencies and multilateral initiatives towards this goal, such as COVAX, on the one hand, and national isolationism, on the other hand.

At the same time, another major critical challenge related to COVID-19 vaccines – referred to as vaccine hesitancy – has emerged.[123] Vaccine hesitancy is the delay in acceptance or refusal of vaccines despite availability of vaccination services.[124] In 2019, it was classified by the WHO as one of the ten threats to global health.[125]

In general terms, the increase in social resistance towards vaccinations – especially in industrialized countries – has forced some States to adopt restrictive policies that imply a vaccination duty, especially with reference to minors. Currently, considerable literature – which analyzes the c.d. "determinants" (psychological, social, cultural, demographical, and economic factors) of vaccine hesitancy – has been developed.[126] Among these – as is well-known – a key role is played by misinformation ("fake news") conveyed by groups against vaccinations through the use of social networks.[127]

In general terms, some individuals are hesitant towards vaccines on scientific grounds (they are reluctant about the safety and efficacy of the vaccines), and others are reluctant for religious reasons. With reference to the COVID-19 vaccines, extremist religious groups have contested the fact that some vaccines (particularly Johnson & Johnson and AstraZeneca) were presumably developed using embryonic or fetal cells. In the United States, historical fetal cell lines were stored in the 1960s and 1970s and have already

---

123 As previously stated, the attainment of herd immunity against the COVID-19 pandemic would require the vaccination of at least 70% of the world's population and is thus a major challenge. OECD, "Access to COVID-19 vaccines: Global approaches in a global crisis", *OECD Policy Responses to Coronavirus (COVID-19)* (OECD Publishing: 2021), https://doi.org/10.1787/c6a18370-en.

124 According to the European Centre for Disease Prevention and Control, "vaccine hesitancy refers to delay in acceptance or refusal of vaccines despite availability of vaccination services. Vaccine hesitancy is complex and context specific varying across time, place and vaccines. It includes factors such as complacency, convenience and confidence". https://www.ecdc.europa.eu/en/immunisation-vaccines/vaccine-hesitancy.

125 https://www.who.int/news-room/spotlight/ten-threats-to-global-health-in-2019.

126 See, among others, Andrea Grignolio, *Vaccines: Are They Worth a Shot?* (Springer: 2018).

127 It is worth recalling that the key scientific publication arguing a causal link between autism and measles, mumps, and rubella vaccines (Andrew J. Wakefield, et al. "Lleal-Lymphoid-Nodular Hyperplasia, Nonspecific Colitis, and Pervasive Developmental Disorder in Children", *Lancet* (1998): 637–641) was retracted. According to the retraction, "no causal link was established between MMR vaccine and autism as the data were insufficient". This is one of the most famous cases of scientific fraud. Dr. Wakefield's claims caused a serious drop in vaccination rates in the United Kingdom since they had a deep impact on public opinion, and Wakefield's findings are still used by people against vaccination as evidence that vaccines are a public health risk. This link has since been refuted by several scientific studies. See, for instance, Anjali Jain, Jaclyn Marshall, Ami Buikema et al., "Autism Occurrence by MMR Vaccine Status Among US Children With Older Siblings With and Without Autism", *JAMA (The Journal of American Medical Association)* 313 (15) (2015): 1534–1540.

been used to fabricate vaccines for several diseases (in particular, hepatitis A, rubella, and rabies). However, the fetal cell lines that were allegedly used to produce COVID-19 vaccines – that relied on adenovirus approaches – have never required or solicited new abortions.[128]

Vaccine hesitancy raises the issue of which strategies can be adopted in order to have the widest coverage of the population immunized (mandatory vaccination policies, mechanisms based on incentives, and an indirect vaccination obligation through the wide use of vaccine passports). In particular, it refers to the relationship between a compulsory and mandatory vaccination for the prevention of the SARS-CoV-2 infection based on public health reasons and individual human rights (such as the right to privacy and the right to conscientious objection by both the patient and the physician). Vaccine hesitancy is a serious threat in the fight against the COVID-19 pandemic and has forced several countries to adopt direct or indirect compulsory mechanisms on vaccinations to prevent SARS-CoV-2 infection.[129]

In this respect, this chapter highlights the importance of science not only in assessing the extent to which pandemic-related measures are proportional to the risks but also in choosing the least restrictive and the most individualized options when restricting civil and political rights because of public health reasons.

This chapter revolves around three key assumptions. First, the collective dimension of the right to health prevails over its individual feature. Therefore, the collective interest in the protection of public health takes precedence over the interest of an individual to (allegedly) protect their own health against the side effects of vaccines, to provide his/her informed consent for medical treatment, and to preserve his/her privacy not to disclose any information about their health status.

Coercion in liberal societies can be justified only in order to prevent harm to other members of a given community. Vaccination generally protects those vaccinated against a given infectious disease but it also affects others. During a pandemic, such as in the case of COVID-19, it is essential to immunize most of the population for two simple reasons: first, people who are infected, even if asymptomatic, can be a deadly threat to others; second, if a large part of the population is affected by the virus, it might overburden the health care system and impede others from having access to essential health assistance.

---

128 https://www.health.nd.gov/sites/www/files/documents/COVID%20Vaccine%20Page/COVID19_Vaccine_Fetal_Cell_Handout.pdf.

129 Charles Shey Wiysonge, Duduzile Ndwandwe, Jill Ryan, Anelisa Jaca, Oumarou Batouré, Blanche-Philomene Melanga Anya, Sara Cooper, "Vaccine Hesitancy in the Era of COVID-19: Could Lessons from the Past Help in Divining the Future?", *Human Vaccines and Immunotherapeutics* (2021): 1–3.

Against this backdrop, under the lens of European interstate relations, Part II of this chapter is divided in three sections. First, it briefly reconstructs the current legal frameworks for administering vaccines against the most common infectious diseases as adopted by domestic authorities to reach the goal of herd immunity, with particular reference to the Council of Europe's Member States, such as Italy, Germany, France, and the United Kingdom. Second, it focuses on the policies of some European countries to tackle the COVID-19 pandemic in the "hot period" of diffusion of the virus between the end of 2021 and early 2022. Third, the chapter specifically focuses on the jurisprudence of the European Court of Human Rights regarding compulsory childhood vaccination and its implication on State policies concerning COVID-19 vaccinations.

A particular focus is devoted to the key case of *Vavřička and Others v. the Czech Republic* (2022), which highlights the Court's approach to the issue of mandatory vaccination, since the Court's decision was adopted at the height of the COVID-19 pandemic.

On this basis, the chapter argues that compulsory COVID-19 vaccination – a path slowly followed by some European countries such as Austria – is perfectly consistent with the ECHR and does not violate fundamental rights.[130] This chapter claims that a vaccine obligation is in line with the evolutionary interpretation of the Strasbourg's Court.

10. A brief history of vaccination policies

An individual's decision to receive or to refuse a vaccine has significant implications for the whole community.

A vaccine provides a direct benefit to the individual and an indirect asset to the community by reducing the risk of spread of a specific outbreak through herd immunity.[131] The security threshold represented by the community immunity is a mechanism according to which, once reached, the coverage of immunized population below 95% of a given infectious disease would not spread either among the subjects that voluntarily or due to health reasons (such as immunosuppressed children) are not vaccinated. It is worth recalling that a few individuals cannot be vaccinated for health reasons and must therefore rely on the indirect benefits of the vaccination.

The maintenance of high vaccination coverage is therefore critically important. Domestic authorities have adopted several strategies to promote and

---

130 With reference to the Council of Europe, it is worth recalling that following the expulsion of the Russian Federation from the Council of Europe on 16 March 2022, as consequence of the invasion of Ukraine, this country ceased to be a party to the European Convention on Human Rights on 16 September 2022, https://www.coe.int/en/web/portal/-/the-russian-federation-is-excluded-from-the-council-of-europe.

131 https://www.nhs.uk/conditions/vaccinations/why-vaccination-is-safe-and-important/.

maintain a higher immunization rate coverage among their populations, including but not limited to mandatory vaccination.[132]

The first compulsory vaccination program was related to smallpox in the XIX Century. Compulsory vaccination is connected to a school of thought developed in Germany according to which the State has a specific duty of taking care of the health of its own citizens, since they were tax payers and potential soldiers. In 1874, vaccination obligation was introduced in the *Reich*.[133] The United Kingdom had instead strong resistances due to its liberal tradition of non-interference by the State in private life. States policies on compulsory or voluntary vaccination must find a delicate balance between different rights and values (individual dimension of health and self-determination *versus* the collective dimension of health).[134]

Vaccination against a given infectious disease can be voluntary or mandatory. Within this spectrum, three different legislative approaches can be highlighted.[135] The first is represented by legal frameworks based on promotional logics through incentives (Australia, Germany, Spain, and the United Kingdom); this means that immunization is not a basic requirement to attend school, but it is highly recommended. The second relates to a legal order with a tendency towards obligatoriness (Canada and the United States).[136] The third is a legal regime with a paternalistic footprint (France and Italy).

In a continuum that goes from the maximum protection of the self-determination of the individual, on the one hand, to the maximum attention to the requirements of public health protection, on the other hand, Germany and the United Kingdom give more weight to the individual dimension of the right to health.

In the United Kingdom, parents – as the trustees of their children's best interests – are entitled to decide whether or not to vaccinate their offspring.[137] The intervention of the public authority can only be registered in certain cases, for instance, of disagreement of views among the parents; in this case, the *favor* towards vaccination emerges considering the jurisprudence of the domestic courts.

---

132 Katie Gravagna, Andy Becker, Robert Valeris-Chacin, Inari Mohammed, Sailee Tambe, Fareed A. Awan, Traci L. Toomey, Nicole E. Basta, "Global Assessment of National Mandatory Vaccination Policies and Consequences of Non-Compliance", *Vaccine* (2020): 7865–7873.

133 Gerard Krause, "The Historical Development of Immunization in Germany: From Compulsory Smallpox Vaccination to a National Action Plan on Immunization", *Bundesgesundheitsblatt – Gesundheitsforschung – Gesundheitsschutz* (2012): 1512–1523.

134 Vaccination Act 1840, 1841, 1853: universal and complimentary vaccination. Obligation abolished in 1898.

135 For more details, see Marta Tomasi, "Vaccini e salute pubblica: percorsi di comparazione in equilibrio fra diritti individuali e doveri di solidarietà", *Diritto pubblico comparato ed europeo* (2017): 455–482.

136 Yilan Peng, "Politics of COVID-19 Vaccine Mandates: Left/Right-Wing Authoritarianism, Social Dominance Orientation, and Libertarianism", *Personality and Individual Differences* 76 (2022): 1–12.

137 Emma Cave, "Voluntary Vaccination: The Pandemic Effect", *Legal Studies* (2017): 279–304.

The idea according to which the choice of whether or not to vaccinate a child is mainly a matter for the parents is also strongly rooted in Germany where there is a strong emphasis on the necessity of a real conscious choice: Germany has not introduced a duty of vaccination but rather advice and consult with the medical staff in order to have a clear understanding of the risks and benefits related to the vaccination. Such an obligation is reinforced by the provision of a financial fine, and it is a pre-condition for the enrollment of a minor at school. However, measles vaccination became mandatory in 2020 for children, teachers, and health professionals.[138]

A compulsory model can be defined as a legal framework that foresees negative consequences because of the refusal of an individual to vaccinate himself/herself or his/her offspring. This duty is not therefore directly imposed through coercion upon an individual, but the legislation levies penalties against those who decide not to fulfill their obligations.

This scheme envisages various degrees of severity spanning from financial penalties, to the exclusion from school services, to the limitation of social and health services, up to the loss of parental rights.[139]

These ranges of penalties have been classified in four categories. The less intrusive are financial sanctions (those that have an impact on the finances of an individual through the imposition of a fine) or educational sanctions (those that have a direct impact on the education of a child through missed enrollment at school).[140] More severe implications imply parental rights' sanctions (such as the loss of parental rights) and liberty penalties (which have a direct implication on the personal freedom of an individual, such as imprisonment).

11. The European model on vaccinations

European countries rely on financial penalties more frequently than any other region of the world (56% of European countries have evidence of a national mandate).[141]

Additionally, Italy is the only country to list temporary loss of child custody as a penalty for non-compliance.[142]

138 Ingrid Torjesen, "German Parliament Votes to Make Measles Vaccination Mandatory", *British Medical Journal* (2019): 367.

139 *Legislative Approaches to Immunization Across the European Region* (Sabin Vaccine Institute: 2018), https://www.sabin.org/sites/sabin.org/files/legislative_approaches_to_immunization_europe_sabin_0.pdf.

140 Katie Gravagna, Andy Becker, Robert Valeris-Chacin, Inari Mohammed, Sailee Tambe, Fareed A. Awan, Traci L. Toomey, Nicole E. Basta, "Global Assessment of National Mandatory Vaccination Policies and Consequences of Non-Compliance", *Vaccine* (2020): 7865–7873.

141 Olivia M. Vaz, Mallory K. Ellingson, Paul Weiss, Samuel M. Jenness, Azucena Bardají, Robert A. Bednarczyk, Saad B. Omer, "Mandatory Vaccination in Europe", *Pediatrics* (2020): 1–16.

142 Fortunato D'Ancona, Claudio D'Amario, Francesco Maraglino, Giovanni Rezza, Stefania Iannazzo, "The Law on Compulsory Vaccination in Italy: An Update 2 Years After the Introduction", *Eurosurveillance* (2019): 1–4.

Among Council of Europe Member States, vaccination is mandatory for a cluster of infectious diseases, such as polio, tetanus, and hepatitis B (in France, Greece, Italy, Portugal, and countries of Eastern Europe, such as Bulgaria, Czeck Republic, Latvia, Poland, and Slovakia).

In Italy, the National Bioethics Committee registered in 2015 in statistical and epidemiological terms a significant drop in the percentage of people vaccinated in relation to infectious diseases considered at high risk of diffusion and contagion.[143] In response to this negative trend, the Italian public authorities introduced measures oriented towards a reinforcement of vaccination duties. The political and normative intervention was structured on two levels. One was of a programmatic nature and was concretized in the updating of the domestic vaccine prevention plan 2017–2019,[144] and the other was a legal intervention represented by the adoption of Legislative Decree n. 73/2017[145] and in the following conversion Law n. 73/2017 that improved the range of compulsory vaccines and reinforced coercive measures. Currently, the National Immunisation Plan (NIP) makes compulsory for children aged under 6 years of age vaccinations against pertussis, measles-mumps-rubella (MMR), varicella, and Haemophilus influenzae type b (Hib), in addition to diphtheria, tetanus, hepatitis B, and polio. This comported with a significant rise in vaccine coverage of over 90% for measles, mumps, and rubella.[146]

In addition, the French legal framework on compulsory vaccinations can be considered basically prescriptive, since vaccination of infants up to two years against 11 diseases (among which are diphtheria, tetanus, and poliomyelitis) is the *conditio sine qua non* for school enrollment, without the possibility of legal loopholes, except for strictly medical conditions related to the existence of counter indications.[147] To reinforce the compliance mechanism, the French

143 *Comitato Nazionale per la Bioetica, Mozione: l'importanza delle vaccinazioni* (24 April 2015), https://bioetica.governo.it/media/1409/m14_2015_vaccinazioni_it.pdf.

144 https://www.salute.gov.it/portale/vaccinazioni/dettaglioContenutiVaccinazioni.jsp?lingu a=italiano&id=4828&area=vaccinazioni&menu=vuoto.

145 Decreto Legislativo n. 73/2017, Ministero della Salute, 19 gennaio 2017, Disposizioni urgenti in materia di prevenzione vaccinale, di malattie infettive e di controversie relative alla somministrazione di farmaci, G.U. Serie generale – n. 130 del 7 giugno 2017, https://www. gazzettaufficiale.it/eli/id/2017/08/05/17A05515/sg.

146 Fortunato D'Ancona, Claudio D'Amario, Francesco Maraglino, Giovanni Rezza, Stefania Iannazzo, "The Law on Compulsory Vaccination in Italy: An Update 2 Years After the Introduction", *Eurosurveillance* (2019), https://www.ncbi.nlm.nih.gov/pmc/articles/ PMC6607737/.

147 Code de la santé publique, Article L3111–2: "I. – Les vaccinations suivantes sont obligatoires, sauf contre-indication médicale reconnue, dans des conditions d'âge déterminées par décret en Conseil d'Etat, pris après avis de la Haute Autorité de santé: Antidiphtérique; Antitétanique; Antipoliomyélitique; Contre la coqueluche; Contre les infections invasives à Haemophilus influenzae de type b; Contre le virus de l'hépatite B; Contre les infections invasives à pneumocoque; Contre le méningocoque de sérogroupe C; Contre la rougeole; Contre les oreillons; Contre la rubéole. "II – Les personnes titulaires de l'autorité parentale ou qui

legal framework envisages criminal sanctions addressed to the parents who have not provided for the given vaccinations. This extremely rigid system has been endorsed by the *Conseil constitutionnel*.[148]

The case of Australia is emblematic of the efficacy of financial sanctions even in the absence of a specific duty.[149] The programme "No Jab No Pay" (no vaccination, no family tax benefits) in the Australian economic-social context where several families cannot afford assistance to their children without such financial exemptions was a remarkable success.[150] Six months after the implementation of the program at the beginning of 2016, total coverage of immunized children aged between 1–5 years was reached.[151]

The liberal model is represented by countries such as Austria, Cyprus, Denmark, Estonia, Finland, Ireland, Lithuania, Luxembourg, the Netherlands, Norway, Portugal, Spain, Sweden, and the United Kingdom.

In the United Kingdom, for instance, according to section 45 *C* of the Public Health (Control of Disease) Act 1984, "the appropriate minister may . . . make provision for the purpose of preventing, protecting against, controlling or providing a public health response to the incidence or spread of infection or contamination in England and Wales". Section 45 *E* ("Medical treatment") states that every health measure under section 45 *C* "may not include provision requiring a person to undergo medical treatment". The term medical treatment includes "vaccination and other prophylactic treatment".

Canada, Germany, and the United States are cases of a mixed model, which mainly focuses on education and appropriate information. Although vaccines are not mandatory, social goods or services offered by the State can be withdrawn to families that choose not to vaccinate their kids.

---

assurent la tutelle des mineurs sont tenues personnellement responsables de l'exécution de l'obligation prévue au I. La preuve que cette obligation a été exécutée doit être fournie, selon des modalités définies par décret, pour l'admission ou le maintien dans toute école, garderie, colonie de vacances ou autre collectivité d'enfants". For details, see Xavier Bioy, "Vaccination obligatoire et droits fondamentaux", *Droit, Santé et Société* (2022): 7–17.

148   Décision n. 2015–458 QPC du 20 mars 2015, https://www.conseil-constitutionnel.fr/en/decision/2015/2015458QPC.htm; Jean-Louis Vildé, "L'obligation vaccinale en question", *Laennec* (2015): 8–23.

149   Kirsten Ward, Brynley P. Hull, Julie Leask, "Financial Incentives for Childhood Immunisation– A Unique but Changing Australian Initiative", *Medical Journal of Australia* 198 (11) (2013): 590–592.

150   https://www.health.gov.au/health-topics/immunisation/when-to-get-vaccinated/national-immunisation-program-schedule. According to the National Immunisation Program Schedule, the increasing of the national immunisation coverage can help to prevent the spread of infectious diseases among the population; https://www.servicesaustralia.gov.au/what-are-immunisation-requirements?context=41186.

151   Timothy J. Cordingley, Mark A.G. Wilson, Kathryn M. Weston, "The Success of Australia's 'No Jab, No Pay' Policy at a Local Level; Retrospective Clinical Audit of a Single Medical Practice Assessing Incidence of Catch-Up Vaccinations", *Health & Social Care in the Community* (2022): 353–359.

In Canada, the States of Ontario[152] and New Brunswick require immunization for several infectious diseases. Valid exonerations are envisaged for health reasons, religious beliefs, and conscientious objection. However, in case of a disease outbreak, unvaccinated children can be exempted from school admission.

The key question is which model works better? According to a report by the Asset Society,[153] a mechanism based on compulsory vaccinations does not always correspond to major coverage. Latvia – which has foreseen 12 compulsory vaccinations – does not reach higher coverage levels compared to the other Baltic States that do not have a mandatory system. At the same time, countries with different policies register the same trend (Austria liberal model versus Romania compulsory model).

Other factors – such as a more or less efficient health system and the level of health literacy in the general population – influence attitudes towards vaccinations.

After this brief overview of selected legislation, in the next section, I focus my analysis on national COVID-19 vaccination strategies and policies.

12. COVID-19 and mandatory vaccinations

The upturn in infections caused by the Delta and Omicron variants in autumn 2021 and early 2022 forced several governments to adopt stringent measures under the form of i) mandatory shots for health workers, high-risk groups, and public servants; ii) an indirect mechanism represented by mandatory COVID-19 certifications (showing vaccination of at least two doses through the Green Pass, a recent negative test, or proof of recovery usually within the past 6 months through a RT-PCR or antigen test); and iii) a reinforced indirect mechanism that allows *de facto* only vaccinated people (not persons with a negative test) the possibility to obtain the Green Pass and to therefore carry on a normal life, such as going to the office, attending sporting events, or having dinner at a restaurant.

The policy of adopting several restrictions for unvaccinated persons has been followed in several EU countries.[154]

---

152 Between 4 and 6 years old, children should receive the following vaccines: tetanus, diphtheria, pertussis, polio, measles, mumps, rubella, and chicken pox. In grade 7, children should receive the following vaccines: meningococcal conjugate (Men-C-ACYW), hepatitis b, and human papillomavirus (HPV). Between 14 and 16 years old, teens should receive the following vaccines: tetanus, diphtheria, and pertussis. See https://www.ontario.ca/page/vaccines-children-school.

153 http://www.asset-scienceinsociety.eu/reports/page1.html.

154 It is worth recalling an upsurge of contagions in China (almost 250 million people infected with SARS-CoV-2 in the first half of December 2022), https://edition.cnn.com/2022/12/23/china/china-covid-infections-250-million-intl-hnk/index.html.

Italy imposed compulsory vaccination for health care professionals.[155] Italy strengthened its Green Pass through the introduction of the Super Green Pass, which requires a third shot of COVID-19 vaccine in order to have access to the workplace, public transportation, and a wide range of social, cultural, and sporting activities (such as restaurants, swimming pools, tennis clubs, and gyms).[156] That is, the strengthened version of the Green Pass is available only after vaccination or recovery; therefore, a negative test result is no longer sufficient.[157]

Ecuador was the first country in the world to make COVID-19 vaccination obligatory except for patients who have a relevant medical condition or an incompatibility.

Austria, which faced one of the lowest rates of a vaccinated population against COVID-19 (around 68%) was eventually forced at the end of 2021 to make COVID-19 vaccines compulsory for people aged from 18 years and above amid a rise of cases; fines of up to €3,600 were envisaged for holdouts. This extraordinary measure was introduced after a targeted lockdown for unvaccinated citizens (the same type of measure was adopted in Germany). Persons who were exempted from this obligation were those who had particular medical conditions, pregnant women, and patients who had been recently affected by COVID-19. The compulsory vaccination mandate was eventually suspended in March 2022, as the Austrian government considered it disproportionate to the threat posed by the Omicron variant.[158]

Vaccination continues to be mandatory in Tajikistan, Turkmenistan, Indonesia, Micronesia, and New Caledonia.

In Costa Rica vaccination is compulsory for persons aged over 5 years; against this backdrop, a specific agreement has been signed with Pfizer to obtain enough shots to immunize all children aged between 5 and 12 years.[159]

In the United States, the Food and Drug Administration (FDA) provided an emergency authorization for children down to 6 months of age.[160]

155 Law of 28 May 2021 No. 76 (conversion into law, with amendments, of decree-law No. 44 of 1 April 2021, containing urgent measures for the containment of the COVID-19 epidemic, on the subject of SARS-CoV-2 vaccinations, justice and public competitions); see Paola Frati, Raffaele La Russa, Nicola Di Fazio, Zoe Del Fante, Giuseppe Delogu, Vittorio Fineschi, "Compulsory Vaccination for Healthcare Workers in Italy for the Prevention of SARS-CoV-2 Infection", *Vaccines* 9 (2021): 1–9.

156 "Misure urgenti per il contenimento della diffusione dell'epidemia da COVID-19 e disposizioni in materia di sorveglianza sanitaria (decreto-legge)", *Legislative Decree, No. 229* (30 December 2021), https://www.gazzettaufficiale.it/eli/id/2021/12/30/21G00258/sg.

157 Simona Zaami, "COVID.19 Vaccine Mandates: What are the Current European Public Perspectives", *European Review for Medical and Pharmacological Sciences* (2022): 643–652.

158 https://www.reuters.com/business/healthcare-pharmaceuticals/austria-scraps-already-suspended-covid-vaccine-mandate-2022-06-23/.

159 https://www.reuters.com/article/health-coronavirus-costa-rica-idUSL1N2LD1HL.

160 https://www.fda.gov/news-events/press-announcements/coronavirus-covid-19-update-fda-authorizes-moderna-and-pfizer-biontech-covid-19-vaccines-children.

13. The European legal framework

13.1. The European Union

The possibility to issue a vaccination mandate with the goal of immunizing a high percentage of the population against infectious diseases was raised within the WHO in the 1960s.[161] To reach the goal of covering at least 70% of the population against the most common infectious diseases, the WHO highlighted two practical solutions: compulsory vaccination and/or persuasion through an expensive campaign of health education.

At a regional level, on 1 December 2014, the Council of the European Union adopted specific conclusions on vaccination as an effective tool in public health, noting, *inter alia*, that

> communicable diseases, including some re-emerging ones, such as Tuberculosis, measles, pertussis and rubella, still present a public health challenge and can cause a high number of infections and deaths, and that the recent emergence and outbreaks of communicable diseases, such as polio, avian influenza H5N1 and H7N9. . . and Ebola virus disease have confirmed that vigilance must remain high also with respect to diseases that are not currently present in the territory of the Union.[162]

The Council recognized that

> many vaccines used in community vaccination programs have been able to prevent disease in individuals and at the same time interrupt the circulation of pathogens through the so-called "herd immunity" phenomenon, contributing to a healthier global society. Community immunity could thus be considered an objective in national vaccination plans.

On 19 April 2018, the European Parliament enacted a resolution on vaccine hesitancy in response to the drop in vaccination rates in Europe, which called on Member States to ensure sufficient vaccination of health care workers, take effective steps against misinformation, and implement measures for improving access to medicines.[163] It also called on the Commission to facilitate a more harmonized schedule for vaccination across the EU.

The importance of vaccines as the most powerful and cost-effective device to protect public health was expressly recognized on 7 December 2018 by

---

161   "Compulsory or Voluntary Vaccinations", *WHO Secretariat, A/13 Technical Discussion* (25 April 1960), https://apps.who.int/iris/bitstream/handle/10665/134370/WHA13_TD-2_eng.pdf?sequence=1&isAllowed=y.

162   Council conclusions on vaccinations as an effective tool in public health. (2014/C 438/04).

163   European Parliament resolution of 19 April 2018 on vaccine hesitancy and the drop in vaccination rates in Europe (2017/2951(RSP)).

the Council of the European Union on a recommendation for strengthened cooperation against vaccine preventable diseases.[164]

Health is, however, a competence of EU Member States (*ex* Art. 168 TFEU), which have the faculty to decide who to vaccinate and whether to impose specific vaccination duties;[165] therefore, the EU cannot directly determine whether the vaccination against COVID-19 or a given infectious disease should be compulsory or not.

EU Member States have – according to public health reasons related to the spread of the COVID-19 pandemic – highly limited the right of free movement of EU citizens. As specified in Recommendation (EU) 2020/1475, such restrictions were based on the principles of proportionality and non-discrimination.

EU Regulation n. 953/2021[166] introduced the EU digital COVID certificate as a necessary tool to freely circulate in the European area.[167] The objectives of Regulation n. 953/2021 are facilitating safe cross-border movement, precluding more restrictive national measures, preventing discrimination, and coordinating the actions of Member States. According to Paragraph 36,

> it is necessary to prevent direct or indirect discrimination against persons who are not vaccinated, for example because of medical reasons, because they are not part of the target group for which the COVID-19 vaccine is currently administered or allowed, such as children, or because they have not yet had the opportunity or chose not to be vaccinated. Therefore, possession of a vaccination certificate, or the possession of a vaccination certificate indicating a COVID-19 vaccine, should not be a pre-condition for the exercise of the right to free movement or for the use of cross-border passenger transport services such as airlines, trains, coaches or ferries or any other means of transport. In addition, this Regulation *cannot be interpreted as establishing a right or obligation to be vaccinated*.

---

164 Council Recommendation of 7 December 2018 on strengthened cooperation against vaccine-preventable diseases (2018/C 466/01).

165 The State's reservation is also confirmed by Article 35 of the EU Charter on Fundamental Rights (Nizza, 2000), according to which "one has the right of access to preventive health care and the right to benefit from medical treatment under the conditions established by national laws and practices. A high level of human health protection shall be ensured in the definition and implementation of all Union policies and activities".

166 Regulation (EU) 2021/953 of the European Parliament and of the Council of 14 June 2021 on a framework for the issuance, verification and acceptance of interoperable COVID-19 vaccination, test and recovery certificates (EU Digital COVID Certificate) to facilitate free movement during the COVID-19 pandemic.

167 Iris Goldner Lang, "EU COVID-19 Certificates: A Critical Analysis", *European Journal of Risk Regulation* (2021): 291–307.

This last wording means that the EU does not take a clear stance on the issue of mandatory vaccination against COVID-19, which lies within the prerogative of each State.

13.2. The Council of Europe

The problem of vaccine hesitancy and the most effective legal options to immunize a wide range of the population has been debated within the Council of Europe (CoE) since the 1990s.

On 19 March 1997, the Parliamentary Assembly of the Council of Europe adopted Recommendation 1317 (1997) on vaccination in Europe.[168]

Two resolutions of the CoE in 2021 address in detail the issue of the compatibility between compulsory vaccinations and human rights: Resolution n. 2361/2021[169] and Resolution n. 2383/2021.[170] Paragraph 4 of Resolution n. 2361 recognizes that "vaccine hesitancy and vaccine nationalism have the capacity to derail the so-far surprisingly fast and successful Covid-19 vaccine effort, by allowing the SARS-CoV-2 virus to mutate and thus blunt the world's most effective instrument against the pandemic so far". Paragraph 7.1.5 encourages Member States to "put in place independent vaccine compensation programmes to ensure compensation for undue damage and harm resulting from vaccination".

With respect to ensuring high vaccine uptake, the CoE takes a clear stance on the fact that citizens must be informed that vaccination is *not mandatory* and that "no one is politically, socially, or otherwise pressured to get themselves vaccinated, if they do not wish to do so themselves" (Para. 7.3.1). Furthermore, States must avoid any form of discrimination if an individual does not want to be vaccinated due to possible health risks (there is no mention of religious beliefs).

In addition, States must adopt effective measures against "misinformation, disinformation and hesitancy regarding Covid-19 vaccines" (Para. 7.3.3). To this aim, transparent information on the safety and possible side effects of vaccines must be distributed (Para. 7.3.4).

---

168 The Assembly considers that efforts to improve the immunization level should not be concentrated solely on the plight of the countries undergoing transition. The immunization level of populations in Western Europe has been steadily declining in recent years. The low percentage of fully vaccinated people, coupled with outbreaks of infectious diseases in the same geographic area, also raise fears of major epidemics in Western Europe. The Assembly therefore recommends that the Committee of Ministers invite member states to devise or reactivate comprehensive public vaccination programmes as the most effective and economical means of preventing infectious diseases and to arrange for efficient epidemiological surveillance.

169 Resolution 2361 (2021), Covid-19 vaccines: ethical, legal and practical considerations.

170 Resolution 2383 (2021), Covid passes or certificates: protection of fundamental rights and legal implications.

Against this backdrop, guidance is also provided by the European Convention on Human Rights and Biomedicine (or Oviedo Convention), namely, Article 5, which recognizes informed consent as a fundamental right of each individual.[171]

The Convention also includes detailed norms devoted to vulnerable persons, such as minors or incapacitated adults (Article 6, "Protection of persons not able to consent"; Article 7, "Protection of persons who have a mental disorder").

Article 26 ("restrictions on the exercise of the rights") affirms that

> no restrictions shall be placed on the exercise of the rights and protective provisions contained in this Convention other than such as are prescribed by law and are necessary in a democratic society in the interest of public safety, for the of crime, for the protection of public health or for the protection of the rights and freedoms of others.

Therefore, compulsory interventions in the field of health are in line with the norms of the Convention if they are "prescribed by law" and are "necessary in a democratic society" in the interest of the protection of public health or the protection of the rights of others, among other reasons (Art. 26).

The problem in the relationship between compulsory vaccinations and the ECHR has been addressed by the European Court of Human Rights (ECtHR) with reference to both the imposition of compulsory vaccinations on minors and the specific case of COVID-19 vaccines.

171 Article 5 of the Biomedicine Convention states that "An intervention in the health field may only be carried out after the person concerned has given free and informed consent to it. This person shall beforehand be given appropriate information as to the purpose and nature of the intervention as well as on its consequences and risks. The person concerned may freely withdraw consent at any time". Article 14 of the Additional Protocol to the Convention on Human Rights and Biomedicine, concerning Biomedical Research (CETS No. 195), adopted on 25/01/2005 and entered into force on 01/09/2007, affirms that "no research on a person may be carried out, subject to the provisions of both Chapter V and Article 19, without the informed, free, express, specific and documented consent of the person. Such consent may be freely withdrawn by the person at any phase of the research". See Roberto Andorno, *Principles of International Biolaw Seeking Common Ground at the Intersection of Bioethics and Human: Seeking Common Ground at the Intersection of Bioethics and Human Rights* (Bruylant: 2013), 21–22; Stefania Negri, "The Right to Informed Consent at the Convergence of International Biolaw and International Human Rights Law", in Stefania Negri (ed.), *Self-Determination, Dignity and End-of-Life Care. Regulating Advance Directives in International and Comparative Perspective* (Brill/Martinus Nijhoff Publishers: 2011), 23–72; Ilja Richard Pavone, *La Convenzione europea sulla biomedicina* (Giuffrè: 2009), 49–58; Solomon E. Salako, "Informed Consent Under the European Convention on Biomedicine and the UNESCO Declaration on Bioethics", *Medicine and Law* (2011), 101–113.

As previously explained, most of the CoE's Member States have in place legislation that envisions compulsory vaccination against specific infectious diseases.

With reference to COVID-19, an individual does not have a specific obligation to vaccinate himself/herself, but in the case of refusal, the State has anticipated a series of indirect sanctions. Indeed, a compulsory vaccination policy against COVID-19 interferes – under a theoretical point of view – with the civil and political rights contained in the ECHR, namely, the right to life (Art. 2), the right to respect of private life (Art. 8, Para. 1), and freedom of thought, conscience, and religion (Art. 9, Para. 1), that enshrines the right to conscientious objection.

Against this backdrop, the Court faced in 2021 three requests for interim measures under Rule 39 of the Rules of the Court[172] presented by a number of professional categories against France[173] and Greece.[174]

In the following section, I argue that the decision by a State to impose compulsory vaccination on health grounds – particularly in a pandemic stage of an infectious disease – does not contrast with the ECHR, and it can be included within the wide margin of control that States enjoy to determine derogations to their rights.

14. Vaccines and the right to life

Many opponents to compulsory vaccination policies ("no vax") argue that the possible side-effects related to a vaccine are a threat to their life. The no vax movement is opposed to vaccination in general, not only compulsory vaccination. There are many people who are favorable to vaccination and want to get vaccinated (and who are therefore not no vax but are opposed to compulsory vaccination).[175]

---

172 Interim measures are urgent measures that, in accordance with the established practice of the Court, apply only where there is an "imminent risk of irreparable damage" (see *Mamatkulov and Askarov v. Turkey*, case No. 46827/99 and 46951/99, Para. 104, 4 February 2005; *Paladi v. Moldova*, case No. 39806/05, Paras. 86–90, 10 March 2009). In the Court's practice, they are generally granted in cases regarding deportation and extradition, serious risk to private or family life, or grave situations of inhumane treatment (such as torture). https://www.echr.coe.int/documents/fs_interim_measures_eng.pdf.

173 On 19 August 2021, the ECtHR received a first complaint by 672 French firemen (members of the *Services départementaux d'incendie et de secours de France*) against the obligation of COVID-19 vaccination imposed by the *Loi n. 2021–1040 du 5 août 2021 'relative à la gestion de la crise sanitaire'*.

174 On 2 September 2021, a similar application was presented before the ECtHR by 30 Greek health care workers who claimed the illegitimacy of the Greek Legislation (Law No. 4820–2021). Silvio Roberto Vinceti, "COVID-19 Compulsory Vaccination and the European Court of Human Rights", *Acta Biomedica* 92 (2021): 1–7.

175 Katrin Schmelza, Samuel Bowles, "Opposition to Voluntary and Mandated COVID-19 Vaccination as a Dynamic Process: Evidence and Policy Implications of Changing Beliefs", *PNAS* (2022): 1–10.

Article 2 of the ECHR affirms that "the right to life is an inalienable attribute of the human beings and forms the supreme value in the hierarchy of human rights". According to the Court's case law, Article 2 is one of the most fundamental provisions of the Convention.[176] It safeguards the right to life as a precondition for the enjoyment of any of the other rights and freedoms protected by the Convention[177]

In addition, the Court has established that Article 2, Paragraph 1 obliges States Parties not only to refrain from intentional and unlawful deprivation of life (duty of *non facere*)[178] but also to take positive steps to safeguard the lives of persons within their jurisdiction.[179]

Under certain circumstances, this duty also entails the undertaking to protect individuals against suicide attempts, especially in the case of detainees.[180]

The right to life has been raised in proceedings before the Court with reference to both beginning and end of life issues in the field of bioethics.[181] The first time that the Court dealt with abortion and beginning of life problems was in *X v. the United Kingdom*,[182] when the former Commission received a complaint by a potential father, who lamented that his wife had been allowed to undergo an abortion for health reasons. The Commission affirmed that the term "everyone" ("toute personne") in the ECHR could not apply to the unborn (embryo/fetus). As to the term "life" and, particularly, the beginning of life, the Commission noted "a divergence of thinking on the question of where life begins" and added "while some believe that it starts already with conception, others tend to focus on upon the moment of nidation, upon the point that the fetus becomes 'viable' or upon live 'birth'" (*X v. the United Kingdom*, Para. 1).

In other cases, the Court has similarly not recognized that the unborn (embryo/fetus) is entitled to "a right to life", considering that "the unborn child is not regarded as a person directly protected by Article 2 of the Convention and that, if the unborn does have a "right" to "life", it is implicitly limited by the mother's rights and interests" (*Vo v. France*, Para. 80), allowing single

176   *Mc Cann and Others v. the United Kingdom*, 27 September 1995, Series A No. 324, Paras. 146 and 147.

177   William A. Schabas, *The European Convention on Human Rights: A Commentary* (Oxford University Press: 2015), 117–163.

178   *L.C.B. v The United Kingdom (1998)*.

179   *L.C.B. v. the United Kingdom*, Application No. 23413/949 June 1998, Para. 36.

180   *L.C.B. v. the United Kingdom*, 9 June 1998, Para. 36, Reports of Judgments and Decisions 1998-III.

181   Ilja Richard Pavone, "Case Law of the Strasbourg Court in the Field of Bioethics and the Biomedicine Convention", in María Isabel Torres Cazorla (ed.), *Bioderecho Internacional y Universalización: el Papel de las Organizaciones y los Tribunales Internacionales* (Tirant lo Blanch: 2020), 119–151.

182   *X v. United Kingdom*, Application No. 8416/78, Decision of 13 May 1980.

States, within their margin of appreciation, to determine in their domestic legislation "when the right to life begins" (*Vo. v. France*, Para. 82).[183]

As to end of life, in the landmark case *Pretty v. United Kingdom* (2002),[184] the Court did not admit a right to die with dignity as a corollary of the right to life; therefore, all of the following cases regarding active euthanasia and assisted suicide (such as *Haas v. Switzerland*)[185] were rejected by the Court on the basis of the general obligation upon States to protect life in an absolute manner, irrespective of the quality of life.

Therefore, the Court stated that

Article 2 cannot, without a distortion of language, be interpreted as conferring the diametrically opposite right, namely a right to die; nor can it create a right to self-determination in the sense of conferring on an individual an entitlement to choose death rather than life.

(Para. 39)

Situations that might only endanger health but not life are, however, not covered by Article 2 ECHR but rather by the scope of Article 8 ECHR.[186]

Positive duties to act imply "all that could have been required of it to prevent the applicant's life from being avoidably put at risk".[187]

In the domain of public health and of a compulsory vaccination, the interpretation of Article 2 implies, first, that States should adopt all necessary precautions to avoid the collateral effects related to the particular health situation of an individual (who might, for instance, have an allergic reaction to vaccines).

Once all necessary safeguards have been adopted on the possible side effects of a given vaccine – which represents a health hazard but does not pose a serious risk to health – it is easy to affirm that this does not correspond to a violation of State duties under Article 2 ECHR.

That is, a danger to life falls within the scope of Article 2 ECHR, while a mere danger to health is included within Article 8 ECHR. For instance, States must adopt additional measures to ensure the physical and mental integrity of patients in hospitals.[188]

183 Jakob Pichon, "Does the Unborn Child Have a Right to Life? The Insufficient Answer of the European Court of Human Rights in the Judgment Vo v. France", *German Law Journal* (2019): 433–444.
184 *Pretty v. The United Kingdom*, Application No. 2346/02, decision of 29 April 2022; Antje Pedain, "The Human Rights Dimension of the Diane Pretty Case", *The Cambridge Law Journal* (2003): 181–206.
185 *Case of Haas v. Switzerland*, Application No. 31322/07.8.
186 William Schabas, *The European Convention on Human Rights: A Commentary* (Oxford University Press: 2015), at 124.
187 *LCB v. the United Kingdom*, Application No. 23413/94, 9 June 1998, Para. 36.
188 Vasileva v Bulgaria App No 23796/10 (EctHr, 17 March 2016), Para. 63.

The former Commission, in *Association of Parents v. the United Kingdom*, clearly argued that if a State sets up a control and monitoring system with the aim of minimizing vaccine-associated side effects, isolated fatalities that were unforeseeable do not amount to a violation of the right to life.[189]

An effective health policy by a given State implies particular attention to single cases and the provision of exemptions for given categories, such as patients who might have adverse immune reactions.

Once it is assumed that a mandatory vaccination policy does not violate Article 2 ECHR, does the right to life imply a specific duty upon the States to immunize their population through their positive obligations or instead to refrain from a vaccination campaign?

States also have specific duties in the health sphere – although a right to health is not envisaged by the ECHR – as affirmed in *Lopes de Sousa Fernandes v Portugal*.[190]

The positive obligation arising from Article 2 may lead to the claim that, in the context of an epidemic or of a pandemic, a vaccine should be made compulsory to protect not only the recipients but also those who rely on herd immunity for protection against a given infectious disease.[191]

In *Calvelli and Ciglio v. Italy* (2002), the Court recognized that States do have specific positive obligations falling within Article 2 ECHR in "the public health sphere" and stated that this duty "requires states to make regulations compelling hospitals, whether public or private, to adopt appropriate measures for the protection of their patients' lives".[192]

15. Vaccines and the right to private life

The Strasbourg Court has over time interpreted in an extensive and dynamic way the rights enshrined in the Convention according to the "living instrument doctrine".[193]

189 *Association of Parents v the United Kingdom* App no 7154/74 31 (Commission Decision, 12 July 1978), 32 et seq.
190 Paragraph 165 of *Lopes de Sousa Fernandes v Portugal* reads as follows: "The Court has stressed many times that, although the right to health – recognized in numerous international instruments – is not as such among the rights guaranteed under the Convention and its Protocols (see *Vasileva v. Bulgaria*, No. 23796/10, § 63, 17 March 2016), the aforementioned positive obligation must be construed as applying in the context of any activity, whether public or not, in which the right to life may be at stake . . . *including in the public-health sphere*".
191 Francesca Camilleri, "Compulsory Vaccinations for Children: Balancing the Competing Human Rights at Stake", *Netherlands Quarterly of Human Rights* 37 (3) (2019): 245–267.
192 *Calvelli and Ciglio v Italy*, Application No. 32967/96 (ECtHR, January 17, 2002), para. 49.
193 *Tyrer v. United Kingdom* (Application No. 5856/72, Judgment of 25 April 1978, Series A No. 26). See Rick Lawson, "The ECHR at 70: A Living Instrument in Precarious Present-day Conditions", *leidenlawblog* (2020), https://www.leidenlawblog.nl/articles/the-echr-at-70-a-living-instrument-in-precarious-present-day-conditions.

Recent decades have particularly registered several rulings of the ECtHR on matters related to bioethics, ranging from beginning of life (abortion, access to reproductive technologies, and the legal status of the human embryo) to end of life issues (right to refuse life sustaining treatments and assisted suicide). These complex problems are increasingly being raised before the Strasbourg Court by invoking breaches of Articles 2, 3, 5, and 6, and most often, Articles 8, 9, and 14.[194]

As a matter of principle, compulsory vaccination amounts to an interference with the right to respect for private life. In 1984, the former Commission had already mentioned that "a requirement to undergo medical treatment or a vaccination, on pain of a penalty, *may* amount to interference with the right to respect for private life".[195] The applicants denied authorization concerning their children to undergo methods of tuberculosis screening – namely, the tuberculin test and chest x-ray. They argued that the Belgian law violated their personal convictions and was an unnecessary interference with private life.

In another case (*Solomakhin v. Ukraine*),[196] the claimant was administered a diphtheria vaccine against his will in an epidemic context. The Court established that physical integrity concerns one of the most intimate aspects of private life, and even a non-invasive medical intervention (such as an injection) amounts to an interference with the enjoyment of this right.[197]

Therefore, the key issue is to evaluate whether such interference is justified under the exemption clause *ex* Article 8, Paragraph 2[198] or under the derogation clause (Art. 15),[199] where the States enjoy a wide margin of authority.

---

194 Research Report, *Bioethics and the case-law of the Court, Council of Europe/European Court of Human Rights* (2012), https://www.coe.int/t/dg3/healthbioethic/texts_and_docu ments/Bioethics_and_caselaw_Court_EN.pdf. See also Thérèse Murphy, Gearóid Ó. Cunn, "Works in Progress: New Technologies and the European Court of Human Rights", *Human Rights Law Review* (2010): 601–638.
195 *Acmanne and others v. Belgium,* Application n. 10435/83, 10 December 1984.
196 Application No. 24429/03.
197 Paragraph 33 of the judgment reads as follows: "Compulsory vaccination – as an involuntary medical treatment – amounts to an interference with the right to respect for one's private life, which includes a person's physical and psychological integrity".
198 Article 8, Paragraph 2 of the ECHR provides that "There shall be no interference by a public authority with the exercise of this right except such as is in accordance with the law and is necessary in a democratic society in the interests of national security, public safety or the economic wellbeing of the country, for the prevention of disorder or crime, for the protection of health or morals, or for the protection of the rights and freedoms of others".
199 Article 15 (derogation in time of emergency) of the ECHR states that "In time of war or other public emergency threatening the life of the nation any High Contracting Party may take measures derogating from its obligations under this Convention to the extent strictly required by the exigencies of the situation, provided that such measures are not inconsistent with its other obligations under international law.
    2. No derogation from Article 2 [right to life], except in respect of deaths resulting from lawful acts of war, or from Articles 3 [prohibition of torture and inhuman or degrading

Analogies can be found with case law on non-psychiatric, mandatory medical treatments: in the case *X and others v. Austria* (1979), the Court claimed that the applicant's compulsory blood testing was justified by the public interest in determining paternity.[200]

It bears recalling that Article 8, Paragraph 2 contemplates derogation according to the well-known three-step test; that is, an interference by a State – demanding compulsory vaccination, for example – can be justified if i) it is provided by law; ii) it is *necessary* in a democratic society; and iii) it pursues a legitimate aim (such as the protection of public health).[201]

Since the norms on compulsory vaccinations are usually envisaged by a law, it must be assessed whether they are *necessary* in a democratic society and whether they *pursue* a legitimate aim.

The notion of necessity in a democratic society is therefore crucial in evaluating the legitimacy of an interference by a State in the private sphere. In *Dudgeon v. the United Kingdom* (1981),[202] the Court argued that the notion of necessity in a democratic society implies "the existence of a 'pressing social need' for the interference in question" (Para. 51). It is up to domestic authorities – that enjoy a wide margin of influence – to assess the pressing social need in each case (Para. 52).

In *Solomakhin v Ukraine* (2012), the Court highlighted two additional criteria to assess the necessity of a compulsory vaccination policy:[203] the first is the protection of public health from the spread of an infectious disease; the second is the suitability of the individual for vaccination. In this framework, one State must evaluate the suitability of the applicant for vaccination and must take the necessary precautions before the medical intervention (Para. 36).

---

treatment or punishment], 4 (paragraph 1) [prohibition of slavery and servitude] and 7 [no punishment without law] shall be made under this provision.

    3. Any High Contracting Party availing itself of this right of derogation shall keep the Secretary General of the Council of Europe fully informed of the measures which it has taken and the reasons therefor. It shall also inform the Secretary General of the Council of Europe when such measures have ceased to operate and the provisions of the Convention are again being fully executed".

200 Anja Krasser, "Compulsory Vaccination in a Fundamental Rights Perspective: Lessons from the ECtHR", *ICL Journal* (2021): 207–233.
201 See David Harris, Michael O'Boyle, Chris Wabrick, *Law of the European Convention on Human Rights* (Butterworths: 2018), 335–355.
202 Case of *Dudgeon v. the United Kingdom* (Application No. 7525/76), Judgment, Strasbourg, 22 October 1981.
203 Spyridoula Katsoni, "What Does the Vavřička Judgement Tell Us About the Compatibility of Compulsory COVID-19 Vaccinations with the ECHR?", *Völkerrechtsblog* (21 April 2021), https://voelkerrechtsblog.org/what-does-the-vavricka-judgement-tell-us-about-the-compatibility-of-compulsory-covid-19-vaccinations-with-the-echr/. See also Rebekah McWhirter, Martin Clark, "Expertise, Public Health and the European Convention on Human Rights: Vavřička v Czech Republic", *The Modern Law Review* (2023): 1035–1048.

As to the proportionality, on sensitive issues, such as the beginning and end of life, States enjoy a wider margin of authority in an inversely proportional measure to the lack of consensus on a given matter.

In the case *Boffa and others v San Marino* (1998), the Court emphasized that the interference related to a compulsory vaccination of minors against Hepatitis B respected the conditions for a valid derogation of *ex* Article 8, Paragraph 2 due to "the need to protect the health of the public and of the persons concerned" (Paras. 8–9).

In the case of *Jehovah's Witnesses of Moscow v. Russia* (2010), the Court stated that there is a specific reference to compulsory vaccination in case of an epidemic and that "the right to private life could in principle be limited for the protection of third parties" (Paras. 36–37).

According to this line of thought, an eventual vaccination campaign against Covid-19 would pursue a legitimate aim.

In the key case of *Vavřička v. the Czech Republic* (2021),[204] the Court clearly explained its position on the issue of mandatory vaccinations.

The judgment is quite relevant to the debate in European countries on compulsory vaccination policies against COVID-19, since it provides a useful legal basis for any legislator to guarantee an appropriate balance between individual rights and the protection of public health.[205]

Apart from COVID-19 vaccines, the CoE's Member States are clearly divided on the issue of mandatory vaccinations, although the judges of the Court emphasized European *favor* towards mandatory vaccination "due to a decrease in voluntary vaccination and a resulting decrease in herd immunity" (Para. 278).

In its judgment of 21 April 2021, the Grand Chamber of the ECtHR took a clear stance on the topic of vaccinations: a State policy that envisages a compulsory vaccination for minors is not in breach of the ECHR. The majority of the judges found the Czech Republic's vaccination legislation to be "fully consistent with the rationale of protecting the health of the population" (Para. 306) and falling within the wide margin of authority provided to Member States on health issues (Para. 274).

The policy struck a fair balance between the protection of children against serious diseases and the protection of families from the consequences of their refusal.

---

204   In this case, the applications were lodged with the European Court of Human Rights by five families – belonging to the no vax movement – between 2013 and 2015. The applicants challenged a violation of Articles 8, 9, 2, 6, 13, and 14 and Article 2 of Protocol 1 to the ECHR. However, the Court asserted the inadmissibility of their claims under Articles 9, 2, 6, 13, and 14 (Paras. 338 and 347) and decided to assess their applications only under Article 8 (right to respect for private life). After this initial assessment, the Court did not deem it necessary to assess their claims also under Article 2 of Protocol 1 (right to education) (Para. 345).

205   Ignatius Yordan Nugraha, Juncal Montero Regules, Merel Vrancken, "Vavřička and Others v. The Czech Republic", *American Journal of International Law* (2022): 579–585.

The judgment was based upon an in-depth investigation that first considered a comparative analysis of the constitutional jurisprudence of the CoE's Member States (such as Italy, France, Hungary, and Slovenia) that basically favor compulsory vaccination.

Then, the Court indicated

> the general consensus among the Contracting Parties, strongly supported by the specialized international bodies, that vaccination is one of the most successful and cost-effective health interventions and that each State should aim to achieve the highest possible level of vaccination among its population.
>
> (Para. 277)

At the same time, the Court concluded that there is no consensus about which is the best vaccine strategy that makes it possible to protect most of the population from a given infectious disease. Paragraph 278 reads as follows: "the Court notes that there is no consensus over a single model".

The role of solidarity and consequently, the collective dimension of health were then reiterated: social solidarity towards the most vulnerable persons requires the rest of the population to assume a "minimum risk" in the form of vaccination.[206]

The Court then considered that the interference with the right to private life was fully justified under Article 8, Paragraph 2 of the ECHR. The derogation is anticipated by law: it has the legitimate goal of protecting public health in its double dimension (as both an individual and collective right), and it is within the margin of authority of States, which is wide in this case for several reasons.

First, there are different positions on vaccination policies; such an approach has limited impact given that it has envisaged only indirect sanctions rather than a direct obligation. Furthermore, the States are in the better position to evaluate their priorities, the use of resources, and the social needs (a decrease in voluntary vaccinations constitutes a pressing social need, as explained in Paras. 283–284).

Finally, the law respects the principle of proportionality because it foresees exceptions (for medical reasons and on religious grounds) and forms of flexibility (the possibility to choose the type of vaccine and when to vaccinate children).

> [I]t cannot be regarded as disproportionate for a State to require those for whom vaccination represents a remote risk to health to accept this

---

206 On the duty of solidarity in the context of a pandemic, see Ming-Jui Yeh, "Solidarity in Pandemics, Mandatory Vaccination, and Public Health Ethics", *American Journal of Public Health* (2022): 255–261.

universally practised protective measure as a matter of legal duty and in the name of social solidarity for the sake of the small number of vulnerable children who are unable to benefit from vaccination specific calendar.

(Para. 306)

The Court evaluated that compulsory vaccination for children was established as a response to a "pressing social need", given that the Czech authorities were bound by positive obligations under the right to health to ensure adequate immunization coverage. According to the experts who provided advice to the authorities, this aim could only be achieved if vaccination were a duty, not a mere recommendation. Therefore, if voluntary vaccination programmes do not suffice to achieve herd immunity, then mandatory schemes may become necessary to protect the best interests of children, both individually and as a group. The interference with the applicants' right was also considered proportionate on the basis of numerous elements, despite the applicants providing reasons related to the lack of trust in science and religious belief.

The concept of the superior interest of the child[207] was also raised by the Court: who decides what is the best interest of a child? Immunization against infectious disease is undoubtedly in the best interest of a minor, since it also allows him/her to be admitted to a *kindergarten*.[208]

Against this backdrop, it is worth recalling that according to Article 24, Paragraph 1 of the UN Convention on the Rights of Children,

> States Parties recognize the right of the child to the enjoyment of the highest attainable standard of health . . . States Parties shall strive to ensure that no child is deprived of his or her right of access to . . . health care services.

Paragraph 2 then affirms that

> States Parties shall pursue full implementation of this right and, in particular, shall take appropriate measures: (a) To diminish infant and child mortality; (b) To ensure the provision of necessary medical assistance and health care to all children with emphasis on the development of

---

207 The principle of "the best interest of the child" is implemented in Article 3 (1) Convention on the Rights of the Child (CRC), which provides that "in all actions concerning children, whether undertaken by public or private social welfare institutions, a court of law, administrative authorities or legislative bodies, the best interests of the child shall be a primary consideration".

208 On the concept of best interest of the minor in *Vavricka*, see David Archard, Joe Brierley, Emma Cave, "Compulsory Childhood Vaccination: Human Rights, Solidarity, and Best Interests", *Medical Law Review* (2021): 716–727.

primary health care; (c) To combat disease . . ., including within the framework of primary health care.

According to General comment Number 15, "the realisation of this right entails the universal availability of immunisation against the common childhood diseases".[209]

The Czech legislation on compulsory vaccination denies permission to enroll unvaccinated children in both private and public schools, making enrollment contingent upon the presentation of a certificate of vaccination. The law does not contemplate an obligation to undergo vaccination, but it imposes a sanction for people who refuse.

According to the applicants' view, "it was not justified to refuse access to nursery schools as a form of punishment for the fact that the children were not vaccinated" (Para. 178). It was a fundamental issue for the applicant *Novotná*, who wanted to pursue a specific educational model.

In practical terms, the applicants argued that the refusal of access imposed a significant burden upon the families that should have taken care of the education of their children at a preschool level. It is worth underlying, however, that *kindergarten* or maternal school is not mandatory in the Czech Republic.

The applicants complained that the Czech legislation violated a series of Articles of the ECHR, namely, Article 8 (right to respect for private and family life) and Article 9 (freedom of thought, conscience, and religion) of the Convention and Article 2 of Protocol Number 1 (right to education) to the Convention. With reference to the last point, the Court did not recognize the necessity of analyzing the issue of the compatibility between compulsory vaccination and the right to education, since it maintained that the issue had already been successfully addressed within Article 8 of the ECHR (Para. 345).

The decision of the Court to abstain from discussing the relationship between private life and the right to education was highly criticized by Judge Lemmens in his partly concurring and partly dissenting opinion.[210]

The arguments of the applicants were based on the concept that vaccinations are an issue that concerns the respect for physical and moral integrity; they particularly recalled the principles of the primacy of the human being over the exclusive interest of science and society (Art. 2 of the Biomedicine Convention) and of informed consent (Art. 5 of the Biomedicine Convention) that envision the right to refuse medical treatment.

---

209 General comment No. 15 by the United Nations Committee on the Rights of the Child in relation to the right of the child to the enjoyment of the highest attainable standard of health, published on 17 April 2013 (CRC/C/GC/15).

210 *Partly Concurring and Partly Dissenting Opinion of Judge Lemmens*, Para. 3.

16. Vaccines and freedom of thought, conscience, and religion

The issue of conscientious objection to vaccination, that is, the refusal to comply with certain vaccination requirements because of personal, moral, or religious views (as opposed to refusal motivated by concerns around vaccine safety or effectiveness) has been discussed in recent years.

The precise stance by the scientific community in recognizing the importance of vaccines as an instrument for the protection of public health and for the balance among health, benefits, and risks is that vaccinations are one of the most efficient and less costly interventions in the health field.

In *Vavricka*, the Court specifically excluded the applicability of Article 9 to the case under examination, establishing that "personal views on compulsory vaccination based on wholly subjective assumptions about its necessity and suitability did not constitute a 'belief' within the meaning of Article 9 of the Convention" (Para. 315). In particular, "the Court finds that his critical opinion on vaccination is not such as to constitute a conviction or belief of sufficient cogency, seriousness, cohesion and importance to attract the guarantees of Article 9" (Para. 335).

The Court confirmed that the emphasis on freedom of conscience must be limited to particular individual situations (for instance, previous adverse reactions that induce an individual to refuse the vaccination); it cannot comprehend a position that is generally critical towards vaccination and vaccination policies that induces the individual to sustain, which are a hazard to the health of the whole population.

The refusal to vaccinate also raises the issues of conscientious objection (*Boffa and Others v. Saint-Marin*); the Court clearly stated on this point that "compulsory vaccination – if applied to everyone irrespective of their beliefs – does not constitute interference with the exercise of freedoms guaranteed by Art. 9".

According to the interpretation of Article 9 of the ECHR, "convictions" must not be confused with the conscience or with mere personal ideas. It is about "firmly held beliefs or opinions to which the activity of conscience leads".[211]

The UN Commission on Human Rights has recognized that conscientious objection "derives from principles and reasons of conscience, including profound convictions, arising from religious, moral, ethical, humanitarian or similar motives" (Res 1998/77).

In Italy, Article 32 of the Constitution is clear on the issue of compulsory vaccinations; the right to health is not considered exclusively an individual right but also an interest of the community according to the Constitutional Court, this allows the imposition of a health treatment if it is directed not only to improve or to preserve individual health but also to preserve the state of health of others.[212] Against this backdrop, collective health prevails over individual health. As specified by the judges of the Constitutional Court, the measures envisaged by the Legislative Decree represent a choice of the domestic legislator. The obligation to vaccinate is a reasonable choice founded on the duty of solidarity to prevent and to limit the spread of serious infectious diseases.

The Italian Constitutional Court in 2018 challenged the validity of a decree-law adopted as an urgency measure because of the worrying drop in the vaccination rate of children; the decree-law increased the number of vaccinations for children from four to ten.

The goal of vaccinations – the prevention of the spread of infectious diseases – is itself a legitimate purpose that must be pursued through measures as indulgent as possible while balancing the protection of health, the respect for private life, and freedom of religion. However, in the case of a public health emergency, such as COVID-19, the protection of public health must always prevail over the considerations or interests of single persons.

In the case of euthanasia and assisted suicide, the decision of an individual, namely, the terminally ill person, to die does not have relevance to third parties, but the situation is different in the case of vaccination. The deliberate choice of an individual not to vaccinate himself/herself or his/her children does have an impact on public health in its collective dimension.

17. Some thoughts on compulsory vaccinations

As public discussions on COVID-19 vaccines multiplied at the end of 2021 and a few States have waveringly leaned towards compulsory vaccinations policies, the Court's judgement in *Vavřička* could not have been any timelier, since it provides useful guidelines on the circumstances under which compulsory COVID-19 vaccinations can be deemed compatible with the ECHR.

In the *Vavřička*'s judgement, the Court did not leave room for generalizations. Instead, it highlighted that its analysis concerned the "standard and routine vaccination of children against diseases that are well known to medical science" (Para. 158) and that "in the present case, which specifically concerns the compulsory nature of child vaccination, that margin should be a wide one" (Para. 280). However, despite such pronouncements, the Court's analysis sheds more light on the formerly established criteria concerning the assessment of compulsory vaccinations' necessity in a democratic society and provides clearer guidelines on the compatibility of compulsory COVID-19 vaccinations with the ECHR.

Throughout its ruling, the ECtHR expressed its view about the "vaccination duty" to protect against contagious diseases that "could pose a serious risk to health", a characterization that could easily apply to COVID-19.

---

212 Constitutional Court, Judgment n. 5/2018 (22 November 2017), https://www.camera.it/temiap/2018/08/03/OCD177-3677.pdf.

What emerges from the judgement in the *Vavřička* case is that there is a scientific consensus on the efficacy of vaccines, although there are different positions on the issue of obligatoriness of COVID-19 vaccines (even though the instrument of the EU COVID Certificate is already a form of indirect enforcement). Indeed, a citizen who wants to have access to particular services, such as travelling on airplanes or trains, or to restaurants or cinemas must either show a Green Pass or must present a valid negative COVID-19 test.

In general terms, according to the judges of Strasbourg in *Vavřička*, the decision whether or not to impose compulsory vaccination against COVID-19 perfectly fits within the wide margin of influence that States enjoy in the sector of public health (Para. 285) in choosing the means by which "to attain the highest possible degree of vaccine coverage".

The margin of authority of States in "sensitive domains", such as life sciences, public health, end of life, and access to artificial procreation technologies, is inversely proportional to the differences among Member States.

The Court was clear on this point: if a policy of voluntary vaccination is not sufficient to achieve and maintain herd immunity or herd immunity is not relevant because of the nature of the disease (e.g., tetanus), then "domestic authorities may reasonably introduce a compulsory vaccination policy in order to achieve an appropriate level of protection against serious diseases" (Para. 288); therefore, compulsory vaccination against COVID-19 can be deemed a "reasonable response" to a public health emergency. In light of i) the ECtHR case law on mandatory medical treatments, ii) the *Vavřička*'s case, and iii) the rejection by the Court of the request for interim measures, one can conclude that State policies requesting compulsory vaccination against COVID-19 are perfectly compatible with the ECHR. The public dimension of the protection of public health prevails over the individual dimension of the right to health.

Furthermore, it is worth recalling that Article 15 of the ECHR explicitly anticipates the possibility to derogate from some ECHR provisions "[i]n time of war or other public emergency threatening the life of the nation", except for peremptory norms (*jus cogens*), such as the right to life, the prohibition of torture and inhuman or degrading treatment or punishment, and the prohibition of slavery and servitude.[213]

Article 15 of the ECHR was triggered because of the COVID-19 pandemic – which exemplifies the notion of "public emergency threatening the life of a nation" – by Albania, Armenia, Estonia, Georgia, Latvia, and North Macedonia.[214]

---

213 Alan Greene, "Separating Normalcy from Emergency: The Jurisprudence of Article 15 of the European Convention on Human Rights", *German Law Journal* (2019): 1764–1785.

214 https://www.coe.int/en/web/conventions/derogations-covid-19. Alan Greene, "States Should Declare a State of Emergency Using Article 15 ECHR to Confront the Coronavirus Pandemic", Strasbourg Observer (2020), https://strasbourgobservers.com/2020/04/01/states-should-declare-a-state-of-emergency-using-article-15-echr-to-confront-the-coronavirus-pandemic/.

On the basis of these considerations, one can conclude that legislative measures imposing a duty of vaccination against COVID-19 (or any other infectious disease that threatens public health) are in line with the ECHR. However, the vaccination must be considered safe by the scientific community, and a mechanism of compensation must be available in case of injuries caused by the vaccine.

18. Concluding remarks

This chapter highlighted the main legal issues raised by the COVID-19 pandemic with reference to the discovery of the new vaccines. One issue relates to the lack of equity in the access to COVID-19 vaccines and medicinal products, and the other refers to the problem of vaccine hesitancy.

In his declaration of 5 May 2023 stating that COVID-19 no longer constitutes a PHEIC, the WHO Director-General confirmed his commitment

> to support development of and equitable access to diagnostics, safe and effective therapeutics and vaccines, through the Access to COVID-19 Tools (ACT) Accelerator; continue to work with all ACT Accelerator partners to provide countries with additional clarity on the processes to enable equitable and timely access to diagnostics, therapeutics, and vaccines, including in humanitarian settings.
>
> (Para. 10)

COVAX – although it has presented structural problems – has managed to deliver vaccines worldwide covering South America and South-East Asia (except for Papua New Guinea with only 375,829 people receiving at least one dose), except for some countries in Sub-Saharan Africa, which still register a low percentage of the immunized population.[215] In Namibia, for instance, only 24% of the population received at least one dose, in Madagascar, this number was 8.4%, and in Niger, this number was 25.3%, while other countries were more successful in immunizing their population (Botswana 82.1%, Zambia 60.3%, Mozambique 59.6%, and Tanzania 56.8%).

Against this backdrop, increased manufacturing capacity that is more equitably, geographically, and strategically distributed could be the solution to guarantee equitable access to pandemic-related products. The principles of equity and solidarity, which are pivotal in the fair and equitable distribution

---

215 The Political Declaration of the United Nations General Assembly High-level Meeting on Pandemic Prevention, Preparedness and Response of 20 September 2023 expressed concern "also that the inequities in access to COVID-19 vaccines are stark, with 22% of the population fully vaccinated in lower-income economies compared to 75% in high-income economies" (PP4).

of COVID-19 vaccines, are included among the core principles in the new pandemic treaty.

The end of the state of emergency in relation to COVID-19 has left unresolved issues that emerged during the pandemic stage. As explained, vaccine nationalism perpetuates the long history of high-income countries securing first treatments and vaccines at the expense of LMICs. These inequalities reveal a fundamentally erroneous perspective of global health and the global economy more broadly, according to which vaccines and essential treatments are considered a market commodity rather than public goods. Accordingly, COVID-19 is a clear example of "Epidemic Orientalism":[216] high-income countries hoarded doses of vaccine to immunize most of their populations against this disease coming from the Far East of the world. At the same time, low-income countries were left behind and relied upon COVAX and donations of excess COVID-19 vaccine doses.

The need for a new paradigm is represented by the negotiations of the WHO Pandemic Agreement, which is the first step towards a decolonization of international law on infectious diseases that is still rooted in the vision of the early sanitary conventions.[217] The hope is that the WHO Pandemic Agreement can determine a change of approach from vaccine nationalism to vaccine equity, representing a genuinely positive step towards a more equitable response to future disease outbreaks.

216 Alexander White, *Epidemic Orientalism. Race, Capital, and the Governance of Infectious Diseases* (Stanford University Press: 2023), 4.
217 More generally, on the necessity to decolonize international law, see Sundhya Pahuja, *Decolonising International Law Development, Economic Growth and the Politics of Universality* (Cambridge University Press: 2011).

VI COVID-19 and infectious diseases as a threat to peace and security

One step behind?

Part I Framing the issue: Infectious diseases and security

1. Introduction

Infectious diseases are a major global public health threat. In today's globalized world, humans and animals – often carrying with them pathogens that cause diseases – are moving around the world more frequently and come into contact with one another more easily than ever before.

The global health emergency related to COVID-19 is a collective threat that is likely to undermine the wealth of States and human beings not only in the short term but also in the long term.

Its rapid spread worldwide has provoked collateral effects beyond the health sphere, such as unprecedented economic crises, an increase in political tensions, widespread human rights violations, and the exacerbation of ongoing conflicts, which all are factors that have hindered or slowed efforts towards its containment. Its impact in developing countries, particularly in those with ineffective health systems, was devastating.

The securitization of COVID-19 in terms of two distinct "referent objects" (humankind vs. citizens) reflects the political tension between the progressive erosion of the *Domaine Réservé* due to the globalization process and the political will in the age of populism to regain some essential functions, among which is health.

Global epidemics and pandemics such as HIV/AIDS, swine flu, SARS, monkeypox, Ebola, and COVID-19 undoubtedly have a dimension related to security.[1]

Several States consider the always wider spread of transmissible diseases a threat to peace and security, not just in the context of developing countries.

---

1 For a wider reflection on the relationship between transmittable diseases and security, see Ilja Richard Pavone, "The Human Security Dimension of Ebola and the Role of the Security Council in Fighting Health Pandemics: Some Reflections on Resolution 2177/2014", *South African Yearbook of International Law* (2014): 56–81; Shantesh Kumar Singh, "Infectious Diseases National Security And Globalisation", *World Affairs: The Journal of International Issues* (2019): 10–23; Anna Hood, "Ebola: A Threat to the Parameters of a Threat to the Peace?" *Melbourne Journal of International Law* (2015): 29–51.

DOI: 10.4324/9781003100645-6

The Central Intelligence Agency (CIA) has identified the problem of the rapid spread of infectious diseases in the United States (with particular reference to HIV/AIDS in the 1980s) due to the ongoing globalization process by highlighting its security aspects.[2]

Undoubtedly, the fear of bioterrorism – among other things recalled by the SG as possible collateral effects of COVID-19 – has contributed to directly link health and security.[3]

In 2000, the SC with the well-known Resolution 1308, highlighted that "the HIV/AIDS pandemic, if unchecked, may pose a risk to stability and security", even if an explicit qualification of HIV/AIDS as a threat to peace and security did not follow at that time.

Action of the SC, with the adoption of the well-known Resolution 2177/2014 – promoted by the United States under the Obama presidency – was requested in 2014 to call the attention of the international community to Ebola and the risk of its spread outside Sub-Saharan Africa to therefore activate mechanisms of solidarity and cooperation.

It is worth recalling that in Resolution 2177, the SC did not directly address Ebola as a threat but rather as a situation that could have triggered political instability in the most affected countries. Indeed, Liberia, Guinea, and Sierra Leone were recovering after years of civil war.[4]

The deadlock within the SC during the COVID-19 pandemic and the delayed adoption of Resolution 2532/2020 (followed by Resolution 2565/2021) has raised serious doubts as to whether the securitization of health represents a consolidated practice within this organ.

The lack of United States leadership in the early phases of the COVID-19 pandemic – which was instead crucial in the process of securitization of health in the cases of HIV/AIDS and Ebola – and the tendency of the former Trump administration to engage in a free-riding strategy had a negative impact in terms of the multilateral response to the pandemic.

In light of the ever-increasing interconnection between pandemics and international security, this chapter offers a critical analysis of the health-security nexus by focusing on the two resolutions enacted by the SC with reference to the COVID-19 pandemic. Reflections on their concrete impact on the fight

---

2 National Intelligence Estimante, "The Global Infectious Disease Threat and Its Implications for the United States" (January 2020), https://www.dni.gov/files/documents/infectiousdiseases_2000.pdf.

3 Stefania Negri, "Emergenze sanitarie e diritto internazionale: il paradigma salute-diritti umani e la strategia globale di lotta alle pandemie ed al bioterrorismo", in *Studi in onore di Vincenzo Starace* (Editoriale Scientifica: 2008), 571–605.

4 For further details, see Pia Acconci, "The Reaction to the Ebola Epidemic Within the United Nations Framework: What Next for the World Health Organization", in Frauke Lachenmann, Tilmann J. Röder, Rüdiger Wolfrum (eds.), *Max Planck Yearbook of United Nations Law* 18 (2014): 405–426.

against these infectious diseases are discussed, and a parallelism with Resolution 2177 on Ebola in Western Africa is drawn.

This chapter argues that framing health issues in a security discourse makes sense regardless of whether the SC is adequately equipped to act very quickly and to provide a strong response using its powers under Article 24 of the UN Charter.

The slow and inefficient response of the SC when facing COVID-19 has epitomized the limits of this UN body, whose actions are greatly hindered by the veto power.

2. New threats to peace and security

The main global challenges to peace and security of the XXI century are new and unpredictable events that demanded a reshaping of the concept of security.

The globalized world must face emerging and unpredictable menaces, such as the growing diffusion of zoonotic diseases, the rise of international terrorism, environmental degradation and climate change, and traditional threats, as exhibited by the Russian military aggression against Ukraine in 2022 and the Israel-Hamas war which began in October 2023.

These new threats, which were, of course, not anticipated when the UN Charter was adopted at the end of World War II, appeared gradually after the end of the Cold War.

The modern threats are less predictable than classic military perils represented by a single enemy State that invades the territory of another State with its troops. They have different sources, ranging from non-state actors (e.g., terrorist entities like ISIS, al Qaeda and Hamas, paramilitary groups such as the "little green men" in southeast Ukraine, pirates, and insurgents) to intangible actors, such as viruses and climate change (even though one might assume that global warming is also the result of the economic activities of States, leading to their refusal to subscribe to and/or implement environmental treaties).

The classic notion of security was strictly related to the realist view of international relations that developed at the beginning of the Cold War. The theory of realism represents an interpretation of international relations that points out its most conflictual and controversial elements. It identifies the world order as a system dominated by anarchy, where a cluster of States – which are merely concerned with their own domestic security and national interests – are in competition among one another for the pursuit of power.[5]

According to this view, security is the protection of the homeland from aggression or attacks by foreign troops. This classic interpretation of national security is recognized by Article 51 of the UN Charter, which has endorsed

---

5 For one of the most influential writings on realism, see Hans G. Morgenthau, *Politics Among Nations: The Struggle for Power and Peace* (Alfred A. Knopf: 1948); Henry Kissinger, "Documentation: Foreign Policy and National Security", *International Security* (1976): 182–191.

the right to individual or collective self-defence in response to an act of aggression.[6]

Currently, the notion of security has radically changed compared to the realist view. It is generally accepted that security agendas should no longer be limited to resisting armed attacks by hostile troops or terrorist groups and preventing armed conflicts, since the array of risks to the survival of a population has multiple sources.

The standard concept of security has failed to protect the human population from the new threats related to the process of globalization, which endangers their lives.[7]

The nature of the threats and their exacerbation of ongoing conflicts have radically changed together with their object. As a matter of fact, the State no longer needs protection but the individuals and their health (and the environment in which they live), according to the emerging concept of Human Security, which considers security as something more than the defence of the territory by an armed attack or an aggression.[8]

The end of the Cold War attested to the idea that if the States were safer than before, then their citizens were not in the same situation.

The SC practice reveals a trend to determine non-conventional threats to peace and security under Article 39 of the UN Charter and to align more closely with the Human Security paradigm. A significant moment of this extension is represented by Resolution 688/1991 on the repression of the Kurds in Northern Iraq, whereby the SC considered "the massive flow of refugees towards and across international frontiers and to cross-border incursions, as a threat to peace and security in the region" (Preamble, Recital 3).

The most consistent developments have been registered through Resolution 794/1992 on Somalia,[9] where the SC recognized a humanitarian disaster consisting of gross violations of human rights and of the rules of international humanitarian law as a threat to peace and security (Preamble). With Resolution

---

6 Article 51 of the UN Charter states, "Nothing in the present Charter shall impair the inherent right of individual or collective self-defence if an armed attack occurs against a Member of the United Nations, until the Security Council has taken measures necessary to maintain international peace and security. Measures taken by Members in the exercise of this right of self-defence shall be immediately reported to the Security Council and shall not in any way affect the authority and responsibility of the Security Council under the present Charter to take at any time such action as it deems necessary in order to maintain or restore international peace and security". See John H. Gibson, "Article 51 or the Charter of the United Nations", *India Quarterly* (1957): 121–138.
7 Karel Wellens, "The UN Security Council and New Threats to the Peace: Back to the Future", *Journal of Conflict and Security Studies* (2003): 15–70.
8 Gerd Obertleiner, "Human Security: A Challenge to International Law?", *Global Governance* (2005): 185–203.
9 Resolution n. 794 of 3 December 1992 on the situation in Somalia.

965/1994 on Rwanda,[10] the SC qualified genocide and the systematic violations of human rights as a threat to peace and security (Preamble).

With Resolution n. 1529/2004 on Haiti,[11] the SC invoked "the deterioration of the political, security and humanitarian situation in Haiti" and established that "the situation in Haiti constitutes a threat to international peace and security and to the stability of the Caribbean" (Preamble).

The tendency by the SC to gradually expand the notion of "threat" since the end of the Cold War found its ideological foundations in the well-known Presidential Statement of 31 January 1992[12] through which for the first time, the SC emphasized forms of instability different from armed conflicts. In the statement, it was clearly indicated that "the absence of war and military conflicts among States does not in itself ensure international peace and security" while quoting "non-military sources of instability" in the economic, social, humanitarian, and ecological fields as new threats to peace and security.

A further expansion in the meaning of a threat took place regarding international terrorism; in particular, Resolution n. 1368/2001 in the aftermath of the Al-Qaeda terrorist attack against the World Trade Center qualified this particular event, and *any other act* of international terrorism, as a threat to international peace and security (Preamble).[13]

This was the first time that an abstract phenomenon was included within the concept of international threats.

The expansion of the notion of threats after the Al-Qaeda attacks ranged from classic security perils, such as the proliferation of weapons of mass destruction (WMD), internal armed conflict, and maritime piracy,[14] to a new category of dangers ("threats to human security"), including gross violations of human rights, illegal exploitation of natural resources, wildlife poaching, and health pandemics.

In line with this tendency, Resolutions n. 2134/2014 and n. 2136/2014, concerning the crisis in the Central African Republic and the equally serious situation of conflict in the eastern part of the Democratic Republic of Congo, respectively, have – incidentally but rather significantly – pointed out the linkage between wildlife poaching and trafficking, ongoing civil wars in

---

10 Resolution n. 955 of 8 November 1994 on the establishment of an International Tribunal and adoption of the Statute of the Tribunal.
11 Resolution n. 1529 of 29 February 2004 on the situation in Haiti.
12 Note by the President of the Security Council, UN Doc. S 23500, 31 January 1992.
13 Resolution n. 1368 of 12 September 2001, on Threats to international peace and security caused by terrorist acts. See also Resolution n. 1373 of 28 September 2001 on Threats to international peace and security caused by terrorist acts, which states in the Preamble that "*any* act of international terrorism constitutes a threat to international peace and security." In this regard, see Raffacle Cadin, *I presupposti dell'azione del Consiglio di sicurezza nell'articolo 39 della Carta delle Nazioni Unite* (Giuffrè: 2008).
14 See, for instance, Resolution 2634/2022 on Peace and security in Africa (Maritime security in the Gulf of Guinea).

the African continent, and the activities of criminal networks and terroristic organizations that operate on an international scale.[15]

The strict relationship between natural resources and conflicts, although the object of growing doctrinal interest,[16] had until now remained unrelated to SC practice, at least regarding the significance raised by living natural resources. In these resolutions, in particular, the SC considered illegal poaching of elephants and smuggling of their ivory as a fuel factor of armed conflicts because it is an illicit source of financing for various armed groups and insurgents often linked to international terrorism.

With Resolution 2347/2017, the SC determined, according to Article 39 of the UN Charter, that the "unlawful destruction of cultural heritage, and the looting and smuggling of cultural property in the event of armed conflicts" constitute a threat to international peace and security.

These resolutions – along with Resolution 2177 – represent a very innovative development of SC practice concerning the idea of threats to peace and security and in particular, the same qualification of the legal concept of international security.[17]

The issue of climate change as a Chapter VII issue has also been debated within the SC,[18] although a thematic resolution on this problem has never been adopted as result of this discussion. The stalemate was due to the opposition of a group of States that prefer to consider environmental issues as traditionally falling within the domain of development cooperation.[19]

There is, however, an *idem sentire* within the scientific community and the international community on three key points in the reconstruction of the relationship between climate change and security. The first is that climate change is a "threat multiplier".[20] As maintained in a 2020 Report, although climate change "is rarely a direct cause of conflict . . . there is ample evidence that its effects exacerbate important drivers and contextual factors of conflict and fragility, thereby challenging the stability of States and societies". In particular, the Report argues that global warming "can increase resource demands,

---

15 Anne Peters, "Novel Practice of the Security Council: Wildlife Poaching and Trafficking as a Threat to Peace", *EJIL Talk* (12 February 2014), https://www.ejiltalk.org/novel-practice-of-the-security-council-wildlife-poaching-and-trafficking-as-a-threat-to-the-peace/.
16 Magnus Öberg, Kaare Strøm, *Resources, Governance and Civil Conflict* (Routledge: 2008).
17 Resolution n. 2347 of 24 March 2017. For further details, see Andrzej Jakubowsky, "Cultural Heritage and the Security Council: Why Resolution 2347 Matters", *Questions of International Law, Zoom-in* 48 (2018): 5–19.
18 UNSC, Verbatim Record UN Doc/S/PV/5663 (17 April 2011).
19 For an analysis of the relationship between climate change and security, see Richard A. Matthew, "Is Climate Change a National Security Issue?", *Issues in Science and Technology* (2011): 49–60.
20 In this sense, see Stephane Hallegatte, Mook Bangalore, Laura Bonzanigo, Marianne Fay, Tamaro Kane, Ulf Narloch, Julie Rozenberg, David Treguer, Adrien Vogt-Schilb, *Shock Waves: Managing the Impacts of Climate Change on Poverty* (World Bank: 2015), 79–95.

environmental degradation and uneven development, and exacerbate existing fragility and conflict risks".[21]

The second point is that climate change (particularly sea level rise) is an existential threat not only for humankind but also mainly for the archipelagic island States of the Pacific region that seriously risk disappearing.[22] Climate change is not therefore a direct cause of conflict but rather a source of extinction of States and populations and a real threat to human security.

Finally, no one doubts that climate change is a progressive threat destined to have negative effects on the governance of resources and, therefore, increasing progressively the risk of conflicts between and within States. If the relationship between climate and security is so intense and strategic, then it is questionable that the SC has so far failed to agree on a thematic resolution on this matter.[23]

3. Resolution 2177/2014 and the securitization of health

Conceptually, the aforementioned trend to expand the notion of security to the domains of environment and health reflects the new challenges emerging from the process of globalization and – as underlined by some scholars – echoes the point of view of the Copenhagen School theory of securitization,[24] which represents the decline of realist thinkers in international relations.[25]

Resolution 2177/2014 on Ebola in Western Africa was evidence at that time that health issues had become increasingly "securitized" within the UN system and that the SC was expanding the notion of "threat" to align more closely with a human security framework.[26] As is well-known, Resolution 2177 has represented a breakthrough in the SC's practice. For the first time in its history, the SC expressly qualified an infectious disease as a threat to peace and security.[27]

21 10 Insights on Climate Impacts and Peace: A Summary of What We Know, Berlin-Potsdam, 2020.

22 David Freestone, Clive Schofield, "Sea Level Rise and Archipelagic States: A Preliminary Risk Assessment", *Ocean Yearbook* (2021): 340–387.

23 For further details, see Raffaele Cadin, "The times they are a-changin', ma la risoluzione tematica del Consiglio di sicurezza sul cambiamento climatico resta una chimera", *Ordine internazionale e diritti umani* 4 (2021): 1048–1055; Paolo Palchetti, "Débattre des changements climatiques au Conseil de sécurité: pour quoi faire ?", *Questions of International Law, Zoom-out* 91 (2022): 39–50.

24 Barry Buzan, *People, States and Fear: The National Security Problem in International Relations* (University of North Carolina Press: 2013).

25 Ashok Swain, *Understanding Emerging Security Challenges. Threats and Opportunities* (Routledge: 2013).

26 Antonietta Elia, "The United Nations Security Council Approach to Global Public Health Crisis: Summary of the Resolution 2177/2014 on Ebola Crisis", *Civitas Europa* (2015): 271–272.

27 Ilja Richard Pavone, "Ebola and the Securitization of Health: United Nations Security Council Resolution 2117/2014 and Its Limits", in Pedro A. Villareal et al. (eds.), *The Governance*

Even if the adoption of this Resolution never implied the adoption of coercive measures under Articles 41 and 42 of the UN Charter or the deployment of troops on the ground, it represents an extraordinary response to an extraordinary event.

Resolution 2177 has since only recommended measures and has not anticipated new duties upon Member States, and it did not have a specific goal to set a precedent with long-term implications on the roles and functions of the SC. This also explains why in the following health emergencies (Zika, wild polio, Ebola in the Democratic Republic of Congo in 2019, and monkeypox in 2022), the SC has not intervened under Chapter VII.

The issue of which criteria might qualify a health emergency as a threat to peace and security by the SC is still the object of debate.[28]

It is evident that the determination of a health emergency as an issue of security depends on the context and mainly on the political will of countries with veto power.

The legal basis for Resolution 2177 and the process of securitization of health can be traced to the Report of the High-Level Panel on Threats, Challenges and Change of 2004,[29] which states that in "extreme cases of threat posed by a new emerging infectious disease or intentional release of an infectious agent, there may be a need for cooperation between WHO and the Security Council in establishing effective quarantine measures" (Para. 70).

The Report recommended that the WHO Director-General should keep the SC informed in the event of any suspicions of overwhelming outbreak of infectious disease.[30]

In the Report of the former Secretary General Kofi Annan of 2005 ("In Larger Freedom"),[31] Paragraph 105 reads as follows: "I myself stand ready, in consultation with the Director-General of the World Health Organization, to use my powers under Article 99 of the Charter of the United Nations to call to the attention of the Security Council any overwhelming outbreak of infectious disease that threatens international peace and security".

However, throughout its existence prior to Ebola, the SC has never endorsed this commitment by dealing directly with previous health pandemics

of Disease Outbreaks. International Health Law: Lessons from the Ebola Crisis and Beyond (Nomos: 2017), 301–323.

28 Gianluca Burci, "Ebola, the Security Council and the Securitization of Public Health", *Questions of International Law, Zoom-in* 10 (2014): 27–39.

29 *The Secretary-General's High-Level Panel Report on Threats, Challenges and Change, A More Secure World: Our Shared Responsibility* (2 December 2004), https://www.un.org/peace building/content/more-secure-world-our-shared-responsibility-%E2%80%93-report-high-level-panel-threats-challenges-and

30 Report of the Secretary-General's High-Level Panel on Threats, Challenges and Change. A More Secure World. Our Shared Responsibility. UN GAOR 59th Sess Supp No 565 Doc A/59 (2004).

31 In larger freedom: towards development, security and human rights for all: report of the Secretary-General (2005).

(i.e., pandemic influenza and SARS). It is only through Resolution 2177 that the SC decided to intervene to react to a situation that could have become a real threat to humankind if not adequately contained. However, in order not to undermine the role of other UN bodies and specialized agencies, the SC expressly decided not to recall Chapter VII of the UN Charter, and as a consequence, it did not adopt any enforcement measures under Articles 41 and 42.

In this regard, it is relevant to clarify that it is quite difficult to contemplate what type of measures the SC could have taken given the absence of a concrete target (such as a terrorist group). In fact, it seems clear that Ebola has not had, to date, any impact on the rules of Chapter VII of the Charter. Rather, the most obvious impact of Ebola was not on collective security but rather on the promotion of human security as an interpretation tool of the notion of threat.

Therefore, this can be considered not a decision but a mere recommendation.

It must be observed that the reference to the typical categories contained in Chapter VII in a resolution aimed at promoting an international response to a viral epidemic not linked to a bacteriological attack seemed to some scholars a paradox, as "the practical value of enforcement actions squarely placed under Chapter VII seems questionable".[32]

Other scholars had no difficulty in drawing the legal foundational nexus between Resolution 2177 and Chapter VII and specifically Article 40 ("Provisional Measures").[33]

In fact, the previous adoption of a resolution under Article 39, qualifying a determined situation as a "threat to the peace, breach of the peace of act of aggression", represents and obligatory procedural step in the adoption of further measures under Chapter VII (in addition or constituting one of the very few limitations of SC powers under Chapter VII), and it does not necessarily call into question the SC powers under Chapter VII to adopt sanctions that do or do not imply the use of force (Art. 41 or 42).

In this case, the provisional measures envisaged by Article 40 could instead be relevant, because they are intended to be a set of actions designed to stabilize a critical situation. The SC simply invited the States of the international community and private entities to adopt provisional measures that would have

---

32 Gian Luca Burci, Jacob Quirin, Ebola, "WHO and the United Nations: Convergence on Global Public Health and International Peace and Security", *ASIL Insights* (2014), https://www.asil.org/insights/volume/18/issue/25/ebola-who-and-united-nations-convergence-global-public-health-and.

33 Ludovica Poli, "La risoluzione n. 2177 (2014) del Consiglio di sicurezza delle Nazioni Unite e la qualificazione dell'epidemia di ebola come minaccia alla pace ed alla sicurezza internazionale", *Diritti umani e diritto internazionale* (2015): 238–245, at 244. Article 40 states that "In order to prevent an aggravation of the situation, the Security Council may, before making the recommendations or deciding upon the measures provided for in Article 39, call upon the parties concerned to comply with such provisional measures as it deems necessary or desirable. Such provisional measures shall be without prejudice to the rights, claims, or position of the parties concerned. The Security Council shall duly take account of failure to comply with such provisional measures".

hindered the further spread of the disease and avoided more incisive measures, such as quarantines, without adopting any binding decision.

4. The conceptual foundation of Resolution 2177

The main global challenges to peace and security in the XXI century – that is, the re-emergence of infectious diseases, the rise of the Islamic State and international terrorism, and environmental degradation – determine a reshaping of the concept of security.

Traditionally, this notion was exclusively related to national security, which was intended as the protection of the territory from aggression or attacks caused by foreign troops.[34]

For this reason, in 1957, Kelsen defined the boundaries of security as "the protection of men against the use of force by other men".[35]

The classic understanding of the concept of international security – which arose after World War II – is strictly related to the foundations of the collective security system, according to which the SC should concentrate within itself the monopoly over the use of force to maintain peace and security.[36]

At present, it is generally accepted that the traditional concept of security as protection of homeland against external military threats does not encompass the array of risks to the survival of a population of a State. In fact, the traditional concept of security failed to protect human populations against new menaces related to the process of globalization that endangered their lives. As such, the nature of the threats and their sources have radically changed, together with their object. It is no longer the State that needs protection but individuals, according to the emerging concept of human security, which considers "security" as something more than the defense of territory by the invasion of foreign troops. Along with the end of the Cold War came the idea that if States were safer than before, then their citizens were not in the same situation.[37]

In general terms, the human security paradigm can be traced to the writings of eminent scholars in the early 1980s and tends to permeate the human rights discourse, the right to health, and security issues.[38]

Health issues can, in fact, be included within the domain of human rights, as recognized in the Alma Ata Declaration of 1978, the major milestone of

34 David A. Baldwin, "The Concept of Security", *Review of International Studies* (1997): 5–26.
35 Hans Kelsen, *Collective Security Under International Law* (U. S. Government Printing Office: 1957), 1.
36 Jean Salmon, *Dictionnaire de droit international public* (Bruylant: 2001), 123.
37 *Canada, Department of Foreign Affairs and International Trade: Human Security: Safety for People in a Changing World* (1999), http://www.summit-americas.org/Canada/Human Security-english.htm.
38 Richard H. Ullman, "Redefining Security", *International Security* (1983): 129–153.

the XX century in the field of public health. Against this backdrop, Ullman affirmed that non-conventional threats – including economic and environmental issues – could be just as dangerous as traditional military ones and consequently deserve special consideration as security issues.

Ullman defined a threat to security as

> an action or a sequence of events that (1) threatens drastically and over a relatively brief span of time to degrade the quality of life for inhabitants of a State, or (2) threatens significantly to narrow the range of policy choices available to the government of a State or to private, nongovernmental entities (persons, groups, corporations) within the State.

Following this reasoning, Mathews argued that environmental degradation should be considered a priority in national security strategies, although she still considers the State rather than human beings as the main object of security policies.[39]

Wars of an international or an internal character, terrorism, and natural disasters (that have a negative impact on the environment) can be included within the first category of threats, which are the most dangerous for human life. A situation with few opportunities for trade, investment, and cultural exchange, and in which important values are threatened falls within the second. The Bruntland Report ("Our Common Future") of 1987 also referred to two great threats facing humankind: "The first is that of nuclear exchange . . . the second is that of environmental ruin worldwide".

The UN Development Programme (UNDP)'s notion of human security promoted by Canada contributed significantly to the evolution of the security concept and "translated into practice" the thoughts of Ullman. The UNDP defined human security in its "Human Development Report" as "safety from chronic threats, hunger, disease and repression" and "protection from sudden and hurtful disruption in pattern of daily life". In delineating human security, the UNDP highlighted five dimensions: economic security; environmental security; energy and resource security; biosecurity; and health security.[40]

The novelty of this notion is characterized by the change in perspective that provides that not only the territory of a State but also the population have the right to be protected from threats.[41]

---

39 Jessica Tuchman Mathews, "Redefining Security", *Foreign Affairs* (1989): 162–177. Supra, note 39, at 133.
40 United Nations Development Programme, UNDP, *Human Development Report* (New Dimensions of Human Security: 1994).
41 Gerd Oberleitner, "Human Security: A Challenge to International Law?", *Global Governance* (2005): 185-203.

This also involved a significant shift in approach: security should no longer be achieved through military means but through sustainable human development.[42]

This broad and inclusive list of sources of human security focuses on the potential of harm to individuals and paved the way to the concept of the responsibility to protect (R2P) (whose effectiveness has been widely criticized due to its complete failure in addressing the humanitarian crises in Libya and Syria).[43]

It is submitted that the most crucial development is the inclusion of health in the human security discourse.[44]

With the growing threat of international terrorism after the end of the Cold War and particularly of bioterrorism, health-related issues have been increasingly dealt with under the security agendas of the United States and the EU.[45]

Predominately, the Anthrax case in the United States acted as the catalyst for the inclusion of health issues in the counter-terrorism strategy.

A further development is evident in the report of the Secretary-General's High Level Panel on Threats, Challenges and Change, 2004, which highlighted global security threats, such as civil wars, the spread of WMD, and international terrorism. The former UN Secretary-General in his 2005 Report "In Larger Freedom" included deadly infectious diseases among the threats to peace and security in the XXI century (Para. 78), giving moral and legal value to the extension of the human security concept to include health. However, in Resolution 2177, the SC, in establishing a link among health, security, and humanitarian crises, extended the boundaries of the notion of threats to peace and security in a highly innovative way by embracing the notion of human security. For example, the Ebola outbreak has been a human security crisis in all respects because – given its unprecedented nature – it endangers the life of entire populations in West Africa. Accordingly, the idea of human security constitutes the theoretical foundation for Resolution 2177, and the novelty is undoubtedly represented by the fact that the SC for the first time considered a natural event as destabilising and therefore dangerous for peace and security. The discourse would obviously have been different if the deliberate spread of a pathogen agent (i.e., a bacteriological attack), such as a WMD, were at the origin of the epidemic.

42 Barry Buzan, Lene Hansen, *The Evolution of International Security Studies* (Cambridge University Press: 2009), 202; Barbara von Tigerstrom, *Human Security and International Law: Prospects and Problems* (Hart Publishing: 2007), 19.

43 Ilja Richard Pavone, "The Crisis of the Responsibility to Protect Doctrine in the Light of the Syrian Civil War", *Global Community Yearbook of International Law* (2014): 115–139.

44 Lincoln Chen, Vasant Narasihman, "Human Security and Global Health", *Journal of Human Development* (2003–2004): 19-25.

45 Daniel M. Gernstein, *Bioterror in the 21st Century: Emerging Threats in a New Global Environment* (Naval Institute Press: 2009).

Part II The Security Council facing the COVID-19 pandemic

5. The stalemate of the Security Council at the onset of the COVID-19 pandemic

The structural limits of the SC in the management of the COVID-19 pandemic have enhanced reflections and parallelisms on the handling of previous health emergencies. Since then, the question has been raised as to whether the precedent represented by Resolution 2177/2014 on the Ebola outbreak could have been replicated with the COVID-19 pandemic.

During the first half of 2020, the SC was deeply divided on dealing with or acknowledging the impact of the COVID-19 pandemic on international peace and security.[46]

On 26 March 2020, the UN Secretary-General António Guterres called for a global ceasefire, demanding a coordinated response and measures to contain the economic and social impact of COVID-19.[47]

He recognized the "unprecedented effects of the pandemic, including the severe disruption to societies and economies, as well as to global travel and commerce, and the devastating impact on the livelihood of people". Similarly, the WHO Director-General, affirmed that COVID-19 represents an "an unprecedented threat, but it is also an unprecedented opportunity to come together as one against a common enemy – an enemy against humanity".[48]

In calling for a global ceasefire, Guterres described COVID-19 as a disease that "attacks all, relentlessly", with some populations most at risk for "devastating losses". At the launch of the global humanitarian response plan on 25 March 2020, Guterres warned that the pandemic threatened to divert international attention and resources from resolving ongoing conflicts and supporting peace processes.[49]

The fact that conflict-affected countries can facilitate the spread of a disease outbreak was already expressed in Resolution 1308/2000 on HIV/AIDS, where the SC affirmed that the "pandemic is exacerbated by conditions of violence and instability, which increase the risk of exposure to the disease through large movements of people, widespread uncertainty over conditions and reduced access to medical care".

46 Bruno Charbonneau, "The COVID-19 test of the United Nations Security Council", *International Journal* (2021): 6–16, at 7.

47 https://psr.org/un-secretary-general-calls-for-a-global-ceasefire/.

48 *WHO Director-General's Opening Remarks at the Media Briefing on COVID-19* (18 March 2020), https://www.who.int/director-general/speeches/detail/who-director-general-s-opening-remarks-at-the-media-briefing-on-covid-19–18-march-2020.

49 https://www.who.int/director-general/speeches/detail/who-director-general-s-remarks-launch-of-appeal-global-humanitarian-response-plan–25-march-2020.

The UN Secretary-General in his remarks to the UN Security Council of 9 April 2020 specifically maintained that "the pandemic poses a significant threat to the maintenance of peace and security", therefore requesting the direct intervention of the SC.[50]

He underlined that the SC's involvement should be "critical to mitigate the peace and security implications" and that "a signal of unity and resolve from the council would count for a lot at this anxious time".

In this regard, he underlined that, although COVID-19 is first and foremost a health emergency, it has more far-reaching consequences "potentially leading to an increase in social unrest and violence".

6. Resolution 2532 (2020)

In this context, the SC adopted with extreme delay a ceasefire resolution on 1 July 2020[51] and a resolution addressed to COVID-19 vaccination campaigns in the context of armed conflicts on 28 February 2021.[52]

Certainly, the crisis in the diplomatic relations between China and the United States in 2020, at the lowest level since the Tiananmen massacre of 1989, had a concrete impact on efforts towards global cooperation in the management of the pandemic.[53]

Resolution 2532 was the outcome of an exhausting negotiation process following the explicit request by the UN Secretary-General António Guterres to discuss this topic within the SC.

The long wait was due to the dispute between China and the United States on the source and name of the novel coronavirus, the strong criticism by the former Trump administration towards the way that the WHO had dealt with the pandemic, and in particular, the charges against the Director-General of the WHO as being under China's control in the wake of the COVID-19 outbreak.

Indeed, attempts to adopt a resolution within the SC have stalled mainly due to the bitter stalemate between China and the former United States administration on the source and name of COVID-19.[54]

The US strongly blamed China for unleashing the pathogen on the world. The initiative – which appeared to be part of a broader strategy of the Trump administration to deflect responsibility for its own slow reaction to the disease outbreak – was blocked by China, which wields veto power.

---

50 https://www.un.org/sg/en/content/sg/statement/2020-04-09/secretary-generals-remarks-the-security-council-the-covid-19-pandemic-delivered.
51 UN Doc S/RES/2532 (2020) (1 July 2020) adopted unanimously.
52 UN Doc S/RES/2565 (2021) (26 February 2021) adopted unanimously.
53 https://foreignpolicy.com/2020/03/27/un-security-council-unsc-coronavirus-pandemic/.
54 Maurizio Arcari, "Some Thoughts in the Aftermath of Security Council Resolution 2532 (2020) on Covid-19", *Questions of International Law, Zoom-out* 70 (2020): 59–76, at 60.

To overcome these divisions, the UN Secretary-General recalled the SC for the purposes of major unity and has expressly requested its intervention by acting on the basis of Article 99 of the UN Charter, which indicates that "the Secretary-General may bring to the attention of the Security Council any matter which in his opinion may threaten the maintenance of international peace and security".

The SG can therefore invite the SC to begin a discussion on a given topic, but it does not automatically imply a direct intervention by the SC.[55]

In practice, Article 99 of the UN Charter has formally been invoked in few cases; the most striking cases date back to 1960 with reference to the Congo question and to the 1979 Iran hostage crisis at the United States embassy.

More recently, in the context of the Rohingya refugee crisis at the border between Myanmar and Bangladesh, SG Guterres has requested concerted action to prevent a further escalation of the humanitarian crisis by requesting the SC "to press for restraint and calm to avoid a humanitarian catastrophe".[56]

China had a lack of transparency in providing information to the WHO on the real spread of the virus considering that reliable sources argued that the virus had circulated in the country since November 2019.[57]

China's decision to leave asymptomatic patients off its coronavirus infection tally also sparked debate.

To further worsen the situation, former President Trump had openly criticized the WHO for its pandemic response – which he considered too soft towards China – and outlined the US's grievances about the WHO's handling of the disease outbreak and its presumed ties to China.

After a lengthy negotiation, the P5 agreed on a very short text that backed the SG's call for a global ceasefire, which appears to have been a watered-down compromise and further evidence of the inadequacy of the voting system within the SC.[58]

To overcome the stalemate within the SC, the compromise was a diplomatic product of "constructive ambiguity".[59] The deal was evident in two elements: first, any mention of the WHO or the IHR was deleted from the final version of the Resolution, and the wording was made more ambiguous to instead refer to the UN system in general rather than to specific agencies. Due to the extreme delay, the momentum was lost, and the practical effect of the Resolution in

55 Benedetto Conforti, Carlo Focarelli, *Le Nazioni Unite*, 9th ed. (CEDAM: 2017), 324–325.
56 Letter dated 2 September 2017 from the Secretary-General addressed to the President of the Security Council, https://www.securitycouncilreport.org/atf/cf/%7B65BFCF9B-6D27–4E9C-8CD3-CF6E4FF96FF9%7D/s_2017_753.pdf.
57 David L Heymann, Nahoko Shindo "COVID-19: What is Next for Public Health?" *The Lancet* (2020): 542–545.
58 Michael Barnett, Martha Finnemore, "Political Approaches", in Sam Daws, Thomas G. Weiss (eds.), *The Oxford Handbook on the United Nations* (Oxford University Press: 2008).
59 Michael Byers, "Still Agreeing to Disagree: International Security and Constructive Ambiguity", *Journal on the Use of Force and International Law* (2021): 91–114.

war-torn countries was minimal, as shown by the Nagorno-Karabakh conflict, where the fighting was at its worst since the ceasefire of 1994.[60]

Second, the COVID-19 pandemic was not labelled as a threat to peace and security under Article 39 of the UN Charter. Paragraph 11 of the preamble of Resolution 2532 (2020) simply maintains that "the unprecedented extent of the COVID-19 pandemic *is likely* to endanger the maintenance of international peace and security".

This is in contrast with the General Assembly, which had adopted four resolutions on COVID-19. Specifically, Resolution 2532 was a missed opportunity, despite being adopted unanimously, because of its weak legal nature (it is a recommendation) and its poor wording (it does not contemplate "further measures" in case of non-compliance).[61]

National egoism prevailed during the negotiation process of Resolution 2532: the United States intended the resolution to be an occasion to globally recognize China's responsibility for the spread of the disease by requesting, among other things, a specific reference to the "Wuhan virus". The United States also strongly rejected any reference to the WHO in the final text following the decision of the former administration to cut ties with the Organization by, first, suspending funding and, later, by withdrawing as a member. Separately, China was eager to avoid any direct or indirect criticism of its handling of the first phase of the disease outbreak and to dismiss any charge of lack of transparency and cover-up of critical information on COVID-19.

Once over the hurdle of the WHO, a compromise was achieved over the idea of supporting the SG's call for a global ceasefire (although all the P5 agreed that it would have not hindered the continuation of counter-terrorism operations).[62]

Despite this, the United States and the Russian Federation were also concerned that a global ceasefire could have hampered their respective military operations in Afghanistan, Iraq, and Syria. The Resolution specifically addresses conflict situations, following the assumption that there is a clear link between violence and instability as a trigger for the spread of COVID-19 and that inversely, the pandemic exacerbates the adverse humanitarian impact of the disease on hostilities.[63]

---

60 The lack of implementation of Resolution 2532 was also explicitly recognized in Resolution 2565 ("expressing concern that the call for a general and immediate cessation of hostilities . . . was not fully heeded").

61 Stefania Negri, "United Nations Security Council Resolution 2532", *International Legal Materials* (2021): 1–6.

62 The United States' full support for a global ceasefire was reiterated in the "Remarks at a UNSC Discussion on Resolution 2532 on COVID-19", 9 September 2020 ("The United States has also been a strong supporter of the Secretary-General's call for a global ceasefire, while acknowledging the importance of continuing counter-terrorism operations"). https://usun.usmission. gov/remarks-at-a-un-security-council-discussion-on-resolution-2532-on-Covid-19-via-vtc/.

63 Erin Pobjie, "Covid-19 as a Threat to International Peace and Security: The Role of the UN Security Council in Addressing the Pandemic", *EJIL:Talk!* (27 July 2020), https://www.

The Resolution demanded "a general and immediate cessation of hostilities in all situations on its agenda" and supported "the efforts undertaken by the Secretary-General and his Special Representatives and Special Envoys in that respect" (Para. 1). The SC then called upon

> all parties to armed conflicts to engage immediately in a durable humanitarian pause for at least 90 consecutive days, in order to enable the safe, unhindered and sustained *delivery* of humanitarian assistance, provisions of related services by impartial humanitarian actors, in accordance with the humanitarian principles of humanity, neutrality, impartiality and independence, and medical evacuations, in accordance with international law, including international humanitarian law and refugee law as applicable.
>
> (Para. 2)

Since the establishment of the UN in 1945, it has been common practice by the SC to request ceasefires by belligerents both in the context of international and non-international armed conflicts. The novelty here lies in the request of a humanitarian pause in a conflict setting, a demand that had never been issued before Resolution 2532. Resolution 2532 also requested the SG to "provide updates to the Security Council on the UN efforts to address the COVID-19 pandemic in countries in situations of armed conflict or affected by humanitarian crises" (Para. 5). In this way, it created a formal mechanism for the SG to monitor and update the SC on the implementation of the ceasefire. This also afforded the possibility of demanding further measures.

7. The legal nature of Resolution 2532 (2020)

In Resolution 2532, the SC expressed "grave concern about the devastating impact of the COVID-19 pandemic across the world, especially in countries ravaged by armed conflicts, in post-conflict situations, or affected by humanitarian crises noting that it could undermine peacebuilding and development gains in countries emerging from armed conflicts" (Preamble).

The legal foundation of this Resolution can be traced to Article 36, Paragraph 1 of the UN Charter, which authorizes the SC to adopt recommendations not only in case of a dispute but also in "*a situation* that might endanger peace and security".[64] It is therefore a recommendation under Chapter VI and not a decision under Chapter VII, and this is evident by the wording

---

ejiltalk.org/Covid-19-as-a-threat-to-international-peace-and-security-the-role-of-the-un-security-council-in-addressing-the-pandemic/.

64 Brigitte Stern, "Article 36", in Jean-Pierre Cot et Alain Pellet (eds.), *La Charte des Nations Unies. Commentaire article par article* (Economica Bruylant: 1991), 603–627; Anders Heriksen, *International Law*, 2nd ed. (Oxford University Press: 2017), 260.

of the operative paragraphs of the Resolution (the SC "demands" and "calls upon").[65] As observed by Morris, ceasefire resolutions issued under Chapter VI are "not binding upon the parties".[66] In light of the low level of compliance with this Resolution, there has been an escalation of new violence around the globe instead of a decrease, indicating that an act under Chapter VII, and specifically under Article 40, would have been more fit for the purpose. In fact, the SC, after having specifically qualified the COVID-19 pandemic as a threat to peace and security, could have invited the parties involved in ongoing conflicts to comply with provisional measures (a ceasefire and humanitarian pause) and could have then threatened the adoption of more stringent measures under Article 41 or 42 in case of non-compliance.

At first glance, there is a striking difference from the wording of Resolution 2177/2014, where it was clearly affirmed that "the unprecedented extent of the Ebola outbreak in Africa constitutes a threat to international peace and security". The terminology is instead more similar to that of Resolution 1308/2000, which emphasized that "the HIV/AIDS pandemic, if unchecked, may pose a risk to stability and security". The SC chose Chapter VI language, since the phrasing of Resolution 2532 textually reproduces Article 33, Paragraph 1 of the UN Charter and Article 4 of the Manila Declaration on the Peaceful Settlement of International Disputes (1982). The object of Chapter VI concerns issues that might "potentially" lead to a threat to peace and security, while Chapter VII is addressed to "ongoing" international crises, such as a "threat to peace, violation of peace and act of aggression" (Art. 39 of the UN Charter.)[67]

Within the framework provided by Chapter VI, the UN has made significant strides towards the prevention of conflicts through "operational prevention" (with the goal of mediating and deactivating tensions and averting disorders) and "structural prevention" (with the objective of addressing political or socioeconomic factors that are the deep-rooted causes of conflicts).[68] Hence, a key role is also played by systemic prevention that aims to address global risks that can fuel conflicts, which possess a transboundary dimension. Over time, the SC has increasingly focused its attention on the security implications of cross-border threats such as illegal poaching, trafficking of persons, environmental degradation, and infectious diseases. Resolution 2532 is part of this recent trend by the SC to address non-conventional threats to peace and

---

65 In this sense, see Erin Pobjie, "COVID-19 and the Scope of the UN Security Council's Mandate to Address Non-Traditional Threats to International Peace and Security", *Heidelberg Journal of International Law* (2021): 117–146, at 123.

66 David M. Morris, "From War to Peace: A Study of Cease-Fire Agreements and the Evolving Role of the United Nations", *Virginia Journal of International Law* (1996): 802–897, at 812–813.

67 Michael Wood, Eran Sthoeger, *The UN Security Council and International Law* (Cambridge University Press: 2022), 90–115.

68 Steven A. Zyck, Robert Muggah, "Preventive Diplomacy and Conflict Prevention: Obstacles and Opportunities", *Stability: International Journal of Security and Development* (2008): 68–75.

security, although these have usually been framed within Chapter VII. However, the SC, despite recalling its primary responsibility for the maintenance of international peace and security, has not explicitly qualified the COVID-19 pandemic as a "threat to peace and security" under Article 39 of the UN Charter. Conversely, Resolution 2532 states that the unprecedented extent of the COVID-19 pandemic "*is likely to endanger* the maintenance of international peace and security". Therefore, the SC has affirmed that the COVID-19 pandemic – if not adequately tackled – has the potential to lead to further turbulence in conflict settings and to threaten peace and security but has not yet reached the threshold for being qualified as a "threat" under Article 39.

The lack of an explicit qualification of COVID-19 as a threat to peace and security and its missed framing within Chapter VII is undoubtedly an element of weakness of this Resolution and has undermined its concrete impact in conflict settings, which is briefly explained in the following paragraph. A determination of COVID-19 as a "threat" under Article 39 would have implied the possibility to rely on Chapter VII powers and to foresee "enforcement measures".

8. Similarities and differences between Resolutions 2177 (2014) and 2532 (2020)

Considering the previously mentioned observations, a brief comparison can be drawn between the SC's action on COVID-19 and on the Ebola outbreak.

The first key contrast between the two resolutions is the different geopolitical landscape. The United States under the former Trump administration exhibited a strong tendency towards unilateralism, as witnessed by the United States withdrawal from UNESCO, the UN Human Rights Council, the Paris Agreement (starting from 4 November 2020), and the WHO (due to take effect in July 2021, although President Biden reversed the process).[69] By contrast, in 2014, the Obama presidency took the leadership of the "securitization of health" process within the SC and promoted the adoption of Resolution 2177/2014 in cooperation with China. For Resolution 2532, the initiative was driven by France and Tunisia, while the United States and China have significantly slowed down the process of adoption of the final text. Furthermore, the lack of any reference to the WHO is also in contrast to Resolution 2117/2014, in which the central role of the Organization was recognized. In the Preamble to the Ebola Resolution, the SC urged States to implement relevant temporary recommendations issued by the WHO. Similarly, Resolution 2439/2018 on Ebola in the Democratic Republic of Congo requested an immediate *cessation*

---

69 John B. Bellinger III, "The Trump Administration's Approach to International Law and Courts: Are We Seeing a Turn for the Worse?" *Case Western Research Journal of International Law* 51 (2019): 7–21. President Biden has decided to rejoin many of the various treaties and international bodies abandoned by the former President Trump. The US, therefore, rejoined UNESCO, the UN Human Rights Council, the Paris Agreement and the WHO. See Stuart Patrick, *Four Contending U.S. Approaches to Multilateralism* (Carnegie Endowment for International Peace: 2023).

of hostilities by all armed groups in light of "the serious concern regarding the security situation in the areas affected by the Ebola outbreak, which is severely hampering the response efforts and facilitating the spread of the virus in the Democratic Republic of the Congo and the wider region" (Para. 4). This Resolution particularly determined that the "ongoing armed conflict", not Ebola itself, was a threat to international peace and security.

The more striking difference is, however, related to the fact that the SC has not specifically recognized the COVID-19 pandemic as a "threat", framing its response within Chapter VI rather than within Chapter VII.

In the precedent of Resolution 2177, the SC acted as a "global health keeper" by pushing the Member States to comply with the IHR and taking the lead in the international response against Ebola.[70]

In view of these mentioned considerations, it is worth considering the added value of Resolution 2532 as part of the global effort against COVID-19. This is particularly because of the long delay in issuing the resolution following the SG's request, the fact that it is not legally binding in its content, and furthermore, the lack of any enforcement measure. The absence of any reference to the WHO is evidence of the pressure by the former United States administration during the negotiation process and the threat to rely on the veto power. This latter point is, however, controversial, given that – in the practice of the SC – the veto power applies only in case of decisions (not of recommendations; *ex* Art. 27, para. 3, of the UN Charter). Therefore, the United States did not have the power to hinder its adoption, and the drafters of the resolution could have insisted on at least a "nuanced" reference to the WHO (even with the United States voting against it), which would have been a signal of vitality by the SC.

This is in stark opposition to the GA, which had already adopted four resolutions on COVID-19 and recognized in the omnibus resolution "the crucial role played by the World Health Organization", despite the United States opposition. In contrast, a Chapter VI resolution could also be considered the most logical solution when the SC faces an "immaterial threat" such as an infectious disease. The possibility to also rely on powers and functions envisaged by the UN Charter apart from Chapter VII in the presence of non-conventional threats was already introduced by South Africa during the debate on the securitization of climate change. South Africa stated that

> Often, the Council has resorted to Chapter VII of the Charter as an umbrella for addressing issues that may not necessarily pose a threat to international peace and security, when it could have opted for alternative provisions of the Charter to respond more appropriately, utilizing other provisions of the same Charter.[71]

---

70 In this sense, Maurizio Arcari, Paolo Palchetti, "The Security Council as a Global 'Health-Keeper'? Resolution 2177 (2014) and Ebola as a Threat to the Peace", *Questions of International Law, Zoom-in* 10 (2014): 1–3.

71 Oli Brown, Anne Hammill, Robert McLeman, "Climate Change as the 'New' Security Threat: Implications for Africa", *International Affairs* (2007): 1141–1154.

One could wonder if it is really appropriate to act under Chapter VII in the case of a disease outbreak. Resolution 2177/2014, representing the culmination of the process of securitization of health, did not eventually envisage coercive measures under Article 41 or 42 or the deployment of troops on the ground. Some scholars had already expressed concern about the risk of overlap between the functions of the WHO, on the one hand, and those of the SC, on the other hand. Fundamentally, they raised an issue about the framing of a health issue within a security framework, arguing that health matters would be better suited for other UN bodies, such as the GA or the UN Economic and Social Council (ECOSOC). Against this backdrop, it is worth recalling that the GA "may discuss any questions or any matters within the scope of the present Charter" (Art. 10).

Through this lens, the lack of any mention of the WHO is not negative in the least and averts the risk of encroachment. It could also mean a clear division of tasks: the WHO would act – in strict cooperation with the GA – as the coordinating body in managing the health response to COVID-19, dealing with specific issues such as vaccine and treatment distribution. The SC, for its part, would then be entrusted with dealing with the collateral effects of infectious diseases in a conflict setting. Aside from the discourse on the clarification of powers and functions in case of disease outbreak, the key fact is that the impact of this Resolution was quite insignificant, since "early signs of compliance in conflict zones have begun to slip, and many countries are actually now experiencing an escalation of violence". It was no coincidence that the SG was forced to repeat on 22 September 2020 his appeal for a global ceasefire. More generally, the SC's inability to provide adequate and prompt support to the SG's call for a global ceasefire highlighted its incapacity to take the lead in the global response to the COVID-19 pandemic, in contrast to its approach during the Ebola epidemic. Despite the formal unanimity in its adoption, Resolution 2532 had shown, instead, a background of sharp contrasts, rivalry among the P5, and the prevailing of domestic interests over the need for coordination. In general terms, the SC's secondary role in the ongoing pandemic is a symptom of the crisis of multilateralism, democracy, and the current architecture of global health governance in what can be characterized as a period of strong unilateralism and weak international law. It will be of great interest to observe whether President Biden will reverse this process and revitalize the United States' role within the international architecture to promote a new age of renewed globalism and multilateralism.

9. Resolution 2565 (2021)

The second resolution of the SC on COVID-19 was adopted as consequence of the election of Joe Biden as United States President and the renewed commitment towards multilateralism by the United States administration.

Resolution 2565 was specifically addressed to suspend armed conflict in order to facilitate the delivery of COVID-19 vaccines in war-thorn countries.

The "Biden effect" on multilateralism was evident in this Resolution, since the specific role of both the IHR (Preamble, 4) and the WHO (Preamble, 6) was explicitly recognized.

Resolution 2565/2021, despite being adopted in a different geopolitical context, does not go further and limits itself to "consider what further measures may be necessary to ensure such impediments are removed and hostilities paused to enable vaccination".

It relied then on the ambiguous formula according to which "armed conflicts can exacerbate the COVID-pandemic, and that inversely the pandemic can exacerbate the adverse impacts of armed conflicts" (Preamble, 3).

In the Preamble, the Resolution emphasized the necessity of international cooperation, recalling the urgency of ensuring "equitable global access to quality, safe, efficacious and affordable vaccines" (Preamble, 5). It then restated that "equitable access to safe, efficacious, and affordable COVID-19 vaccines is essential to end the pandemic" (Preamble, 7). It then recalled the Role of the Act Accelerator (Preamble, 6) and COVAX.

Furthermore, it stated that extensive immunization against COVID-19 is a global public good. As is well-known, immunization is an effect of vaccines, and the reference to immunization was a specific policy choice since a direct reference to vaccines as a GPG would have implied a clash with the IPR.

The Resolution then considered that the "unprecedented extent of the COVID-19 pandemic is likely to endanger the maintenance of international peace and security", replicating the formulation of the previous resolution and abstaining from expressly qualifying the disease outbreak as a threat.

Next, it called for the "strengthening of national and multilateral approaches and international cooperation" by expressly quoting the COVAX facility to facilitate the roll out of vaccines in situations of armed conflicts (Art. 1).

There is a consistent SC practice as represented by the "days of tranquility": safe corridors to allow the delivery of medicines and vaccines and to facilitate the work of health workers. Three UN-negotiated days of tranquility in Sudan allowed the immunization of over 5 million children in Sudan through the administration of anti-polio vaccines.[72]

Against this backdrop, to facilitate the delivery of vaccines, the SC reiterated its demand "for a general and immediate cessation of hostilities" (Art. 2), it demanded that all parties to armed conflicts "engage immediately in a durable, extensive and humanitarian pause" (Art. 3), and it called for a "safe and unhindered humanitarian access for the humanitarian personnel and medical personnel" (Art. 4).

It called for the protection of civilian infrastructure, which is critical to the delivery of humanitarian aid for essential services concerning vaccinations and "related medical care" (Art. 4, Para. 2).

---

72 https://reliefweb.int/report/sudan/un-call-days-tranquility-bears-fruit-more-five-million-children-have-been-vaccinated.

The SC then reserved the possibility to "consider what further measures may be necessary" where hostilities and activities of armed groups would hinder the delivery of COVID-19 vaccines.

This Resolution is the outcome of the "Biden" effect on UN diplomacy after the strong unilateralism of the former President Trump.[73] It is evident by the wording of Resolution 2565 that it is in stark contrast with the previous Resolution, since the crucial role of the WHO and multilateral instruments, such as the ACT Accelerator, were expressly recognized.

Despite the renewed United States leadership, diplomats and negotiators decided not to replicate the model of Resolution 2177 and chose a resolution focused on facilitating the vaccination campaign against COVID-19 in the context of armed conflicts.

Specifically, if the SC took the leadership of the global response to tackle the epidemic during the 2014 Ebola outbreak in Western Africa, then during the COVID-19 pandemic it manifestly failed to do so. In the Ebola case, it is true that the role of the SC was eventually symbolic, since no measures under Article 41 or 42 were issued, but the SC's function was crucial in coordinating international efforts, gaining additional funding, and building momentum in the global community.

Therefore, Resolutions 2532 and 2565 were undoubtedly a downsizing of the process of the "securitization of health" and a step behind when compared to Resolution 2177 (2014) on the Ebola outbreak. The SC's disarray has brought to the forefront the key question of the role that the SC can play in dealing with the spread of infectious diseases with global implications ("non-traditional security threats").

10. Concluding remarks

As the UN organ entrusted with the primary responsibility for the maintenance of international peace and security, one might have expected strong leadership to address the common threat represented by the COVID-19 pandemic.

The COVID-19 pandemic clearly revealed that the process of securitization of health within the SC – which gained momentum with Resolution 2177/2014 – came to a standstill for a set of reasons.

The first is related to the lack of a strong United States leadership in the early phases of the disease outbreak due to the unilateralism of the former Trump administration and the dispute with China over the name and source of the novel coronavirus. The slow reaction by the SC facing the global spread of COVID-19 confirmed the impossibility – more or less explicitly foreseen by the drafters of the Charter – of any meaningful reaction by the SC when

73 See *Remarks by President Biden Before the 76th Session of the United Nations General Assembly* (21 September 2021), https://www.whitehouse.gov/briefing-room/speeches-remarks/2021/09/21/remarks-by-president-biden-before-the-76th-session-of-the-united-nations-general-assembly/.

the concerned State is a P5. The SC struggles to react when there is attrition among the P5. This case heightened a deep contrast between the two most powerful permanent members over how to characterize the origins of the pandemic.

The second factor is represented by the Russia-Ukraine war and the Israel-Gaza war, that heavily questioned the human security paradigm, which is the conceptual foundation of SC resolutions on health issues, and determined a resurgence of a Cold War concept of threat related to an armed attack by a State or a terrorist group like Hamas against the territory of another country.

Accordingly, the centrality of the SC as the main actor in responding to disease outbreaks with a global impact – which gained momentum with Resolution 2177 – was heavily questioned during the COVID-19 pandemic. Its peripheral role in the global response to the COVID-19 pandemic with slow and ineffective action[74] clearly demonstrated that the SC is not the most appropriate forum to address infectious diseases and their nexus with security.

In contrast, Resolution 2177 was an extraordinary response to an extraordinary event, but the drafters of the SC did not intend to set a precedent. The subsequent practice of the Council facing the transnational health crises after Ebola, such as Zika, wild polio, COVID-19, and monkeypox, has denoted a progressive retreat by the SC.

Resolutions 2532 and 2565 have instead shown a narrow field of intervention of the SC when facing transnational health crises that is limited in dealing with the impact of infectious diseases in war zones. The SC's practice therefore denotes a lack of intention to use Chapter VII language when dealing with infectious diseases, which does not mean, however, a complete indifference towards the matter health. As outlined in a paper by Voss, Kump and Bochtler, health issues are increasingly been discussed within the SC,[75] which denotes a trend to address issues related the delivery of vaccines and treatments, the protection of health care professionals, and the health of peace keepers in conflict settings. The fact that Resolutions 2532 and 2565 failed to qualify the COVID-19 pandemic as a threat to peace and security has thus definitively put an end to the possibility that Resolution 2177 would have represented a precedent and the beginning of a process of securitization of health with the SC as the central body in charge in the global arena.

The COVID-19 pandemic has shown two different approaches and two different narratives: on the international level, the UN and the WHO have called States to multilateralism and global cooperation and solidarity towards what was labelled as a "threat to humankind" and a "threat to peace and security".

---

74 Jeremy Farrall, Christopher Michaelsen, "The UN Security Council's Response to COVID-19: From the Centre to the Periphery?", *The Australian Year Book of International Law Online* (2021): 214–230.

75 Maike Voss, Isabell Kump, Paul Bochtler, "Unpacking the Framing of Health in the United Nations Security Council", *Australian Journal of International Affairs* (2022): 4–10.

On the domestic level, governments have instead acted on a unilateral basis, with a different timing and recalling of concepts such as sovereignty, borders, and framing the outbreak as a national security issue (governments responded to it by asserting almost unprecedented national authority).

As previously explained, vaccine nationalism was a key feature of the States' response to the pandemic. On the European continent, the European Union was unable to coordinate a health response among its Member States or to provide appropriate solidarity.[76]

Notably, COVID-19 was declared by the former U.S. President, Donald J. Trump, a "national emergency", employing the metaphor of the United Stated being "at war" and himself as a "war-time president".[77] In fact, the concepts of homeland and security require a concrete enemy as the main cause of the threat, namely, China and the WHO.

China, for its part, pursued (and continues to pursue) a policy of extensive cover-up of data and information. The lack of transparency in China's policy-making process,[78] although it experienced a surge in COVID-19 infections between the end of 2022 and early 2023, contributed (and still contributes) to the global spread of the disease.

This is not a case where autocratic States were (apparently) more successful in dealing with the pandemic by imposing severe measures and limitations to civil and political rights. The Chinese zero-covid policy comported with a low rate of immunization among the population and a deep economic crisis.

One might wonder, therefore, whether COVID-19 has witnessed a shift towards a more authoritarian international law as foreseen by Tom Ginsburg, who outlines the decline of democracies and the rise of authoritarian States worldwide.[79] The problem is that this new landscape in international relations has an impact on multilateralism, globalism, and the potential role of the SC (where the two authoritarian States of China and Russia have veto power) in managing as a leader of future epidemics and pandemics.

76 It is worth recalling that within the EU, a specific body, the Health Security Committee (HSC), should coordinate the European response to epidemics and pandemics ("serious cross-border threats"); see Decision No. 1082/2013/EU on serious cross-border threats to health and repealing Decision No 2119/98/EC. CoViD-19 Wuhan virus, https://edition.cnn.com/2020/03/25/politics/g7-coronavirus-statement/index.html.

77 CoViD-19 Wuhan virus, https://edition.cnn.com/2020/03/25/politics/g7-coronavirus-statement/index.html.

78 China data 'under-represents' true impact of Covid outbreak – WHO, *The Guardian* (4 January 2023), https://www.theguardian.com/world/2023/jan/05/china-data-under-represents-true-impact-of-covid-outbreak who.

79 Tom Ginsburg, "Authoritarian International Law?" *American Journal of International Law* (2020): 221–260.

Concluding observations

Without specifying when and where or the degree of severity, in 2019, the WHO predicted that the world would face another influenza pandemic. In early 2020, an outbreak of a new corona virus (SARS-CoV-2) was reported from China. The world community, including the WHO, was ill-prepared to appropriately cope with what quickly became a global pandemic, as declared by the WHO Director-General on 11 March 2020.

On 5 May 2023, the Director-General proclaimed the termination of the state of emergency with reference to the COVID-19 pandemic. The downgrading of COVID-19 marked the end of the pandemic more than three years after the declaration of PHEIC of January 2020 – about six weeks before characterizing it as a pandemic.

The "day after" of the COVID-19 pandemic left many unresolved issues, such as the unpreparedness of States and of the international community as a whole in managing and tackling the new disease, the lack of equity and solidarity in the distribution of COVID-19 vaccines, the origins of the virus, and the problem of how to prevent a new pandemic.

This volume has retraced the three years that have changed the world and the perception of infectious diseases as a global threat with nearly 7 million deaths and 765 million confirmed COVID-19 cases. As the COVID-19 pandemic began, the whole world abruptly tilted away from normal. Over the following three years, the discovery of highly effective vaccines in record time allowed most of the world to come back to normal life, with globally 13.3 billion doses of COVID-19 vaccines administered as the WHO Director-General declared the end of the emergency, many of which rolled out through the channels of the ACT Accelerator and COVAX. Despite the immunization of a high percentage of the world population, COVID-19 remains a disease that increased inequalities and discrimination between high-income countries and the rest of the world, as witnessed by the phenomenon of vaccine nationalism.

The book focused particularly on the repercussions of the COVID-19 pandemic on the HEPR architecture by highlighting what went wrong and what was done in order to strengthen the WHO and to prevent future pandemics.

COVID-19, which hit every country in the world, has raised several issues as to the efficiency of international law and global health governance

DOI: 10.4324/9781003100645-7

in preventing and managing disease outbreaks. The pandemic displayed a plethora of shortcomings in the governance of disease outbreaks with the WHO at the epicenter. In particular, the WHO failed to exercise its international public authority to convince States to cooperate during the pandemic and to respect their duties arising from the IHR. In fact, the exercise of international public authority by the WHO during the COVID-19 pandemic was largely ineffective, since its response was delayed, and its recommendations were, for the most part, unapplied. States reacted slowly and unilaterally to the pandemic by closing their frontiers and isolating their citizens, without any sort of coordination with other countries or within regional fora. As witnessed by previous outbreaks, a collective and multilateral reaction in the management of infectious diseases is critical, since viruses do not recognize borders. The failure of the WHO in tackling the COVID-19 pandemic, the lack of global cooperation, and the rise of vaccine nationalism questioned the whole global health architecture. Given the collective nature of international law, the world community felt the urgency to review the efficacy of global health law and to assess whether its legal framework based on the IHR represents a valid tool in the containment of modern global pandemics such as COVID-19. The call for reform, however, has not addressed the roots of the problems, among which are health sovereignty and statism. I have contended that the "globalist" approach of the new pandemic treaty is illusory and utopian since it is at odds with the "nation-state first" approach that dominated the response to the COVID-19 pandemic. The Westphalian State-based system that permeates international relations was not minimally scrapped by a major global pandemic, which has instead reinforced State nationalism, and it is not questioned in the new pandemic treaty, which recalls "health sovereignty" as one of the key principles. Specifically, the treaty does not give to the WHO the authority to control domestic policies during a pandemic, including those on vaccines, lockdowns, contact tracing, or school closures or to carry out on-site inspections in case of a suspected pandemic risk.

There are also unresolved matters that pertain to the way that human beings interact with the environment, which I have underscored in this volume. We are entering a new age of pandemics related to factors such as the process of globalization, habitat destruction, and exploitation of animals, which are the hallmark of the Anthropocene. Against this backdrop, this volume has recalled that COVID-19 is the epitome of the asymmetric relationship between human beings and the nature – as demonstrated by the anthropocentric approach in international law – which can be considered the dark side of globalization. I have outlined that the notion of deep prevention – set up within the broader One Health concept – must be translated into practice through the establishment of specific obligations upon States to prevent the spread and the transmission of severe disease outbreaks. However, this raises additional problems that are still unsettled, starting with a complete change of perspective of international law at the human-animal-environment interface.

The WHO Pandemic Agreement recognized, in line with the One Health concept, that human health is strictly interrelated with animal welfare and environmental protection, but it failed to clearly recognize that human activities are the main cause of the resurgence of zoonotic pathogens (this would have opened new frontiers in the field of State responsibility, namely, the "liability" of a State for lawful acts).

As the International Panel on Climate Change (IPCC) acknowledged that the climate crisis is unequivocally caused by human activities, the international community should clearly state that emerging infectious diseases do have an anthropocentric footprint and that it is the "common concern of humankind" to prevent, reduce, and control the spread of epidemics and pandemics.

After millions of deaths and the devastating impact of COVID-19 on our daily lives, global health law has a tall order to fill. Providing concrete and effective tools for managing in a coordinated manner future epidemics and pandemics if and when they occur would be an appreciable step forward.

By identifying legal gaps and providing legal arguments, this book has contributed to the historical and conceptual foundation and the practical development of international law in the new age of COVID-19, with the goal of stimulating legal reform in this vital new era.

Index

Note: Notes are indicated by n and note number following the page number.

For Product Safety Concerns and Information please contact our EU
representative GPSR@taylorandfrancis.com
Taylor & Francis Verlag GmbH, Kaufingerstraße 24, 80331 München, Germany

www.ingramcontent.com/pod-product-compliance
Ingram Content Group UK Ltd.
Pitfield, Milton Keynes, MK11 3LW, UK
UKHW021847100825
461702UK00010B/187

* 9 7 8 0 3 6 7 6 0 8 2 9 3 *